THE ROOTS OF URBAN DISCONTENT

THE WILEY SERIES IN URBAN RESEARCH

TERRY N. CLARK, Editor

PETER H. ROSSI
RICHARD A. BERK
BETTYE K. EIDSON

THE ROOTS OF URBAN DISCONTENT

Public Policy, Municipal Institutions, and the Ghetto

A Publication of the Center
for Metropolitan Planning and Research of
the Johns Hopkins University

A WILEY-INTERSCIENCE PUBLICATION

JOHN WILEY & SONS, New York • London • Sydney • Toronto

Library of Congress Cataloging in Publication Data:

Rossi, Peter Henry, 1921-
   The roots of urban discontent.

   (The Wiley series in urban research)
   "A publication of the Center for Metropolitan Planning and Research of Johns Hopkins University."
   "A Wiley-Interscience publication."
   1. Cities and towns—United States—Case studies.
2. United States—Social conditions—1960-
3. Sociology, Urban. I. Berk, Richard A., joint author. II. Eidson, Bettye K., joint author.
III. Johns Hopkins University. Center for Metropolitan Planning and Research. IV. Title.

HT123.R67   301.36'0973   73-22219
ISBN 0-471-73770-4

Printed in the United States of America

10 9 8 7 6 5 4 3 2 1

To the immigrant generation of our families, urban ghetto dwellers of an earlier age

THE WILEY SERIES IN URBAN RESEARCH

Cities, especially American cities, are attracting more public attention and scholarly concern than at perhaps any other time in history. Traditional structures have been seriously questioned and sweeping changes proposed; simultaneously, efforts are being made to penetrate the fundamental processes by which cities operate. This effort calls for marshaling knowledge from a number of substantive areas. Sociologists, political scientists, economists, geographers, planners, historians, anthropologists, and others have turned to urban questions; interdisciplinary projects involving scholars and activists are groping with fundamental issues.

The Wiley Series in Urban Research has been created to encourage the publication of works bearing on urban questions. It seeks to publish studies from different fields that help to illuminate urban processes. It is addressed to scholars as well as to planners, administrators, and others concerned with a more analytical understanding of things urban.

TERRY N. CLARK

ACKNOWLEDGMENTS

Our foremost debt is to the public officials, institutional agents, and rank-and-file citizens who gave freely of their time to answer our questions. Although many have by now forgotten the occasion of their interviews, we hope that this text will remind them of their contribution and justify the time that each donated.

We are also grateful to the Ford Foundation who provided funds for the collection of the basic data in 1968. The research was supported by the Center for the Study of Metropolitan Mental Health Problems, National Institute of Mental Health, primarily through Grant MH16549 which supported the research staff through the difficult and overly long period of data analysis. To the Kerner Commission, and particularly staff members David Ginsburg and Victor Palmieri, we are indebted for the opportunity of working with them and for their help in obtaining funds.

Angus Campbell and Howard Schuman of the Institute for Social Research of the University of Michigan graciously allowed access to data collected from sample surveys in each of the fifteen cities. Without these data, this volume would not be possible. This exchange is a tribute to their sense of intellectual colleagueship.

Many persons worked on the project. David Boesel ably supervised the field operation in which public officials in the fifteen cities were interviewed. Boesel also conducted some of the preliminary analyses that are the foundation of the chapter on educators. W. Eugene Groves helped to

ix

design the instrument used in interviewing policemen and conducted some of the preliminary analyses of the resulting data.

Initially, the senior author was joined by James S. Coleman in designing and conducting the research reported here. Unfortunately, other interests and obligations kept Coleman from full participation beyond the first phase of study design. As a consequence, this study shows only slight traces of the great research skill at Coleman's command. We are sure the study would have been better for his full participation in the enterprise.

We enjoyed the pleasure of working with Audits and Surveys, Inc., of New York who undertook the hard task of carrying out structured interviews with samples of institutional agents in each of the fifteen cities involved. We are especially appreciative of the interest shown by Solomon Dutka and Lester Frankel, as well as the hard work of Richard Hess who supervised the data collection activities of Audits and Surveys.

The preparation of the final manuscript has been the primary responsibility of the senior author. However, the chapters on the retail merchants and the employers rests so heavily upon the analyses undertaken, respectively, by Richard A. Berk and Bettye K. Eidson in their dissertations, that these chapters are more their work than that of the principal investigator. In addition, all three authors spent time preparing drafts of other chapters, as well as editing and providing critical comments on all parts of the manuscript. The final product is the result of a cooperative endeavour that has survived the dispersal of the cooperators among three universities spread across the Northeastern region.

The research reported here was started originally in the Department of Social Relations and later was carried out under the auspices of the Center for Metropolitan Planning and Research.

Finally, we must acknowledge the diligence, patience, and jovial spirits of Ms Shirley Sult who saw the manuscript through so many drafts.

Our debts are many. We hope that we have acknowledged fairly the help that we have received.

Our faults also may be many, but they are our own.

PETER H. ROSSI
RICHARD A. BERK
BETTYE K. EIDSON

Center for Metropolitan Planning and Research
The Johns Hopkins University
Baltimore, Maryland
December 1973

CONTENTS

LIST OF TABLES

LIST OF FIGURES

THE ROOTS OF URBAN DISCONTENT

Chapter 1

INTRODUCTION

Some cities, especially the great metropolises, develop distinctive reputations, based partially on their physical appearances and partially on certain critical events in their histories. San Francisco is regarded widely as America's most beautiful city, a city whose climate matches its beauty. New York's distinctive skyline along with its being the headquarters of so many corporations gives it the reputation of being the most sophisticated and cosmopolitan American city. At the other extreme, some cities are known for their faults: Radio and television comics often draw a laugh from an audience by referring to Peoria or Hoboken, presumably symbols of dullness and parochialism. W. C. Fields could easily bring down the house by stating that he would rather be dead than spend Sunday in Philadelphia, whose puritanical "blue laws" prohibited the selling of liquor on Sundays.

But reputations and "images," no matter how widely shared, do not really indicate what it is like to live in one city or another. The skyline of Manhattan or the hills of San Francisco may look appealing on an airline travel poster, but the reality of living in either of those two cities may have nothing to do with the attractiveness of those features. After all, life is not lived against the background of a panoramic view of a city's skyscrapers, except perhaps by the very rich whose luxury apartments may provide such views as amenities. For the vast majority of a

1

city's population, everyday life is lived against backgrounds that are far less spectacular. For the poor and for minorities who have few choices concerning where they can live, one city may be just as bad or just as good as another.

Does the city in which one lives make a difference? This is the central question to which the research described in this volume is addressed. We are concerned particularly with one segment of an American urban population—blacks—and with the larger metropolitan areas of the north and west, concerns that arise out of the historical origins of the study, described more fully in a later section of this chapter.

A city may be regarded as a design for living: at least, the purposes of a city (or for that matter, any human community) are so diffuse that they cover almost all aspects of human life. The elements of city design include its topography, physical plant, industrial and business enterprises, local political structures, and networks of connections between individuals, households, and larger social organizations. To live in a city means to be influenced to some degree or another by these elements of design.

To examine the extent to which living in a particular city affects its inhabitants requires singling out a few aspects of city design for more careful examination. In this volume we have chosen to examine three aspects of city design—local government and certain municipal institutions, industrial and business enterprises who are major employers of local inhabitants, and retail enterprises who provide goods and services to neighborhoods.

The rationale for choosing these aspects of city life for detailed examination in relationship to the lives of blacks in cities is based largely on the assumption that these aspects represent institutions that affect strongly life in urban ghettos. The local government represents the city as a corporate entity. Municipal institutions, such as the police, schools, and social welfare, provide important services. Employers provide or restrict access to employment, hence income. Retail merchants provide goods and services.

Of course, these are not the only local institutions that have an impact on inhabitants of a city. We could have studied the transportation system, how the layout of streets, highways, and mass transit facilities provided access to employment, shopping, and other necessary functions. We could have studied the impact of those institutions that comprise the housing market and examined how realtors, builders, landlords, and housing inspectors condition the lives of blacks in urban places. However, because, as usual, resources are limited, we chose a set of life areas that we could handle within resource limitations.

\ The central concern of this volume is to examine the interrelationships between three levels of urban social structure: (1) local public policy makers, comprised of elected public officials, the heads of major municipal departments, and "civic notables," or persons who play important roles in urban civic life; (2) "institutional agents," or persons who operate on the grass roots levels of important urban structures, for example, policemen, teachers, case workers, retail merchants, and personnel offices of major employers; and (3) rank-and-file black citizens.

The design of the study is comparative. We examine fifteen cities, representing thirteen of the fifteen major metropolitan areas of the United States. The cities can be viewed as a sample of cities or as almost an entire universe.

The historical context is early 1968 when the field work for our study was undertaken. The relationships that our data uncover are those which obtained at that point in time. How much change has taken place since then we must leave to future researches.

The central concerns of the research as described above were not as intended at the time the study was designed and fielded. Circumstances and findings themselves forced a change in the direction of the analysis. Of course, this change in focus is not unusual in social research, for social scientists are still fumbling about in a twilight of understanding.

The research reported in this volume grew out of a concern over a series of events which shook deeply American society in the 1960s. Beginning with a few minor disturbances in 1963, occupying the center of public attention with the extended disorders in Watts in 1965, and reaching a climax with the great riots in Washington, Chicago, Baltimore, and Pittsburgh in 1968, a great amount of public attention was drawn by the civil disorders that broke out in black neighborhood after black neighborhood in city after city. At the end of the decade, few American cities in the North and West did not have their local versions of the great riots that shocked the nation in 1967 and 1968. Some cities— New York, Chicago, and Los Angeles—had several major disorders. Southern cities were not entirely exempted from the troubles of the times: Atlanta, Tampa, Miami, and New Orleans had their bouts as well. By the end of 1969, the total number of civil disorders involving blacks since 1962 had reached over 2500.[1]

---

[1] As tabulated by the Lemberg Center for the Study of Violence, Brandeis University. This count includes incidents involving five or more people and is culled from newspaper accounts in the major papers in the United States. The count thus includes incidents of a very minor nature (e.g., a high school disturbance) as well as the major disorders of the period.

Public concern with urban civil disorders reached a high with the major riots in Newark and Detroit in the summer of 1967 and did not descend until the early 1970s. The disorders presented a problem in understanding to almost everyone in the society. It was easy to understand why there were civil disorders in Newark and possibly in Chicago where local municipal administrations had reputations of being particularly insensitive to their black constituencies. Indeed, because most of the major disturbances began with incidents involving the police, local sources seemed to provide the forces that gave rise to the civil disorders. However, when liberal municipal administrations became subject to civil disorders, understanding the meaning of the disorders became more problematic. Indeed, liberal municipal administrations—for example, that of Mayor Cavanaugh in Detroit or of Mayor Lindsay in New York— that had made a public point of being attentive to black constituencies had some of the worst of the 1960s troubles.

At the peak of public concern and puzzlement over the meaning of these troubled events in the fall of 1967, President Johnson appointed a National Commission headed by Governor Otto Kerner of Illinois to probe into the causes of the riots and to suggest remedies that might prevent their reoccurrence. The historical context is worth noting. In the summer of 1967 more than 150 civil disorders involved blacks, eight of which had been deemed serious enough by local authorities to justify calling upon military forces to supplement (and in some cases to supplant) local and state police. By the end of August 1967 the American public had been treated to a month's display of looting, arson, and property damage on their television screens, centering mainly around the events of Newark and Detriot. The Kerner Commission[2] immediately sought answers to the question "Why?"[3] and were spurred on by the hope that the diagnoses found and the remedies devised might prevent the summer of 1968 from being even hotter than the summer of 1967.

The Kerner Commission quickly put together a staff which was headed by David Ginsburg, launched a series of field investigations in cities that had had serious disorders in 1967, and began to hold hearings in cities that had been hit by the most serious riots. In addition, early in the fall of 1967, David Ginsburg called together a group of social scientists to

---

[2] Known officially as The National Advisory Commission on Civil Disorders.

[3] Two perceptive, although different in tone, accounts of the Kerner Commission can be found in Michael E. Lipsky and David Olson, "Riot Commission Politics," in *Ghetto Revolts*, Peter H. Rossi (Ed.), Aldine Press, Chicago, 1970, and in Andrew Kopkind, "White on Black: The Riot Commission and the Rhetoric of Reform, *Cities Under Siege*," in David Boesel and Peter H. Rossi (Eds.), Basic Books, New York, 1971.

advise the Commission on the directions that its research activities should take. Out of this meeting came the plans for the research to be described in this volume.

The main concern of the meeting between the Kerner Commission staff and the social scientists was to discover why some cities had had disorders and why others did not. The arguments for a comparative study of cities were apparently so persuasive that Ginsburg queried the Ford Foundation about support for the researches.

The general ideas that stimulated the research plans devised at that time had to do with the roles played by local municipal administrations in affecting the moods of residents of black ghettos. In cities where blacks had many grievances and in which local public officials were relatively unresponsive to such grievances, civil disorders were likely to occur. In cities with opposite characteristics, civil disorders were unlikely to occur. What were the areas of public life in which critical grievances would arise? What were the municipal institutions to which the moods of blacks were particularly responsive? What was the role of black leaders? There were the open questions to be answered by a comparative study of a relatively large group of cities varying in their 1967 civil disorder experience, ranging from the cities that had experienced major disorders to the cities that had been entirely peaceful.

With financing furnished by the Ford Foundation, two groups of researchers were to study the worth of this general explanation and to provide answers to the critical questions raised. Angus Campbell and Howard Schuman of the University of Michigan's Survey Research Center surveyed small samples of black and white citizens in each of fifteen cities. The senior author of this volume and James S. Coleman of Johns Hopkins University agreed to study the political elite and municipal administrations (plus two critical parts of the private sector) in the same fifteen cities, concentrating on those portions of the local institutions that were in direct contact with black ghetto residents.

The researchers were sent into the field in the winter of 1967–1968 in a set of cities chosen to represent three groups as follows:

I: Cities that had experienced serious civil disorders in 1967
    Newark
    Detroit
    Milwaukee
    Cincinnati
    Boston

II: Cities that had experienced no disorders in 1967 but had experienced disorders in earlier years

Brooklyn, New York (Bedford-Stuyvesant)
Cleveland
Chicago
San Francisco
Philadelphia

III: Cities that had experienced no disorders in 1967 or earlier

Washington, D.C.
Baltimore
Gary, Indiana[4]
Pittsburgh
St. Louis

The design and detailed plans for the Hopkins survey are described in the next chapter.

A perceptive reader, looking at the list of cities, will discover that this study (and the one undertaken by the Survey Research Center) can not show why it was that some cities had civil disorders and others did not. Very shortly after the field work had been conducted, some of the most serious of the civil disorders of the 1960s broke out, following the assassination of Martin Luther King, in precisely those cities which had been included because they were models of civil quietude. In April 1968, Baltimore, Washington, and Pittsburgh had extremely serious disorders. In addition, Chicago had the worst of the series of riots that it was to suffer in that period.

In short, the study as originally designed was a failure almost before the data had been completely collected. The failure was caused not so much by the capriciousness of human events as the naiveté of the original conceptions that guided its design. The central idea behind the study was that *civil disorders were local phenomena, or responses by blacks to local institutions and the conditions in local ghettos.* There is now ample evidence that this central idea was wrong. The civil disorders of the 1960s were generalized political responses to conditions that were common to blacks in general rather than to blacks in some particular locale.

The *report*[5] of the Kerner Commission, issued in March 1968, in a very general way recognized the fact that the roots of disorders sprang from the longstanding poor living conditions of black Americans caused by

---

[4] Chosen more because a black (Richard Hatcher) had recently been elected to the mayor's office than for any other reason. Thus in Gary's administration, black residents would have especially high levels of trust.

[5] *Report of the National Advisory Commission on Civil Disorders*, Government Printing Office, Washington, D.C., 1967.

a society that was prejudiced against this minority. The "centuries of neglect" were the long-term causes of the civil disorders, according to the report, with more proximate causes left somewhat unspecified.

In retrospect, the events of the 1960s can be interpreted as the northern version of the civil rights movement, much less organized, more chaotic, less "nonviolent,"[6] but representing a massive wave of protest by the black against being the "low man" on the totem pole of our society. Indeed, as Spilerman[7] has shown, the best post hoc predictor of whether a city experienced a riot in the 1960s is the proportion of blacks in the city's population. In short, the more blacks, the more likely was a city to have had a civil disorder.

The supralocal sources of the civil disorders was also documented amply in the results of both the Hopkins and Michigan surveys. In reports on the studies published by the Kerner Commission[8] no differences could be shown between the three types of cities. Cities that had experienced serious disorders were likely to report a higher amount of tension, most intelligently interpreted as a consequence of the disorder, but police, case workers, ghetto merchants, and such differed not at all in the three groups of cities in the attitude and reported behavior measures. Similar results were presented by Campbell and Schuman[9] from statistics from their interviews with blacks and whites in the fifteen cities.

It was also quite obvious from our studies that there were differences among the fifteen cities. In some places, black citizens had little faith in local administrations while in others blacks regarded their mayors and other officials as sympathetic and at least "trying." Similarly, we found in our studies that police departments varied considerably from place to place; some pursued rigid law and order policies while others were more conscious of the civil rights of citizens. *These differences from city to city, however, were simply not related to whether the city had experienced civil disorders in 1967, 1968, or in any other year.*

Although it took some time for the Hopkins research staff to adjust to

---

[6] It must be kept in mind that the major violence of the civil disorders were acts directed toward property and the police. Considering the extent and the mass involvement of the disorders, there were remarkably few personal injuries and deaths, far fewer, for example, than in the Civil War draft riots in New York or the Post-World War I riots in Chicago or East St. Louis.

[7] Seymour Spilerman "The Causes of Racial Disturbances: Test of a Theory," Institute of Research on Poverty, University of Wisconsin, Discussion Papers 58–69, December 1969.

[8] National Advisory Commission on Civil Disorders, *Supplemental Studies*, Government Printing Office, Washington, D.C., 1968.

[9] *Ibid.*

the failure of the original main purpose of the research, we gradually began to look at the sources of intercity differences. The present concern of the research partially results from paying attention to what the data were telling us, partially is a matter of rescuing ourselves from a failure, and partially is a matter of pursuing latent interests that had led to the design in the first place. The exact motivation of this volume is hard to state. All we can say now is that these are legitimate sociological concerns, and that the volume is whatever proof we can muster that those concerns can be served by the research as designed.

The research described in this volume tends to support three major conclusions:

First, the central institutions of different cities treat their black citizens quite differently.

Second, black citizens keenly appreciate those differences, expressing alienation and dissatisfaction in cities in which they are slighted and expressing the opposite in cities with more tolerant views and policies toward blacks.

Third, the different treatment of blacks in place to place depends on the political strength that they can muster. In cities where blacks are a large proportion of the electorate, municipal administrations tend to be more attentive to black leaders. In cities where blacks are poorly organized or constitute a small minority, black citizens tend to get short shrift at the hands of officials and low-level bureaucrats.

Although failing to explain local patterns in civil disorders, such findings should not be casually dismissed. When large numbers of Americans, especially large numbers claiming a similar identity, feel mistreated, there are compelling reasons for concern on at least moral grounds. When complaints can be linked to the actions of important local institutions, a variety of administrative and political issues emerge which reflect fundamental societal malfunctions. As a highly urbanized nation with overlapping and interdependent organization, local problems cannot be considered isolated problems. All Americans are affected. Civil disorders are not the only medium for expressing grievances. Indeed, they may have only short-run consequences. The patterns that we have uncovered in our research may condition the nature of local political events long after the civil disorders of the 1960s will have faded from the salient portions of our political memories.

Chapter 2

STUDY DESIGN AND METHODS

The research described in this volume arose out of the widespread public need to understand the meanings of the civil disorders of the summer of 1967. The research proposed to discover why some cities had experienced major civil disorders that summer and others did not. Thus the design focused on differences among a set of cities, selected to vary in their experiences with civil disorders in 1967. The differences among cities were studied on three levels: (1) political and civic elites; (2) institutional agents; and (3) rank-and-file black and white citizens.

It cannot be said that the design was illuminated by a highly sophisticated theory of civil disorders. The model underlying the explanatory model stressed three potential factors leading to disorders. First, black citizens in each community had accumulated a reservoir of grievances arising out of the discrepancies between their *de jure* rights as full citizens of our society and their *de facto* positions as a discriminated against minority. Second, the attention that political and civil elites gave to black grievances and the remedies that they put forth to ameliorate the conditions giving rise to those grievances varied from city to city. Third, local institutional structures (employers, police, welfare agencies, etc.), influenced partially by the policies as set forth by civic and political elites, varied in their treatment of blacks.

The design of the three studies was accomplished in detail by a division of labor among the two major research groups—the University of Michigan and Johns Hopkins University—aided by advice and consultation with the staff of the Kerner Commission. As always, the best of intentions can deteriorate due to distance and time pressure. Although the efforts of the two research groups were to be closely coordinated, each group quickly developed its own pacing; thus the style of work and coordination between the two groups was not as close as initially desired. The individuals involved cannot be blamed, but again cooperative research efforts are difficult to carry out (even without time pressure) when separate groups are constituted with a clear division of labor and located some hundreds of miles apart. The Michigan group had a clear mandate to carry out population surveys, and the Hopkins group to carry out elite and institutional agent surveys. Considering the time constraints on both studies, it is even more understandable that the two research groups should drift apart.

The time constraints on the studies were quite severe. Although the broad outlines of the two studies were completed in the late fall of 1967, it was not until mid-December (in the case of the Michigan group) and early January (in the case of the Hopkins group) that funds were available to start the active phases of design and implementation. The Kerner Commission had a report deadline of June 1968, but decided in December to issue its main report in March 1968, hoping that it would be possible thereby to persuade Congress to pass appropriate legislation before the summer of 1968. Although studies originally were intended to go into the final report, it was decided to release their findings in a supplemental report to be issued before the Commission went out of existence in the summer of 1968. Thus these deadlines dictated that we were to conduct the studies and write reports to be published in the summer of 1968. The total time available from design to report was about 6 months, scarcely allowing for a leisurely pace.

Selection of the Fifteen Cities. The design called for a comparison among cities, especially major metropolitan areas where the most serious and extensive civil disorders had occurred in 1967. Cities in the South were ruled out because they had experienced few civil disorders and were thought to manifest local political patterns peculiar to that region.[1]

---

[1] At the time, blacks in southern cities had just begun to play some role in local politics but not enough—outside of especially "progressive" cities such as Atlanta or Miami—to make them a significant local political force. Thus we anticipated that all southern political and civic elites would show a pattern of ignoring black constitu-

Since a comprehensive study of a city was costly, limited funds restricted the design to a relative small number of cities.

There was nothing sacred about the number fifteen. We cannot report that the sample size was chosen by using the rigorous techniques that statisticians suggest. Rather, fifteen cities represented the best compromise between budget constraints and educated guesses about the relative importance within and between city variance. Clearly, compromises had to be made; the greater the number of cities, the shallower the coverage of each.

The actual selection of the cities in the study was accomplished in a meeting with the two research teams and the Kerner Commission staff. The decisions made at that meeting were not complete products of rationality. Although there was complete agreement on including both Newark and Detroit—indeed the Kerner Commission's existence was largely in reaction to the very extensive and dramatic disorders in those two cities—it was not as easy to choose what other cities to include.[2] Some cities were included because there was particular interest in what impact a black mayor would have—Gary, Washington, D.C., and Cleveland. Others were omitted because they had been studied extensively earlier, for example, Los Angeles. This patch-work decision-making process finally settled on the following three groups:

Group I: Severe disorder cities
             Newark
             Detroit
             Milwaukee
             Cincinnati
             Boston

Group II: Minor disorders or disorders in years prior to 1967
             Brooklyn, N.Y. (Bedford-Stuyvesant)
             Cleveland
             Chicago
             San Francisco
             Philadelphia

---

encies. We also reasoned that no civil disorders had occurred in such cities because local police forces would have suppressed any such disorders with considerable dispatch and force.

[2] The recollection of the senior author (who was present at the meeting) was that the decision-making process was free of conflict. Rather, it was more a matter that rational values for making positive choices were missing.

Group III: No disorders experienced
             Washington, D.C.
             Baltimore
             Gary
             Pittsburgh
             St. Louis

Of the eighteen non-Southern metropolitan areas (SMSAs) with 1,000,-000 or more population in 1960, thirteen are in our sample, with the two largest metropolitan areas (New York–New Jersey and Chicago–Northwestern-Indiana) each represented by two central cities. The large metropolitan areas omitted are Seattle, Los Angeles, San Diego, Kansas City, and Buffalo. Beyond the obvious bias against West Coast cities, the cities chosen are a rather dense sample of major metropolitan areas of the south.

Of course, this characterization of the fifteen cities as a "dense sample" of major metropolitan areas is a *post hoc* one. Initially the cities were not recognized as such a sample. Yet, the fact that the sample covers so large a proportion (almost 75%) is not one that can be ignored. We are going to take the posture in this volume that the processes that we have uncovered as descriptive of our fifteen cities can be reasonably generalized to the central cities of the largest metropolitan areas in the United States.[3]

Interviewing Political and Civic Elites.   The research design called for a study of the political and civic elites in each of the fifteen cities. In each city, we wanted to know the following information. First, what were the attitudes of public officials and civic figures toward blacks in their cities? Second, how much communication was there between the public officials and civic leaders and the leaders of the black community? Third, what were the issues involving blacks or race relations that were on the local political agendas in each city?

The data to answer these questions were obtained from qualitative interviews with public officials, civic leaders, and black leaders in each of the fifteen cities. Teams of interviewers[4] hired and trained by the

---

[3] Another way of characterizing the cities in the sample is to say that they constitute a sample of fourteen out of the 20 central cities with 500,000 or more population in 1960 (the population of Gary, Indiana did not reach that limit).

[4] Recruited from among former research staff members of the Kerner Commission. Interviewers included Patricia Bennett, Ann Bernstein, Esther Carter, Andrew Hogan, Anthony Jones, Diane Phillips, and Bruce Thomas. In addition, the authors conducted many of the interviews in Baltimore and Washington, D.C.

Hopkins research group were sent out to each of the fifteen cities to interview respondents; each interviewer was to use a broad interview guide constructed by the senior author. Appointments were made in advance of their arrival in a city and the teams interviewed from 20 to 40 individuals in each city. The interviewing began with a fixed set of respondents; and then fanned out to other persons who were mentioned in the interviews with the fixed set. Persons occupying the following positions constituted the fixed set:

Mayor
Police chief
School superintendent
Key persons in the city council
Key persons on the school board
Head of local welfare department
Head of department of public works
President of the local NAACP chapter
President of the local Urban League chapter
Editor(s) of local newspapers
Heads of local TV and radio stations

Using their discretion in the field the teams would fan out from these respondents to between 20 and 40 interviews in each city. Typically, in each city the respondents would mention leading members of the business and industrial elite who were important in community decision-making, black leaders of organizations outside the traditional NAACP and Urban League (e.g., CORE or SLCC), and persons active in politics who were not holding down a public office in local government at the time (e.g., former mayors or heads of local political parties). As many as possible of these designated persons were interviewed in the 5- to 10-day period allocated for field work in that city. In addition, the Kerner Commission made available to the Hopkins Research staff interviews that had been conducted by staff members of the Commission in some of the same cities.

Interviewers took notes during the interview; then at the end of each interviewing day they dictated accounts of the interviews which were then transmitted to Hopkins and transcribed there. For each city, the transcribed interviews amounted to about 100 to 150 manuscript pages.

The interviewing team met with a range of success both in fulfilling the interviewing plan set out for them in each city and in obtaining information from respondents. In some cities, notably Boston, respondents were almost uniformly uncooperative in setting up appointments, meeting the interviews at the appointed time, and, when interviewed in giving full and reasoned answers to the general questions posed by the interviewers. In other cities, notably Cincinnati, the exact opposite conditions prevailed. The variability from interview to interview within a city was considerable. Some respondents either were unwilling to talk about particular topics or were not very knowledgeable about those topics. For example, a police chief would ordinarily know very little about the employment situation facing blacks, and major businessmen or industrialists would usually be very reluctant to make statements about police treatment of blacks. As a consequence, it became apparent that we could not use individual interviews as the unit of analysis. The coverage of topics varied greatly from interview to interview; in some cities, key officials refused to be interviewed or claimed to be too busy to grant an interview. Missing data within interviews and missing respondents within a city set forced a treatment other than the conventional treatment of these interviews.

Upon reading through the transcribed interviews for each city, the research staff discovered that while each individual interview left much to be desired, the total set for each city presented a fairly consistent and complete coverage of the main topics for a city. Thus while the police chief may not have been knowledgeable about employment opportunities for blacks, the head of the Urban League and the president of the local Chamber of Commerce could provide ample and consistent accounts of black employment prospects.

Because the total set of interviews for a city was revealing, the research staff adopted a rather unique way of handling these qualitative interviews. They developed a coding scheme which covered a large number of variables; this scheme was applied to the city sets of interviews.[5] Each member of the research team applied separately the coding scheme to each set of community interviews. Thus a member of the team might read through the interviews with political and civic elites of Boston and rate the mayor of Boston on a nine point scale, according to the rater's judgment of how much power the mayor had in local political decision-making as revealed generally in the total set of city interviews. No attempt was made to reconcile by discussion differences among raters.

The separate ratings made by each of the five members of the staff[6] were then subjected to one-way analysis of variance. Only those ratings

---

[5] A more detailed description of this procedure and the rationale behind it is contained in Peter H. Rossi "Some Issues in the Comparative Study of Community Violence," in *Problems in Research on Community Violence*, R. W. Conant and M. A. Levin (Eds.) Praeger and Company, New York, 1969.

[6] David Boesel, Bettye K. Eidson, Richard A. Berk, W. Eugene Groves, and Robert L. Crain.

that showed significant intercity differences were used in the analysis in this volume.[7] A very large proportion of the ratings (more than half) showed significant intercity versus interrater differences, substantiating the impressions that led to the use of this technique.

These ratings form the data base for the analysis in Chapter 3. They are also used throughout the volume, especially to get at the salience of issues in each city and at the nature of the local political regime. Appendix B contains the rating schemes used.

Surveys of Institutional Agents.   The surveys of institutional agents sampled persons whose jobs involved either delivering important services to ghetto residents in each of the fifteen cities or whose job activities "controlled" important resources that urban blacks needed. These persons and their activities were to illustrate the critical ways in which the institutional structure of the city impinged upon the lives of ghetto residents.

The institutions chosen were those who were involved directly in the issues currently on the political agenda in large metropolitan areas. The choices made were not systematic, although we venture that there would be considerable overlap between our set and any other picked using the same criterion. We decided that the following groups were of particular importance:

Police
Welfare workers
Retail merchants
Major employers
Educators
Political party workers

In retrospect, it is clear that we omitted several institutional areas of considerable importance and conversely spent resources on some which

---

[7] The analysis of variance used city as a "treatment" and coder variance around the mean for each city as the error term. Although technically there are some problems with this application of one-way analysis of variance (e.g., since the same coders rated each city the "treatments" are probably correlated), it seemed the only way to gauge the existence of useful between-city variation. Standard reliability coefficients indicated substantial rater consensus, but failed to decide whether the consensus reflected important city differences. In short, consensus was a necessary but insufficient condition for a useful coding outcome. Or putting it another way, if the disagreement among coders was larger than the difference between cities, one would not have much faith in coder means showing between city variation. A copy of the coding scheme used in this process is appended to the volume. (See Appendix B).

turned out to be relatively unimportant. The especially glaring omissions include the housing industry[8] and health care institutions. Conversely, it was not efficient to spend as much resources as we did on either the educators or the political party workers. Indeed, the sample size used within each city for political party workers was too small to allow inter-city comparisons; hence in the analysis, there are generally no break-downs by cities of political party workers.

Although it is fairly easy, given sufficient resources, to carry out a sample survey of the population of the United States as a whole or of any major subdivision within this country, it is more difficult to draw samples of special groups, especially when those groups are not concen-trated in small geographical areas; this difficulty was obviously encoun-tered in designing this study. Most of the persons we wanted to interview worked in the ghetto areas of the cities. However, they were likely to live in places dispersed widely throughout the city. Furthermore, each group constituted so small a fraction of the populations of the cities selected that population surveys gave little help in locating them. The sampling strategy that was dictated by these considerations was to sample them on-the-job. Interviewers had to approach them through the institutions that employed them.

Municipal agencies—police, education, and social welfare depart-ments—were approached through contacts initiated with mayors and heads of the departments involved. As a preliminary to the survey a letter from the Kerner Commission was sent to each mayor, police chief, school superintendent, and head of public welfare departments in each of the fifteen cities; the letter asked for cooperation in drawing a sample for interviewing of their personnel serving ghetto areas. In each city, school systems and welfare departments cooperated fully and allowed interviewers from Audits and Surveys to select personnel according to plans which we drew up (described more fully below). The heads of police departments were considerably less willing to cooperate. Indeed, in Milwaukee and Boston, the police chiefs not only refused to cooperate but issued orders to members of the department not to grant interviews upon pain of dismissal from the force.[9] As a consequence the analysis

---

[8] Institutional agents from the housing market were considered as a possible group but rejected mainly because of the complexity of the housing market with its separate mechanisms for distributing rental and owner-occupied units and its mixture of public and private suppliers of housing. At the time housing appeared to present especially difficult sampling problems.

[9] Rather than risk the jobs of any respondents we did not try to interview policemen in either of these two cities. It was quite possible, although not very efficient, to attempt to interview policemen in their homes or on patrol. In Milwaukee five inter-

of police departments and their functioning in the ghetto areas of their cities are based upon the thirteen cooperating cities.

Since our task was to interview personnel who worked in ghetto areas, we had to define for municipal departments what those areas were. The sampling department of Audits and Surveys prepared maps for interviewers in each city outlining those census tracts which contained 50% or more blacks in 1960. These maps helped the interviewers explain to the agencies where respondents should be working to be eligible for selection in the sample.

The selection of retail merchants, political party workers, and major employers had to be accomplished differently, since these are decentralized and autonomous units. Since the selection of each group was accomplished somewhat differently, the specific ways used are described in greater detail below.

Selecting Police. Interviewing supervisors on the national staff of Audits and Surveys called upon heads of each police department. They reminded them of the letters sent by the Kerner Commission and then asked for the location of precincts (or comparable units) that served the areas outlined on their maps. Supervisors then went to senior officers in each precinct and requested a list of names of personnel eligible for interview.[10] Supervisors also requested appropriate space within each precinct headquarters within which to conduct interviews. Respondents were then selected randomly from lists and interviewed by interviewers of the same race.

Although the procedures described above were followed in a majority of the police departments, modifications were often made to accommodate local problems and sometimes the adamant wishes of police officials. For example, in Chicago it was not possible to interview police officers selected from lists, since the Chicago Police Department refused to supply

---

views with policemen were obtained before the police chief's orders were promulgated. These interviews were not used in analyses which touch on intercity difference in police departments.

[10] To ensure that interviews were distributed among policemen of supervisory and patrolmen rank as well as according to race, the following quotas were established for each police department:

	Black	White
Supervisors	1	4
Patrolmen	9	26
Totals	10	30

lists. In that city interviewers had to arrange for interviews with police-men on an individual basis, often by intercepting them as they left pre-cinct headquarters to go on patrol. In other cities, commanding officers of precincts insisted on the right to choose individual policemen to be inter-viewed, apparently in order to present their "best" men. In still other cities, it was not possible to select specific respondents in a systematic way; the selection was then made according to those who were available when interviewers appeared on the scene and who were not needed on urgent precinct tasks.

The necessary modifications of our sampling plan due to actual field conditions lead one to question strongly whether the samples obtained were unbiased. However, the biases involved most likely represented policemen as more tolerant toward blacks. If one postulates that the police departments tried to provide us with policemen who would present their "best" side (presumably least prejudiced against blacks), then our find-ings of the relatively illiberal views and practices of policemen actually understate the attitudes of police in the thirteen cities. In fact, were a more representative sampling available, policemen might prove more intolerant toward blacks.

Selecting Educators.   Much the same procedures were followed in con-tacting the school systems in each city. The superintendent's office was visited to obtain locations of schools in ghetto areas. Each school prin-cipal was contacted and asked to provide lists of persons who fitted particular quotas[11] of position and race. Interviews were conducted in the schools. Two senior and/or junior high schools and two elementary schools were selected in each city. Respondents were to be selected at random from lists provided.

As in the case of the police, there were many departures from the ideal. Some principals insisted on doing the selection of respondents personally, possibly with a view toward "pleasing" the Kerner Commission or even the Johns Hopkins researchers. The extent and the strength of the biases introduced by these departures are not known.

Selecting Welfare Workers.   The procedures followed in the case of welfare workers were identical with those followed in the case of police

---

[11] Quotas for educators were set as follows:

	Black	White
Principals or assistant principals	2	2
Classroom teachers	8	8
Totals	10	10

or departments of education. However, in some states (e.g., Illinois and Pennsylvania), welfare was either a county or state function. In other states, welfare offices were highly centralized with no branches in local neighborhoods or with suboffices which covered very large areas. In such cases we were supplied lists of welfare case workers working in ghetto areas by central or very large district supervisors.[12]

Welfare departments were considerably less concerned than either police or education departments that "proper" respondents be selected. Hence selection of respondents in this institution involves less of a bias than in the case of police or educators.

Selecting Personnel Officers of Large Employers. The purpose of this sampling was to interview persons with decision-making and policy-setting responsibilities in the hiring and upgrading of employees in large employing organizations in each city. We concentrated on large employers to obtain efficient coverage of the policies governing the hiring and advancement of a large segment of each city's work force.

Since employment opportunities for blacks (and other residents) of a central city could be located anywhere within the metropolitan area defined by that central city, we sampled among business enterprises (but not government units except in Washington, D.C.) in each city's metropolitan area. Lists of establishments were obtained from Dun and Bradstreet. The largest ten establishments and 20 of the next 90 largest establishments were chosen for our sample, making a total of 30 employing establishments in each city. The heads of the establishments were contacted by Audits and Surveys supervisors and asked to cooperate by allowing us to interview their personnel (or comparable) officer.[13] The cooperation of employing establishments was excellent.

Selecting Ghetto Retail Merchants. Audits and Surveys is particularly experienced in the sampling of retail establishments, since one of its main continuing activities is periodic auditing of the stocks of retail stores measuring the turnover of high volume retail products. Sampling experts

---

[12] Quotas set for welfare case workers were as follows:

Black	White	Total
10	10	20

[13] In Washington, D.C. where the largest employer is obviously the federal government, the personnel officer of the General Services Administration was interviewed. Since he does not directly hire and upgrade personnel in the wide variety of agencies under his general jurisdiction, it would have been more sensible to interview personnel officers in constituent agencies.

of Audits and Surveys determined from maps the main commercial streets within each of the ghetto areas of each city, established quotas of types of retail establishments,[14] and directed interviewers to select establishments on main commercial streets to fulfill those quotas.

Thirty retail merchants—owners or managers—were selected in each city. It is difficult to relate how many retail stores were contacted to complete these thirty interviews. Because there were "refusals" or problems in completing interviews, the possibility of self-selection and interviewer biases exists.

Selecting Political Party Workers. Police precinct captains, retail merchants, and school principals were asked the names of local political clubs and local political party officials in the neighborhoods in which they worked. Three clubs (or similar organizations) were selected from lists collected in this fashion. Ten respondents were selected by contacting three clubs in each city and selecting the officers of those clubs.

Because of the relatively unorganized nature of some of the political parties in some of the cities, it was sometimes difficult to obtain names of persons who were political party officials at a local level. For example, in Washington, D.C., political clubs hardly exist. Thus interviewers had to interview elected public officials, in this case members of the City Council.

Fulfillment of the Sampling Plan. No sampling plan is ever fulfilled to perfection. There are just too many ways for things to go wrong. This survey is no exception. The interviewing was interrupted in some cities by the April 1968 riots. In others, public officials cooperated but only in their peculiar ways. The sample in each city is flawed in some way that may affect results. The best argument we can give for using the data is that the analysis makes sense. Indeed, many of the results given in the remaining chapters could not have been obtained were our data subject to severe biases.

The numbers of interviews obtained in each city are shown in Table 2.1. We started out to obtain 2250 interviews and received 2161, the main segments missing being the police samples in Milwaukee and Boston.

---

[14] Based upon the overall distribution of retail establishments in each city. Quotas were established for merchants as follows:

Black	White	Total
8	22	30

In other cities, by and large, the proper numbers of interviews with the proper persons were obtained.

The Survey Research Center Population Surveys. The data from rank-and-file citizens in each of the fifteen cities were obtained by the University of Michigan's Survey Research Center. The Survey Research Center has had a vast amount of experience in conducting sample surveys and enjoys a worldwide reputation as possibly the foremost sample survey organization.

The procedures employed by the Survey Research Center in sampling black and white residents in each of the fifteen cities are based upon area probability sampling methods, described more fully elsewhere.[15]

The population within each city represented consists of persons 16 through 69 years of age living in households within the 1960 corporate limits of the city. Persons with no place of residence, people in institutions, and persons living in group quarters are not included in the population sampled. Two thousand eight hundred interviews were obtained from black persons, defined as above, in the fifteen cities; the numbers of blacks by city ranged from 110 to 255. Two thousand six hundred interviews were obtained from white persons in the sample cities, the numbers ranging from 120 to 240 per city.

The data from the Survey Research Center city surveys are used in this volume primarily in aggregated forms, percentages, or averages computed for each city.

A Note on Modes of Analysis Used in This Volume. The data used in the chapters to follow are amenable to a variety of analyses, the mode chosen at a particular point being dictated by the limitations of the data and the kinds of questions asked.

The main purpose in this volume is to understand the differences among the fifteen cities in the ways in which the political and civic elite, institutional agents, and black citizens interact with each other around issues that are critical to urban existence. Along these lines, the basic unit of analysis is the city and the total number of observations is therefore fifteen. The smallness of this number is a serious limitation on the depth to which analysis can be pursued. For example, many of the regression analysis shown in later chapters are based upon fifteen observations,

---

[15] Angus Campbell, *White Attitudes Toward Black People*, Institute for Social Research, Ann Arbor, 1972, Appendix B.

TABLE 2.1

Numbers of Interviews with Institutional Agents Obtained in Each City

	Police	Educators	Social Workers	Political Workers	Retail Merchants	Personnel Officers	Total
Desired Number =	40	20	20	10	30	30	150
Number Obtained in Each City							
Baltimore	40	20	20	10	29	30	149
Boston	0	20	20	10	30	31	111
Brooklyn	40	20	28	8	37	34	167
Chicago	38	20	21	10	30	28	147
Cincinnati	40	20	20	10	30	30	150
Cleveland	40	20	20	8	30	30	148
Detroit	40	16	20	10	30	29	145
Gary	42	20	18	11	30	32	153

TABLE 2.1 (Cont'd)

Desired Number =	Police 40	Educators 20	Social Workers 20	Political Workers 10	Retail Merchants 30	Personnel Officers 30	Total 150
Milwaukee	5*	20	19	5	31	30	110
Newark	41	20	22	7	29	28	147
Philadelphia	40	20	19	10	33	29	151
Pittsburgh	40	20	20	5	29	30	144
San Francisco	39	21	19	10	29	30	148
St. Louis	40	20	21	10	30	30	151
Washington, D.C.	37	21	20	5	31	26	140
Totals	522	298	307	129	458	447	2,161

*Obtained before police chief forbid further interviewing. These 5 cases are not used in most of the tabulations.

providing a very small number of degrees of freedom with which to work. We can only be confident that we have found an empirical relationship when the correlations are very high, much higher than is usually deemed acceptable in typical social science researches.

The criteria that should be applied to our data to judge whether a difference among the fifteen cities has been explained by its relationship to other intercity differences is an open question. If we were to regard the fifteen cities as a sample of an infinite universe of cities, it takes a correlation of .5 or above to reach statistical significance at the .05 level of confidence. Yet, there is good reason to regard the fifteen cities as more than a sample drawn from such an infinite universe. In fact, there are a rather small number of large metropolitan areas in the United States—only eighteen had populations of 1,000,000 or more in 1960, and our sample represents thirteen of the central cities involved. Hence it also makes sense to regard our findings as descriptive statistics, whose statistical significance in the traditional sense is not an issue. There are good and compelling reasons to take one or the other of these two positions. Indeed, it is tempting to argue strongly for the second position, since it presents a more sympathetic view of our data. However, in the interests of making conservative statements about our findings, we have employed consistently conventional statistical tests to our data, sometimes reporting them when they do not meet conventional criteria but, providing at the same time, information that will help the reader judge whether to go along with our interpretations.[16]

Unfortunately, the representativeness of our sample are not the only issues. Since some of the respondents were generated through nonprobability techniques, biases in estimated standard errors, as well as means, are possible. Therefore, interpretations of significance tests take on additional complexity. When nonprobability techniques produce inflated sample variance, significance tests are conservative. In contrast, artificially reduced sample variances produces misleadingly powerful significance tests. In our case, it is hard to know how the sample variances were affected. Where officials made available only their "best" people, variance was probably decreased. Where officials tried to present a "cross-section," variance may have been increased. Regardless of intent,

---

[16] Our ambivalent use of significance tests is conservative in another sense. Had we chosen to define our sample of cities as taken from a finite universe of large American metropolitan areas, we could have employed finite sample corrections on our significance tests and increased markedly the number of findings leading to rejection of the null hypothesis.

officials achieved their aims to some unknown degree. Given these complications, our decision to employ significance tests was undertaken with considerable ambivalence. Technically, they are often inappropriate. Yet, cautiously handled, they can provide a rough gauge of the extent of sampling error.

The role of sampling error becomes still more complicated when analyses are made at the city level. City characteristics are often aggregate statistics based on individual respondents, and consequently are subject to sampling error. There is no direct way to consider this sampling error in aggregate statistics used as variables at the city level when multivariate techniques are employed. Hence our use of multiple regression obscures some indeterminancy. This is a common difficulty for statistical techniques that take sample statistics as their raw material. Typically path analysis, for example, has the same problem. The correlation matrix on which it is based usually involves sample correlations whose sampling errors are ignored.

Throughout the manuscript multiple regression is the most common multivariate technique. The underlying linear model can generate a wide variety of statistics with different substantive interpretations. We have chosen to emphasize variance measures rather than slope measure; this should please some methodologists and annoy others.[17] With little initial theory, questionable sampling, and unknown amounts of measurement error, we felt that slope measures might too easily lend themselves to "spuriously specific" interpretations. There is too much "wiggle" in our data to support predictions of a certain number of units change in a dependent variable for every unit change in the independent variable. In addition, many of our measures come in arbitrary metrics, ruling out plausible interpretations for at least unstandardized regression coefficients. In short, although slope measures and variance measures are

---

[17] The variance versus slope debate has been raging for some time and will likely continue. There are many parties involved with important differences of opinion even between alleged allies. Usually arguing for variance measures are James S. Coleman ("Reply to Cain and Watts," ASR, 35:242–249), Richard B. Darlington ("Multiple Regression in Psychological Research and Practice," Psych. Bull., 69:161–182) Richard C. Pugh ("The Partitioning of Criterion Score Variance Accounted for in Multiple Regression," Amer. Educ. Res. J., 5:639–646), and Otis Dudley Duncan ("Path Analysis with Sociological Examples," AJS, 72:1–16). Arguing for slope measures are Glen G. Cain and Harold Watts ("Problems in Making Policy Inferences from the Coleman Report," ASR, 35:228–242), H. M. Blalock ("Causal Inferences, Closed Populations and Measures of Association," ASPR, 61:130–136) and John W. Tukey ("Causation, Regression, and Path Analysis) in Statistics and Mathematics in Biology, Oscar Kempthorne et al. (Eds.), Iowa State College Press, 1954.

similar in their algebra, variance partitions[18] seemed more likely to encourage prudence.

A final methodological issue involves one "ecological fallacy." Many of the analyses presented are based on aggregated data. Indices are formed from the sample survey interviews which represent the level of complaints about the police, for example, and are related to indices formed over police interviews relating aggregated police attitudes to these levels of complaints. Obviously what are being related in such an analysis are collective characteristics rather than individual characteristics. Thus finding that complaints about the police are more frequent in cities whose policemen show relative intolerant attitudes toward blacks means just that. It does *not* mean that individual blacks are complaining about the attitudes that they observe manifested by the police. Our conventional language is not congenial to making statements about aggregates, and it is very easy to slip grammatically from the aggregate level to the level of individuals. We hope that the reader will forgive those lapses in language precision: Some of them were used to avoid ponderous English.

From time to time through the volume we present analyses of data that are intended to be heuristic rather than definitive. In some cases the data are not extensive enough to anchor firmly a set of findings, although the findings are quite provocative. We have included these analyses, qualified hopefully with enough *caveats* that the reader is not misled too easily. This applies particularly to the several variance partitioning that are found at the end of some of the chapters.

---

[18] The process of partitioning variance begins by allocating to each independent variable in mutliple regression its "unique" contribution to explained variance. The unique contribution has been called "usefulness' by Richard Darlington ["Multiple Regression in Research and Practice," *Psych. Bull.*, 69 (3) (1968)] and is the additional variance explained when a given variable is added *last* to the regression equation. Unique contribution can also be defined as the square of the part (not partial) correlation or the square of the correlation between the variability of a given independent variable orthogonal to all other independent variables and the *unadjusted* variability in the dependent variable. After each variable's unique contribution has been determined, the unique contribution of all pairs, triplets, and so on, are calculated by dropping each "cluster" in turn from (or adding it last to) the regression equation. Finally, by subtraction the total explained variance can be divided among all variables independently and among all combinations of variables. It is probably worth noting in passing, the unique contribution usually less than (and never greater than) the squared partial correlation and the squared standardized regression coefficient (see Pugh *op. cit.*) Hence the unique contribution provides the most conservative estimate of variance attributable to each independent variable.

Chapter 3

SOME URBAN STRUCTURES:
Politics, Power, and Influence

When one visualizes a city, he most naturally pictures the profile of a downtown central business district.[1] The visualization of Chicago is the Loop, of New York the impressive profile of lower Manhattan, and of San Francisco the bridges and the hills of the business district. Because their central business districts do not contain as many monumental structures, lesser cities have less distinct images. But the downtown area forms the picture nevertheless. The distinctive profiles of higher buildings, the ambience created by intense activity, and the attraction of shops, stores, and theatres all make the central business district the visual symbol of the city.

There are good reasons for the symbolic dominance of downtown. Most frequently people travel toward the central business district, as the traffic jams on major business streets eloquently testify. The distinctive architecture of downtown is another reason for its dominance. Compared to other parts of a city, downtown provides more landmarks to serve as mnemonic visual aids to picturing the city.

From an organizational point of view, downtown is dominant because

---

[1] See Kevin Lynch, *The Image of the City* The MIT Press, (Cambridge, 1960) for a pioneering attempt to study how the residents of a city visualize their urban environments.

it serves as the headquarters for so many significant urban activities. The central offices of major business enterprises and public utilities are located in the city center. But, even more important, downtown is political headquarters. City hall is usually a monumental building (or at least intended as such). Police headquarters, and the state, local, and federal court buildings also remind one that law and order emanates from the city center. Downtown is the headquarters of the city—the place where major business and political decisions are made. Here is where we find the mayor, city councilmen, the police chief, and heads of government agencies. Here we also find the heads of businesses and public utilities (at least during daylight hours on weekdays).

In a perceptive essay, Norton Long[2] characterized the decision-making structure of American cities as an "ecology of games," observing that a local community is in effect a set of "games," each centering about a major institution where players follow out their roles according to rules that determine how resources are to be divided among players. Thus there is a "local government game" whose players are local officials and whose rules are the city charter, local ordinances, and other pertinent legislation. There is a "finance game," centering around the city's banks and banking officials, a "merchants' game," and so on.

The "games" of the local community are performed mainly on the playing field—downtown. A prominent part of the field is city hall where the mayor, city council, and major local government officials play out the major portions of their critical roles.

Thus this chapter focuses mainly on activities that take place downtown in the fifteen cities that we studied. The main purpose of this chapter is to describe some critical features of civic life in each of the fifteen cities, especially as they bear upon the relationships of the local structures to the black communities of the cities. In other words, we are concerned with major local political officials, civic leaders drawn from the private sector, and black leaders and rank-and-file members of each community. The viewpoints described are the perspectives of persons who are "active" in local political and civic affairs. In other words, we show how the elites in each of the cities view themselves, the decision-making apparatuses of their cities, and the relationships that these elites hold to the leaders and rank-and-file blacks in those cities.

The Data. The descriptions of the civic arenas are formed from interviews with the civic and political leaders (and other notables) within

---

[2] Norton Long, "The Local Community as an Ecology of Games," *Amer. J. Sociol.,* **64**: 251–261 (November 1958).

each of the cities. Early in 1968, a team of researchers interviewed as many of the major actors in each of the fifteen cities as they could within a period of 5 to 10 working days for each city. In addition we were permitted access to field reports from the interviews which the Kerner Commission conducted in certain cities.

The respondents interviewed were members of the city's elite, persons holding positions of importance (e.g., mayor, police chief, and school superintendent) or who were brought to the attention of field workers because they were mentioned frequently by such persons. Thus the field team would conduct interviews initially with persons on the list of job holders in the city and then branch out to the chains of referrals. On the average about 40 such 1- to 2-hour interviews were conducted in each of the fifteen cities.[3]

The main body of data discussed in this chapter are ratings of cities based upon the information contained in the qualitative interviews of members of each city's elite. The interviews obtained in a city were read carefully by four members of the research team, and then each member rated independently each city along a large number of rating scales. Thus on the basis of the total amount of information available concerning the mayor's power position in the community, each rater gave a numerical value from 0 through 10 which expressed his best opinion of how the elite members interviewed viewed the mayor's power position.

This procedure was used because the interviews varied so widely from each other in length, coverage of subject matters, and, frankly, the honesty with which respondents answered the questions put to them. For example, it was rare that a police chief knew much in detail about the local school system, while the school superintendent or a member of the school board might know a great deal about the school system. This method of handling qualitative interviews is very similar to that of social anthropologists handling their field notes, except that because four research staff members were involved, the reliability of the judgments made can be better estimated by the procedures that we employed. (These procedures are described in greater detail in Chapter 2.)

It is important to bear in mind throughout this chapter that the ratings are based upon interviews obtained during the early part of 1968. These findings do not necessarily describe any of the fifteen cities today (1973), although we can expect some degree of continuity from year to year. It is also important to recognize that the ratings are accomplished on an arbitrary scale; thus it is difficult to make any conclusions other than those based on comparisons among the fifteen cities studied. In other words, a rating of 10 on a particular dimension given to a city

---

[3] See Chapter 2 for detailed discussion of field work procedures.

has some meaning in relationship to the ratings given to other cities, but is difficult to interpret alone. Finally, the reader should also be aware that these ratings are framed from the opinions of the elites of a particular city. Although there is some correspondence, often very close, between these ratings and the views of rank-and-file city residents, usually elite perceptions and evaluations of their cities diverge from those of the rank-and-file to some degree.

Who Runs the City?   Our cities have grown so complex, and urban problems correspondingly have become so massive that it is problematic how they function at all. Yet function they do despite the dire predictions of some urban problem "specialists" that our cities are on the verge of collapse. Somehow, residents are fed; goods are produced and distributed; families are formed, grow, die, and are replaced; and incredible numbers of people and amounts of goods are moved about each day. Although the central decision-making apparatus of local government seems impotent to affect rapid and/or far-reaching changes, it does make decisions that are more or less faithfully translated into policy that guides behavior.

The complexity of the city and its sluggish response to purposive attempts to attack urban problems leads to the bothersome question of how decisions are made and carried out. To many researchers and scholars concerned with the urban scene, the problem of where power lies seems especially elusive. Since World War II several score researches have tried to determine how community decisions are made.[4] The results of these studies have not been very clear cut. Some researchers find that major city officials, for example, the mayor, play important roles in decisions involving urban renewal projects or fluoridation of the water supply. In other cities, it appears as if a "shadowy" elite of businessmen and merchants influence the decision-making structure far more than their numerical strength in the population would indicate.

The results of different studies have produced such varying descriptions of American cities that whether a pluralist or power structure model fits best the American urban scene has become an issue.

As a guide to the interpretation of the data to be presented in this volume, the literature comprising American community studies suffers

---

[4] See the articles by John Walton and Claire Gilbert in *Community Structure and Decision Making*, Terry N. Clark (Ed.), Chandler Press, San Francisco, 1968, for analyses of the degree to which there is consensus among community power analysts and researchers.

from two main disabilities. First, most of the community studies that have touched upon the critical questions of decision-making and political power have been conducted in cities well below the size range considered here. With the exception of Los Angeles, all of the ten largest central cities in the North are included among the fifteen cities in our sample. Neither political scientists or sociologists studied these major metropolitan centers.[5] Second, most of the studies have been of single cases. The absence of a comparative perspective makes the interpretation of any findings a hazardous affair. For example, viewed alone, a particular city may appear to be dominated by a mayor and a powerful political machine, while viewed in a comparative perspective, the power of the mayor and his political machine may be only fair or middling in a set of cities which would span the full range of variation in these respects.

It is difficult to see how the present study can contribute very much to the controversies over community power. The methods employed in this study are eclectic. In one sense, this is a study in power "reputations," since we rely heavily on the preponderance of the evidence in the set of interviews conducted in each city. In another sense, it is a study of specific decisions, because our elite informants often cited specific decisions behind their statements about the influence positions of various individuals and groups. The exact proportions that go into this mixture of decisional techniques and reputational methods is hard to discern.

On balance, it appears to us that our study is closer to the reputational power studies in which power is attributed to individuals and groups; we rely mainly on attributions of power (or of other characteristics) that are reflected in interviews conducted with elites in each of the fifteen cities. In other words, our study is based largely on the images that informed and active individuals have of the roles played by various groups in the communities in question. Of course, we expect that there is some correspondence between "image" and "reality," but this correspondence is not probed empirically.

Figure 3.1 illustrates the kind of data toward which attention is directed in this chapter. The bar in Figure 3.1 is calibrated from 0 through 10, representing the rating scale used by our research group as they read each set of interviews from each city and made judgments about the

---

[5] This statement is not entirely accurate. Studies have been made of specific decisions in some of the major cities, Chicago being a favored city for such studies. See Edward A. Banfield, *Political Influence*, The Free Press of Glencoe, New York, 1961, and Peter H. Rossi and Robert A. Dentler, *The Politics of Urban Renewal*, The Free Press of Glencoe, New York, 1962. Both volumes are concerned with how sets of rather specific decisions, for example, concerning urban renewal and public hospital policy, were made in Chicago during the earlier years of Mayor Daley's long regime.

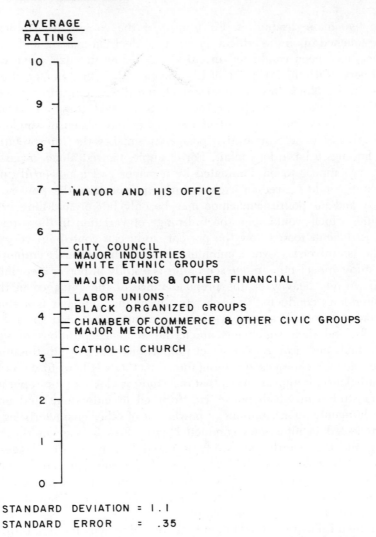

Figure 3.1. Elite interviews: average ratings given to importance of groups in city decision-making. Standard deviation = 1.1. Standard error = .35.

importance of each of ten groups in city decision-making. Each of a set of groups within the cities is placed on the bar according to the average rating given to that group in all of the cities combined. Thus the highest group on the bar is "mayor and his office," which is rated 6.9 on the average by the five raters. At the bottom of the bar are shown the standard deviations and standard errors of the distribution of the ten average ratings.[6] The size of differences among the ratings can be roughly judged by using the standard deviation of the ratings. Thus two ratings that are more than two standard deviations (22) apart are quite different given the distribution's variability. In addition, the standard errors for each mean (treating the five ratings as a sample) are typically quite small, of the order of .30, indicating that differences between means larger than 1.2 units (4 standard errors) are very unlikely to have occurred by chance.

Using these criteria it is abundantly clear that the "mayor and his office" on the average is the most important group in city decision-making. Although the remainder of the groups are spaced close together, "major industries" are probably more important than "major merchants," and "white ethnic groups" are usually considerably more important than the "Catholic Church," and more important than "black organized groups."

These averages computed across all the ratings in all fifteen cities conceal more than they reveal, as Figure 3.1 indicates, wherein the ratings given to the ten groups in each of the fifteen cities is shown.

In Figure 3.2 each bar represents the ratings given to one of the ten groups. The cities are located along those bars according to the average of the five ratings given to that group in that city. Thus on the first bar on the left-hand side of Figure 3.2, the ratings are of the importance in decision-making of the "mayor and his office." The first rating on the top of the bar is given to Chicago (CHI) whose mayor (then as now, Richard J. Daley) received the highest rating, 9.75, of any of the fifteen mayors. At the opposite end of the bar is the average rating received by the then Mayor of Cincinnati (CNC) 2.25.

For the sake of space and simplicity, we have abbreviated the cities as follows:

Baltimore   BAL
Boston   BOS

---

[6] The rating for each group (e.g., 6.9 for the mayor) is based on the coded qualitative interviews with elites. Each mean was calculated from the individual scores given to each group by the five raters. Technically, if the ratings for each group are viewed as a sample, each mean is subject to sampling error. If variability in ratings is viewed as measurement error, adjustments for attenuation are appropriate. In either case, the "instability" of each mean rating is ignored in this graph (though as described in Chapter 2, crucial in determining which ratings were used). Each mean is a point estimate; graphed and then treated as raw data from which a standard deviation and standard error are calculated. Therefore, the standard deviation of 1.1 is the standard deviation of the ten means used as raw data and the standard error is the estimated deviation of the sampling distribution of these means used as point estimates.

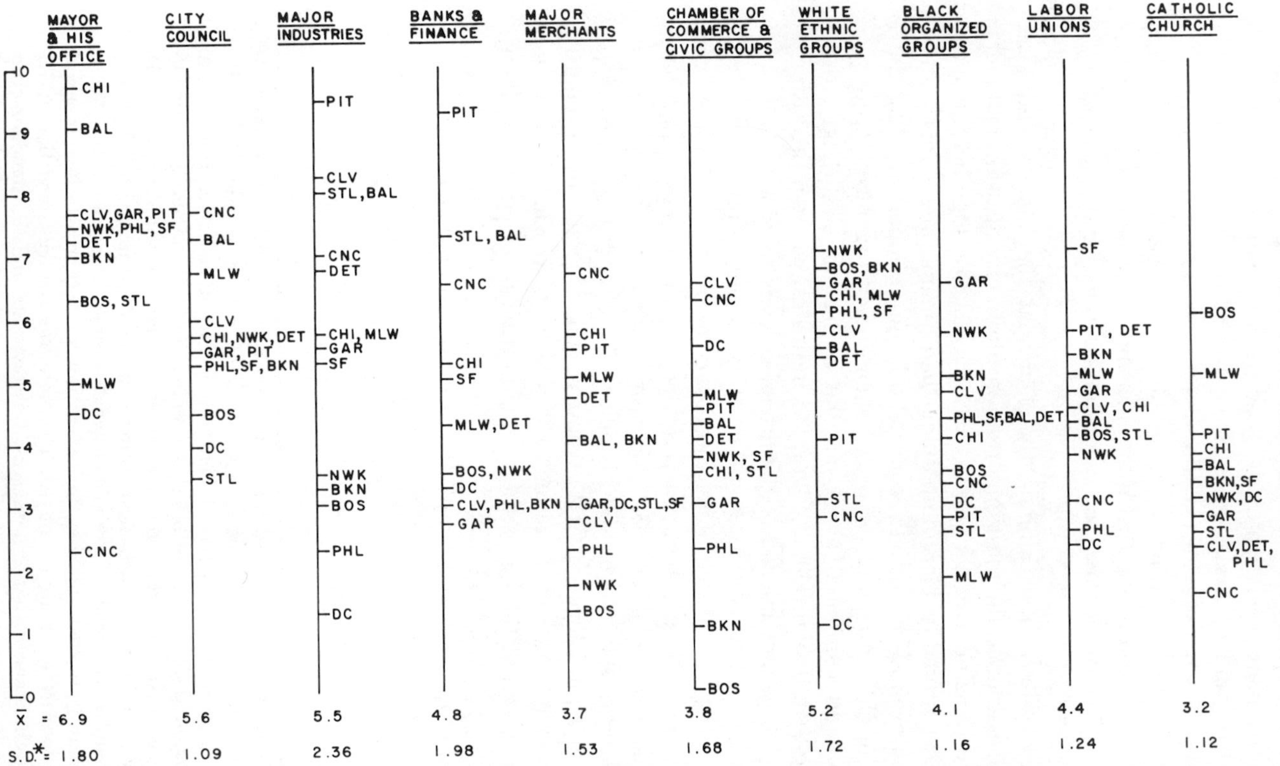

Figure 3.2 — Elite interviews: importance of groups in city decision-making.

Column headers (left to right): MAYOR & HIS OFFICE, CITY COUNCIL, MAJOR INDUSTRIES, BANKS & FINANCE, MAJOR MERCHANTS, CHAMBER OF COMMERCE & CIVIC GROUPS, WHITE ETHNIC GROUPS, BLACK ORGANIZED GROUPS, LABOR UNIONS, CATHOLIC CHURCH

Means ($\bar{X}$) and standard deviations (S.D.) for each column:

Group	$\bar{X}$	S.D.
MAYOR & HIS OFFICE	6.9	1.80
CITY COUNCIL	5.6	1.09
MAJOR INDUSTRIES	5.5	2.36
BANKS & FINANCE	4.8	1.98
MAJOR MERCHANTS	3.7	1.53
CHAMBER OF COMMERCE & CIVIC GROUPS	3.8	1.68
WHITE ETHNIC GROUPS	5.2	1.72
BLACK ORGANIZED GROUPS	4.1	1.16
LABOR UNIONS	4.4	1.24
CATHOLIC CHURCH	3.2	1.12

*S.D. = The standard deviation which can facilitate comparisons across as well as within distributions. Using the means and standard deviations provided the reader can transform the location of any city into a Z score based on a standardized distribution (mean = 0, SD = 1.0)

Figure 3.2. Elite interviews: importance of groups in city decision-making. S.D. = the standard deviation which can facilitate comparisons across as well as within distributions. Using the means and standard deviations provided the reader can transform the location of any city into a Z-score based on a standardized distribution (mean = 0, S.D. = 1.0).

34

Brooklyn	BKN
Chicago	CHI
Cincinnati	CNC
Cleveland	CLV
Detroit	DET
District of Columbia	DC
Gary	GAR
Milwaukee	MLW
Newark	NWK
Philadelphia	PHL
Pittsburgh	PIT
St. Louis	STL
San Francisco	SF

By using two or three key letters from city names (much in the style of airline baggage tags) we hope that the abbreviations suggest enough of the name so that the reader can easily interpolate the missing vowels and consonants.

The results displayed in Figure 3.2 show that the cities vary considerably both in the groups that were important in the decision-making of each city and in the variation in a particular type of rating from city to city. For example, Chicago and Baltimore are cities in which their mayors occupy considerably greater than average positions of importance. It would indeed be fatal to the validity of our study if Mayor Daley had turned out to be a figure of minor importance in the ratings given by our research group. Pittsburgh is a third city that shows an unusual pattern—one of preeminence of major industries and banks.

A few of the cities stand out because of the comparative unimportance attributed to one or more of the groups. Washington, D.C., shows a pattern in which the mayor, city council, and almost every group are given low ratings. Of course, this finding is no mystery, since decision-making in Washington, D.C., is so heavily influenced by the Congress and other federal government officials.[7] The low importance accorded to the mayor

---

[7] The term "major industries" as used in these ratings refer to the "private sector" of the economy. Obviously, Washington, D.C.'s major "industry," the federal government and its agencies, is preeminent in a variety of ways, including constituting through the Congress and its committees the major law-making body for the district. The preeminence of the federal government accounts for the low ratings given to almost every other potential actor in Washington, D.C. Indeed, the almost total lack of any home rule for the district puts this city outside of many of the general trends shown by the other fourteen cities. It can be very legitimately argued, we believe, that had we been perceptive enough to treat the federal government (and especially the congress) as one of the major actors on the local scene, the deviant patterns of

in Cincinnati has already been noted,[8] but the rating of 0 given to the chamber of commerce and other civic groups in Boston deserves some attention.

The diversity of patterns among cities and across rating dimensions is supported by the analysis of variance in Table 3.1 in which highly significant F-ratios (using interrater variance as the error term) are shown both for city means and for rating dimension means. It should be especially noted that the F-ratio for the interaction between city means and rating dimension means is also significant, indicating that the cities tend to be rated in unique ways by the raters. In short, the pattern is one of diversity with individual cities tending to show unique profiles expressing the comparative importance of groups in city-decision making.

Table 3.2 presents yet another way of looking at the ratings of Figure 3.1. In this table we show the intercorrelations among ratings, computed by using the city average ratings on each of the dimensions. The correlations thus express the extent to which each pair of rating dimensions vary together. For example a high correlation between the importance of the mayor and the importance of white ethnic groups, indicates that when the mayor is considered important, white ethnic groups are also important, and vice versa. Two major patterns stand out. First, apparently when the mayor is considered important, both white ethnic groups and black organized groups are considered important. Second, the various business groups (industries, banks, merchants, and chamber of commerce) vary together, so that when one business group is considered powerful so are the others. Cities in which the mayor and solidary groups are important are usually not cities in which the business groups are important.

In short, there appear to be two types of cities—one in which the mayor is preeminent along with white ethnic groups and black organized groups, and the other in which business groups are dominant while the mayor plays a subordinate role.

However these tendencies are by no means strong enough to construct clearcut typologies. The cities show enough idiosyncrasies (e.g., Cleve-

---

this city as shown here would be lessened. Washington, D.C., would have resembled the pattern of Pittsburgh whose major industries tend to dominate the city. Unfortunately, we did not modify our rating scheme at the time to take into account the peculiarly unusual situation of Washington, D.C.

[8] Cincinnati is virtually the only major northern city that has a council-manager form of city government. Cincinnati's mayor is elected by city councilmen from among council members. The mayor's duties are primarily to preside over council meetings and to represent the city on ceremonial occasions. An appointed city manager is the city's chief administrative officer.

TABLE 3.1

Results of Two Way Analysis of Variance of Ratings
of Importance of Groups in City Decision Making
(See Figure 3.2)

Source	Degrees of Freedom	Mean Square	F-Ratio	P
Total	599	5.16		
Rating Dimensions	9	85.8	45.2	<.01
Cities	14	18.6	9.8	<.01
Interaction (Cities and Dimensions)	126	9.5	5.0	<.01
Error	450	1.9		

Note: Analysis of variance was computed using the individual ratings given
by members of the research group thereby allowing an estimate of the
error variance separate from the interaction between cities and
dimensions. F-ratios were computed by dividing appropriate mean
squares by the error mean square.

land where the mayor *and* major industries are both rated above average
in importance) that each city may be said to show a unique patterning,
with only three cities showing clearly different patterns from all the
others: Chicago, with its mayor, Richard J. Daley, overshadowing other
actors; Pittsburgh, with its dominant industries and banks; and Washington, D.C., with its relatively powerless groups. The other cities fall in
between these extreme cases, on the one hand more of a structure of
importance than Washington, D.C., and on the other less of a concentration of power than in Chicago or Pittsburgh.

Evaluating the importance of particular groups in the decision-making
process is one critical way of looking at the central decision-making processes in a city. Yet, such ratings show far from the complete story. We
also need to take into account the typical ways in which issues are
settled, whether through conflict or through the building of consensus.
To round out the portrait of decision-making in the fifteen cities, additional ratings along these lines are shown in Figure 3.3.

Each of the raters gave a numerical value from 0 to 10 which expressed the extent to which he thought each of the following statements
applied to the "styles" of decision making in each of the cities.

TABLE 3.2

Elite) Inter-Correlations Among City Ratings
Interviews) of Importance of Groups in City Decision Making (N = 15)

	City Council	Major Ind.	Banks	Major Merch.	Ch. of Comm.	White Ethnic	Black Groups	Labor Unions	Catholic Church
Mayor	-.08	.18	.04	-.21	-.30	.58	.52	.51	.10
City Council		.38	.21	.58	.43	.20	.07	.28	-.18
Major Industry			.72	.51	.47	-.12	-.11	.53	-.17
Banks				.53	.28	-.39	-.38	.38	-.01
Major Merchants					.45	-.30	-.32	.20	-.15
Chamber of Commerce						-.54	-.22	-.06	-.47
White Ethnic							.52	.39	.34
Black Groups								.16	-.30
Labor Unions									.18

NOTE: Correlations were computed using city average ratings and hence are based on N = 15.
Applying ordinary tests of significance a correlation must be above .5 in order to be
significantly different from 0 at the .05 level.

Issues are usually controlled by a political machine.
Issues are usually controlled by a civic elite.
Issues usually involve great public conflict.
Issues tend to be settled by gradually building consensus rather than
forcing through decisions over the opposing groups.

The resulting average ratings received by each of the cities are shown in
Figure 3.3. Note that analysis of variance (as shown at the bottom of

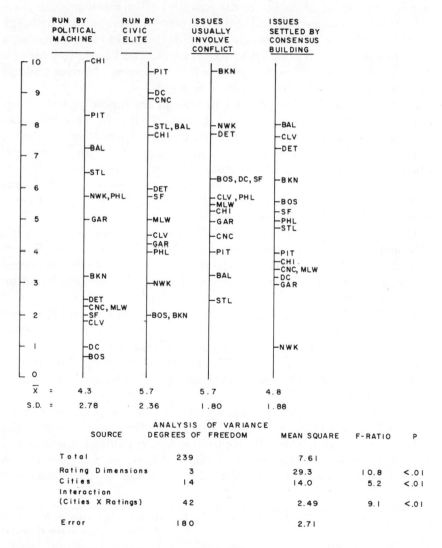

RUN BY POLITICAL MACHINE	RUN BY CIVIC ELITE	ISSUES USUALLY INVOLVE CONFLICT	ISSUES SETTLED BY CONSENSUS BUILDING

X̄ = 4.3   5.7   5.7   4.8

S.D. = 2.78   2.36   1.80   1.88

ANALYSIS OF VARIANCE

SOURCE	DEGREES OF FREEDOM	MEAN SQUARE	F-RATIO	P
Total	239	7.61		
Rating Dimensions	3	29.3	10.8	<.01
Cities	14	14.0	5.2	<.01
Interaction (Cities X Ratings)	42	2.49	9.1	<.01
Error	180	2.71		

Figure 3.3.   Elite interviews: styles of decision-making.

Figure 3.3) indicates the statistically significant differences obtained among ratings among cities, and that there is a significant amount of interaction between cities and ratings.

According to these ratings, Chicago is (each rater giving Chicago a rating of 10) run to a greater extent by a machine as compared to any other city. Indeed, it would have been quite surprising and disturbing if Chicago had turned out otherwise, given the national reputation of that city as a stronghold of the last of the powerful urban machines. Considerably below Chicago, but still quite above the average, is Pittsburgh (with a score of 8.25). Pittsburgh also heads the list of cities in having a predominance of a civic elite who settles issues. The long lasting alliance between Pittsburgh's industrial elite and a succession of urban political machines is expressed in this pattern of ratings.[9]

In stark contrast to Chicago and Pittsburgh are Boston and Washington, D.C. (with ratings of .75 and 1.0, respectively). In these two cities the raters could find little evidence that political machines dominated the settling of issues. Despite the long heritage of Mayor Curley and other well known local political figures, Boston's present local politics is characterized by the absence of long-standing coalitions and lasting political factions among its major local politicians. The peculiar situation in Washington, D.C., needs no comment.

Civic elites are reputed to control the settling of issues in Pittsburgh, Washington, D.C.,[10] and Cincinnati, but play negligible roles in Boston, Brooklyn, and Newark. Indeed, civic elites are somewhat more important on the average than political machines, as the greater average rating for the former indicates.

Regarding the ways in which issues are worked out, some cities, such as Brooklyn, Newark, and Detroit, experience much public conflict among long-standing alignments of local groups, while St. Louis and Baltimore experience very little. The settlement of issues through consensus is typical of Baltimore, Cleveland, and Detroit and least characteristic of Newark.

Looking at the correlations among ratings (Table 3.3), we can see that conflict over issues is negatively related to the dominance of political machines or civic elites. By controlling issues, political machines and civic elites lessen the degree of conflict. This is one interpretation of these findings. Note, however, that the cities that have conflicts over

---

[9] See Bruce M. Stave, *The New Deal and the Last Hurrah*, University of Pittsburgh Press, Pittsburgh, 1971, for an account of Pittsburgh machine politics in the transition to the New Deal period.

[10] The civic elite of Washington, D.C., consists of a loose coalition of federal officials, merchants, lawyers, and other local notables.

TABLE 3.3
Elite   ) Inter-correlations Among Ratings of
Interviews) Decision Making Styles (Figure 5.3)
             (N = 15)

Styles of Decision Making

	Run by Pol. Mach.	Run by Civic Elite	Issues Involve Conflict	Issues Settled Through Consensus
Political Machine		.34	-.42	-.15
Civic Elite			-.66	.01
Conflict				-.14
Consensus				

issues are only slightly less likely to decide issues through consensus, as the correlation of −.14 between these two ratings seem to indicate. For example in Detroit issues produce conflict among long-standing alignments in the citizenry, yet Detroit is also rated among the highest of cities that decide issues through the building of consensus.

The reader with a good memory may recall that the same cities in which the mayors were rated as important in decision-making tended also to be the same cities in which political machines were reputed to dominate the decision-making process. Indeed, a strong political machine ordinarily needs a powerful high official, such as the mayor, to where the two ratings are plotted one against the other. achieve results. This impression is probed more deeply in Figure 3.4,

Strong political machines are rarer than dominant mayors. Although there is an overall tendency for cities with dominant mayors to have strong political machines, as shown by a correlation of .66, many cities with strong mayors do not have strong political machines, for example, Cleveland, San Francisco, Detroit, and Brooklyn.[11]

---

[11] Brooklyn, it must be kept in mind, does not have a local mayor, because it is a part of New York City. The ratings referring to Brooklyn sometimes have an ambiguous meaning, on occasion pertaining to New York City as a whole, and sometimes to the subcommunity of Bedford-Stuyvesant, the neighborhood upon which this study is focused. Thus the ratings in this chapter refer mainly to New York City as a whole, even though our interviews with agency personnel are with those who serve in Bedford-Stuyvesant, and the Survey Research Center's sample of rank-and-file blacks and whites refers to the borough of Brooklyn, a much larger area but still only one of New York City's five boroughs.

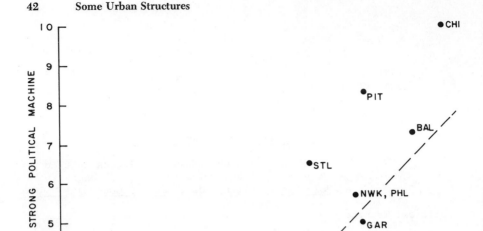

Figure 3.4. Elite interviews: relationship between importance ratings of mayor and "issues controlled by strong political machine." Correlation = .663. Dotted line = regression.

The ratings of the importance of civic elites in the settling of issues is in large part an expression of the importance of major industries in decision-making, as Figure 3.5 indicates. Although the overall correlation between these two ratings is not very high (.483), this coefficient is unduly influenced by the idiosyncratic patterns shown by two cities: Washington, D.C., stands out as a city in which major industries play a minor role in decision-making but in which a civic elite is important in settling issues. Cleveland shows the exact opposite syndrome with a

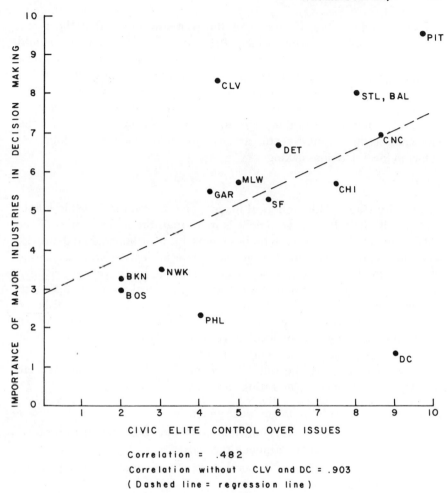

Figure 3.5. Elite interviews: relationship between importance of major industries in decision making and importance of civic elite in settling issues. Correlation = .482. Correlation without CLV and DC = .903. Dotted line = regression line.

high rating of importance given to the major industries but not much influence credited to Cleveland's civic elite. Indeed, if we remove Cleveland and Washington from Figure 3.5 correlation between the two ratings jumps to .903. Apparently, in Washington, D.C., a strong civic elite is not dominated by major industries in the private sector, and in Cleveland, a weak civic elite is composed of groups not from the major industries.

It is clear from the discussion of the past few pages that the power structures of all fifteen cities have been stamped from no one mould. Each city shows an almost unique pattern, ranging at the one extreme of Chicago with its preeminent mayor to the other extreme of Washington, D.C., in which very little power is held by any of the major actors. If there are any overall trends, however, they indicate that mayors ordinarily play an important role and that major industries and other elements of the business sector are usually influential, if not dominant, actors in local decision-making.

Inside City Hall.   Although local mayors may be the most visible inhabitants of city hall, local government is more than the mayor's office alone. City councils (or equivalent bodies) pass local ordinances and provide a forum for the discussion of local issues. Special legislative bodies, especially school boards, hold sway over important local service organizations. Appointed department heads administer local agencies that carry out, more or less faithfully, pertinent local, state, and federal legislation. The mayor may be more of the focus of attention within local government, but the apparatus of local governmental institutions is a complex large enough to have some degree of autonomy in action.

Figure 3.6 compares the relative strengths of the mayors in each city and their city councils. The ratings are defined as follows:

Autonomy: the ability to act independently

Potency: ability to carry out decisions and cause action to be taken by local government agencies

Competence: reputation of general competence and leadership ability in office

As the average ratings shown in Figure 3.6 indicate, mayors overshadow city councils both in autonomy and in potency. From the viewpoints of the elites whom we interviewed, mayors appear to be preeminent not only in the decision-making process in general but also within local government.

The overall high ratings given to mayors obscures a number of interesting differences among cities. As usual, Chicago stands out because it has a mayor who is regarded as highly autonomous, potent, and competent. At the other extreme, Washington, D.C., because of its peculiar position as a creature of the federal government, is seen as having a competent mayor who lacks autonomy and the ability to carry through a

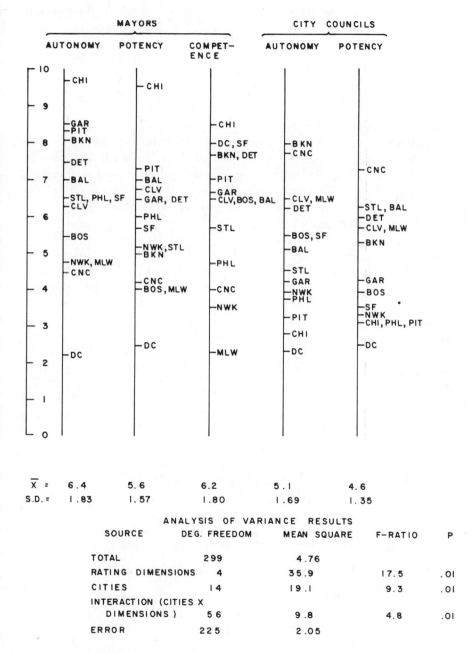

	MAYORS			CITY COUNCILS	
	AUTONOMY	POTENCY	COMPET-ENCE	AUTONOMY	POTENCY

$\overline{X}$ = 6.4   5.6   6.2   5.1   4.6
S.D.= 1.83   1.57   1.80   1.69   1.35

ANALYSIS OF VARIANCE RESULTS

SOURCE	DEG. FREEDOM	MEAN SQUARE	F-RATIO	P
TOTAL	299	4.76		
RATING DIMENSIONS	4	35.9	17.5	.01
CITIES	14	19.1	9.3	.01
INTERACTION (CITIES X DIMENSIONS)	56	9.8	4.8	.01
ERROR	225	2.05		

Figure 3.6. Elite interviews: mayor and city council: autonomy, potency, and competence.

decision to action. Nor is Washington's mayor relegated to this position through the dominance of its city council. The Washington, D.C., city council shares the same low position of its mayor.

Still a third pattern is shown by Cincinnati, whose relatively powerless mayor is overshadowed by an autonomous and potent city council. This pattern is undoubtedly due to structural characteristics of Cincinnati local government, a council-manager form of government.

The correlations among ratings shown in Table 3.4 show that autonomy and potency are almost synonymous, with correlations of .87 for mayors and .81 for city councils. Competence, however, is much less closely related to the other two ratings for mayors, the correlations involved being .45 and .36. These correlations are undoubtedly depressed by the high competence rating given to Washington's mayor along with very low autonomy and potency ratings.

There is an overall tendency for the ratings of mayors and of city councils to be slightly negatively related. However, when we examine the joint distribution of such ratings, as in Figure 3.7, where the autonomy ratings of city councils and mayors are plotted against each other, it becomes obvious that Washington, D.C., represents a very deviant point in an array that shows a rather general negative relationship. Indeed, if we omit Washington, D.C., from our computations, the correlation jumps from −.03 to −.43. Furthermore, if we omit Brooklyn, a point that deviates in the opposite direction from Washington, D.C. (i.e., both the mayor and the city council are rated as highly autonomous), the

TABLE 3.4

Elite   )   Inter-Correlations Among City Ratings
Interviews)   of Autonomy, Potency and Competence of
             Mayor and City Council (See Figures 3.9 and 3.10)
             [N = 15]

	Ratings of Mayor			Ratings of City Council	
	Autonomy	Potency	Competence	Autonomy	Potency
Mayor Autonomy		.87	.45	-.03	-.007
Mayor Potency			.36	-.23	-.10
Mayor Competence				-.24	-.33
Cty. Cncl. Autonomy					.81
Cty. Cncl. Potency					

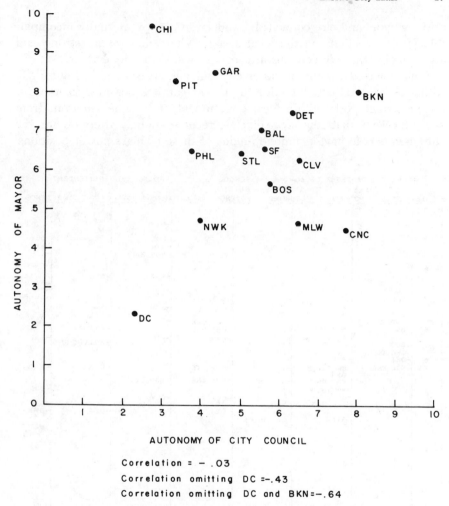

Figure 3.7. Elite interviews: autonomy of mayor and autonomy of city council. Correlation = .03. Correlation omitting DC = −.43. Correlation omitting DC and BKN = −.64.

correlation turns even more in the negative direction, −.64.[12] In other words, the peculiar situations of Washington, D.C., and New York City

[12] There is an important statistical point here. With but fifteen cases, altering one or two of the data points can make substantial differences in the correlation coefficient. This will become especially problematic later in multiple regression .equations with N's of 15.

aside, mayors and city councils by and large occupy mutually incompatible power positions on the local scene. Where mayors are strong and autonomous, the city councils are seen as weak and dependent.

Some selected ratings on other city officials are shown in Figure 3.8. Although we originally intended to present parallel measures for most of the important posts within local government, it became apparent from our interviews that few local officials receive enough attention for the elite members to have definite opinions of these official's power positions.

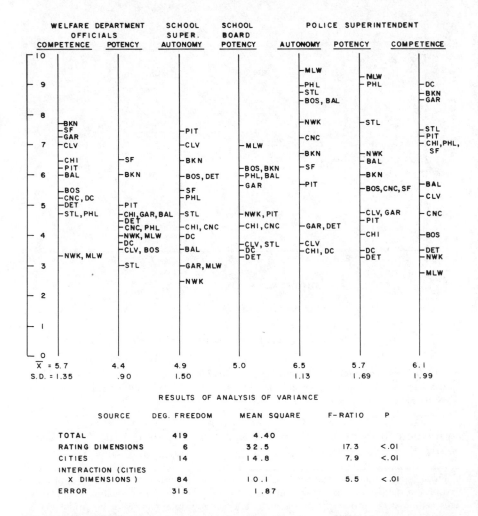

Figure 3.8.   Elite interviews: ratings of public officials in welfare department, education, and police departments.

For example, although each of the cities had local versions of the Model Cities and Community Action Programs, the directors of these agencies were not sufficiently well known to be mentioned by elite members within each city or across different cities. As Figure 3.8 indicates, we were able to obtain some ratings concerning welfare officials, school superintendents, and police chiefs. For an uncomfortably large number of cities, there was insufficient information upon which to base ratings of welfare officials and school superintendents; hence these ratings must be viewed with some suspicion.[13]

Welfare officials and school superintendents hold relatively weak positions as compared with either mayors (see Figure 3.8) or with police superintendents. Note that although the analysis of variance results (shown in the bottom of Figure 3.8) indicate that city differences, rating differences, and city-rating interactions are significant, the largest F-ratio is attached to ratings, which indicates that the difference among the four types of actors in the table are far less likely to have occurred by chance. Furthermore, although cities do show idiosyncratic tendencies, the differences among cities are less significant than the differences among actors.

The interrelationships among the ratings are shown in Table 3.5. The weakness of intracity patterns is upheld in this table by the generally

---

[13] Of course, one may take the position that an official ought to be potent (or competent) enough to come to the attention of local elite members; hence the absence of a rating expresses the extent to which the position in question is a weak and impotent one. Mindful of the possibility that there may be powerful but relatively quiet public officials whose activities would not come to the attention of even those elite members who are deep into local politics, we have preferred to omit ratings rather than make unverified assumptions about what a missing rating may mean.

TABLE 3.5

Elite) Ratings)	Inter-Correlations Among Strength Ratings of Welfare Officials, School Superintendents, Police Chiefs and Mayors (N = 15)				
	Welfare Officials Autonomy	School Superintendent Autonomy	Police Chief Autonomy	City Council Autonomy	Mayor Autonomy
Welfare Officials		.19	-.16	.17	.45
School Super.			-.21	.23	.30
Police Chief				.25	-.24
City Council					-.02

low correlations among ratings. When mayors are autonomous, welfare officials and school superintendents also tend to be autonomous. In contrast there is a slight tendency for the autonomy of police chiefs and mayors to be negatively related, for example, when the mayor is rated as autonomous, police chiefs are likely to be seen as relatively subordinate and correspondingly weak.

The relationships of city officials to the City Council are even weaker than their relationships to the Mayor. There are very slight tendencies for police chiefs, school superintendents, and welfare officials to be autonomous when the city councils are autonomous, but the correlations involved are so small that they are quite far from statistical significance. Note also that the relationship between the autonomy of the mayor and the autonomy of the City Council is essentially zero. Autonomous city councils are to be found in cities that have autonomous mayors about as frequently as in cities that have weak mayors.

In short, a strong, autonomous mayor dominates the local scene at the expense of the chief of police, but reinforces the autonomy of public welfare officials and school superintendents. In contrast, where a mayor is weak, police chiefs are strong, while welfare and public education lose autonomy. Public welfare departments and school systems act in this respect as if they functioned closely with the mayor's office, while police departments behave as if they were quasigovernments competing for power with the mayor's office. Indeed, as we show in later chapters, citizens react to police departments and mayors with more sensitivity involved than to either welfare departments or public education. Apparently a strong mayor provides supportive backing to the latter and close supervision over the former.

City Hall and the Ghetto.   For most of our metropolitan areas—especially for those with central cities containing high proportions of black residents—the problems faced by city hall are intimately connected with race relations. To political conservatives, urban problems are restoring law and order, rehabilitating the central city so that it becomes attractive again to the middle class now located in the suburbs, and rehabilitating a new set of immigrants to "normal" middle-class standards of work and behavior. To political liberals, urban problems center around the depressed socioeconomic position of black residents and around programs designed to bring blacks into parity with whites. In either perspective, the black subcommunities are central to any detailed specification of "urban problems" because the term itself has become a synonym for race relations.

The relationships between black subcommunities and local political structures are of central concern in this volume. The ways in which city councils and mayors relate to their black constituencies vary considerably among cities. Both range widely in their accessibility to black leaders, their sympathetic response to black demands, and their knowledgeability and sophistication about their black constituencies.

Figures 3.9 and 3.10 present ratings, respectively, of the mayor and the city council of each of the cities. The analysis of variance results presented at the bottom of each of the figures show that there are statistically significant differences among the ratings and among the cities.

The cities are particularly well differentiated in the ratings of the mayor (see bottom of Figure 3.9), indicating that differences among cities (hence among mayors) constitute the source of the largest amount of the variation in the ratings.

The intercorrelations among ratings of the mayor, as shown in top half of Table 3.6, are all .88 or above, indicating that the mayors tend to line up in remarkably similar ways on each of the dimensions rated.[14] Furthermore, with respect to four of the mayors' ratings, the cities divide clearly into two groups. In six cities the mayor is rated as being markedly less accessible to black militants, less sympathetic and responsive to black demands, and lacking in knowledge and sophistication about the black community. These six are St. Louis, Philadelphia, Chicago, Cincinnati, Newark, and Milwaukee. In contrast, the other nine cities are all rated as having mayors who are considerably more sympathetic and accessible to blacks; Gary, Cleveland, Washington, D.C., Baltimore, and Brooklyn are regarded as having the most sympathetic and accessible mayors of the total group of nine.

The images of city councils are much less clear as indicated in the bottom half of Table 3.6. City councils appear less consistent to our raters, as the generally lower intercorrelations among ratings indicates. Nor do the councils separate themselves into groups in Figure 3.10, as did the mayors.

In contrast to city councils, it is clear that mayors are regarded as more

---

[14] It is difficult to decide between two alternative interpretations of these high relationships. On the one hand, these high correlations may be interpreted as representing a "halo effect" in which the "general reputation" of a mayor, as sympathetic or antagonistic to his black constituents, lead raters to regard a mayor as positive or negative in each particular respect. On the other hand, the correlations may reflect the fact that a mayor's "general reputation" is made up precisely of such attributes. We suspect that both processes are at work; hence we use mainly the ratings of "responsiveness to black demands" as representing the general reputation of the mayor vis-a-vis the black subcommunity of his city.

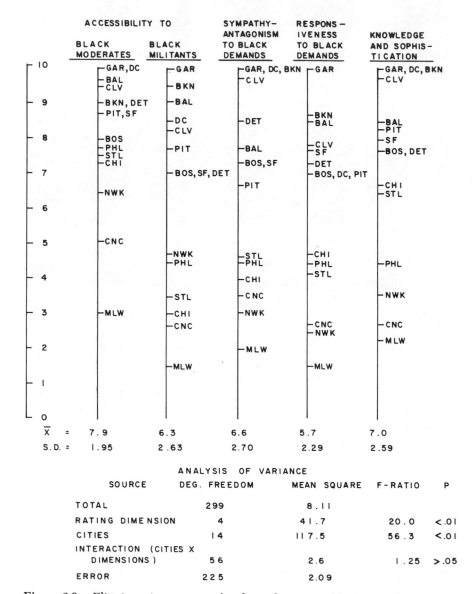

Figure 3.9. Elite interviewers: mayor's relationship to city black community.

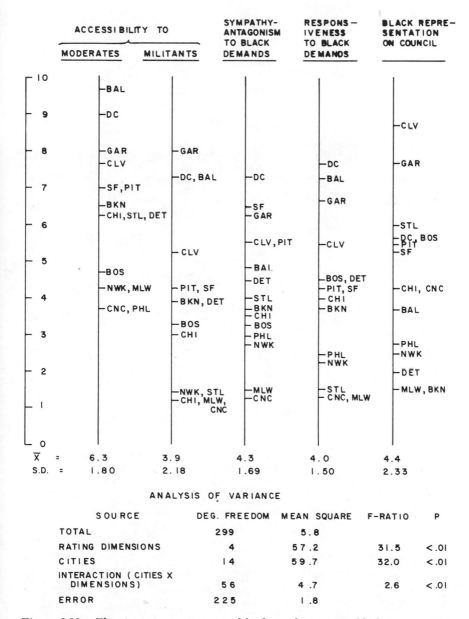

SOURCE	DEG. FREEDOM	MEAN SQUARE	F-RATIO	P
TOTAL	299	5.8		
RATING DIMENSIONS	4	57.2	31.5	<.01
CITIES	14	59.7	32.0	<.01
INTERACTION (CITIES X DIMENSIONS)	56	4.7	2.6	<.01
ERROR	225	1.8		

Figure 3.10. Elite interviews: city councils' relationships to city black communities.

TABLE 3.6

Elite)	Inter-correlations Among Ratings of
Interviews)	Mayor and City Council Relationships
	to Negro Communities (N = 15)

A.   Inter-Correlations Among Ratings of the Mayor:

	Accessability to				Information &
	Moderates	Militants	Sympathy	Responsivness	Sophistication*
Access: Mods		.90	.90	.88	.94
Access: Mils			.93	.91	.88
Sympathy				.91	.94
Responsiveness					.92

B.   Inter-Correlations Among Ratings of City Councils:

	Accessability to				Black*
	Moderates	Militants	Sympathy	Responsivness	Representation
Access: Mods		.38	.81	.73	.54
Access: Mils			.81	.84	.56
Sympathy				.86	.63
Responsiveness					.72

*Note that these variables are not identical in each matrix. It was not possible for our raters to make ratings of the "knowledge and sophistication" of the City Councils, because not enough information was available in the elite interviews. Nor was it possible to get a sensible analogue to the rating of "black representation" for the mayors office, although three of the mayors (Gary, Cleveland, and Washington, D.C.) were black.

accessible, more sympathetic, and more responsive to black demands. Comparable average ratings are generally considerably lower for city councils than for mayors. Nevertheless, cities that have responsive mayors tend to have responsive city councils, even though the level of responsiveness of the former exceeds that of the latter. The correlation between the two ratings is .87, a magnitude of the same order as the correlations among separate ratings of the mayor and among ratings of the city council. In short, city administrations and legislatures vary according to their reputations for accessibility to black leaders, and sympathy and responsiveness to their demands.

Of course, these ratings are based upon reputations reflected through the preceptual screens of the elite respondents whom we interviewed, the interviewers who recorded their responses, more or less faithfully, and finally the possibly selective readings of the interview protocols by our research staff. After all, it doesn't take very much additional information from our interview protocols to rate Mayor Daley of Chicago as a powerful mayor who is not one of the most liberal mayors concerning the position of blacks in his city; hence our findings in this respect may reflect the general image of Chicago and Mayor Daley in the mass media.

To assess the worth of these ratings, we examine the way in which the ratings coincide with the images held by the black populations of each city, as in Figure 3.11. In the Survey Research Center interviews with samples of blacks in each city, respondents were asked:

> Do you think the mayor of (CITY) is trying as hard as he can to solve the main problems of the city, or that he is not doing all he could to solve these problems?

Figure 3.11 relates the proportion of those who replied that the mayor was doing all that he could to the ratings derived from the elites interviewed on the mayor's responsiveness to black demands. It is important to keep in mind that these two variables come from quite different sets of data and were generated completely independently from each other. Indeed, the ratings of the elite interviews were accomplished before we knew the survey results.

In spite of the fact that the two variables are not quite identical in content—the elite ratings refer to responsiveness to the demands of black leaders, and the sample survey ratings refer to the mayor's effort to solve city problems of an unspecified nature—the relationship is remarkably high. The correlation between the two variables is .79, and there are no points which lie very far off the regression line of Figure 3.11.

The elite ratings may not refer to the "real" situation in each city, but they certainly appear to reflect widely held views of the mayor; they include not only opinions of the elite of high-level political participants but also the rank-and-file of the black population of the fifteen cities.

The two cities that deviate most from the regression line of Figure 3.11 are New York and Milwaukee. To the elite New York's Mayor Lindsay appeared to be more responsive than acknowledged by the black residents in the Brooklyn area according to the Survey Research Center's sample.[15]

---

[15] Indeed, this may be the clue to the difference between the ratings—the sample survey respondents are all drawn from an area of New York City where the plight of blacks may have been especially acute.

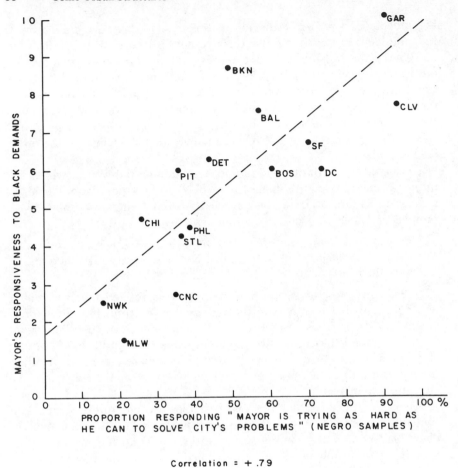

Correlation = +.79

Figure 3.11. Elite interviews and population survey. Rating of mayor's responsiveness to black demands and survey responses "mayor is trying as hard as he can to meet city's problems" (black sample). Correlation = +.79.

Milwaukee's Mayor Maier suffered from (or enjoyed) quite a different dissimilarity between the two variables: the elite respondents considered him much less responsive than the rank-and-file of Milwaukee's black residents did.

Additional evaluation of the worth of the elite ratings can be obtained from considering the correlation between the ratings of the responsiveness of the mayor and answers to this question—"Do you think city officials pay more, less, or the same amount of attention to a request by or

a complaint from a Negro as from a white person?" The correlation between these two measures across the fifteen cities was +.55. When we
consider that black rank-and-file residents were rating city officials as a
group—a group that consists of the mayor, city council, department
heads, and minor administrative officials—the correlation must be regarded as a very high one.

The relatively high relationship between ratings derived from the elite
interviews and corresponding ratings from the Survey Research Center's
surveys of black subcommunities in our fifteen cities is very encouraging.
At minimum, the relationship raises the credibility of the elite interview
ratings. At maximum, it lays the foundation for the central theme of this
monograph—the political leadership of a city has profound effects on
the actions of governmental agencies, which in turn are reflected in popular positive or negative assessments of the responsiveness of local
institutions.

Black Leadership and Popular Moods.   In each of the fifteen cities,
the black subcommunities had developed some sort of leadership structure and formed civil rights organizations. In every city, a chapter of the
NAACP existed. Most cities had chapters of the Urban League. And all
cities had branches of one or more of the newer, more militant black
organizations. Because race is an urban "problem," these organizations
and black leaders are squarely in the center of local politics. Our elite
interviews reflected this important position by treating extensively the
style of the local civil rights movement and offering many statements
about the mood of the local black population. Black subcommunity
leadership was rarely seen as a monolithic structure by the elite respondents. Indeed, many were puzzled about who the "real" leaders of the
local black subcommunities were. Local black leaders and would-be
leaders caused more confusion by claiming and counterclaiming local preeminence.

In addition, the black leaders often advanced opinions about the mood
of their followers that exaggerated the militancy of black rank-and-file.
In this respect, black leaders are not very much different from the
leaders of other groups. White political leaders, however, for some reason
or other, expected and believed that there was more consensus among
blacks than among any other subgroup within the community.[16]

---

[16] It is possible that the outbreak of civil disorders in the middle of the 1960s gave
rise to these expectations of consensus among blacks. Collective behavior on the
scale of the civil disorders in Newark or Detroit which involved so many people in

Figure 3.12 presents ratings of the styles of local civil rights "movements" in each of the fifteen cities. Five different styles were distinguished in the ratings:[17]

Integration oriented: Directed toward getting policy statements from white leaders which would make integration in public accommodations, housing, schools, and employment a matter of public policy.

Autonomy oriented: Directed toward having separate but black controlled sets of community institutions (schools, retail business, neighborhood police forces, etc.).

Grievance oriented: Directed mainly toward correcting specific conditions (e.g., discrimination in specific organizations, increased welfare payments, better equipment for Ghetto schools).

Participation oriented: Directed mainly toward having the ghetto community and its leaders consulted on issues involving the black community.

Radical goal oriented: Directed toward rejecting the present social order as "sick" and substituting an alternative social order of a radically different kind.

Looking at the averages for all the cities shown in Figure 3.12, it is clear that the civil rights movements in most cities achieved highest scores on grievance orientations and lowest scores on radical orientations. The 1968 civil rights movements of the cities were also highly oriented toward "participation": that is, black leaders wanted to be consulted on issues that related to the ghetto communities. In short, the typical city's civil rights movement was not separatist or radical move-

---

the same activity, appears in stark contrast to the everyday experience of individuals pursuing their individual ends that it is difficult to appreciate that such outbreaks can occur without self-conscious leadership. The apparent unanimity of behavior in civil disorders may have led white political officials to see behind the disorders more organization in the black subcommunities than in fact existed. It certainly caused officials to exaggerate the extent to which rank-and-file blacks subscribed to the more militant varieties of black nationalist and radical ideologies.

[17] These rating dimensions were selected because they seemed to the research staff to cover the then current differences among civil rights movements and ideologies. It is obvious that separatist movements were to be equated with movements which had high "autonomy" orientations. The NAACP, in contrast, could be characterized as a movement that was strong in grievance and integration orientations. We expected that the black communities would be a mixture of orientations, depending in part on the organizations which had come into prominence within each of the cities, and in part on the ideologies of the more prominently known black leaders.

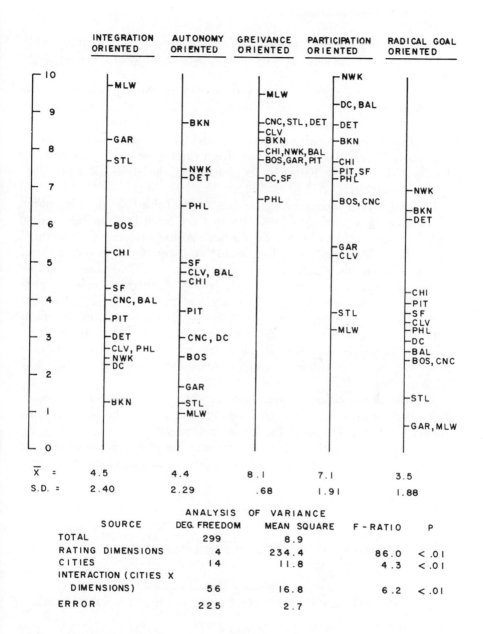

	INTEGRATION ORIENTED	AUTONOMY ORIENTED	GREIVANCE ORIENTED	PARTICIPATION ORIENTED	RADICAL GOAL ORIENTED
$\overline{X}$ =	4.5	4.4	8.1	7.1	3.5
S.D. =	2.40	2.29	.68	1.91	1.88

ANALYSIS OF VARIANCE

SOURCE	DEG. FREEDOM	MEAN SQUARE	F-RATIO	P
TOTAL	299	8.9		
RATING DIMENSIONS	4	234.4	86.0	< .01
CITIES	14	11.8	4.3	< .01
INTERACTION (CITIES X DIMENSIONS)	56	16.8	6.2	< .01
ERROR	225	2.7		

Figure 3.12. Elite interviews: styles of civil rights movement.

ment in the eyes of the community's elites, but was more concerned with the correction of specific grievances and participating in the settlement of issues.

The analysis of variance results presented in the bottom of Figure 3.12 indicates that there were strong differences among ratings and among cities with significant interaction between ratings and cities. In short, the different civil rights movement orientations varied widely from each other, cities were different from each other, and cities showed a rather idiosyncratic pattern with respect to the styles that predominated in each city.

The correlations among ratings are shown in Table 3.7. The patterning is unusually clear in this table: Cities that are rated high on Integration and Grievance tend to be low on Radical, Autonomy, and Participatory Orientations. Similarly, cities that are high on any one of the latter three are also high on the others of that group, but low on Grievance and Integration. Indeed, if we examine the patterning of individual cities in Figure 3.12, it is clear that Milwaukee, Gary, and St. Louis show high scores on Grievance and Integration Orientations but low scores on the more radical Autonomy, Participation, and Radical orientations. In contrast Newark, Brooklyn, and Detroit show the most radical styles, because they are rated relatively high on Autonomy, Radical Goals, and Participation.

The remaining cities do not show as clear a pattern. For example, Baltimore's scores fall near the average on all of the style ratings although it is rated high on Participation Orientation.

Using our data it is difficult to account for the differences among styles of the predominant civil rights movement among cities at any one

TABLE 3.7

Elites   ) Inter-Correlations Among Ratings of
Interviews) Civil Rights Movements (N = 15)

| | Styles of Civil Rights Movements | | | |
	Integration	Grievance	Radical	Autonomy	Participation
Integration		.42	-.77	-.81	-.77
Grievance			-.11	-.24	-.49
Radical				.91	.73
Autonomy					.69

time. In 1968, it is clear that the most militant civil rights movements were to be found in Newark and Detroit—cities that had experienced the most severe civil disorders of the summer of 1967. Whether the predominant styles in those cities antedate the disorders and emerged as a consequence of them is not answerable with our data. There is some hint, however, that the militant styles emerged as a consequence of civil disorders. Baltimore, Washington, D.C. and Pittsburgh were to suffer very extensive civil disorders in the spring of 1968, after our data from the elites in those cities had been collected. It is clear that these three cities are far from the most militant; thus militancy may be one of the consequences of a disorder.[18]

Not only do the styles of the civil rights movements differ in each city, but also the issues at stake in race relations differ. For some cities, the critical issues revolve about relations between the police and black communities. In other communities, housing, or employment may be the major issues. In part, the issues that are salient indicate the objective problems faced by the city. In part, they represent those issues accented by civil rights leaders.

Figure 3.13 contains ratings of the salience of eight different issues in each of the fifteen cities. Analysis of variance of these ratings indicate significant differences among issues and cities, and a significant amount of interaction between cities and issues. The average salience ratings for the eight issues (as well as the F-ratio for rating dimensions) show strong differences among issues—some tend to be high in salience among all cities and others relatively low in all cities. Thus the issue that received the highest salience rating is "police brutality," and reaches the highest possible rating (10) in three cities, Philadelphia, Newark, and Detroit. In contrast the issue that is least salient on the average is "community control over schools," an issue that agitates the black community of Brooklyn, but is scarcely mentioned in the cities of Milwaukee, Gary and St. Louis.

The four issues that are important everywhere are "police brutality," "housing," "police protection," and "exploitation by retail merchants." The four that are less salient are "discrimination in private employment," "school desegregation," "adequacy of public welfare," and "community control of schools."

It is difficult to discern a pattern of issue salience characteristic of

---

[18] Of course, it is possible that militancy levels remain the same before, during, and after civil disorders, and all that changes are the elite's images of the levels of militancy. The high levels to be found in Detroit and Newark may be mainly attempts on the part of the elites of those cities to explain why the black communities in their cities erupted in disorder.

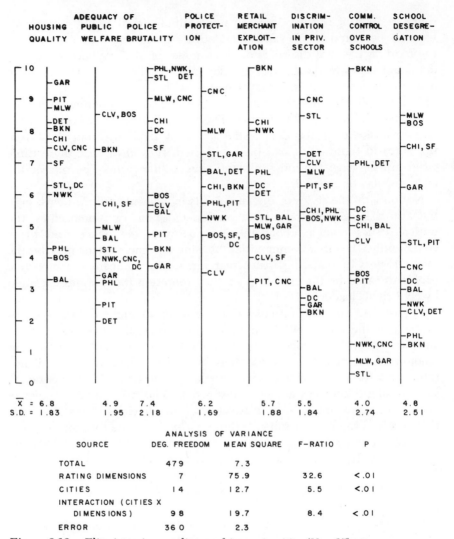

	HOUSING QUALITY	ADEQUACY OF PUBLIC WELFARE	POLICE BRUTALITY	POLICE PROTECT-ION	RETAIL MERCHANT EXPLOIT-ATION	DISCRIM-INATION IN PRIV. SECTOR	COMM. CONTROL OVER SCHOOLS	SCHOOL DESEGRE-GATION
X =	6.8	4.9	7.4	6.2	5.7	5.5	4.0	4.8
S.D. =	1.83	1.95	2.18	1.69	1.88	1.84	2.74	2.51

ANALYSIS OF VARIANCE

SOURCE	DEG. FREEDOM	MEAN SQUARE	F-RATIO	P
TOTAL	479	7.3		
RATING DIMENSIONS	7	75.9	32.6	< .01
CITIES	14	12.7	5.5	< .01
INTERACTION (CITIES X DIMENSIONS)	98	19.7	8.4	< .01
ERROR	360	2.3		

Figure 3.13.   Elite interviews: salience of issues in cities ($N = 15$).

either particular cities or of pairs of larger groupings of issues. Table 3.8 which contains the intercorrelations among salience ratings tends to bear out this judgment. By and large, the correlations among ratings are small and inconsistent in sign pattern. In short, few issues "hang together" in the sense that they tend to be both present or absent. The highest correlation in Table 3.8 is between the salience ratings of "police brutality" and "discrimination in private sector employment." Given the small

TABLE 3.8

Elite)   Inter-Correlations Among Salience Ratings
Interviews)   of Issues (N = 15)

	Housing Quality	Public Welfare	Police Brutality	Police Protection	Retail Mchts.	Private Sector Discrim.	Comm. Control	School Desegregation
Housing Quality		-.21	-.19	.28	-.08	.14	-.16	.20
Public Welfare			-.38	-.44	.12	-.13	.20	.14
Police Brutality				.21	.10	.58	-.17	-.06
Police Protection					.09	.26	-.38	.14
Retail Merchants						-.50	-.38	-.42
Private Sector Discrimination							-.41	.16
Community Control								-.47

number (15) on which these correlations are based, a correlation of
.58 is barely significant. Indeed, most of the correlation coefficients in
Table 3.8 are not significant.

The fifteen cities varied in the extent to which issues in general were
salient, as the average salience ratings for each city shown in Table 3.9
indicate. The cities are arranged in order of descending salience ratings.
At the one extreme, Chicago, Milwaukee, and Brooklyn get the honors
for having the highest saliency ratings, indicating that more topics are
at issue or at higher levels of visibility to the elites in those cities than
elsewhere. At the one extreme, Baltimore and Gary appear to be sleepy
little towns with little agitated race relations.

Of course, averages, as usual, can be quite deceptive. For example,
Gary's low rating is achieved despite the fact that the quality of housing
is more salient as an issue in that city than in all the others. Similarly,
Brooklyn has a very high average, even though employment discrimination and school desegregation are least salient in that city.

TABLE 3.9

Elite)	Average Salience Ratings Across Eight
Interviews)	Issues for Each City

City	Average Salience Ratings
Chicago	6.78
Milwaukee	6.47
Brooklyn	6.19
Detroit	6.19
San Francisco	6.12
Cincinnati	6.12
St. Louis	5.75
Boston	5.62
Philadelphia	5.50
Cleveland	5.38
Washington, D.C.	5.34
Newark	5.28
Pittsburgh	5.03
Gary	4.81
Baltimore	4.56
Grand Mean =	5.68
Standard Deviation =	.60

By definition, issues are those topics that enter upon the agenda of public discussion in legislative bodies and in protest meetings, and are reflected in the amount of attention given to them in the mass media. The presence of any issue or a large number of issues on a public discussion level, however, is not necessarily a measure of the extent to which such matters reflect an agitated state of the general population. Indeed, as we show in subsequent chapters, the relationship between popular opinion and public issues is a complicated interplay among leadership initiative, objective conditions, and subjective importance of the area of life in question.

An astute political man neglects public opinion at the peril of losing out in the voting booth. At least part of the proper assessment of a political situation involves estimating the direction, height, and shifts in the tides of mood and confidence that may be sweeping through a constituency or its subdivisions. The elite interviews were almost obsessed with such concerns, centering mainly around degree of tension in relations between blacks and whites.

Ratings of these tension levels and degrees of confidence in local leadership as reflected in the elite interviews are shown in Figure 3.14. It is abundantly clear from the analysis of variance of these ratings that these ratings are significantly different from each other, that cities differ strongly, and that the interaction between cities and ratings is also significant. It is also clear that Newark and Detroit have both black and white populations who were regarded as very tense and uneasy.[19] In contrast, Cincinnati has a tense black population but its whites, while above average in tension, have yet to reach the high tension level of their black fellow citizens. The opposite pattern is shown in Chicago where whites are uneasy and apprehensive but blacks are less so.

In Newark and Detroit white leaders appeared to have lost the confidence of their black constituents, while in Detroit and Brooklyn the confidence of whites seems to have deteriorated the most.

By almost every criterion, Detroit in early 1968 was apparently the most "uptight" of the fifteen cities, as both whites and blacks evidenced high levels of tension and low levels of confidence in public officials.

---

[19] The high tension ratings for the populations of Newark and Detroit are undoubtedly influenced by the fact that these two cities suffered from severe civil disorders the summer previous to our interviews with elites. We know very little about the transiency of tension and hence cannot judge whether a high level of tension which may have preceded a period of civil disorder might have been dissipated by the time sample survey interviewers questioned rank-and-file residents in those two cities. In short, the half life of tension may be shorter than the half life of the *perception* of tension held by major civic actors.

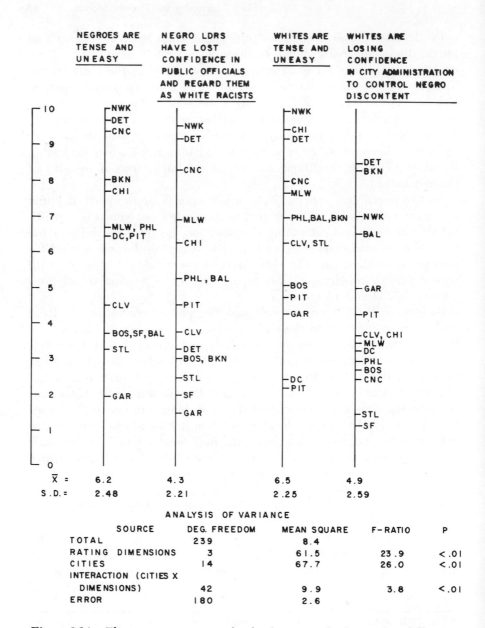

SOURCE	DEG. FREEDOM	MEAN SQUARE	F-RATIO	P
TOTAL	239	8.4		
RATING DIMENSIONS	3	61.5	23.9	<.01
CITIES	14	67.7	26.0	<.01
INTERACTION (CITIES X DIMENSIONS)	42	9.9	3.8	<.01
ERROR	180	2.6		

Figure 3.14. Elite interviews: tension levels of Negro and white rank and file.

Newark and Brooklyn come close to Detroit in some respects but were different in others.

In contrast no city shows a clear pattern of low tension and high confidence in public officials. Gary, which had just elected its first black mayor, showed low levels of black tension and high levels of black confidence in public officials, but whites in Gary were somewhat uneasy and less confident of public officials. Perhaps the closest to an "all round calm" city is St. Louis, where elite interviews generated ratings which were all at or below the average in each of the ratings.

In Table 3.10 it can be seen that the ratings are all positively related, indicating that to the elites, at least, a high level of tension in one race is matched by a high level of tension in the other. Similarly a decline in confidence on the part of blacks in the political leadership of the city is matched by a similar decline among whites.

There is a positive relationship between the level of tension of the black population and the average saliency of issues, as discussed earlier. The correlation between the two measures is +.45, indicating the cities whose average issue saliency was high were the cities where the black masses were tense and uneasy.[20] From the point of view of elite participants in the political process, issues and tensions are closely related.

---

[20] Some of the issues considered are more closely related to the tension level of the black population than others. For example, if we consider the saliency ratings of three of the issues—police brutality, the quality of housing, and exploitation of retail merchants—the multiple correlation with tension levels of the black subcommunities is .69, whose F-ratio just barely misses significance at the .05 level.

TABLE 3.10

Elite)   Inter-Correlations Among Tensions
Ratings)   Level Ratings of Rank-and-File
           (N = 15)

	Blacks Tense	Black Leaders Losing Confidence	Whites Tense	Whites Losing Confidence
Blacks Tense		.87	.68	.43
Blacks Losing Confidence			.73	.34
Whites Tense				.48

The Survey Research Center interviews with rank-and file blacks and whites in the fifteen cities again provide a means of evaluating the elite ratings. Table 3.11 presents a number of correlations between the elite ratings and some direct measures of tension levels among the general populace—black and white. Because the Survey Research Center interviews did not question directly individual respondents about their levels of tension, uneasiness, sense of outrage, or other possible direct measures of mood, we have been forced in Table 3.11 to rely on rather indirect measures. Most of the questions refer to relationships between whites and blacks, surely one of the points at issue, but not necessarily the full measure of tension level for either blacks or whites. As a consequence

TABLE 3.11

Elite Interviews &) Relationships Between Elite Ratings of
Sample Surveys   ) Black and White Tensions and Sample
                      Survey Related Questions

A.   Correlations Between Elite Ratings of Black Rank-and-File Tension
     and Selected Measures from Sample Survey Interviews with Blacks

     "Few Whites can be Trusted"*   .15
     "Index of Institutional Self-Determination"**   .49
     "Index of Separatism"***   .21

B.   Correlations Between Elite Ratings of White Tension and Selected
     Measures from Sample Surveys with Whites

     "Many Negroes Dislike Whites"****   .46
     "Many Whites Dislike Negroes"****   .68

The items used are as follows:

     *"Do you personally feel you can trust most white people, some
     white people or none at all?"

     **Composed of questions asking whether blacks should be served
     by black principals, teachers and black storeowners in
     situations where blacks are in the majority.

     ***Composed of questions which ask whether blacks should have
     "anything to do with whites" and whether "there should be a
     black nation here".

     ****"Do you think only a few Negroes (whites) dislike white (Negro)
     people or almost all dislike white (Negro) people?"

the low correlations may reflect some combination of poor measurement and lack of fit between elite perceptions and "objective reality," as the exact proportions of the combination is impossible to discern.

Despite the fact that the correlations are low, it is at least comforting that they are all in the right direction. By and large, in cities where tension levels are high, the opinions of rank-and-file black and white residents are reasonable indicators of tension. Note that the correlations for the white residents is higher than those for blacks, possibly indicating that local elites are possibly better informed about their white constituents. Considering that most of the elites interviewed were whites, this interpretation at least appears plausible.

Inspecting the raw data lying behind Table 3.11, one is inevitably left with the impression that the elite ratings exaggerate severely the amount of tension in each city. For example, in none of the cities—including Newark and Detroit—did a majority of the black respondents indicate that they thought most whites could not be trusted. Of course, it does not take a clear majority to have a civil disorder. Indeed, all of the surveys of riot participants indicate that the proportion who participated could not exceed more than 25%. This exaggerated view of the currents of popular unrest inside a city is part and parcel of the rhetoric of local community politics. Elites tend to magnify ripples into tidal waves just as our political commentators interpret a bare majority victory of a presidential candidate as a drastic reorientation of the national mood.

Urban Leadership Styles. The purpose of this chapter was to introduce the reader to the data amassed on city differences in leadership styles. We have shown that there are significant differences between cities like Chicago, in which the mayor dominates the local scene, and cities, like Cincinnati and Washington, D.C., where the locus of power and influence is not so neatly concentrated in one position. We have also shown that these leadership styles have some impact on public opinion among whites and blacks in the same cities. The task of the remainder of this monograph is to trace out the links between local leadership and popular responses.

Some, if not most readers, may question what accounts for the differences among cities? Our own data are peculiarly unable to provide the answers. Part of the answer undoubtedly lies in the particular histories of each city. For example, the dismantling of New York's great Tammany political machine took place at the same period of time that Mayor Richard Daley of Chicago was strengthening his party's hold on Chicago.

Similarly, the weak position of the mayor of Cincinnati seems to be a carry over of a local tradition—Cincinnati has been the only major city to be run by the city manager plan for an appreciable period of time.

In part, structural differences among cities account for their differences. Detroit has been locally nonpartisan. Washington, D.C., is uniquely dependent on Congress and its committees. The strong interest taken in Pittsburgh by the Mellon family is not matched in any of the other cities in the study by an equally prominent and involved financial and industrial elite.

To unravel the chains of cause and happenstance that produced these city differences requires more than a one-time survey. We need to look at history, economic structure, demography, and group formation. The best we can do—and we hope it is not inconsiderable—is to examine the *consequences* of this patterning of urban differences, a task that occupies central attention in the chapters to come.

Chapter 4

THE AGENTS OF URBAN
SYSTEMS IN THE GHETTO

There are many levels on which one experiences a city. As a visitor we may see mainly those things located along the main highways. We may be impressed, horrified, or amused by the massive downtown monuments to the headquarters of businesses and of municipal government. However, a visitor rarely sees more than the interiors of a few homes, perhaps hotel or motel rooms, and possibly the inside of a few offices or factories. It would be unusual for a casual visitor to experience a city the way a resident does, nor would he ordinarily experience in the same way its central institutions.

To a native, his city may be mainly his home, the routes he takes to work, shop, play, visit, go to school, or to obtain medical treatment. The institutions that he knows intimately are those which are related to the central activities of family life, work, education, health, and play. Rarely does he experience directly more than a highly restricted part of the total complex of institutions that make up a city. Of course the local mass media supply some of those broader experiences vicariously, but still it is the more "newsworthy" aspects of the city that receive most attention. For example, police department headquarters receive more media space than local police precincts.

The main direct and enduring contacts that a citizen usually has with city institutions are in the context of acting out his main routines of work, sociability, school, and play. Unless he works downtown, he may see the city center only on special trips to shop or to go to a downtown movie. His contact with central urban institutions occur on their peripheries. His children go to the local schools and his contacts with the public education system of his city may be exclusively through the teachers, principals, and specialized school personnel that his children come in contact with. Most citizens meet the police as traffic regulators, and less frequently one encounters local precinct patrolmen enforcing other laws or rendering assistance. The city's political life is ordinarily a newspaper game, and the citizen's direct contact with politics may be entirely through his local party officials and candidates for city council.

A native may have more contacts with the organized economic life of the city than with any other major institutions. The retail market is tied to him through the stores he patronizes, a good many of which may be in his local neighborhood. The business establishment for which he works is probably his prime contact with the labor market, but there are also the establishments with which he has had contact in the past and with which he might seek employment in the future. The housing market has provided him with his home or apartment, and stands ready to provide him with alternatives through classified ads, real estate brokers, and real estate management firms.

These peripheral points of major local institutions are the main points of contact for the rank-and-file citizen. Thus the police system is represented by local patrolmen, the retail market by local retail merchants, the schools by neighborhood teachers and principals, the labor market by those who hire and fire in business establishments, and so on. Policy may be made in the downtown area, but the administration of policy takes place at the periphery.

To gain an appreciation of the level of direct experience contacts between urban institutions and rank-and-file citizens, one must examine the quality of the relationships between the peripheral agents of such institutions and the clients, customers, or employees with whom they come into contact. This is the main purpose of this chapter and those that follow. Using personal interviews with such *agents* in each of the fifteen cities, we present data on their views of the "urban problems" and the citizens with whom they are in contact. The term agent is used here mainly for want of a better term for these persons who deal in a very direct sense with citizens. The agents with which we are concerned are those who deal mainly with black citizens. The occupational roles are as follows:

(40) *Policemen*:   Patrolmen and minor police officials whose assignments are in black residential areas

(20) *Teachers*:   Classroom teachers and supervisory personnel who are assigned to elementary or high schools in black areas

(30) *Retail Merchants*:   Owners or managers of retail stores who are located in black neighborhoods

(20) *Welfare Workers*:   Case workers and immediate supervisors who are employed by public welfare departments whose assignments are to black clients

(30) *Personnel Officers*:   Persons who are in charge of hiring policy in a sample of major establishments in the private sector of each city. (*Note*: Personnel officers do not deal only with blacks.)

(10) *Political Party Workers*: Party officials who are in political subdivisions of the city largely inhabited by blacks (usually on the precinct or ward level)

The numbers in parentheses represent the projected sample size of each group in each of the fifteen cities, the size representing rough estimates on the part of the research staff about the relative importance of information from each group of agents. Thus by setting the sample sizes for police as the largest of all groups, we were estimating that information on police attitudes was more important than that of other groups.

In retrospect, it is hard to justify the omission from this list of other types of institutional agents. Particularly conspicuous in their absence are the agents of the housing market and medical care systems; both institutional complexes have been at the focus of public interest over the past few years. It also seems wasteful to have studied so small a sample of political party workers, the data from whom have not yielded as much understanding as that from the other agent groups studied.[1] Hence it should be borne in mind that these agents are not the only points of contacts between ghetto residents and the larger institutional complexes of the urban centers involved. We believe they are important ones,

---

[1] Indeed the analyses of these data produced such weak results that none are presented in this volume.

but we are all too conscious that important parts of the urban scene have been omitted.

With the exception of personnel officers in large firms, all of the agents chosen were from among those who had the closest contact in their occupational group with the black areas of each city. The details of how samples were selected (and in some cases, were selected for us) are given in Chapter 2.

Socioeconomic Profiles of Institutional Agents. Although the institutional agents all are part of the interface between central urban institutions and residents of their cities' black ghettos, they differ considerably one from the other in their social origins. In part, these differences are sampling artifacts, since we specified that we wanted a certain proportion of some of the occupational groups to be black (e.g., educators, social workers, and policemen). However, other characteristics are findings in the sense that they were free to vary.[2]

Table 4.1 presents some of the important socioeconomic characteristics of the six occupational groups. Note that the items marked with an asterisk (*) are items that were used in setting sampling quotas and hence do not describe the group as much as they describe the research staff's estimate of the overall proportion of blacks in that group. Thus, although the findings shown in Table 4.1 are descriptive of the samples of occupational groups whom we interviewed, they are unrepresentative of the total cadres in the fifteen cities, because they represent (with the exception of personnel officers) agents that are assigned to the black neighborhoods of the cities. Furthermore, their representativeness of this more restricted group is questionable due to the purposive sampling used. However, because the remainder of this chapter is concerned with comparisons among the six occupational groups in their views of the city and of blacks, it is important to bear in mind that the socioeconomic compositions of the groups vary. Hence the differences among the occupational groups are only partly occupational in character but are to some degree generated by different socioeconomic mixtures.

Most of the occupational groups are predominantly male—personnel officers and policemen are almost completely male. Retail merchants and party workers were mainly men, but up to one in three were women. Only among educators and social workers do women predominate. The

---

[2] To the extent that these other characteristics are correlated with the sampling criteria, however, they are not entirely free to vary. Thus if black educators are more likely to be female than whites from the same occupational group, setting a quota on blacks alters the sex composition of the occupational groups.

sex composition of the occupational groups constitutes the most striking differences shown in Table 4.1.

The occupational groups differ considerably in age. Social workers are among the very young (under 30), a difference that is reflected in a very low average age of 37.5 years. Policemen are the next youngest group averaging a little below 38 years, followed by educators who average midway between 40 and 41. The remaining occupational groups are considerably older. Several political workers and retail merchants are in their seventies, although the averages for these two groups is 49. Personnel officers are also mainly in late middle age, averaging slightly under 48.

Few educators and social workers have not finished college, while few retail merchants and even fewer policemen have earned their bachelor of arts degrees. The political party workers have the most heterogeneous educational distribution; one fourth have completed some postgraduate work, usually attending law school. College graduates predominate among personnel officers with almost two out of five having had some postgraduate experience.

Only policemen are predominantly lifetime local residents. All the other occupational groups are composed mainly of people who have been born elsewhere and have migrated to their cities. At the one extreme, three out of four political party workers are migrants to their cities while at the other extreme two out of three policemen were lifetime residents.[3]

No surprises are to be found in the religious composition of the occupational groups. Almost stereotypically, policemen are predominantly Catholic, while ghetto retail merchants are more than one-third Jewish.[4] The remainder of the occupational groups display Protestant majorities, influenced to some degree by the proportion of blacks (who are predominantly Protestant) within a group.

The household incomes of social workers are the lowest of the six occupational groups, in contrast to personnel officers, who usually earn over $15,000 per year. Teachers enjoy a better income level than one might expect, although one must bear in mind that income data reflect not only the earning of the persons involved but also that of their spouses. Political

---

[3] Since so many of the adult black residents of the fifteen cities have migrated to their present residences since World War II, this pattern is not surprising. Although ordinarily political party workers would contain a large proportion of native born, the fact that the political agents in this sample are black leads to a different pattern.
[4] In many of the large cities, blacks have succeeded Jewish neighbors with the latter leaving behind many small businessmen who shifted customers rather than follow their old clientele to newer locations. Jewish retail merchants tend to be concentrated among the oldest group, perhaps expressing the inability of older persons to reinvest in a new location with all the capital, effort, and so on that would be involved.

TABLE 4.1

Agent)   Selected Socio-Economic Characteristics of
Interviews)   the Six Occupational Groups

Characteristic:	Police	Educators	Social Workers	Party Workers	Retail Merchants	Personnel Officers
A. Race:*						
White	76%	50%	50%	0%	74%	99%
Black**	24	50	50	100	26	1
B. Sex:						
Male	100%	43%	37%	67%	79%	96%
Female	0	47	63	33	21	4
C. Age:						
Average =	37.9 yrs.	40.5 yrs.	35.7 yrs.	49.1 yrs.	49.0 yrs.	47.6 yrs.
50 or over	8%	18%	17%	48%	44%	42%
40-49	27	25	16	30	30	34
30-39	36	30	23	14	17	19
Under 30	28	22	43	6	7	4
DK & NA	1	4	2	3	3	1

TABLE 4.1 (Cont'd)

Characteristic:	Police	Educators	Social Workers	Party Workers	Retail Merchants	Personnel Officers
D. Educational Attainment:						
Did not Finish High School	9	0	0	16	26	1
High School Grad	55	0	1	22	32	5
Some College	34	1	10	33	24	17
College Grad	1	31	62	5	13	38
Post Graduate	1	68	27	24	4	39
DK & NA	#	0	#	0	#	0
E. Place of Birth:						
Born in City	63	44	33	25	40	38
Elsewhere	37	54	66	74	59	58
DK & NA	#	2	1	1	1	3
F. Religion:						
Protestant	38	59	61	74	36	58
Catholic	57	24	25	21	23	25
Jewish	1	10	6	2	38	11
Other & None	3	6	8	3	2	5
Refusals & NA	1	#	#	0	1	1

*NOTE: Since race was used as a sampling control, the findings with respect to race are almost entirely an artifact of sampling.

\# = less than 1%.

**Includes a few Orientals, American Indians and other non-whites, not amounting to more than 0.2% of the sample.

TABLE 4.1 (Cont'd)

Characteristic:	Police	Educators	Social Workers	Party Workers	Retail Merchants	Personnel Officers
G. Household Income:						
Less than $5,000	0	#	#	11	8	0
$5-7,4999	12	8	33	14	14	1
$7.5-9,999	49	14	23	16	14	3
$10-12,4999	22	19	10	12	15	11
$12.5-14,999	11	23	17	15	9	15
$15,000 & over	6	34	15	27	22	66
Refusals	#	1	1	2	16	3
DK & NA	#	#	0	2	1	1
H. Organization Membership:						
Belongs to at least one organization	84	93	72	89	53	81
DK & NA	#	0	#	2	#	1

TABLE 4.1 (Cont'd)

Characteristic:	Police	Educators	Social Workers	Party Workers	Retail Merchants	Personnel Officers
I. Home Ownership:						
Owns	67	68	37	75	72	85
Rents	31	32	62	24	27	15
DK & NA	#	#	1	1	1	1
J. National Party Identification:						
Democrat	45	50	51	71	53	14
Republican	13	11	7	20	14	48
Independent	41	38	39	8	29	36
DK & NA	1	1	2	0	4	2
K. Local Party Identification:						
Democrat	47	44	46	67	49	13
Republican	12	9	8	20	1	39
Independent	39	44	42	10	35	45
DK & NA	2	3	3	3	5	3
100% =	(522)	(299)	(307)	(129)	(458)	(447)

workers and retail merchants display a considerable range in household income, with the latter containing a fair proportion of high income earners.

Members of the six occupational groups are joiners, a majority of each belonging to at least one organization. More than nine out of ten educators belong to organizations, displaying the highest level of membership. In contrast, retail merchants show the least tendency to join associations, with a bare majority (53%) joiners.

With the exception of personnel officers, five of the six occupational groups are predominantly Democratic on both the national and local political scene. As one might expect, party workers are most heavily Democratic, reflecting the last 30 years of heavy support for Democratic national party candidates on the part of black voters.

No clear portrait emerges out of the data in Table 4.1 concerning the "typical" agent of urban institutions. The best that can be said is that the agents are in their middle years; tend to be somewhat better educated than their clients, customers, or employees; and are not to be found among the poor or the very rich. Beyond this very general description, it is necessary to develop different vignettes for each of the occupational groups. Urban policemen assigned to ghetto precincts tend to be high school graduates, in their middle thirties, locally born, Catholic, and Democratic. Ghetto educators are college graduates, most likely women, from Protestant backgrounds, and migrants to the city. Social workers are similar to educators in background but are younger. Political workers are the most heterogeneous, varying considerably in education, income, and age, and are homogeneous only in their loyalty to the Democratic party. Ghetto merchants are also heterogeneous, because they are older on the average, but they also span a wide age range, with a wide range in household income; however, they are relatively wealthy on the average.

Although the backgrounds of urban institutional agents are of some interest, they are only part of the information presented to their clients, customers, or employees. Indeed, these aspects of the agents may be of the least interest to citizens; of greater importance are the ways in which they regard their constituents and in which they perform their occupational roles. In other words, it may not matter too much from which social backgrounds an occupational group may be recruited, if in their behavior toward their clients or customers, they all act in much the same way.

Agents' Definition of the "Urban Problem."   With the exception of the personnel officers, the institutional agents we surveyed ply their trades inside the ghettos of their cities. We should expect therefore that the agents would be especially sensitive to the "urban problem," because the experiences of work bring them daily into contact with that problem in its most extreme form.

The agents' perceptions of the major "problems" facing their cities are shown in Table 4.2, as responses to the question "What are the major problems facing (CITY)?" As one might expect, no major surprises emerge from the responses in Table 4.2. The "urban problems" syndrome of "race relations," "poverty," "crime," "housing," and "local government" are most frequently cited by all of the occupational groups.

The institutional specializations of the agents are reflected in the different frequencies with which particular kinds of problems are mentioned. "Crime" is the most frequently mentioned problem by the police, far more than by retail merchants who are the next most likely group to mention it. Poverty and housing are given most frequently as a problem by the educators, social workers, and party workers, and less frequently by the police, retail merchants, and personnel officers. Public education is a problem most mentioned by the educators, although political party workers also give this response frequently.

In short, while there is general consensus among institutional agents concerning the broad definition of the "urban problem," each group stresses that particular part of the broad problem which impinges most directly on their occupational roles. Thus retail merchants stress business conditions, police stress crime, and so on. Furthermore, there is a liberal–conservative split among occupational groups. Educators, social workers and party workers are more likely to stress problems relating to the depressed conditions of urban populations, while retail merchants, personnel officers, and police stress problems like crime.

This split among the occupational groups is also shown in the correlations presented at the bottom of Table 4.2, which expresses the extent to which pairs of groups agree on the relative importance of each of the component problems. Note that there are high correlations between the pairs formed by educators, social workers, party workers, and personnel officers, while these groups show lower levels of agreement with the retail merchants and the police. The latter pair show more agreement with each other than with any of the other groups studied.

The problems that their cities now handled better are shown in Table 4.3, which contains the answers to the question, "Thinking back over the past few years and the problems your city has had to face, what have been the major improvements?" The last row of Table 4.3 contains the proportions in each occupational group who saw *no improvements* in their cities. Retail merchants, policemen, and political party workers

TABLE 4.2

Agent Interviews) "Major Problems Facing the City" As Seen by The Six Occupational Groups

Major Problems Facing the City	Police	Educators	Social Workers	Party Workers	Retail Merchants	Personnel Officers
Race Relations	37%	49%	31%	29%	27%	32%
Poverty	32	52	63	62	32	37
Crime	53	13	9	19	33	13
Housing	25	52	59	58	28	38
Local Government	32	25	23	22	22	28
Education	15	43	27	34	16	27
Civil Disorders	13	6	7	4	9	11
Traffic	6	3	5	2	4	18
Business Conditions	2	6	7	2	28	11

TABLE 4.2 (Cont'd)

Major Problems Facing the City	Police	Educators	Social Workers	Party Workers	Retail Merchants	Personnel Officers
Environment	2	3	3	3	2	3
Welfare & Recreation	8	3	13	8	8	6
Miscelanneous	2	6	6	2	#	6
100% =	(522)	(299)	(307)	(129)	(458)	(447)
Average Number of Responses =	2.3	2.5	2.5	2.4	2.1	2.3

Inter-correlations* Among Occupational Groups (N = 12)

	Police	Educators	Social Workers	Party Workers	Retail Merchants	Personnel Officers
Police		.55	.46	.57	.76	.56
Educators			.91	.93	.64	.93
Social Workers				.98	.62	.89
Party Workers					.67	.89
Retail Merchants						.64

*Computed by inter-correlating columns in the upper half of this table.

TABLE 4.3

Agent)
Interviews)

"Major Areas of Improvement in City"
Cited by Six Occupational Groups

Major Improvement Areas Cited	Police	Educators	Social Workers	Party Workers	Retail Merchants	Personnel Officers
Race Relations	10	12	11	16	7	9
Poverty	21	29	28	32	18	25
Crime	2	2	2	1	2	2
Housing	33	25	31	22	32	40
Local Government	20	29	34	33	7	23
Education	11	29	18	11	8	13
Civil Disorders	#	#	#	0	1	2
Traffic	11	10	5	9	10	21

TABLE 4.3 (Cont'd)

Major Improvement Areas Cited	Police	Educators	Social Workers	Party Workers	Retail Merchants	Personnel Officers
Business Conditions	1	2	1	0	2	5
Environment	2	1	1	2	3	3
Welfare & Recreation	9	8	14	5	5	6
Miscellaneous	4	6	6	5	4	14
No Improvement Seen	21	15	13	24	32	12
100% =	(522)	(299)	(307)	(129)	(458)	(447)
Average Number of Improvements Cited	1.2	1.2	1.5	1.4	1.0	1.3

showed the most despair about their cities, with 20 to 30% claiming that there had been no improvements in their cities.

The improvements seen were primarily in housing, local government, and education. Although crime and race relations loomed large as problems facing the city, few of the institutional agents saw any improvements in these areas over the past few years.

The general impression that emerges from the comparison of Table 4.2 to Table 4.3 is one of pessimism. More problems are cited than improvements noted. Few saw much improvement in the major problems that they cited—race relations, poverty, and crime.

The perceived problems and local improvements cited in Tables 4.2 and 4.3 are those which were spontaneously mentioned by the agents interviewed in response to rather broad questions. While these questions did not suggest to the respondents what problems to mention and hence record problems in terms of their salience to the respondents, they are subject to some degree of ambiguity. We asked the respondents what were the "two or three" major problems, an assumption which puts an upper limit on the number of problems and relies on the memories of the respondent.

To compensate for these defects and to round out the account of urban problems, we followed up these two general questions with a series of specific questions; each was addressed to a single problem and asked the respondent to rate whether the problem in question was "very serious," "somewhat serious," "slightly serious," or "not at all serious." The proportions within each occupational group who rated each of the ten problems as "very serious" are shown in Figure 4.1.

The relative importance of various specific conditions that make up the "urban problem" displayed in Figure 4.1 is not very different than that in Table 4.2. The major differences lie in greater weights given to the problem of controlling "violence and civil disorders" and "finding tax funds to support municipal services"—both topics received very slight levels of mention in response to the broad question of "what are the major problems" of the city.

Crime, civil disorders, and race relations head the list, with each more than half of the respondents rated them "very serious." At the opposite extreme, one in five considers the "corruption of city officials," and one in three regards "traffic and highways" or "air pollution" serious problems. Some of the topics generate considerable disagreement among institutional agents, for example, unemployment and public education, while others are characterized by relative consensus, for example, crime control, traffic, and corruption.

Figure 4.2 contains the same information for each city, pooling the

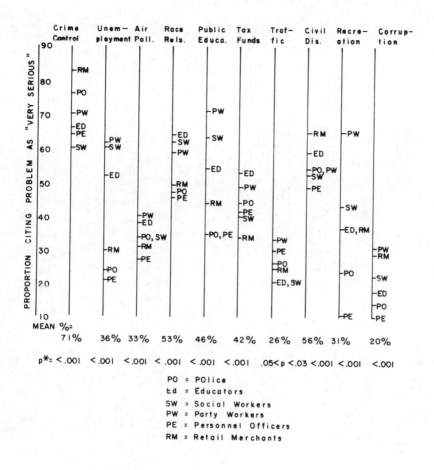

* based on Chi—Square using three categories of responses (usually collapsing the last two categories). Indicates the extent to which the distribution departs from hypothesis that the subgroups' response distributions are essentially identical.

Figure 4.1. Agent interviews: proportion citing problems as very serious by six occupational groups.

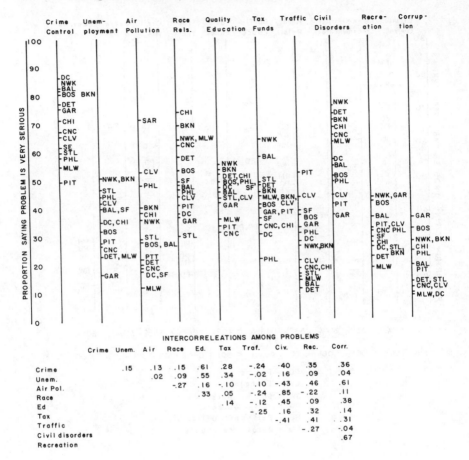

INTERCORRELEATIONS AMONG PROBLEMS

	Crime	Unem.	Air	Race	Ed.	Tax	Traf.	Civ.	Rec.	Corr.
Crime		.15	.13	.15	.61	.28	-.24	.40	.35	.36
Unem.			.02	.09	.55	.34	-.02	.16	.09	.04
Air Pol.				-.27	.16	-.10	.10	-.43	.46	.61
Race					.33	.05	-.24	.85	-.22	.11
Ed						.14	-.12	.45	.09	.38
Tax							-.25	.16	.32	.14
Traffic								-.41	.41	.31
Civil disorders									-.27	-.04
Recreation										.67

**NOTE: All distributions in this table are significantly different from random distributions, as tested by Chi-SQuare, beyond the .001 level.

Figure 4.2. Agent interviews: seriousness of selected problems in fifteen cities.

information from the specific occupational groups for each city.[5] The findings of Figure 4.2 indicate that for most problems the cities show rather individualized profiles of seriousness. The correlations shown on the bottom half of Figure 4.2 tend to be positive and small, indicating

---

[5] Note that because the numbers of each occupational group interviewed in each city was approximately the same and the proportions black within each occupational group are approximately identical, the comparisons among cities are not confounded with either occupational or racial differences. The only exceptions are Milwaukee and Boston, where it was not possible to obtain interviews with policemen.

that cities that have one problem tend to have another; however, these tendencies are rather weak. Only a few of the correlations are high, for example, +.85 between the seriousness of the problems of "race relations" and "violence and civil disorders," with the majority of the entries in the correlations matrix falling between +.5 and −.5.

Despite the fact that the cities show relatively idiosyncratic patterns of perceived problem severities, some cities show more severity on the average than others. In Table 4.4, the average proportion citing individual problems as serious has been computed and presented. The table is arranged in order of descending average problem severity. In only one city—Newark—does a majority regard all the problems as serious on the average. At the opposite end of the list, in Milwaukee only one in three of the institutional agents see local problems as "very serious." Although the spread between the top city in the list in Table 4.4 and the bottom is undoubtedly statistically significant, it is not at all clear whether such a spread represents a clear substantive difference.

TABLE 4.4

Agent   )   City Average Proportions Rating Problems
Interviews)   as "Very Serious"

City	Average Percent "Very Serious"
Newark	53%
Brooklyn	49
Boston	45
Chicago	44
Gary	43
Baltimore	42
Philadelphia	41
San Francisco	40
Cleveland	40
Detroit	40
Washington, D.C.	37
Cincinnati	37
Pittsburgh	36
St. Louis	35
Milwaukee	34

Grand Means =   41%

Both the idiosyncratic profiles of Figure 4.2 and the unclear patterning of Table 4.4 demonstrate a need to approach the data from yet another vantage point. Perhaps the particular character of each city contributes to the differences among the proportions who rate each problem as "very serious," but that the idiosyncratic characteristic of these differences is not apparent in the data presented so far. To ferret out the contributions made by cities, occupational groups, and background differences among individual institutional agents (e.g., age, sex, and educational attainment), we have undertaken a multiple regression analysis whose results are presented in Table 4.5.

It is important to understand the findings presented in Table 4.5. The entries in columns 1 to 10 contain variance partitions (see note 18 in Chapter 2) and indicate the proportion of the total variation in the seriousness ratings of the problem in question which is explained uniquely by various combinations of race, background factors, occupation, and city. Background factors include age, sex, educational attainment, household income, and religion, all of which were considered as one group in the computations. The occupations are the six occupations with which this chapter has been especially concerned. "City" is a set of dummy variables with each city representing a single dummy variable. For example, the first entry in the first column (0.02%) states that 0.02% of the total variation from individual to individual in their ratings of the seriousness of the problem of crime control is uniquely explained by the race of respondent. "Unique" indicates statistical orthogonality from all the other independent variables (and groups of independent variables), and can be calculated by entering the variable or entire cluster *last* in the regression equation. The next to last row of Table 4.5 contains R^2, or the total amount of variance explained by all the variables—race, background, occupation, and city. The last row contains the proportion of the total explained variance that is accounted for by the group of dummy variables labelled as "city." In other words, the last row compares the contribution of characteristics of various cities to the opinion of the institutional agents whom we interviewed as to which problems were very serious.

A great deal of information is packed very tightly into the columns of Table 4.5. For example, comparisons among the first four rows of any column permits assessments of the relative independent (unique) contributions to the ratings made by the race, background, occupation, or the city of residence of the respondents to their seriousness ratings. The next six rows show unique joint contributions—the extent to which combinations of pairs of these variables explained variance independently of the variables. The next four rows contain similar information for combinations of triplets of variables (also called joint contributions) and the last row of combinations takes into account all the variables together.[6]

The sets of variables considered account jointly for relatively modest amounts of variation among individuals in their ratings of problem severity; the R^2 row ranges from .27, in the case of unemployment ratings to .07, in the case of tax funds ratings, averaging out to .14. Note however, that an R^2 of .14 is equivalent to an R of .38, a not inconsiderable correlation for most survey data.

In six out of the ten problem areas, city characteristics account for the major part of the explained variance; the variables in question are crime control, air pollution, race relations, traffic and highway conditions,

---

[6] At least two clarifications of the statistical results are needed. First, all of the data entries in Table 4.5 (columns 1 to 10) are in variance metrics, analogous to squares of correlational measures (in this case the square of the part correlation). Therefore, there should be no negative signs. Note that the negative signs occur for combinations of variables, for instance, background and race in column 1, and are typically associated with tiny amounts of variance. The appearance of these negative variance partitions can be understood through the equation $R^2 = b'_1 r_{01} + b'_2 r_{02} + \cdots + b'_n r_{0n}$ where b' is the standardized regression coefficient, and r is the zero order correlation between an independent variable and the dependent variable. If the sign of the zero order correlation between a given independent variable and the dependent variable is different from the sign of the standardized regression coefficient, adding the variable to the regression equation can *reduce* the amount of variance explained. This is likely to occur when the independent variables are at least moderately intercorrelated and when some of the partial correlations with the dependent variable are negative. In other words, the standardized regression coefficient, which is a partial measure, will be of a different sign from the zero order correlation and their product will be negative. The reduced R^2 causes the subtractions required for partitioning variance to occasionally produce negative signs. Typically the negative explained variances are so small that they can be safely ignored: certainly such is the case with this table. However, when the intercorrelations among the independent variables are high and each variable is highly associated with the dependent variable, the negative variance can become considerable. Usually this indicates substantial multicolinearity and suggests that the results of the regression equation are unstable. In later chapters where occasionally the negative variances are as large as 3% (with an R^2 of around 80%) we take pains to interpret the findings cautiously. For a detailed discussion of these problems, see Robert A. Gordon's, "Issues in Multiple Regression" (*AJS*, **73**: 592–616) and Chapter 10 in Jan Kmenta's *Elements of Econometrics* (MacMillan, New York, 1971). We also need to clarify "joint contribution." Joint contributions are *not* interaction effects. Interaction effects reflect a nonlinear (usually multiplicative) relationship between two (or more) independent variables used in predicting the dependent variable. Joint contributions result from the correlation between two independent variables and the ability of this overlapping component to explain variance on the dependent variable. Joint contributions are explained variances that cannot be uniquely attributed to any one independent variable.

TABLE 4.5

Agent) Relative Contributions of Race, Background
Interviews) Occupation and City to Seriousness Ratings
of Ten Urban Problems (N = 2161 Respondents)

Independent Variables				Dependent Variables									
Race*	Back-ground	Occup.	City	(1) Crime Control	(2) Unemploy-ment	(3) Air Poll.	(4) Race Relations	(5) Educ.	(6) Tax Funds	(7) Traf-fic	(8) Civ. Dis.	(9) Recreation	(10) Corruption
+	0	0	0	0.02%	2.7%	0.06%	0.0%	1.7%	0.09%	0.07%	0.1%	3.4%	0.6%
0	+	0	0	0.9	1.7	0.7	2.7	3.4	0.7	0.09	0.4	1.0	1.4
0	0	+	0	1.2	2.4	0.5	0.4	1.7	1.1	0.42	0.5	2.5	2.6
0	0	0	+	5.3	7.7	12.2	7.9	3.1	4.0	6.6	8.6	3.1	10.3
+	+	0	0	-0.01	0.8	-0.02	0.03	0.6	-0.02	0.3	0.1	0.6	0.6
+	0	+	0	-0.02	3.5	-0.06	0.1	2.4	-0.01	-0.06	-0.09	4.1	0.7
+	0	0	+	-0.01	0.6	-0.05	0.02	0.3	-0.06	0.03	-0.05	0.2	0.3
0	+	+	0	0.9	4.2	1.0	2.0	1.2	0.81	0.6	0.4	1.0	0.8
0	+	0	+	0.5	0.5	0.01	0.4	0.4	0.11	0.3	0.3	0.2	-0.1

TABLE 4.5 (Cont'd)

| Independent Variables | | | Dependent Variables | | | | | | | | | |
| Back- | | | (1) Crime Control | (2) Unemploy-ment | (3) Air Poll. | (4) Race Relations | (5) Educ. | (6) Tax Funds | (7) Traf-fic | (8) Civ. Dis. | (9) Recreation | (10) Corruption |
Race*	Occup.	City										
0	+	+	0.04	-0.2	0.3	-0.02	0.02	0.12	0.2	-0.04	-.07	-0.1
+	+	0	0.03	3.2	0.05	0.2	1.2	0.02	-0.3	-0.06	2.3	0.9
+	+	0	0.01	-0.5	0.05	-0.03	-0.3	0.05	-0.3	0.06	-0.3	-0.3
+	0	+	-0.1	0.05	0.04	0.07	0.2	0.05	-0.03	0.02	0.07	0.1
0	+	+	-0.06	0.1	-0.4	0.07	-0.05	-0.14	-0.4	0.07	-0.04	0.2
+	+	+	0.1	-0.03	-0.02	-0.07	-0.1	-0.05	0.2	-0.04	-0.02	-0.09
R^2 =			.0881	.2685	.1437	.1368	.1581	.0677	.0778	.1042	.1814	.1771

Proportion of Explained
Variance Uniquely

	(1)	(2)	(3)	(4)	(5)	(6)	(7)	(8)	(9)	(10)
Ascribed to City =	60%	29%	84%	58%	20%	23%	84%	82%	17%	58%
Race	#	10%	#	#	10%	1%	#	#	18%	3%
Occupation	13%	8%	3%	2%	10%	16%	3%	2%	13%	14%

= less than 1%

* "+" = cluster included as an independent variable. "0" = cluster not included as independent variable.

violence and civil disorders, and corruption of city officials. For these variables city differences override those generated by the personal characteristics and occupations of the institutional agents. Objective conditions existing in the city appear to be especially determinating with respect to air pollution, where 84% of the explained variance in this rating is taken up by city characteristics. Indeed, looking back at Figure 4.2, we may surmise that the especially high ratings of "very serious" given by the institutional agents in Gary, Indiana, as well as the considerable spread in ratings among other cities, leads to this finding. Of course, anyone who has visited a reasonable number of the cities involved can verify the fact that on almost any given day the amount of air pollution produced by Gary's steel mills is considerably more than that to be found in the typical American city.

In none of the ratings does the race of the respondent account for more than a minor proportion of the explained variance, with the highest percentage (18%) occurring with respect to the adequacy of recreational facilities; this is the only case in which the contribution of the race of the respondent exceeds the contribution of city as a variable.

Occupational characteristics also contribute only modest amounts to the seriousness ratings, although on the average they contribute more than race.

Thus far we have discussed the unique contributions of variables taken one at a time. The joint contributions of combinations of variables occupy the larger proportion of the entries in any one column, although with very few exceptions the joint contributions do not amount to very much. Only with respect to unemployment, education, and recreation can significant proportions of explained variance be attributed to combinations of variables. For example in the severity ratings of the problem of public education, the combination of race and occupation accounts for 13% of the explained variance, more than either of the two variables taken singly. Indeed, looking at Figures 4.1 and 4.2 we can surmise that it is black educators who regard the problem of the quality of public education with particular gravity. The joint contributions of race and occupation to the ratings of unemployment is another example; this combination contributes 15% of the explained variance in that rating.

The overall characterization that emerges is as follows: The institutional agents regard crime control, race relations, violence and civil disorders, and public education as urban problems of particular severity. Although the six occupational groups vary one from the other in the extent to which they perceive these problems as serious, the major proportions of the variation among institutional agents in these ratings are a result of characteristics of the cities involved. In other words, variations from city to city in, say, the severity of the problem of race relations, override either differences among the occupational groups or the race and background of the individual men and women who make up the occupational groups.

This critical role played by characteristics of the cities in the evaluations of severities of local urban problems leads quite naturally to the question of how well local communities are coping with the problems of urban life. Institutional agents were asked a series of questions[7] concerning the governments of their cities. From these questions a scale was constructed, a high score designating a favorable opinion of city government, and a low score the opposite. Scale scores, expressed in Z-scores are shown in Figure 4.3 for cities, occupational groups, and blacks and whites.

The Z-scores that are used in Figure 4.3 have little substantive meaning (unlike the percentages in Figures 4.2 and 4.3) because the absolute scale values express the extent to which average scores for the units involved are above or below the mean for all institutional agents expressed in terms of percentages of standard deviations. For example, the Z-score for St. Louis is +.50 indicating that the average score for the institutional agents interviewed in St. Louis is one half a standard deviation above the mean scale score for all the cities combined.

The vertical bar on the extreme left side of Figure 4.3 represents the city averages. St. Louis ranks the highest in the esteem of its institutional agents while Boston achieves (or suffers from) the lowest esteem. Note that the cities which have serious problems according to either the elite or the institutional agents, are not necessarily the same cities that are

---

[7] The questions employed in constructing the scale were as follows:

Q4   Compared to other cities of the same size, how well do you think (City) is meeting the problems it faces? . . . much better than average, about average, or less than average?

Q27a   The political leaders of our city are imaginative and are always coming up with new ideas on how to meet the city's problems. Completely true, mostly true, somewhat true, or not true?

Q27b   This is a city which has always been among the last to try new ideas like urban renewal, educational reforms, and so on. (Same response categories as above.)

Q27c   One of the good things about this city's government is the tremendous cooperation various agencies give to each other.

Q27f   The average citizen can always find someone in the city government who is willing to help him solve his problem.

Responses to the four questions were positively intercorrelated and seemed to be expressing much the same dimension. Response to the items were scored to represent degrees of approval of city government and a scale score constructed by adding together item scores.

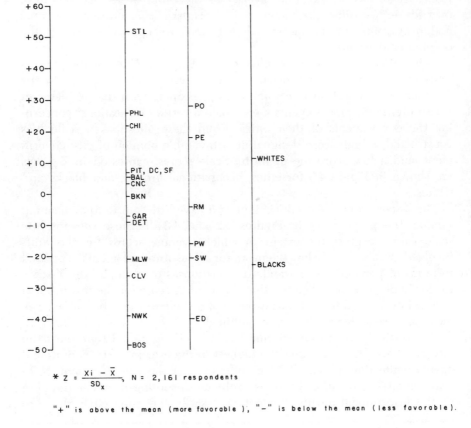

$$* \; Z = \frac{X_i - \bar{X}}{SD_x}, \quad N = 2,161 \; respondents$$

"+" is above the mean (more favorable), "−" is below the mean (less favorable).

Figure 4.3. Agent interviews: evaluation of city government scale (Z-scores).

regarded as having poor government. Indeed, the correlation between the scale scores shown in Figure 4.3 and the average severity proportions shown in Table 4.4 is a modest −.449, indicating that cities with lower levels of perceived problem severity also have a tendency to have more highly regarded city governments.

The middle vertical bar of Figure 4.3 contains Z-scores for the six occupational groups. Policemen and personnel officers apparently have charitable views of their city governments, while educators especially have unfavorable views. The racial differences shown in the right hand vertical bar indicate that whites more favorably regard city government than do blacks.

To determine the relative contributions of race, background, occupation, and city in the responses of the Evaluation of City Government Scale, a regression analysis was undertaken, the results of which are shown in Table 4.6. The four sets of variables together account for a very modest 15% of the variance ($R^2 = .1531$). Although each of the variables contribute somewhat an explanation of the responses to the items included in this scale, the largest proportion of the explained variance (38%) is accounted for by the characteristics of cities. The background characteristics of the respondents accounts for another 22% of the explained variance, while race and occupation accounts for 4 and 10%, respectively.

The results of the analysis of the Evaluation of City Government Scale are similar to the results of the analysis of the perceived severity of local manifestations of the urban problem. By and large the characteristics of the cities lie behind the perceptions of problems and the perceived worth of local government. These findings override the considerable differences that exist among the institutional agents with respect to race, occupation, and such individual attributes as age, sex, and educational attainment. In short city characteristics to which the institutional agents are reacting is a reality.

Views of Blacks and Civil Rights. Although there are obvious racial undertones to the urban problems discussed with the institutional agents (and for some of the cities, where prominent public officials are blacks, the discussion of city government necessarily involves racial attitudes), by and large in the previous section we were concerned with problems not intrinsically involved with the evaluation of blacks and their position within the fifteen cities. After all, both those who are unsympathetic to blacks and those who are sympathetic may both view race relations as a "very serious" problem. Even those problems that have a stronger tone of racial partisanship, for example, crime control and unemployment, are more affected by the characteristics of individual cities than by those of race or individuals in the evaluation of severity ratings.

We now turn to items that are directly and explicitly related to the black populations of the fifteen cities. Several dimensions of attitudes toward blacks and their civil rights are considered. First, there is the question of whether the institutional agents perceived blacks as relatively equal, inferior, or superior to whites as reflected by the ways in which they are treated by important institutional sectors. Second, we consider how much progress toward equality of treatment has been experienced by blacks in each of the cities.

A Scale of Opportunities for Blacks and a Scale of Perceived Rate of Black Progress are shown in Figure 4.4 which presents scale scores for cities, occupational groups, and races. The Scale of Opportunities is made up of items which asked the respondent,

> Compared to other groups in the city of the same income and education, do you think Negroes are about as well off, less well off, or better off, with respect to (educational opportunities, employment opportunities, treatment by the police, housing, treatment by public officials, medical care, and recreation)?

A scale score was constructed for each respondent; a high score indicated that the respondent saw blacks as relatively well off and a low score reflected deprivation. Conceivably, this scale should be relatively neutral with respect to racial attitudes, since it might be assumed that the items pertained to the "facts" of racial differences in education, employment, and so on. Despite this obvious possibility, the unobvious in fact occurred: The more sympathetic a respondent was to blacks, the less likely he was to see them as relatively well off. No scale in our study discriminates as well between whites and blacks as their positions on the vertical bar on the extreme right of Figure 4.4 indicate. Blacks average .70 standard deviations below the mean score and whites attain an average of .67 standard deviations above the mean score.

The occupational groups show also a wide spread in scores, with the police, retail merchants, and personnel officers asserting that blacks are relatively well off, and educators, social workers, and party workers take the opposite pole. The pattern that emerges is one of relative denial that local ghetto members suffer any disabilities because of race.[8]

Because the racial and occupational mix of institutional agents is approximately identical from city to city, the city scores of opportunities for blacks cluster together quite closely with only one city—Washington, D.C.—showing a marked departure from the mean score; oddly enough

---

[8] Since the Z-scores do not yield an appreciation of the extent to which the content of the raw responses bolsters this pattern of denial, we present below the proportions who replied that blacks were better or as well off in each of the areas questioned:

Area	Percent Perceiving Blacks "As Well Off," or "Better Off"
Educational opportunities	55
Employment opportunities	39
Treatment by the police	54
Housing	24
Treatment by public officials	65
Medical care	68
Recreation	53

TABLE 4.6

Race*	Combination Background	Occupation	City	Proportion of Variance Uniquely Explained
+	0	0	0	0.6%
0	+	0	0	3.3
0	0	+	0	1.5
0	0	0	+	5.8
+	+	0	0	0.3
+	0	+	0	1.0
+	0	0	+	0.08
0	+	+	0	1.9
0	+	0	+	-0.3
0	0	+	+	0.2
+	+	+	0	0.7
+	+	0	+	-0.09
+	0	+	+	0.02
0	+	+	+	0.3
+	+	+	+	-0.09
		R^2 =		.1531

Percent of Explained Variance Uniquely Attributable to....

Race	4%
Background	22%
Occupation	10%
City	38%

* "+" = cluster included as independent variable. "0" = cluster not included as independent variable.

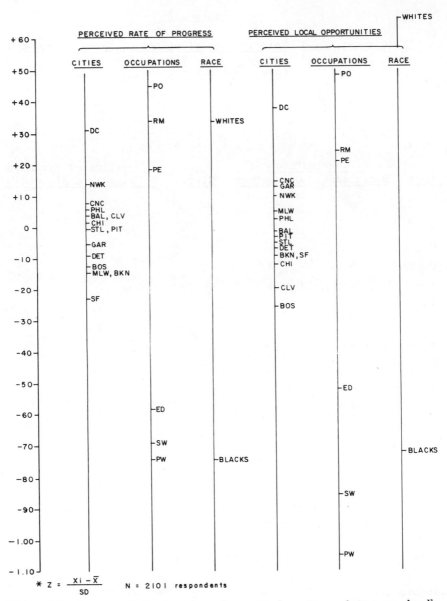

Figure 4.4. Agent interviews: scales of perceived position of Negroes locally (Z-scores).

it is a direction that indicates that the institutional agents perceived relatively greater opportunities for blacks in that city.

The three vertical bars on the left side of Figure 4.4 contain average scores on a Scale of Perceived Black Rate of Progress, an index composed of answers to three questions concerned with the extent to which the respondent perceived blacks improving their positions, have improved their positions, and respondents' satisfaction or dissatisfaction with the rate of improvement.[9]

The average scale score differences for whites and blacks are especially widely apart on this scale as well. The average score for whites is .34 standard deviations above the mean and the corresponding figure for black respondents is .74 standard deviations below the mean. We can interpret high scale scores as indicating further instance of pattern of denial of the depressed positions of blacks in the cities.

As in the case of the previous scale discussed, policemen, retail merchants, and personnel officers are most likely to see their city's blacks in position of equality, while educators, social workers, and political party workers see blacks in a relatively inferior position.

City averages tend to cluster closely about the mean, with the exception of the average for Washington, D.C. Despite the small spread in city averages, there is a fairly high correlation across cities in the city average scale scores for the Scale of Perceived Black Rate of Progress and Scale of Perceived Black Opportunities the correlation is .005.

A regression analysis of the two scales using the familiar independent variables—race, background, occupation, and city—is shown in Table 4.7. Note that considerably greater proportions of the variance in scale scores have been explained by these independent variables than shown in the multiple regressions presented earlier in this chapter, with R^2 for each scale being around .4, equivalent to a correlation coefficient of about .65. As could be anticipated from the fact that the two racial groups were

---

[9] The items included in the Scale of Perceived Black Rate of Progress are as follows:

Q5   In your opinion, how well are Negroes treated in (CITY)? . . . better than any other part of the population . . . equally . . . as other people of the same income, . . . worse than other people of the same income . . . treated worse than any other part of the population?

Q7   Compared to about five years ago, would you consider Negroes in this city a lot better off, generally better off, about the same?

Q11   Now in terms of Negroes gaining what they feel to be equality, do you feel that Negroes have tried to move much too fast, too fast, too slow, or has it been about right?

The scale is scored so that a high score indicates a belief that blacks are well off and/or are moving too fast in their struggle for equality.

TABLE 4.7

Agent   )   Relative Contributions of Race, Background,
Interviews)   Occupation and City to Scores on Scales of
                 Black Opportunities and Perceived Black Rate
                 of Progress (N = 2161 respondents)

Race*	Combination Background	Combination Occupation	City	Proportion of Total Variance Uniquely Attributed Perceived Black Opportunities	Proportion of Total Variance Uniquely Attributed Perceived Rate of Progress
+	0	0	0	9.1%	9.6%
0	+	0	0	2.8	3.9
0	0	+	0	3.2	2.6
0	0	0	+	1.9	1.1
+	+	0	0	3.4	4.3
+	0	+	0	5.7	5.4
+	0	0	+	0.3	0.4
0	+	+	0	7.2	8.6
0	+	0	+	0.1	0.2
0	0	+	+	0.1	0.07
+	+	+	0	5.9	6.4
+	+	0	+	-0.3	-0.2
+	0	+	+	0.2	0.2
0	+	+	+	0.01	0.04
+	+	+	+	-0.1	-0.16
		$R^2 =$		.3956	.4246

Percent of Explained Variance Uniquely Attributable to....

Race	23%	23%
Background	7%	9%
Occupation	8%	6%
City	5%	2%
Background and Occupation	18%	20%
Race and Background and Occupation	15%	20%

* "+" cluster included as independent variable. "0" = cluster not
  included as independent variable.

so far apart in Figure 4.4, the independent variable which accounts uniquely for the largest proportion of the variance is race, accounting in each scale for 23% of the explained variance. Combinations of variables play a stronger role in the regression analysis than has been the case in previous analyses. For example, the combination of background and occupation accounts for 18% and 20% of the explained variance. Race and background and occupation together account for 15% and 20%. In contrast, city as an independent variable shows very weak effects on the scale scores, accounting uniquely for 5% of the explained variance in the Scale of Perceived Black Opportunities and 2% of the explained variance in the Scale of Perceived Black Rate of Progress.

Clearly, sympathy for the position of blacks and desires for their progress are functions of race, occupation, and background. Black institutional agents feel that their brothers (or sisters) are lagging in progress and are still at a point where equality of opportunity and treatment has yet to be attained. Police, retail merchants, and personnel officers are less sympathetic than the other occupational groups, even when we take into account the differences in racial mixes that characterize the occupational groups. Finally, the better educated and younger institutional agents tend to be more sympathetic to the position of blacks.

The posture that is presented by some of the major institutions impinging on the ghettos (especially the police, retail merchants, and the personnel officers of major employers) is one of *optimistic denial*—things are not bad at all for blacks in their cities. Furthermore, blacks are pushing too hard against the barriers to equality.

These attitudes of optimistic denial are not merely particular to the content of the scale items involved. They also affect other ideological matters. We present one example here, a Scale of Persons Versus System Blame as applied to civil disorders. A "person–blame" explanation of civil disorders is one phrased in terms of the characteristics of participating individuals (e.g., outside agitators, criminal elements, and lack of self-control) as opposed to explanations in terms of characteristics of social systems (e.g., institutionalized racism, and unresponsive city government). The scale was constructed from a series of items posing a number of explanations for (then recent) civil disorders; a high score represented a tendency to blame systemic conditions and a low score a tendency to blame persons.[10]

---

[10] The items employed were as follows:

Q21 One view of the riots is that they occur because Negroes feel that their complaints are not being paid sufficient attention to by local authorities.

Q22 Another view . . . is that they are mainly the result of the criminal element in

Figure 4.5 presents the average scale scores attained by each city, the six occupational groups, and the two races. As in the other scales, blacks take a more sympathetic position vis-a-vis their group, seeing the cause of the civil disorders as defects in the system that surround the black community while whites tend to blame personal characteristics of blacks. The line-up of occupational groups by now also is very familiar: policemen, retail merchants, and personnel officers are the occupational groups that cluster on the person–blame side of the scale while educators, social workers, and political party workers cluster at the other end. The city averages show a larger dispersion than in the other scales reported so far with much the same line-up of cities.

The regression analysis reported in Table 4.8 is also a somewhat familiar pattern: Race alone accounts for more (20%) of the explained variance than any other single variable, followed by occupation (12%). But more of the explained variance is accounted for by the combination of background and occupation (23%) than for any of the variables singly. Furthermore, the triplet combination—race, background, and occupation—accounts for a rather large percentage (15%) of the total explained variance.

In short, the personal theories of the causation of civil disorders held by the institutional agents are ones which stress the personal deficiencies of riot participants. The theories are a reflection of attitudes toward blacks and their civil rights.

Public and Private Sector Leadership for Civil Rights. In northern cities the issue of whether blacks should have formal equality before the law

---

the Negro ghetto getting out of hand and taking advantage of minor incidents to provide opportunities for looting.

Q23 Still another view of the riots sees them mainly as a result of the agitation of Negro nationalists or other militants who are taking advantage of the grievances of the Negro population to create the conditions for a rebellion.

Q25 Another view sees the riots as mainly provoked by police brutality in handling arrests and other problems in the Negro community.

Q26 Yet another view sees most Negroes as basically violent with little respect for the laws and mores of our society. Riots occur mainly because authorities have been too permissive.

Responses categories for each of the questions were as follows:

Largely true but not the main reason?
The main reason?
True but not a major reason?
Not true at all?

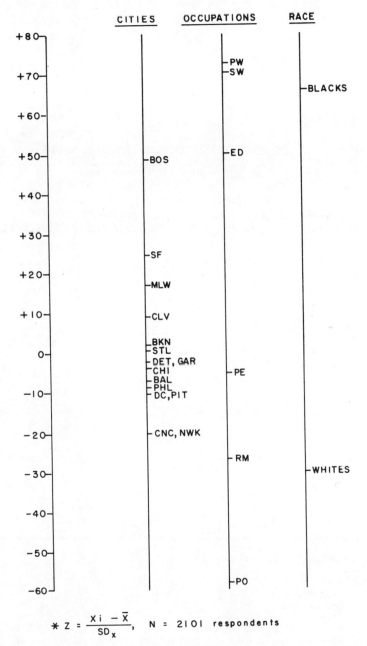

$$* Z = \frac{X_i - \bar{X}}{SD_x}, \quad N = 2101 \text{ respondents}$$

Figure 4.5. Agent interviews: perceived causes of riots scale: system versus persons blame: Z-scores. (High score = high system blame.)

TABLE 4.8

Agents) Relative Contributions of Race, Background,
Interviews) Occupation and City to Scale of Person Versus
System Blame (N = 2161 respondents)

Race*	Combination Background	Occupation	City	Proportion of Total Variance Uniquely Attributed
+	0	0	0	7.7%
0	+	0	0	2.6
0	0	+	0	4.6
0	0	0	+	1.5
+	+	0	0	3.3
+	0	+	0	3.4
+	0	0	+	0.08
0	+	+	0	9.0
0	+	0	+	0.0
0	0	+	+	0.1
+	+	+	0	5.9
+	+	0	+	0.1
+	0	+	+	0.3
0	+	+	+	0.7
+	+	+	+	0.1
		R^2 =		.3916

Proportion of Explained Variance Uniquely Attributable to....

Race	20%
Background	7%
Occupation	12%
City	4%
Background and Occupation	23%
Race and Background and Occupation	15%

* "+" cluster included as independent variable. "0" = cluster not
included as independent variable.

is no longer alive. By and large the majority of public leaders and the public itself has conceded that blacks and whites in principle should be treated equally. The issue which arises in this period is whether the present position of blacks fits that principle or not. As we have seen in the last few pages, white and black institutional agents differ in opinion as to whether blacks have in fact achieved a sufficient degree of equality or whether they are still suffering from disabilities in present day society. We have also seen that some of the occupational groups involved tend toward a position that we have called *optimistic denial* while others tend toward a position which stresses that ghetto blacks suffer still under the penalties of a variety of discriminatory practices.

Under these circumstances we can expect that the question of which groups within each city are providing leadership in the movement for greater equality for blacks produces considerable disagreement among institutional agents. Those who see the position of blacks as close to the condition of equality may expect groups which provide leadership to mainly stand for the maintenance of the status quo, while those who believe that blacks are deprived have different and quite variant definitions of what is appropriate leadership.

Institutional agents were asked a series of questions concerning major groups within each city and the leadership that they provided in "working for equal treatment of all citizens regardless of race or color." The responses to these items provided the bases for two additional scales. A Scale of Public Sector Civil Rights Leadership, and a similar scale for the private sector.[11] Each scale expressed the extent to which the respondents believed the sector in question provided strong leadership (a high score) or was relatively indifferent or "dragging their feet" (a low score). Figure 4.6 contains the average scores for cities, occupational groups, and the two races on each of the two scales.

White institutional agents are more likely to accord more positive lead-

---

[11] Based on responses to an item as follows:

Q10   In every city there are groups that are leaders in working for equal treatment of all citizens regardless of race or color. Other groups are less apt to be concerned with this. How about various groups in this city? Are the (Group) . . . leaders, active in this area but not necessarily leaders, indifferent to the problem or are they dragging their feet on it?

Groups in the private sector:
Police, social workers, elected officials like the mayor, and teachers in the public schools.

Groups in the public sector:
Major employers, major retail businesses, and bankers.

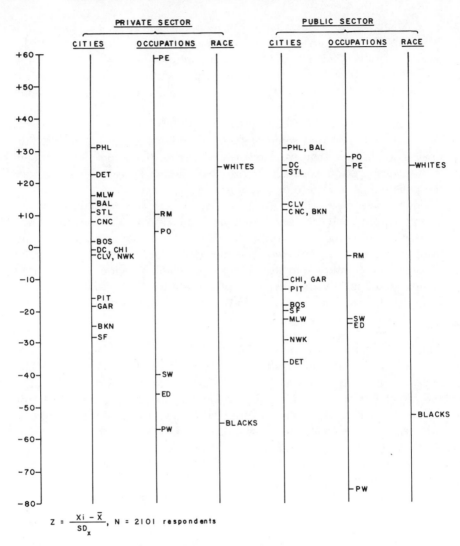

Figure 4.6. Agent interviews: perceived leadership for equality provided by private sector. Score and public sector (Z-scores).

ership to both the private and the pubilc sector, while blacks are less likely to see either sector as providing leadership in this area. The line-up of occupational groups should now be very familiar to the reader: policemen, personnel officers, and retail merchants believe that groups in the private sector and in the public sector provided stronger civil rights leadership than do social workers, educators, and political party workers.

The line-up of cities, however, is less familiar, reflecting more the kinds of leadership in *fact* provided by the public and private sector than the levels of prejudice of the institutional agents in each of the cities.

The results of the regression analysis shown in Table 4.9 indicates that the usual sets of four variables were not able to account for as much of the variance in these two scales as in some of the scales discussed earlier, 25% for the private sector leadership and 22% for the public sector. More of the explained variance can be attributed uniquely to the influence of city characteristics: 11 and 23%, respectively, for the private sector and the public sector. This last finding indicates that there is significant city-to-city variation in the perception of leadership activities provided by the public and private sector, likely reflections of real leadership configuration.

Conclusions. This chapter mainly described what the sets of institutional agents were like. In this sense, it is a portrait of the kinds of people and the range of attitudes which blacks face in the cities' ghettos when they have contacts with major urban institutions. Although we cannot tell how much of themselves the agents reveal in such contact situations, we can be sure that some of the differences among cities and among occupational groups are perceived by their black clients, customers, and employees.

Several findings stand out in this chapter. First, it is abundantly clear that there are pervasive differences among cities. Local environments as determined by the institutional agents are different and presumably have their impact on local residents. It is especially striking that the same cities do not appear either at the top or the bottom of each of the measures that we considered. In Chapter 3, it appeared that Newark and Detroit were obviously the most troubled of all the fifteen cities; yet with respect to their institutional agents, Newark and Detroit appear distributed throughout the range of cities and are not consistently regarded as having the most problems.

Second, there are clear and consistent differences among occupational groups. Indeed, the groups tend to cluster into a liberal set—educators, social workers, and political party workers—and a more conservative set—retail merchants, police, and personnel officers. The liberals express a more sympathetic view of blacks while the conservatives are more likely to deny the existence of problems for blacks and regard whatever disadvantages blacks suffer as caused by the personal characteristics of the group itself. The conservatives are characterized by what we have called a pattern of "optimistic denial."

TABLE 4.9

Agent   ) Relative Contributions of Race, Background,
Interview) Occupation and City to Scales of Public Sector
            and Private Sector Leadership in Civil Rights
            (N = 2161 respondents)

| | | | | Proportion of Total Variance Uniquely Attributed | |
Race*	Combination Background	Occupation	City	Private Sector	Public Sector
+	0	0	0	4.5%	5.3%
0	+	0	0	1.7	1.5
0	0	+	0	3.9	1.3
0	0	0	+	2.8	5.0
+	+	0	0	0.5	2.0
+	0	+	0	6.1	4.5
+	0	0	+	0.2	0.02
0	+	+	0	1.9	0.6
0	+	0	+	0.2	0.01
0	0	+	+	-0.04	0.3
+	+	+	0	3.0	1.8
+	+	0	+	-0.2	-0.1
+	0	+	+	0.1	0.2
0	+	+	+	-0.05	-0.11
+	+	+	+	-0.2	-0.2
		R^2 =		.2465	.2208

Proportion of Explained Variance Uniquely Attributable to....

Race	18%	24%
Background	7%	7%
Occupation	16%	6%
City	11%	23%
Race and Occupation	25%	20%

*Cluster included as independent variable. "0" = cluster not included as independent variable.

Third, race plays a large, often determinative role, in how the institutional agents view their cities and the position of blacks in the ghetto. Understandably, blacks are more sympathetic to blacks, and whites are less so. Indeed, one of the major reasons why the occupational groups differ one from the other is because they also differ in the proportion of blacks in their midst. However, the liberal occupations are still liberal when you take race into account, and blacks are more liberal than whites within each of the occupational groups.

This chapter necessarily ends on an inconclusive note. We now know that the occupational groups differ one from the other. But we do not know the consequences of those differences. The next chapters of this volume are dedicated to the task of discerning.

Chapter 5

GHETTO POLICE:
Social Characteristics and Police Practice

The police constitute a critically important urban institution in contemporary black ghettos. Not only are they a constant visible source of authority, but they are also a 24-hour-a-day source of help and aid. Schools are open ordinarily in the daytime on weekdays and closed during weekends and summer. Retail stores open only during business hours. But, the police are there *all* the time, maintaining patrol, helping in emergency sickness, and even giving on-the-spot marital counseling. The only general purpose urban service institution in the ghetto is usually the police department; because of the police's ubiquity, availability, and, significantly, low or no cost, in poorer neighborhoods they perform the functions that in better neighborhoods are the responsibility of a variety of other institutions.

Although service is an important part of police activities in the ghetto, obviously it is not the main reason for their presence there. The main tasks of the police are the maintenance of order, enforcement of laws, the detection and apprehension of offenders, and the prevention of crime and misdemeanors. Urban ghettos are high crime areas, and urban ghetto residents are much more likely to be the victims of both crimes against the person and crimes against property, than are the residents of other areas.[1] As a corollary, ghetto residents are more likely to be offenders. This purely statistical view, however, masks a great deal of variation: Not every ghetto resident is victimized and even fewer are offenders. The delicate task of making distinctions among various types of offenses, between offenders and ordinary citizens, and between what is essentially a "private" matter and what is an offense is left in the first instance in the hands of the police.

The hard lot of the policeman results from the contradictory tasks that he has to perform. On the one hand, he must prevent wrong doing and—apprehend wrong doers, but he should make no errors in doing so. On the other hand, he must perform a variety of services, but he must not be too intrusive into what may be defined as essentially private matters. Obtaining and maintaining a delicate balance between appearing arbitrary and capricious and being efficient in performance is a difficult task perhaps best performed by men who are intimately conversant with local cultures and are able to make fine distinctions among local residents.[2]

Potentially the police can make a positive contribution to the quality of life in the ghetto or can rub raw the sores of resentment. It is therefore entirely understandable that the police constitute a critical institution, an important first interface between the local ghetto and the larger community.

This chapter describes the characteristics of samples of policemen in thirteen of our cities drawn from among those whose main duty assignment is in predominantly black sections of their cities. We also show how the behavior of the police is, on the one hand, conditioned by the political leadership of the city (more particularly the mayor and police chief) and, on the other hand, has an important effect on the ways in which black residents react to their cities.

The Sample. Interviews with 522 ghetto policemen[3] selected from thir-

---

[1] *Field Surveys II: Criminal Victimization in the United States,* President's Commission on Law Enforcement and the Administration of Justice, Washington, D.C., Government Printing Office, 1967.

[2] The dilemmas of the policeman's role has been treated at length in a variety of social science publications, upon which we have leaned very heavily for ideas in this introductory section. See especially James Q. Wilson, *Varieties of Police Experience,* Harvard University Press, 1968; Jerome Skolnick, *Justice Without Trial,* John Wiley and Sons, New York, 1967, and Egon Bittner, *The Functions of Police in Modern Society,* GPO, Washington, D.C., 1970.

[3] Five interviews were obtained with policemen in Milwaukee before the police chief forbade his men to grant interviews. These interviews are included in tables which concern the characteristics of policemen in general and are excluded when differences among cities were studied. For the latter purpose the effective size of our sample is 517.

teen cities are the main body of data with which we work in this chapter. Two of the police departments, Milwaukee and Boston, refused to cooperate with the Audits and Survey field interviewers and hence had to be omitted in most cases from the analysis. In each city, interviewers were instructed to interview 40 policemen, five of whom were to be above the rank of patrolman, and one fourth were to be blacks.[4] All of the policemen to be interviewed were to be chosen from among those assigned to precincts covering the areas of the city with the highest proportions of blacks.

Access to policemen for the purpose of interviewing was difficult to obtain. Not only did the police departments of two cities (Milwaukee and Boston) refuse to cooperate with the interviewing field staff, but the two police chiefs also forbade men under their command from cooperation on their own time. Some of the cities, notably Chicago and Detroit, repeatedly postponed arranging for interviewing and the interviews from those two cities did not take place until well into the summer of 1968.

We hoped to draw probability samples from all eligible policemen in each of the cities. Seldom, if ever, was this possible. Police commands were reluctant to turn over lists of policemen for sample selection. Rather it was typical for police department officials to select the men and to arrange these men to be interviewed. Hence our final sample expressed to some unknown degree the biases of the police captains and higher level officials who in fact selected the samples for our staff. Although we cannot assess how much bias in the responses were generated by this mode of selection, we can assume that the selectivity reflected the images that the police departments in question consciously wished to project to the public. Police officials were very much aware that our survey was conducted at the behest of and under the sponsorship of the Kerner Commission and, although they may not have read the Commission Report, the attention rendered the Report in the mass media provided the officials with some basis for assessing the viewpoints represented by the Commission.[5] However this discussion of selection does not mean that the

---

[4] These quotas were set to enable comparisons within each city on the basis of rank and race. These proportions, of course, do overrepresent both higher ranks and blacks in the police forces of the cities. In only Chicago and Philadelphia have the proportions of blacks on the police force reached above 20%.

[5] Since 1968, most of the major city police departments have become even less accessible, as police have become more and more defensive because of criticism from blacks and others concerned with civil rights, and at the same time more independent because of the support of those public officials who have made "law and order" a major plank in political platforms.

resultant data are close to worthless; we can present some empirical evidence that the biases have not washed out critical differences among police departments.

The selection of the police samples and some potential resulting biases are discussed in greater detail in Chapter 2.

The Social Characteristics of Urban Police. As we saw in Chapter 4, the police showed more biographical characteristics of working class whites than any other occupational group.[6] Most of the policemen (63%) were born in the cities in which they were serving. Although most (91%) had earned high school diplomas, few had gone to college (35%) and a still smaller proportion (2%) had obtained any college degrees. The majority (57%) were Roman Catholic in religion and only 1% were Jewish.

Politically, the policemen tend toward the Democratic column nationally and locally (45%), with a very small proportion (12%) identifying with the Republican Party. The policeman's median income (around $9000) rounds out the portrait of the lower middle or middle-middle class. In most of the socioeconomic indicators policemen appear to be slightly above the national urban medians, and their religious affiliation suggests that many have been recruited from among the second and third generation descendents from immigration at the turn of the century from Southern and Eastern Europe. In short, police appear to be recruited heavily from among the "ethnics," [7] a term which has almost become the liberal intellectual euphemism for reactionaries (especially in the civil rights sense) among the working class.

How much the social origins of the police affect their relationships with ghetto residents is hard to gauge without a reference point of persons of similar origins who are not policemen. Nor do we know whether ghetto residents perceive them in terms of their jobs or in terms of their social backgrounds. Nevertheless, it is reasonable to speculate that the

---

[6] See Table 4.1 for detailed distributions on the characteristics discussed in this section.
[7] In a strict sense of the term, everyone has ethnicity simply by being a descendant of ancestors of a particular background and immigration history. However, the term "ethnic" is commonly used as a blanket term, referring to mainly the late nineteenth century and early twentieth century Southern and Eastern European stocks and their descendants. It is also used in a slightly disparaging way indicating that whatever an ethnic groups characteristics, it is the peculiarities of their backgrounds that cause faults.

police share with their working class brothers and neighbors the similar economic binds of many blue collar workers who earn enough to be clearly above the poverty level but who still have a difficult time in making ends meet. Their ethnic and racial ties may make it difficult for them to identify and empathasize with blacks who are their social competitors for jobs, housing, and educational opportunities for their children. In any event, it is clear from the analysis of Chapter 4 and from the evidence presented in this chapter that ghetto policemen are hardly sympathetic to blacks and, to the contrary, often see the population of the ghetto as hostile and unfriendly.

The Policeman's Lot.   Given the objective difficulties that ghetto policemen face in meeting almost contradictory demands, it would be surprising if they saw their jobs as sinecures. Indeed, most of the policemen were able to point to at least one major problem that they faced while doing their jobs in the ghetto precincts to which they were assigned, only 6% could not think of major problems,[8] and the policemen on the average thought of 1.4 problems to relate to our interviewers. The problems cited are shown in Table 5.1.

In Table 5.1 the major problems cited by the police are divided into three broad groupings: those dealing with the police system itself; those dealing with police relations with other systems, including the general public; and those concerning social conditions with their precincts. It is clear that police regard their external relations more frequently as a problem than any other category and two out of three policemen cite this area as problematic. "Lack of support from the general public" is particularly a sore point to the police. Of course, it is difficult to discern from these response frequencies precisely what the police had in mind by "general public": was it the public residing in their particular precincts or, more inclusively, all of the city's residents. The policemen also complained about the legal system which they believe frustrate the proper pursuit of their occupational activities.

The second major grouping of problems pertain to the social conditions within the areas to which they are assigned, cited by two out of five policemen. Crime and juvenile delinquency in their precinct is the major complaint here, cited by 16% of the policemen. Race relations runs

---

[8] Or, were unwilling to indicate what they were to the Audits and Surveys interviewers.

TABLE 5.1

Police   )   Major Problems Facing Police in Precinct
Interviews)

Major Problems:		Percent Citing Problem
I: **Police System Problems:**		
Manpower Shortage		10.9%
Equipment Shortage		5.1
Personnel Policies		8.8
Low Pay		.5
Other		2.4
	Subtotal	27.7%
II: **External Relations of Police:**		
Lack of General Public Support		44.4%
Lack of Support from Public Officials		2.4
Defects in Courts, Laws		19.9
Other		1.1
	Subtotal	67.8%
III: **Social and Economic Conditions:**		
Poverty, Social Disorganization		6.8%
Crime and Juvenile Delinquency		15.5
Race Relations		13.7
Riots and Civil Disorders		1.9
Other		2.2
	Subtotal	40.1%
No Problems Cited		6.1%
100% =		(522)*
Average Number of Problems Cited =		1.4

*Since policemen could give more than one response to this question, the percentages add up to considerably more than 100%.

a close second (14%). Poverty and social disorganization (e.g., broken families and lack of motivation for education) is seldom cited (7%), as one might have anticipated from the responses of the police shown in Chapter 4.

Internal problems of the local police system is the third category of responses, cited by 28% of the policemen. Here the police appear to be concerned primarily with a manpower shortage (11%) and defects in the personnel policies of the police department (e.g., favoritism and poor discipline).

Thus policemen find that problems in their jobs come from deficiencies in the citizens that they serve and that should support them. Any defect in the police departments themselves, is too few policemen to do the job.

The police may see themselves as having problems, yet they are not seething with dissatisfaction, as Table 5.2 indicates. Nor are they enthusiastic. One in three are very satisfied with their jobs as policemen, another one in three are somewhat satisfied, a distinct minority (21%) express some dissatisfaction, and a very small minority (6%) indicate that they are very dissatisfied. Of course, such figures can be misleading: After all, these are policemen who are still on-the-job; perhaps those who were

TABLE 5.2

Police   )   Satisfaction with Job as Policeman in
Interviews)   This City

Level of Satisfaction	Whites	Blacks	Total
Very Satisfied	37%	32%	36%
Somewhat Satisfied	34	46	37
Somewhat Dissatisfied	23	15	21
Very Dissatisfied	5	6	6
DK & NA	1	2	1
100% ▪	(397)	(125)*	(522)

*Chi Square   .10 > p > .05

*Significance of differences between whites and blacks.

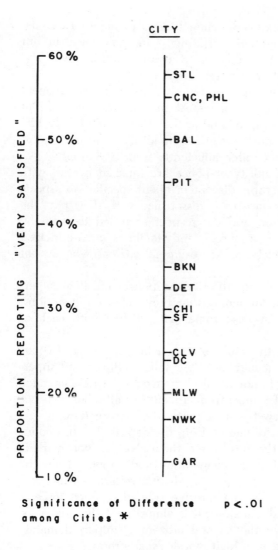

CITY

Significance of Difference   p < .01
among Cities *

* Computed using Chi Square testing the hypothesis
that cities differ from each other only through
sampling error. Full response categories used
in computing Chi Square

Figure 5.1 Police interviews: proportion "very satisfied" with jobs as policeman in each city.

greatly dissatisfied did not stay long enough to accumulate to a significant proportion at any one point in time. The policemen in our sample have been in their occupations for an average of 10.2 years and hence can scarcely be classed as neophyte "rookies."

Satisfaction with their jobs varies considerably from police department to police department as Figure 5.1 shows. At the one extreme, 58% of St. Louis' policemen are very satisfied and at the other extreme only 12% of Gary policemen are very satisfied with their jobs. According to this range conditions of police work differ sufficiently from city to city.

Despite the fact that the majority of police are satisfied overall with their jobs, there is still considerable discontent about specific job aspects as Table 5.3 shows. Policemen are most dissatisfied with their pay, the physical danger they encounter, and the respect accorded to them by citizens. Working conditions, resources and facilities are criticized moderately, but not as extremely, as, for example, citizens who do not give policemen due respect.

Policemen are most satisfied with their fellow policemen, their supervisors, and the flexibility and autonomy that they enjoy on their jobs; a majority of policemen are at least somewhat satisfied with each of these job aspects.

Not all is harmony within the ranks of the police, however. In particular, black policemen do not find that their fellow officers and supervisors are as congenial a bunch, nor do black policemen express as much dissatisfaction with the lack of respect from citizens.[9] In all other respects, however, black policemen show the same patterns of satisfaction.

The impression that begins to emerge from the data is that the police (particularly the whites on the force) see themselves as poorly paid, hamstrung in their jobs by lack of cooperation and support from the general public and the specific population whom they are serving, and as beset by physical danger. On the positive side, the police force is seen as congenial to work with. In short, it is almost as if the police see themselves as walled off from the general citizenry, supported mainly in their work by participating in a high morale work group.

[9] Black policemen gave the following distributions of response to these items:

	Very Satisfied (%)	Somewhat Satisfied (%)	Somewhat Dissatisfied (%)	Very Dissatisfied (%)
Fellow officers	27	48	22	3
Respect from citizens	19	34	35	12
Supervisors	39	43	11	6

All of the distributions above are significantly statistically different from the responses given by white policemen (P less than .01 in each case).

TABLE 5.3

Police) Levels of Satisfaction with Eight
Interviews) Aspects of Job

Aspect of Job	Very Satisfied	Somewhat Satisfied	Somewhat Dissatisfied	Very Dissatisfied	DK	100% =
Pay	10%	37	27	25	1	(522)
Working Conditions	10%	44	33	12	#	(522)
Other Policemen Worked With	51%	34	12	3	1	(522)
Physical Danger	10%	26	33	19	12	(522)
Flexibility you have in doing Job	23%	38	22	16	1	(522)
Supervisors	50%	35	10	3	2	(522)
Respect from Citizens	9%	31	34	24	2	(522)
Resources and Facilities to Help on Job	18%	35	26	20	1	(522)

*Based on answers to Q33 "Each job has its advantages and disadvantages. Consider several aspects of your particular job as a policeman, compared to other jobs in this city. Are you generally very satisfied, somewhat satisfied (etc.) with how this job is treating you with respect to (pay, etc)?"

Undoubtedly because race often forms a barrier to friendships, black policemen are less attracted to the fellowship offered by police work. Partially compensating for the lack of fellowship, black policemen feel less of a sense of isolation from the population they serve.[10] Perhaps as a consequence, black policemen, as we saw in Table 5.2, are nevertheless as generally satisfied with their jobs as whites.

The city-by-city patterns of job satisfactions are shown in Figure 5.2 where the proportions of the police in each city who are satisfied (combining "very satisfied" and "somewhat satisfied") are plotted for each of the separate aspects of job satisfaction.

Members of various police departments differ widely in their satis-

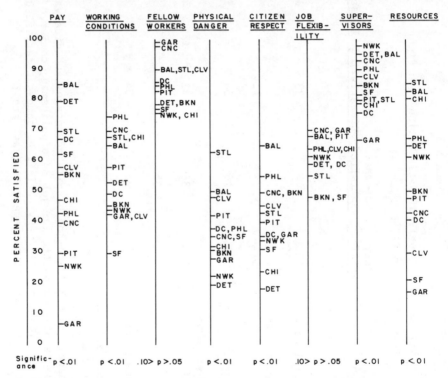

Figure 5.2   Police interviews: specific aspects of job satisfaction by cities.

---

[10] It should be emphasized that this relative statement emphasizes the differences between white and black policemen. In an absolute sense, as note 9 indicates, almost half (47%) of the black policemen express dissatisfaction with the respect given to them by citizens. Furthermore, our sample comes from inner city precincts; thus black police should feel less isolated from citizens.

faction with pay, working conditions, physical danger, and supervisors and resources available to policemen. The variation in satisfaction with pay is especially striking, ranging from a satisfaction level of 7% in Gary to 85% in Baltimore.[11]

The thirteen police departments differ least with respect to satisfaction with fellow workers and with flexibility on the job. In the case of the former, it appears that the levels of satisfaction are uniformly high, while in the case of the latter, the police departments cluster around the middle of the scale.

From the bars in Figure 5.2 it is difficult to see any particularly strong patterns in the positions of particular police departments. For example, while Gary's policemen express lowest satisfaction with pay, they are the most enamoured of their fellow workers, and around middling concerning citizen regard for the police. The individualization of police department patterns is borne out more clearly in the correlations shown in Table 5.4.

As Table 5.4 shows, the correlations among dimensions of satisfaction across cities are neither uniform in sign or in size, which indicates that individual cities tend to vary in their position from vertical bar to vertical bar. When we consider that a correlation coefficient has to be above .52 to be significant at the .05 level, most of the correlations in Table 5.4 do not meet this criterion. Indeed, only the correlation between levels of satisfaction with working conditions and satisfaction with resources made available to the police (.72) is clearly significant.

Despite this zero order pattern of interrelationship among the dimensions of satisfaction on a city level there are nevertheless relatively high relationships between the dimensions and the ratings of general satisfaction that we considered earlier (see Figure 5.1). By and large cities which have police departments which have high individual satisfaction dimensions also have high general satisfaction. Indeed it is possible to predict the level of general satisfaction with a fair degree of accuracy by considering only three of the separate dimensions: the multiple correlation (R) between a police department's general level of satisfaction (Y), working conditions (X_1), physical danger (X_2), and satisfaction with

---

[11] This intercity variation reflects to some degree the objective differences between the pay scales of the several police departments. The correlation between the median level of household income reported by police in each department and the levels of satisfaction is .507, indicating a strong reality base to the satisfaction levels. It should be pointed out that median household incomes reflect earnings of other working members of the household as well as the pay scales of the policemen; hence the correlation might well be higher, if we had direct information on pay scales.

TABLE 5.4

	Police Interviews)	Correlations Among Dimensions (Computed on City Proportions Satisfied) [N = 13]						
	Pay	Working Conditions	Fellow Police	Physical Danger	Citizen Respect	Flexibility	Supervisors	Resources
Pay		19	-23	20	02	-26	25	51
Working Conditions			07	33	37	13	21	72
Fellow Police				40	42	53	-30	-43
Danger					53	-04	15	27
Citizen Respect						12	25	15
Flexibility							-02	-27
Supervisors								40

supervisors (X_3) is .88,[12] and yields the following regression equation:[13]
$$Y = -57.6 + 65X_1 + .54X_2 + .44X_3$$
In short, for every additional percentage point of satisfaction with working conditions, physical danger, and supervisors, the proportion of police in the department in question who are generally satisfied with their jobs goes up about one half of a percentage point.

In an attempt to find out whether the sources of dissatisfaction with the policeman's lot stemmed from the general role of policeman or from the specific assignment, the police were asked a set of items which called for explicit comparisons between their ghetto precinct assignments and other assignments in their cities. Table 5.5 contains the answers to four such questions. A clear majority of the police claim that their ghetto assignments are harder (62%) and only a small minority (6%) claim that they are easier. Black policemen are more likely to see these assignments as "about the same" as other assignments (40%), although half (50%) believe that their assignments are more difficult.

About the same majority (63%) see their ghetto assignments as more hazardous than other assignments, and only a small minority (6%) claim they are safer. As before, black policemen are more likely to claim there is no difference between ghetto and other assignments, but the differences between whites and blacks are not as great on this question.

When asked whether they would prefer some other assignment, less than half the policemen (48%) would prefer to remain on their present assignment. Another one fourth would prefer another assignment and the remaining one fourth do not care one way or the other. Black policemen are slightly more likely to prefer another assignment, but the difference involved does not reach the high levels of statistical significance.

The last question of Table 5.5 asks whether the police are regarded by the residents of their precincts with respect or with contempt. On the whole, the majority see a respectful set of precinct residents (52% of police see the residents regarding them with respect), as opposed to a contemptfull set of residents (32%). Yet, the balance perhaps is not as important as the very large proportion (one in three) of the police who feel that their clients regard them with contempt. It is difficult to imagine that the best and most careful efforts of such policemen must obtain under those circumstances. To some extent, this perception is a function

---

[12] Significant beyond the .01 level. Note city averages are used in this computation; hence $N = 13$. This particular equation is the "best" in predicting overall satisfaction from its components. Since the three independent variables produced the largest R, adding more variables would have lowered the F ratio. (The decrease in degrees of freedom did not compensate for the increase in variance explained.)

[13] Raw regression coefficients are used in this equation.

TABLE 5.5

Police .) Comparisons Between Ghetto Assignments
Interviews) and other Assignments

A. Q2a "Compared to other assignments in other precincts of the city,
how do you regard this particular assignment?"

	Whites	Blacks	Total
Harder	66%	50%	62%
Easier	5	6	6
About the Same	27	40	30
DK & NA	2	3	2

Chi Square Significance of Racial Differences $p < .01$

B. Q2b "Is the work safer, isn't there any difference, or is it more
hazardous than elsewhere in the city?"

	Whites	Blacks	Total
Safer	6	6	6
No Difference	28	40	30
More Hazardous	66	52	63
DK & NA	1	2	1

Chi Square Significance of Racial Differences $.05 > p > .01$

TABLE 5.5 (Cont'd)

C. Q4 "Would you prefer working in this precinct for several more years (or maybe even permanently), would you prefer some other assignment in this city, or doesn't it matter to you where you work?"

	Whites	Blacks	Total
Prefer Present Assignment	51%	40%	48%
Prefer Another Assignment	25	27	26
Doesn't Matter	24	32	26
DK & NA	#	2	1

Chi Square Significance of Racial Differences .20 > p > .10

D. Q5 "How much respect does the average resident of this precinct have for the police?"

	Whites	Blacks	Total
Great Deal of Respect	9%	16%	10%
Some Respect	39	52	42
Neither Respect nor Contempt	14	6	12
Some Contempt	23	16	21
A Great Deal of Contempt	12	9	11
DK & NA	3	1	2

Chi Square Significance of Racial Differences p < .01

N for whites = 397
N for blacks = 125

of the characteristics of the police, as the differences between black and white policemen indicate: 48% of the whites see their clients as regarding them with respect as compared with 68% for black policemen. Black policemen either experience different things in the ghettos or perceive the same things differently.

Figure 5.3 presents data for each of the thirteen cities from which we have police interviews. Significant differences appear among the cities

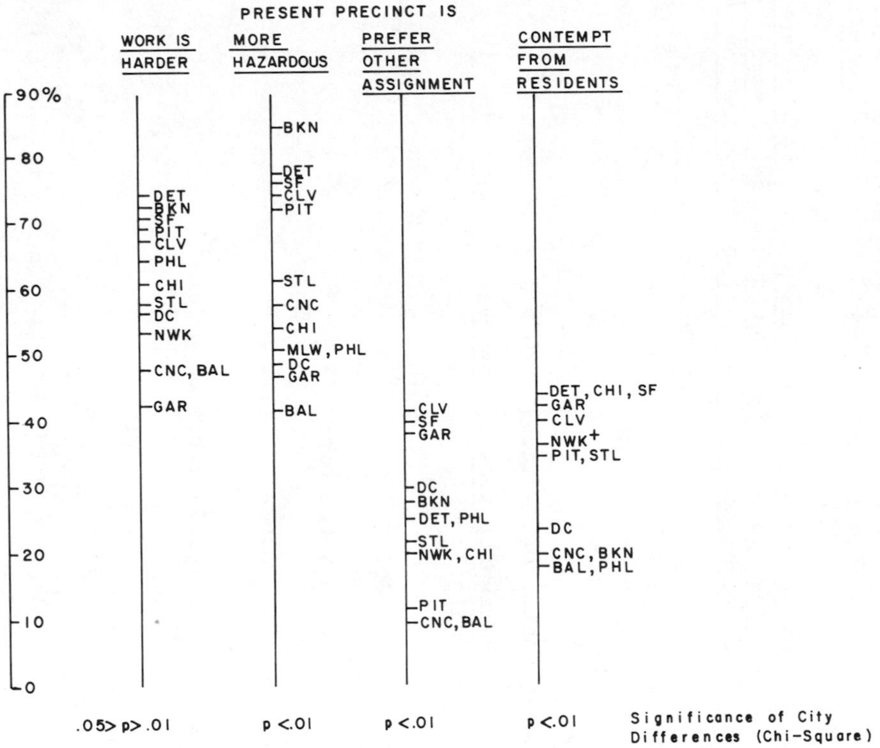

CITY LEVEL CORRELATIONS AMONG LEVELS OF SATISFACTION WITH PRECINCT ASSIGNMENT (N = 13 CITIES)

	MORE HAZARDOUS	PREFER ANOTHER ASSIGNMENT	CITIZENS HAVE CONTEMPT	ASSIGNMENT IS HARDER
HAZARDOUS		.32	.25	.76
PREFER OTHER ASSIGNMENT			.47	.20
CITIZENS HAVE CONTEMPT				.14

Figure 5.3 Comparison between ghetto precinct assignments and other police assignments by city.

to the extent that such variations are unlikely to have been statistical arti-facts. As we saw in the case of the variables presented in Table 5.4, the levels of satisfaction with precinct assignments tend to correlate across cities; thus cities with high levels of dissatisfaction in one respect are likely to manifest high levels in another respect. Those tendencies are not very strong, however, as the correlations at the bottom of Figure 5.3 are not impressively high; thus each city tends to display a more or less idiosyncratic profile. The major relationship among the four variables in Figure 5.3 is between the levels claiming the assignment to be more diffi-cult and claims that the assignment is more hazardous ($r = .76$).[14]

The relationships with which we have been concerned up to this point are among levels of variables across cities. Thus the regression equation presented earlier described the relationship between the proportion of a city's police department who were satisfied with their jobs as policemen and the proportion of a city's police department who were satisfied with their working conditions. In presenting information of this sort, we are primarily concerned with the characteristics of *police departments*, espe-cially those portions of the departments which deal with the city's ghettos, and *not* with *individual policemen*. It is important to realize that whether an individual policeman is satisfied with his job may depend on quite different factors, although one may expect that at least the same patterns of relationships among variables are shown.

Table 5.6 presents an analysis of the contributions to general satisfac-tion by individual policemen in a set of variables which are correlates of individual levels of satisfaction with the job of policeman. Together the set of variables "account" for about 32% of the total variation among individual policemen.

The major portion of the explained variance (18.6%) is accounted for by the same factors which predicted levels of police department satisfac-tion. The more satisfied a policeman was with working conditions, his fellow policemen, his supervisors, respect from citizens, and so on, the

---

[14] One may raise the question whether these variables which purport to relate to the particular precincts to which the police were assigned are really different from the more general ratings of the job of the policeman as shown earlier in Figure 5.3. That they are different to a large extent can be shown in the form of correlations between the levels of disenchantment shown in Figure 5.4 and corresponding levels from Figure 5.3. For example, the correlation across cities between the proportions claiming the policeman's job to be more subject to physical danger and the proportion who state that their precinct work is hazardous is .10, a very low relationship indeed. The same sort of correlation computed between respect received from citizens in general and respect from people in the precincts is .23, similarly low. Apparently these pairs of measures are sensitive to different aspects of police work, at least as reflected in differences among the thirteen cities.

TABLE 5.6

Police   )   General Job Satisfaction: Relative Contributions
Interviews)   of Satisfaction with Specific Aspects of Job,
              City, Background and Other Variables   (N = 522)

Satisfaction with Specific Aspects of Job *	City	Background**	Race	Proportion of Total Variance Uniquely Attributable
+	0	0	0	18.6%
0	+	0	0	4.6
0	0	+	0	0.9
0	0	0	+	0.1
+	+	0	0	6.1
+	0	+	0	-0.4
+	0	0	+	-0.1
0	+	+	0	0.5
0	+	0	+	0.1
0	0	+	+	-0.1
+	+	+	0	0.3
0	+	+	+	0.0
+	0	+	+	0.0
+	+	0	+	-0.2
+	+	+	+	-0.2

Total Variance Explained (R^2) = .316

R   = .554

* "+" = presences of the factor as an independent variable.
   "0" = absence of the factor as an independent variable.

**Includes having relatives in precinct, having friends in
   precinct, attending meetings in precinct, having a desk job
   or being on patrol, and years on the force.

more likely he was to express a high level of general satisfaction with his job as policeman.

City differences in policeman job satisfaction persist when other individual level factors are taken into account. The variation from city to city accounts uniquely for about 4.6% of the total variance among individual policemen. The remaining sets of factors, which include, race, education, social ties with residents of their precincts, and such account uniquely for so little interindividual variance that they may be regarded as negligible factors in job satisfaction.

The joint contribution of city differences and levels of satisfaction with specific aspects of the policeman's job account for the only other large amount of variance (6.1%) which expresses the extent to which these two factors co-vary so closely that it is difficult to unravel the separate threads of their influence.

It is difficult to resist the temptation to write about these findings in causal terms. Yet, it would be unwarranted to do so. From our own data it is not possible to tell whether policemen first assess how satisfied they are with particular aspects of their jobs and then come to a general assessment or whether the process is reversed. Indeed, the process may be one of mutual interaction between an overall assessment of job satisfaction and contentment or discontent with specific job features. Furthermore, since we only have policemen in our sample who serve in the ghetto precincts of their cities, it may well be the case that we are understating the role of such assignments in the generation of job satisfaction. After all, the policemen who are in our sample may be precisely those to whom such features of the precinct as the danger of the work may not be important, as others may have been either transferred out because of poor performance or selfselected themselves out.

One finding in Table 5.6 of considerable importance to the analysis in this chapter is the persistent effect of city differences after other differences among departments have been taken into account. The results we have obtained so far indicate that police departments vary considerably in the general level of satisfaction with their roles displayed by rank-and-file policemen. By and large, policemen are satisfied when they view "working conditions" as good and when they have supervisors whom they regard as satisfactory. Of course, with hindsight we may wish that we had measured "working conditions" more specifically. It would also be useful to have a more precise image of what in the supervisory levels of the police department leads to satisfaction on the part of the rank-and-file.

Although we cannot attack the last question directly, we can use ratings derived from the elite interviews to shed some important light on what is meant by satisfactory supervision. Table 5.7 presents correlations of the proportions satisfied with supervisors and of two elite ratings of the police chief (used because these were the only data relevant to the supervisory levels of the police department available in the elite ratings) —the "autonomy" and "competence" ratings. At the bottom of Table 5.7 the regression of the two elite ratings on the proportion satisfied with

TABLE 5.7

Police & Elite)	Correlations Among "Satisfaction with
Interviews)	Supervisors", "Autonomy" Ratings of

Correlations Among "Satisfaction with Supervisors", "Autonomy" Ratings of Police Chief and "Competence" Ratings of Police Chief (Based on Correlations Computed with Cities as Units) [N = 13]

	Police Satisfaction with Supervisors	(Elite) Autonomy of Police Chief	Competence of Police Chief
	Y	X_1	X_2
Satisfaction with Supervisors		.44	-.81
Autonomy of Police Chief	X_1		-.13

Multiple Regression on "Satisfaction with Supervisors" (Raw Regression Coefficients)

$$Y = 99.9 + .037 X_1 - .015 X_2$$

$$R = .881$$

supervisors is presented. Note that these are correlations computed with cities as units ($N = 13$ cities).

Table 5.7 contains some surprising relationships. To begin with, the correlation between satisfaction with supervisors and ratings of the competence of the police chief is high—*but negative* ($-.81$). The relationship of supervisor satisfaction with ratings of the police chief's autonomy ratings is smaller—*and positive* ($.44$). Together the two ratings predict the satisfaction proportions with a fair amount of accuracy ($R = .881$). Apparently, whatever makes up a competent police chief according to elites provokes relative dissatisfaction with supervision among the rank-and-file ghetto policemen! Furthermore, a relatively autonomous police chief leads to high levels of satisfaction with supervision!

At this point, it is difficult to interpret properly these findings; nevertheless, we are tempted to speculate. Earlier, police were shown to feel somewhat isolated from the public while very chummy with each other. If these attitudes are as prominent as the data suggest, police may sometimes react as if they were an ethnic minority group. In this instance, police would favor supervisors whose primary commitment was to the police department, not city hall nor the public. In contrast, city elites would generally prefer police officials who were responsive first to broad community needs (hence competent and not autonomous) and second to the parochial needs of the police department. Therefore, the correlations in Table 5.7 may indicate considerable tension between cities and their police departments. Since these data were collected, police organizations of various sorts (the P.B.A., police unions, etc.) have become far more visible which suggests that indeed police often see their interests as quite distinct from city elites and the public.

Regardless of one's interpretations of Table 5.7, the data indicate that the job satisfaction rating levels found in metropolitan police departments are related to the general features of the departments involved and the way in which department commands are related to the political structure of the city. We return to considerations of this sort later in this chapter.

What Do Policemen Do?   Although the major exposure of members of the general public to policemen is through their patrol activities, a policeman covers a variety of specific activities. Although most policemen are on patrol, there are many precinct and central headquarters jobs; some policemen are detectives and other specialists, some are stationed in the courts and in other municipal buildings, and some also often run the municipal jail. Our sample of policemen was deliberately restricted to those who worked out of precinct headquarters, mainly as patrolmen.[15] Table 5.8 indicates that the quotas set in sampling were fairly successful: Two out of three policemen in our sample are solely on patrol, 12% have desk jobs only, and the remainder have some combination of patrol and desk responsibilities.

Patroling ghetto precincts is sometimes a solitary activity (almost two out of five patrolmen are on patrol by themselves), but mainly a group activity, three out of five patrolmen sharing their beat with at least one partner.

While on duty a policeman spends most of his time in a patrol car; in

---

[15] Sampling quotas were set at 75% patrolmen and 25% precinct headquarters personnel.

TABLE 5.8

Police   )   Selected Characteristics of Police
Interviews)   Activities and Training (N = 522)

A.   Assignment in Precinct:*

Has regular beat only   65%
Has desk job only   12
Combination   24

B.   Characteristics of Patrol:

   1.   Solitary or Partner Patrol
         Patrols by self   33%
         Patrols with partner   55
         Does not apply   12

   2.   Racial Mixture of Patrol Groups
         Patrols only with same race
              partner   15%
         Patrols sometimes with other
              race partner   73
         Desk job or patrols by self 27

   3.   Proportion of Time on Patrol on Foot and in Patrol Car
         Average proportion spent on
              foot patrol   16%
         Average proportion spent in
              patrol car   54
         Average proportion spent in
              court, in precinct offices
              and in other activities 30

C.   Residence of Police:

	Whites	Blacks	Total
Lives in precinct	12%	36%	17%
Lives elsewhere	88	64%	83
100% =	(397)	(125)	(522)

D.   Special Training Experiences

Proportion with special training in riot control   87%
Proportion with special training in human
     relations, psychology, counselling, etc.   88

*These proportions were set primarily by sampling quotas in
which we limited the proportion who had primarily desk jobs
in the precinct headquarters.

fact, policemen claim that they spend about half of their time in their patrol cars. Only a small proportion of the time is spent on foot patrol (16% on the average is spent walking a beat). The remainder of the time is spent in the precinct headquarters, in court, and on other related duties.

Most (73%) of the policemen have had at least some experience patrolling in racially mixed patrols, but only a small proportion (16%) on a regular basis. The typical patrol team is racially homogeneous.

Most of the police, white and black, do not live in the neighborhoods in which they are stationed. Black policemen are more likely to be residents of their precincts (one out of three) than white policemen (12%), but for both groups neighborhood residence is distinctly a minority pattern.

From the information presented in Table 5.8, some degree of distance appears to exist between the patrolmen and their precincts. Few of the patrolmen spend much of their time on foot patrol. Mainly they ride around in the company of a partner (who is also white) and maintain surveillance over their beat through the windshields and side windows of their patrol cars.

On patrol, police officers may be called upon to do a variety of tasks. At some point during the day they may be directing traffic, writing up traffic and parking violations, answering calls for assistance from other policemen, investigating a complaint phoned in to the police dispatcher by a citizen, and so on. Much of the time may be spent on vigilant surveillance—cruising the streets in a patrol car watching for the cues that would call for investigation or for active intervention on their part.

Whether to take action toward enforcement of the law or toward the apprehension of an offender is often the decision of the policeman on the beat. Whether to take this step requires a quick judgment of whether the officer is making a correct move or an error. If someone "looks suspicious," he may either be about to engage in some illegal activity or have in fact engaged in such activity; therefore, the officer would be right to interrogate him. Or he may be proceeding in a completely law abiding fashion, in which case the officer would upset an innocent person. Even though the decision in any one particular case may not call for a conscious choice of one or the other alternative, the decision does, in effect, weigh the risks of not enforcing the laws or of antagonizing either a citizen or the witnesses to an intervention.

Knowing that in many urban ghettos the relationships between the police and the citizenry are far from optimum, we asked the police in our sample how frequently they engaged in a series of practices that we thought might produce some resentment on the part of ghetto citizens. Table 5.9 contains the results. Note that the policemen were not asked about their own individual practices, but about what was customary in their precincts. Furthermore, the categories of response are unfortunately more vague than ideally desired. We do not know how frequent "frequently" is, although we can be sure that "never" means at least "hardly ever."

All of the practices in Table 5.9 are claimed to be employed by the police: With varying degrees of regularity, the police intervene in domestic quarrels, search with and without a warrant, stop and frisk suspicious people, break up loitering groups, and interrogate suspected drug users. Almost all (more than nine out of ten) policemen claim that they are called upon frequently to intervene in domestic quarrels, a majority so great that one must judge this to be a standard practice in any of the departments. The next highest frequency activity is breaking up loitering groups, a practice which 63% of the policemen say is a frequent occurrence. The other practices in Table 5.9 are claimed to be frequent by only a minority of the policemen. The practice judged (19%) to be least frequent, but engaged in by most departments on a "sometimes" (43%)

TABLE 5.9

Police   ) Frequency of Potentially Controversial
Interviews) Police Actions   (N = 522)

| Activity* | Frequency | | | | |
	Frequently	Sometimes	Seldom	Never	DK & NA
Intervene in Domestic Quarrels	92	5	1	1	#
Search with a Warrant	19	43	31	6	1
Search on Suspicion But Without a Warrant	28	34	23	14	1
Stop and Frisk Suspicious People	38	31	20	10	#
Break up Loitering Groups	63	27	8	1	#
Interrogate Suspected Drug Users	37	34	23	6	1

*Based on answers to Q9: "Since the problems differ from precinct to precinct in this city, some of the practices of the police department will naturally differ somewhat. In your precinct are policemen called in frequently, sometimes, seldom or never to......?"

or "seldom" (31%) basis is "searching with a warrant." "Searching on suspicion without a warrant" is cited by one in four policemen as a "frequent" practice, although only 14% claim that the practice "never" occurs in their precincts. A little more than one in three policemen claims that "breaking up loitering groups" and "interrogating suspected drug users" are "frequent" practices.

In Figure 5.4 differences in practices among cities are shown. Note that the proportions shown vary in definition from dimension to dimension: The proportion "frequent" is shown for "domestic quarrels" and "interrogate suspected drug users" while the other percentages refer to the combined "frequent" and "sometimes." This variation in definition facilitates comparisons among cities.

As one may have suspected, the difference among cities with respect to intervention in domestic quarrels was scarcely large enough to reach statistical significance. However, with respect to *each* of the other five

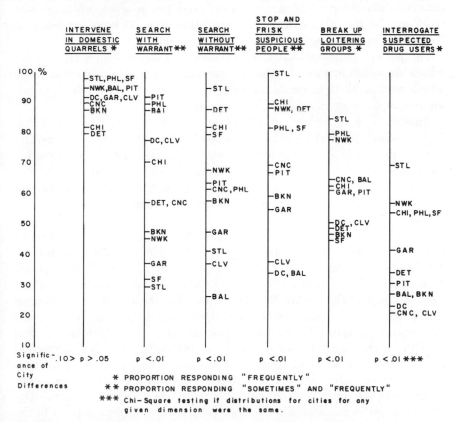

Figure 5.4   Police interviews: frequencies of selected police practices by city.

dimensions of police practices, the cities varied in a highly nonrandom fashion. For example, 92% of the Pittsburgh policemen claim that searching with a warrant is a "frequent" and "sometimes" activity, contrasting with only 32% of the St. Louis policemen. Apparently in St. Louis the practice of police is to search without a warrant as expressed by the 98% of the St. Louis policemen who claim this to be either a "frequent" or "sometimes" activity. Only 27% of the Baltimore policemen claim the same levels of frequency for that practice.

Although at first glance, the city levels of police practices appear to be idiosyncratic, there are patterned differences among cities. Table 5.10 presents the correlations among the levels of practices, computed using cities as units. Note that the practices can be so arranged that the correlations among the main diagonal are very high positive, and that the correlations to diminish and turn negative with distance from the main diagonal. Thus at the one extreme, there is a close relationship (+.87) between "searching without a warrant" and the practice of "stop and frisk" and, at the other extreme, a correlation of − .65 between levels of "searching without a warrant" and "searching with a warrant."

The pattern indicates that some practices go together in a city (those which are adjacent to each other in the matrix of Table 5.10) and those which are not likely to be found with high levels in a city (those which are one or more steps removed in the order of Table 5.10).

Another way of looking at the same relationship is shown in Table 5.11, in which pairs of cities are correlated with each other. The correlations in that table are computed by pairing up the levels of practices for pairs of cities and computing correlations. A high correlation indicates that a pair of cities have similar profiles of practices and a low correlation indicates that the cities are relatively dissimilar. Although the correlation is unstable because of the small N, a very clearly defined cluster of cities is shown in the triangle lower right-hand corner of the correlation matrix, where the correlations among Washington, D.C., Baltimore, Pittsburgh, Cleveland, and Philadelphia are all high (.85 and above) indicating that these cities show very similar profiles of police practices. Looking back at the Figure 5.4 we can see that these cities tend to have low levels of searching without a warrant, stopping and frisking, and interrogating suspected drug users. Another type of city is defined in the triangle in the upper left-hand corner of the matrix which is composed of Newark, Gary, St. Louis, and San Francisco. These cities tend to show high levels of police activities of another sort—searching without warrants, stopping and frisking, and breaking up loitering groups. The other four cities are somewhere in between the two groups defined in the larger triangles of 5.11. The two smaller triangles highlight pairs of cities

TABLE 5.10

Police)
Interviews) Correlations Among City Levels of
Potentially Controversial Police Practices*
[N = 13]

	Stop and Frisk	Interrogate Drug Users	Break up Loitering Groups	Intervene in Domestic Quarrels	Search with Warrants
Search without Warrants	.87	.74	.29	-.26	-.65
Stop and Frisk		.82	.44	-.14	-.47
Interrogage Drug Users			.58	.20	-.44
Break up Loitering Groups				.43	-.01
Intervene in Domestic Quarrels					-.002

*See Figure 5.5 for "breaks" used in establishing levels for cities.

TABLE 5.11

Police) Correlations Across Levels of Potentially
Interviews) Controversial Police Practices Computed
Between Pairs of Cities (N = 5)

	GAR	STL	SF	CHI	DET	CNC	BKN	DC	BAL	PIT	CLV	PHL
NWK	83	87	80	56	55	67	71	21	12	24	26	40
GAR		71	77	46	53	73	83	46	45	34	52	44
STL			84	49	56	40	47	-23	-25	-22	-15	-07
SF				73	76	52	69	04	-02	07	14	15
CHI					98	75	78	25	22	40	36	44
DET						74	78	70	71	73	78	80
CNC							95	70	71	73	78	80
BKN								69	67	69	77	74
DC									97	95	99	93
BAL										88	98	85
PIT											94	98
CLV												92

whose profiles are highly similar—Chicago and Detroit, and Cincinnati and Brooklyn.

It is tempting to refer to the five cities contained in the lower right-hand triangle as the "civil rights oriented" cities. The lowest practice levels found in those cities are precisely in the practices which have come under fire in the recent liberal decisions of the Supreme Court. In contrast, the four cities in the upper-hand triangle show relatively high levels in precisely the same practices, a finding which tempts one to characterize these cities as having "law-and-order" oriented police departments. However, the cities are not very clearly differentiated, with some of the cities showing contradictory patterns. The main finding in the data in this section is the considerable variation from city to city in the levels of five out of the six police practices, a variability which should be reflected in the responses of ghetto residents to their police departments. We consider this question at some length later in this chapter.

The police practices under scrutiny in this section were selected because they had the *potentiality* of being abrasive to ghetto residents. However, whether they are in fact such is at least in part dependent on the ways in which the practices are carried out and the nature of the problems with which they are supposed to deal. Thus one can expect that a sensitive and discriminating police department, confronted with high rates of crime and domestic disorders could operate at very high levels of engaging in such practices if the residents of the precincts involved were convinced that the levels were justified by the problems of law enforcement and that the police carried out the practices while still protecting the innocent. According to this view the methods and efficiency of police department activities would be important to the ghetto residents' interpretation of the intention the practices.

Style or tone is a difficult attribute to measure with the sample survey method. Ideally, one would prefer to observe how the police comport themselves on patrol when they are called upon for help. In the absence of such direct observations, we rely on responses reflecting attitude, such as those shown in Table 5.12.

One in three (36%) of the policemen interviewed believe that most people respond to reason. A little more than half (55%) claim that some people respond to reason, while others have to be confronted with power and force. A definite minority (8%) state that only force and power are respected in this world. The predominant ideology lying behind these responses is tilted more to the liberal than to the authoritarian side in the age old controversy over the relative efficacy of reason versus force in the maintenance of social control. The modal police ideology is one which recognizes differences among their clients, for some only force and power is appropriate, and, for others, a reasoning approach.

The same liberal ideology is displayed in the answers to the second question shown in Table 5.12. Few police (12%) believe in approaching suspects belligerently: Most (87%) believe that aggressiveness should be shown by the police only in response to aggression displayed by a potential suspect.

The last question listed in Table 5.12 is concerned with police estimates of the typical popular response to stop and frisk. Less than one in ten policemen (8%) believe that the typical citizen does not mind being stopped and frisked. Two out of five believe that citizens are willing to give information but do not like being frisked. The remainder either find that it is necessary to threaten (31%) or actually use force (11%) to obtain cooperation.

It seems clear that stop and frisk is not popular with the typical citizen who may be the object of the activity. Half the policemen think that citizens willingly give information, even though the majority do not like being frisked. But two out of five policemen believe that some rough handling is typically necessary, a tactic which is bound to ruffle more than a few feathers.

Figure 5.5 contains the city-by-city distributions of responses to the three questions contained in Table 5.12. For only one of the questions, are there clearly distinctive city differences. By and large the police in each city do not differ in their estimation of citizen response to stop and frisk. Nor is there very much intercity difference in the technique of stop and frisk. The main differences among city police departments are based on the belief that people respond better to reason or to force.

The policemen who frequently engage in stop and frisk are the policemen who believe that reason is less efficacious than force. The correlation between city proportions believing in the efficacy of reason and the frequency of stop and frisk activities is −.56. It is obviously difficult to unravel the cause and effect relationships implied by such a correlation. It may well be that stop and frisk activities are a response to a hostile environment, or that the ideology of social control adjusts to justify the current practices. All that can be said at this point is that cities tend to have police departments which have ideologies of social control consistent with their practices.

By and large policemen believe that stop and frisk activities are productive from a law enforcement point of view. Table 5.13 presents police estimates of the proportions of stop and frisk operations which are productive. The top half of Table 5.13 contains estimates of the proportion of stop and frisk incidents which yield some evidence that the per-

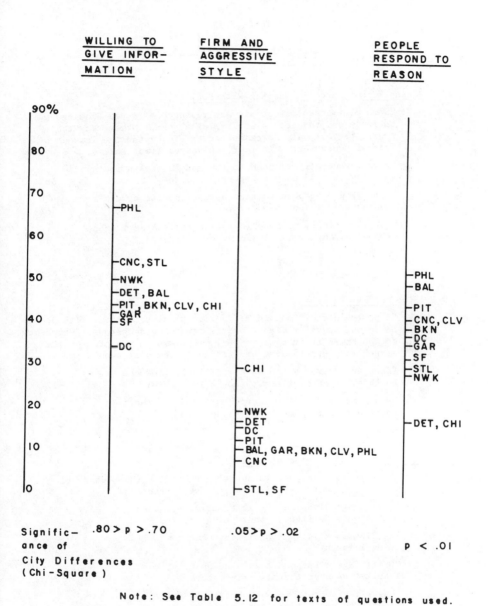

WILLING TO GIVE INFORMATION	FIRM AND AGGRESSIVE STYLE	PEOPLE RESPOND TO REASON

90%

80

70

—PHL

60

—CNC, STL
50 —NWK   —PHL
—DET, BAL   —BAL
—PIT, BKN, CLV, CHI
—GAR   —PIT
40 —SF   —CNC, CLV
                                                           —BKN
                                                           —DC
—DC   —GAR
                                                           —SF
30   —CHI   —STL
                                                           —NWK

20
                      —NWK
                      —DET
                      —DC
                      —PIT
10   —BAL, GAR, BKN, CLV, PHL   —DET, CHI
                      —CNC

0   —STL, SF

Signific-   .80 > p > .70   .05 > p > .02
ance of
City Differences   p < .01
(Chi-Square)

Note: See Table 5.12 for texts of questions used.

Figure 5.5 Police interviews: style and tone of police practices by city.

TABLE 5.12

Police   )   Style and Tone Measures of Police
Interviews)   Practice

A. Reason Versus Force in Dealing with Public:

Q13 "Some claim that all people are reasonable if you show enough
patience and respect in working with them. Others say that
people respect only force and power -- obeying the law out of
fear of punishment. In your job do you find that....

"People generally respond in the end to reason and
very few respond only to power and force   36%

"Some people respond to reason and respect; others
respond only to power and force   55%

"Very few people respond to reason and respect. Most
people respond primarily to power and force   8%

DK & NA   1%

100% =   (522)

B. "Stop and Frisk" Style:

Q11 "A police officer should be in control of situations with people
he suspects are criminals or are otherwise dangerous. Which way
do you think it is best to deal with someone you sto p on the
street for questionning or frisking? That is, should you....

"Deal aggressively and authoritatively from the start
so that the suspect knows who is in control   12%

"Deal firmly from the start, but be polite until a
hostile move is made by the suspect?   87%

DK & NA   1%

100% =   (522)

C. Popular Response to Stop and Frisk:

Q12 "When you stop people to question and frisk them, which of the
following...best describes their usual reaction?

"Willing to give you any information you want
without any hesitancy about being frisked   8%

"Willing to give you information but don't like
being frisked   40%

"Unwilling to respond to you adequately, but
finally do under threats or pressure   31%

"Unwilling to respond and physically resist your
efforts to get information and if you were to search
them, they would injure you or escape if not restrained   11%

DK & NA   1%

100% =   (522)

TABLE 5.13

Police   ) Estimates of Yields from Stop and
Interviews) Frisk Practices

A. Estimates of Possession of Weapons on Persons Stopped:

Q10a "Of every ten people you stop to question and frisk,
about how many actually turn out to be carrying something on them that might have lead to a crime or some
sort of trouble (gun, knife, etc.)?

None	2%
One of Ten	10
Two of Ten	8
Three of Ten	9
Four of Ten	5
Five of Ten	12
Six of Ten	7
Seven of Ten	10
Eight of Ten	10
Nine of Ten	8
Ten out of Ten	2
Don't Know	8
Desk Job: Does not Frisk	8
100% =	(522)

B. Estimates of Criminals Detected Among Persons Stopped:

Q10b "Of every ten people you stop to question and frisk,
about how many actually turn out to be criminals you
are looking for, or people engaged in illegal
activity, such as carrying marijuana or stolen goods?

None	4%
One in Ten	16
Two in Ten	11
Three in Ten	8
Four in Ten	7
Five in Ten	14
Six in Ten	2
Seven in Ten	4
Eight in Ten	6
Nine in Ten	5
Ten in Ten	2
Don't Know	12
Desk Job: Does not Frisk	8
100% =	(522)

145

sons stopped may have been engaged in or were going to engage in a criminal activity. The median estimate lies between 50% and 60%, indicating that half the police believe that 50% or more of the stop and frisk incidents are productive.

A very similar claim of productivity is shown in the bottom half of Table 5.13, where the police estimates of the proportion of incidents which turn up criminals who are wanted or persons who are obviously engaged in criminal activity. The median lies between 40 and 50% productivity.

In short, a large proportion of the police believe that in more than one of two stop and frisk incidents, something justifies the incident and may lead to the prosecution of a wrong doer or the prevention of a crime.

Surprisingly, there are little city differences in the estimates of productivity with respect to weapons found on the persons frisked, but considerable differences with respect to the persons frisked being wanted or potential criminals. Figure 5.6 contains these findings.

The productivity of stop and frisk activities is only slightly related to the frequency of engaging in such practices. For example, the correlation between levels of frequency (by city) of the practice and the levels of productivity for finding weapons is $-.11$ and the corresponding correlation involving productivity with respect to criminals is $-.239$. Neither of these correlation coefficients are statistically significant, although the fact that both have negative signs suggests that productivity decreases with increasing frequency.

With some exceptions, the analysis so far indicates that the major factor in levels of police practices of one sort or another are the differences among cities and among police departments. Of course, we have neglected to look very carefully at the ways in which individual policemen differ in their perceptions of local police practices. It may well be the case that any of the many ways in which police departments could differ in composition from city to city may generate these differences. To see to what extent city differences are independent of other factors, a multiple regression analysis was undertaken using an index of Potentially Controversial Police Practices (PCPP) as the dependent variable. The index was constructed for each policeman, using his answers about frequency of searching without a warrant, spotting and frisking, breaking up loitering groups, and interrogating suspected drug users. These items were used in the index, since they are the least libertarian practices and potentially most likely to be resented by those toward whom the policies may be directed.

Table 5.14 presents the results of the multiple regression analysis in the form of the unique contributions of blocks of variables—background, city, and "neutral police practices"—at the top of the table, and a break-

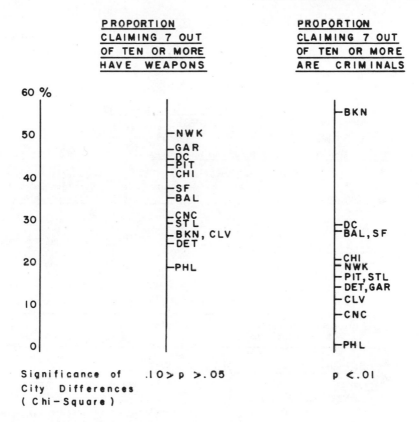

Figure 5.6 Police interviews: estimated yields of stop and frisk operations by city.

down of the grouped variables into the unique contributions of their components in the bottom half of Table 5.14.

To make sure that we were not capitalizing on some peculiarity of cities that we had not already detected, the analysis drew on as wide a range of variables as possible. The "background" group contained such factors as race, rank, age, education, and tenure. The "neutral police practices and attitudes" group contained an almost indiscriminately mixed set of items, ranging from estimates of the productivity of stop and frisk to the proportion of time spent on foot in the precinct. Nevertheless, it is abundantly clear in the analysis that city differences account for most of the explained variation in responses among policemen. In other words, the background of the policemen, his particular estimates of frisk productivity, or his view of reason versus force as instruments of social control matters little; what mattered most, and overwhelmingly so, is the

TABLE 5.14

Police   )   Relative Contributions of Background,
Interviews)   Neutral Police Practices and City Toward
              Potentially Controversial Police Practices (PCPP)

A.   Unique Contributions of Blocks of Variables:*

Background	City	Combination Neutral Police Practices	Proportion of Total Variance Uniquely Attributable
+	0	0	.0250
0	+	0	.1838
0	0	+	.0232
+	+	0	.0307
+	0	+	.0004
0	+	+	.0119
+	+	+	.0004

$$R^2 = .2757 \qquad (R = .5251)$$

Proportion of Explained Variance Uniquely
Attributable to City   67%

B.   Unique Contributions of Individual Variables:

Background Variables Unique Contributions		Neutral Police Practices Unique Contributions	
Race	(-).0087	Productivity Frisk (criminals)	.0074
Rank	.0107	Worry that people in precinct	
Desk Job	(-).0087	might complain about	
Age	(-).0007	police	(-).0036
Protestant	(-).0015	Mixed racial patrol	
Catholic	(-).0010	participation	.0020
Local Born	.0005	Does not attend meetings in	
Education	.0002	precinct	.0021
Renting Home	(-).0002	Power and force vs reason	.0012
		Has friends living in precinct	.0006
		Frisk productivity (weapons)	.0002
		Citizens react violently to	
		frisk	(-).0001
		% of time spent on foot in	
		community	.0000
		Does not live in precinct	.0000

*Dependent variable is index composed of frequencies of
  "Searching on suspicion without a warrant"
  "Stop and frisk suspicious people"
  "Break up loitering groups"
  "Interrogate suspected drug users"
Thus a high score on the index was given to a policeman who claimed that the
frequency of these practices was high in his precinct.

city from which the policeman was selected. The Variation in Potentially Controversial Police Practices Index is then characteristic of the city and its police department.

The multiple correlation coefficient for the entire set of variables is .53, indicating that about 28% of the variation from policemen to policeman can be accounted for by the set of independent variables. The strength of city differences can be seen in the fact that 67% of the explained variance (or 18% of the total variance) is accounted for by the cities.

The background variables and the "neutral police practices" group account for about the same amount of variance, 2.5% and 2.3%, respectively. Among individual variables, only race and rank account uniquely for any significant portion of the variance in answers from policeman to policeman.

Conclusions.   The findings of this chapter make it abundantly clear that the police are local institutions, sensitive to local conditions, hence variable more from city to city than from policeman to policeman. Even black policemen, whose racial identity might be thought of as possibly overriding the characteristics of their police departments, are sensitive to city differences.

The policemen are locals in another sense as well. Their social origins place them squarely in the lower middle class. Furthermore, of all the groups of institutional agents we are studying in this volume, the police are most likely to have been born and (presumably) lived all their lives in the cities in which they serve.

There might be many reasons for the intercity variability that has been observed in this chapter. But the main explanation must be related to the organizational form of police departments. The police are a paramilitary force characterized by a strong chain of command. Police officials expect and get prompt compliance with their commands. The variation from city to city then is a function of the kinds of police policies promulgated by police officials.

Why the police are different from city to city in their police practices is studied in Chapter 6.

Chapter 6

POLICE AND THE GHETTO:
Police Practices and Local Politics

The police and their occupational activities were described in the preceding chapter. This chapter probes into the effects of different police practices on ghetto residents and into the sources of these differences. In short, do ghetto residents experience the police differently from city to city? And why do cities differ in the ways in which police departments behave?

The value of the analysis in Chapter 5 rests heavily on the validity of police reports on the prevalent practices (in 1968) in their precincts. In Chapter 2 we indicated that in many cities the police samples were chosen by police officials according to some criteria unknown to the researchers. It may then be asked whether the results of the analyses reflect mainly the biases of police sample selection.

Fortunately we can provide fairly convincing documentation for the validity of the measures of prevalent police practices. In part the population survey conducted by the Survey Research Center asked respondents whether they had ever been personally subjected to abusive treatment at the hands of their local police.[1] An index measuring the level of police

---

[1] The index is composed of questions asking whether the respondent had ever been insulted by the police, stopped and frisked for no good reason, or roughed up by the police.

abuse experienced by the Negro populations of the thirteen cities was constructed, and its relationship to the Potentially Controversial Police Practices (PCPP) Index is shown city by city in Figure 6.1.

The correlation between the two indices is .638, indicating a fairly high (although not perfect) relationship. In other words, in cities whose police claim that stop and frisk practices, searching without a warrant, and interrogating suspected drug users are prevalent practices, the black population experiences high levels of what they consider to be abusive behavior on the part of the police.

Each of the two indices shown in Figure 6.1 come from completely independently collected data. The Potentially Controversial Practices Index is based upon interviews with the police, and the Experience with Police Abuse Index is derived from sample surveys of black residents in the same cities. The correspondence between the two sets of data is high enough to support a claim of some validity for the PCPP index. In other words, whatever biases were displayed in the selection of policemen as respondents and by the individual policemen in their answers, these biases did not geratly affect the ordering of cities in the extent to which the police claim do engage in certain types of police practices which probably are considered abusive by citizens.[2]

Later in this chapter we explore deeper the relationship between police practices and popular experiences with the police. The fact that the relationship is not perfect (indeed the common variance is but 41% of the total variance) means that other factors intervene between popular experiences with the police and popular interpretations of that experience.

The Police and Their Clients.   Whether true or not, the nostalgic image of the urban policeman before mechanization was of a paternal but firm neighborhood fixture who knew most of the residents by sight and had a fairly accurate idea of the characteristics of the people with whom he had to work. Indeed, one of the major problems in the development of "professional" police forces in the metropolitan United States was that

---

[2] Recall the meaning of the correlation coefficient. It measures the degree to which two sets of numbers tend to correspond to relative magnitude. The correlation transforms the data into Z-scores and then takes the mean cross product. Therefore, the positive correlation of .638 indicates that high scores on the PCPP tend to correspond with high scores on the index of experience with police abuse, but says nothing about the absolute amount of either. Either or both measures may be underreporting or overreporting the real incidence of events. In short, our sampling problems with police did not wipe out relative correspondence between cities on these measures, although it may have affected the estimates of absolute incidence.

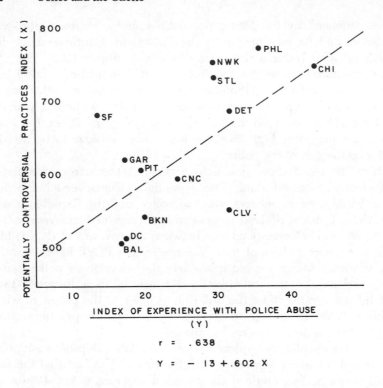

r = .638

Y = − 13 + .602 X

Note: Index numbers have no direct substantive meaning.

Figure 6.1 Police and population interviews: PCPP Index and Population Survey Index of Experience of Police Abuse. *r* = .638, *Y* = −131 + .602X. Note: index numbers have no direct substantive meaning.

local policemen were often too deeply embedded in the social structure of the neighborhoods that they patrolled.[3] Given the social lines between blacks and whites, and the fact that none of the cities in our sample had police forces with more than one fourth black, the chances are quite low that policemen in ghetto precincts would develop the same sorts of embeddedness to the same depths that led to the reorganizations of police departments in the nineteenth century. In addition, the mechanization

---

[3] The English solved this problem by forbidding the members of the metropolitan police force to marry and by rotating assignments frequently. The police forces of Boston and New York had to be reorganized several times on a city wide basis to break the entirely too close ties between local policemen and their precincts. See James F. Richardson, *The New York Police: Colonial Times to 1901*, Oxford University Press, New York, 1970.

of the police patrol, while undoubtedly raising the efficiency of police in the pursuit of criminals fleeing by car, also lowered the chances of policemen knowing residents intimately in their precincts as they may have in preautomobile days.

Nevertheless an intimate acquaintance with the people who live in the precincts the policeman patrols can be very useful to him and to the administration of law enforcement. Knowing "who is who" is likely to reduce the errors that could lead at the one extreme to false arrest charges and at the other to charges of harassment. Furthermore, the better known the police are to their clients, the more likely the residents are to interpret police actions as benign. A remote and impersonal police force which makes many law enforcement "errors" (even though they be "honest" errors) is likely to be looked upon with suspicion and even active dislike by the residents whom they serve.

Table 6.1 contains three measures of the extent to which ghetto policemen are related to their patrol neighborhood through the ties of kinship, friendship, or associational life. The majority of policemen have neither friends, relatives, or associational ties in the ghetto neighborhoods. Three fourths of all policemen have no relatives living in the areas they patrol, a figure which rises to 84% for white policemen and is still a majority (55%) for black policemen.

The policemen are more likely to have friends who live in their precincts, with 42% claiming to have such friends whom they see socially. Black and white policemen contrast sharply in this respect; only 33% of the whites as compared to 72% of the blacks have friends in their precincts.

Finally, only 29% of the policemen attend meetings of organizations[4] in their districts. The proportion drops down to 24% when we consider white policemen only and is 44% for the black policemen.

Nor are there strong differences among the thirteen police departments in these respects, as Figure 6.2 relates. When considering relatives living in districts and attendance at associational meetings the differences among the thirteen cities are not statistically significant. However, the city police departments do vary with respect to friendships with people in their patrol districts. Policemen in Cleveland are especially likely to claim to have friends in their patrol districts (65%), followed by Gary (55%), with Detroit (28%), and St. Louis and Philadelphia (22%). It is not clear what affects high or low levels of friendship. For example, it might be

---

[4] Of course, we do not know the extent to which attendance at such meetings is in the line of duty—perhaps as part of community relations work—or arises out of a concern with problems in the districts or need to socialize.

TABLE 6.1

Police   )   Kinship, Friendship and Associational
Interviews)   Ties to Precincts

	Whites	Blacks	Total
A. **Relatives Living in Precinct:**			
None	84%	55%	75%
Some	15	45	24
DK & NA	1	-	1

Chi Square Significance of Race Differences: p $<$.001

	Whites	Blacks	Total
B. **Friends Seen Socially Living in Precinct:**			
None	66%	28%	57%
Some	33	72	42
DK & NA	1	-	1

Chi Square Significance of Race Differences: p $<$.001

	Whites	Blacks	Total
See Friends a Lot	6%	27%	11%
Just Sometimes	27	45	31

	Whites	Blacks	Total
C. **Attend Meetings of Organizations in Neighborhood:**			
Does not Attend	76%	56%	71%
Attends Some Meetings	24	44	29

Chi Square Significance of Race Differences: p $<$.001

	Whites	Blacks	Total
100% =	(397)	(125)	(522)

thought that cities with high proportions of blacks in their populations, hence most likely to have large black ghettos, would reflect the lowest probability of police friendships with their clients. However, the order of the cities in Figure 6.2 bears no relationship to the proportion black in the city populations.

Although social and organizational ties are important, it is possible for policemen to have considerable knowledge about an area without being deeply embedded in its social structure. Knowing who people are, who potential leaders and trouble makers are, and who ordinary residents are,

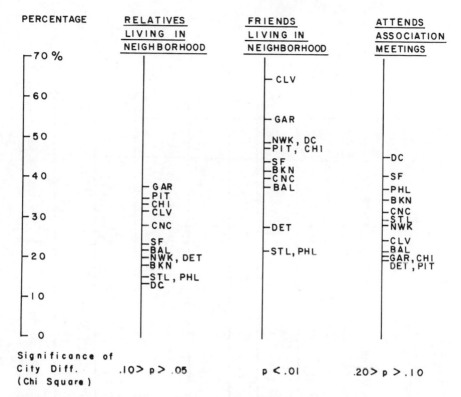

PERCENTAGE	RELATIVES LIVING IN NEIGHBORHOOD	FRIENDS LIVING IN NEIGHBORHOOD	ATTENDS ASSOCIATION MEETINGS

Significance of
City Diff.   .10> p > .05   p < .01   .20> p > .10
(Chi Square)

Figure 6.2   Police interviews: kinship, friendship, and associational ties in each city.

as opposed to strangers in the neighborhoods, are of considerable use in police work. Table 6.2 presents the numbers of various residents who are known to the police "well enough to speak to them when you see them." These data indicate that the police typically know more local business men (usually nonresidents) and more "continual trouble makers" than they know adult or youth leaders, or criminals engaged in organized crime. Of course, it is difficult to evlauate these numbers without knowing how many persons are in each category. Nevertheless it seems fairly obvious that local merchants are a relatively small number, compared, for example, to the "residents in general." Yet the average known are 28 and 44, respectively, while it is most likely that general residents outnumber local merchants on the order of at least 100 to 1.

The patterns in Table 6.2 indicate that in many cities the police are relatively unaware of the structuring of the black communities which they patrol. Although it is often asserted that one of the problems of black ghetto communities is a lack of leadership, often this assertion means that the speaker does not have enough familiarity with the com-

TABLE 6.2

Police   ) Numbers of Residents of Various Types
Interviews) Known Well Enough "To Speak To" (N = 522)

Resident Types	Percentages who know well enough to speak to							Median Number Known	DK
	None	1-5	6-10	11-25	20-50	51-100	101		
Shop Owners, Managers and Clerks	2	9	11	22	22	16	16	28	1
Important Adult Leaders in the Neighborhoods	16	32	21	13	10	5	2	6	2
Residents in General	5	8	8	14	18	13	31	44	2
Important Teenage and Youth Leaders	31	29	15	10	6	3	3	3	3
Government and Private Agency Workers in Neighborhood	20	31	20	13	9	4	2	5	1
"Continual Trouble Makers"	6	9	13	24	19	13	13	24	2
Criminals in Organized Crime	31	26	14	11	7	5	3	4	4

*Based on Q23: "...about how many people among (..........) do you know well enough to speak to when you see them?"

munity in question to have discerned any leadership patterns. The police apparently suffer from this disability as well.

Figure 6.3 presents city averages in numbers of persons known in most of the categories of persons discussed in Table 6.2. In addition, the bar on the extreme right-hand side of the figure is a composite index consisting of the sum of persons known in all of the categories in the bars to the left. Thus a Combined Acquaintance Index of 200 indicates that the police in the city in question on the average know about 200 persons in their precincts, a figure arrived at by adding together the merchants, residents in general, adult leaders, youth and agency leaders, and trouble makers known.

All of the distributions in Figure 6.3 are significantly nonrandom—that is, the police departments of the several cities are statistically different from one another. The location of the points on each of the bars represents numbers of persons in the category in question known on the average by the police. The groups of points tend to cluster in different areas of the bars, reflecting the fact that the police generally know more of some category of precinct residents than others.

Presented at the bottom of Figure 6.3 are the intercorrelations among indices. Note that the correlations are all positive, indicating that police departments which are knowledgeable in one respect tend also to be knowledgeable in another respect. The highest correlation is between numbers of adult leaders known and numbers of youth leaders known which indicates that knowledge about one segment of leadership goes along with knowledge about another segment. Knowing "trouble makers" is least related to knowing residents, merchants or leaders, perhaps more expressive of the police practices and the nature of the law enforcement problems presented than of knowledge generally about their districts.

The Combined Acquaintance Index, shown on the bar to the extreme right of Figure 6.3, most clearly differentiates among cities. At the high end are a cluster of three—St. Louis, Baltimore, and Washington, D.C.—all of which have police departments with very high levels of knowledge about their "clients." At the opposite, lower end of the bar are a group of five cities—Brooklyn, Philadelphia, Chicago, Detroit, and San Francisco—with relatively very low levels of acquaintance in their patrol districts. The remaining cities are spread unevenly in between the two clusters of high and low cities.

The distribution of cities on the Combined Acquaintance Index leads to the suspicion that the size of cities and the proportion of blacks in their populations are affecting the position of cities on the index. The larger cities—Brooklyn, Chicago, Philadelphia, and Detroit—are on the low end and medium sized cities are on the upper end. Furthermore,

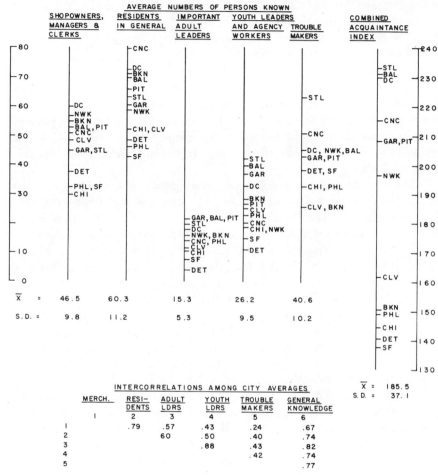

Figure 6.3 Police interviews: police knowledge of persons in precinct patroled by city.

cities with high proportions of blacks in their population tend to be on the upper end—Baltimore, Washington, D.C., Gary, and Indiana. This insight is more than adequately borne out in Table 6.3 where the correlations of city size, proportion black, and the Combined Acquaintance Index are shown. Indeed, these two variables, combined in a regression analysis, account for 52% of the variance among cities, with $R = .718$. In short, the larger the city, the lower the Combined Acquaintance Index, and the higher the proportion black, the higher the Index.

Unfortunately we can do little to investigate these relationships further, although the speculative urge argues for at least laying out a line of interpretation. It may well be the case that the relationship of population

TABLE 6.3

Police   ) City Size, Proportion Black and
Interviews) Combined Acquaintance Index (N = 13)

Correlations

		Combined Acquaintance Index (1)	City* Size (000) (2)	Proportion Black (3)
Combined Acquaintance Index	(1)		-.631	.515
City Size (000)	(2)			-.298

Regression Analysis

$$Y = 175 - .021X_1 + .942X_2$$

X = General Acquaintance Index

X_1 = City Size (in thousands)

X_2 = Proportion Black

R^2 = .516

R = .718

$.05 > p > .01$

*City size in 1968 is an interpolated estimate using 1960 and 1970 Censuses and calibrated in thousands.

**Proportion black in city using an interpolated estimate.

size to the Combined Acquaintance Index is a phenomenon embracing the relationships between service agencies and the public generally. The larger the city, the more difficult it is to get to know other people, including persons in especially visible positions—for example, local merchants— and to understand the leadership structure of any urban neighborhood. Or, it may be that in larger cities, police departments are generally more autonomous and less sensitive to the population of particular neighborhoods, and are more tuned to headquarters than to the people on the beat. The importance of the proportion black in the population may mainly reflect the political power of the black community. The larger the proportion of blacks of the electorate, the more blacks are taken into account in the political decision-making process, and indirectly the more sensitive police departments and individual policemen become to their black "clients."

Obviously, it is difficult to determine the worth of these explanations without additional information. It would be particularly important to learn how the size of the city affects the acquaintanceship ranges of policemen with residents of white neighborhoods. Unfortunately we do not have such data available.

However, it is possible to gain some additional insights into the meaning of the correlations of Table 6.3 by examining the ways in which the separate indexes which go into the Combined Acquaintance Index are each related to population size and the proportion black. Table 6.4 presents these correlations.

TABLE 6.4

Police   ) Acquaintance Indices Related to City
Interviews) Size and Proportion Black (N = 13 cities)

	Correlation With	
Index	City Size	Proportion Black
Number of Merchants, etc. Known by Police	-.47	.46
Residents "In General" Known	-.25	.30
Adult Leaders	-.40	.32
Youth Leaders	-.29	.38
"Trouble Makers"	-.58	.25

Unfortunately, the patterns of Table 6.4 are not very clear. In addition, none of the correlations in Table 6.4 are statistically significant. It appears that the size of the city affects strongly the numbers of merchants and trouble makers known and is not very strongly related to number of "residents in general known." This suggests that in the smaller urban areas, merchants and trouble makers stand out against the background of the mass of "clients" in a patrol district.

The proportion black in a city does act as if it were a political variable. The larger the proportion of blacks, the more merchants, youth leaders and adult leaders the police will know. Of course this last interpretation is somewhat forced, since the meaning of knowing more merchants as political variable is somewhat obscure.

A more direct approach to the problem is to examine the effects of other police characteristics on the number of people a policeman knows. In Table 6.5, the variation among individual policemen in the Combined Acquaintance Index is analyzed through multiple regression methods. Four clusters of variables are used in this analysis—city, race, background (age, education, local birth, and rank), and community participation (whether policemen has kinship, friendship, and associational ties in neighborhoods). The four variables together account for 19.3% of the variation among individual policemen. Among the variables used, city accounts uniquely for more of the total variance than any other cluster—6.1%. Next in importance is the unique contribution of the Community Participation Index, which contributes to 5.2% of the variance in the scope of police acquaintance. The background cluster accounts for 4.4%, and race for a small 0.5%.

Note that because of the close association between race and community participation, the overlap between these two factors contributes an additional 3.0%.

The analysis in Table 6.5 indicates three main factors affecting the numbers of persons known by policemen in their districts. First, there are significant differences in this respect by city, reflecting in part the demographic relationships between population size, proportion black, and the scope of acquaintanceship discussed earlier. In part this finding also shows the effects of departmental policies. We see later that departments with high levels of potentially abusive patrol practices are also departments in which policemen have narrow acquaintanceship ranges.

Second, certain types of policemen are more likely to have developed more extensive knowledge of their patrol beats. Older policemen are more likely to know more residents, possibly because they are more likely to have been on the same beat for longer periods of time.

Third, black policemen are more likely to have ties in the community,

TABLE 6.5

Police   ) Combined Acquaintance Index:
Interviews) Relative Contributions of City, Race,
            Background and Community Participation (N = 522)

		Combination		
City ***	Race	Background*	Community Participation**	Proportion of Total Variance Attributable
+	0	0	0	6.1%
0	+	0	0	0.5
0	0	+	0	4.4
0	0	0	+	5.2
+	+	0	0	0.0
+	0	+	0	0.8
+	0	0	+	-0.7
0	+	+	0	-0.4
0	+	0	+	3.0
0	0	+	+	0.5
+	+	+	0	0.0
+	+	0	+	-0.3
+	0	+	+	0.2
+	+	+	+	0.3

Total Variance Explained (R^2) = .193

R = .439

*"Background" variable cluster includes Rank, Grade, Education, Religious
  Affiliation and Local Birth

**"Community Participation" in an index composed of having relatives,
  friends, and attending association meetings in neighborhood. (See
  Table 7.15 for description of items.)

***"+" indicates the presence of the factor as an independent variable. "0"
  indicates the absence of the factor as an independent variable.

hence wider scopes of acquaintanceship. Independently of such community ties, black policemen are only slightly more likely than white
policemen to know more residents. The effect of race is channeled mainly
through such community ties.

We have dealt at great length with the levels of acquaintanceship that
policemen have built up with persons living or working in the precincts
they patrol, because we were proceeding on the assumption that such
ties were important generally in setting a tone for police-community rela-

tionships within ghetto areas. The worth of that assumption, of course, has yet to be demonstrated.

In an earlier analysis in this chapter we saw that the more police departments engaged in potentially abusive practices, the more likely were residents to claim high levels of police abuse, shown in the interviews conducted by the Survey Research Center with samples of blacks in each of the thirteen cities. Indeed the correlation between the Potentially Controversial Police Practices Index and Index of Experienced Police Abuse (computed from the Survey Research Center data) was .64. The relationship, while high, was far from perfect, leaving considerable room for the operation of other variables. We speculated at that point that whether individuals who experienced "abusive" law enforcement contacts with the police depended in part on how they interpreted the actions of the police. Thus if the police are generally regarded as friendly and understanding, a particular action, for example, stopping and interrogating someone, might be interpreted quite differently than the same action occurring where the police are generally regarded as hostile and unfriendly. We also speculated that in communities in which the police had many ties of acquaintanceship a more benign interpretation of police actions would be more likely. If many residents know policemen, they may be less likely to distrust their actions and suspect their motives.

Acquaintanceship can work in another way as well. Where the police know the people in their precincts, they may be much less likely to make errors in their law enforcement activities which lead to unnecessary harassment. Knowing that a particular resident is locally regarded as a law-abiding citizen, a patrolman might be less likely to interpret (and possibly thereby misinterpret) some act on his part as "suspicious behavior." Hence errors in treating law-abiding citizens as if they were potential offenders would be lessened.

If these speculations are of any worth, then the addition of measures of acquaintanceship ranges to measures of police behavior ought to account for significantly more of the variation from city to city in the levels of police abuse and in general beliefs about abusive local police departments. The empirical results substantiating these expectations are shown in Table 6.6.

A police department's level of acquaintance with precincts' residents makes a significant difference in the residents' interpretation of police practices. Where the level of potentially abusive practices is low and where the police know many persons in their precincts, residents are not likely either to experience personally police abuse or to believe that police are generally abusive to them. Both the objective practices of the

TABLE 6.6

Police &   )   Relationships Between Police Abusive
Sample Survey)   Behavior Indices. General Acquaintance
Interviews   )   Index and Black Residents Experiences
                   with and Beliefs About Police Abuse (N = 13 cities)

A.   Correlations Among Indices:*

	Police Interviews		Survey Interviews		
	PCPP Index	Combined Acquaintance Index	Direct Experience Abuse	Observe Police Abuse	General Beliefs About Police Abuse
PCPP Index		-34	.69	.59	48
Gen. Acq. Index			-73	-56	-.72
Experience Abuse				.66	.68
Observe Police Abuse					.90

B.   Regression on Direct Experience with Abuse Index:

$$Y = 2.5 + .398X_1 - 1.271X_2$$

$$R = .87 \quad p < .01$$

where Y = Index of Direct Experience with Police Abuse (Survey Data)

X_1 = Index of Potentially Controversial Police Practices Index
      (Police Interviews)

X_2 = Combined Acquaintance Index (Police Interviews)

C.   Regression on Index of General Beliefs About Police Abuse:

$$Y = 3.5 + .121X_1 - .779X_2$$

$$R = .76 \quad p < .01$$

where Y = General Beliefs About Police Abuse

X_1 = Potentially Controversial Police Index

X_2 = Combined Acquaintance Index

*Variables are defined as follows:
    Potentially Controversial Police Practices (PCPP) Index: Combination of
        frequencies of breaking up loitering groups, stopping and frisking
        and searching without warrant
    Direct Experience with Police Abuse: Survey Items asking about
        personal experiences of police abuse
    Observed Police Abuse: Survey items asking respondents' about police
        abuse seen, but not experienced directly
    General Beliefs About Police Abuse: Survey items asking respondents'
        assessments of police abuse in their neighborhoods

police and the extent to which they know persons living and working in their precincts independently affect experiences and beliefs.[5]

The regression analyses presented in Table 6.6 are based upon an implicit assumption of causality in which the dependent variables are assumed to be the outcome of the independent variables. The perceptive reader will already have noticed that this is an assumption open to question. For example, it may well be the case that police practices are responses to the reactions of precinct residents to the police: Where residents are hostile and uncooperative, the police in turn are repressive and abusive. Similarly the levels of acquaintance within precincts may be a function of the residents' willingness to be friendly to the police who patrol their neighborhoods.

The causality directions assured in Table 6.6 can only be tentatively viewed as sensible at this point in the analysis. With three variables, it is not possible to construct sophisticated models which would test more powerfully these assumptions of causality. In the last section of this chapter we present data to substantiate more strongly the causal sequences posited here.

These findings indicate that the more instances of abuses are observed and the less widely acquainted are the police with residents of their beats, the more likely blacks are to believe highly that they and their neighbors are abused at the hands of the police. The more the police are embedded in the social networks of their patrols, the more residents they are acquainted with, and the less likely residents will enlarge their observations of specific instances of police abuse into a general characterization of the police as abusive.

Police Views of Their "Clients." The preceding sections of this chapter have been concerned mainly with reports from the police on their behavior toward residents of their patrol districts. We have deliberately steered away from considering any attitudinal dimensions of police-community relations, although it must be admitted that behavioral reports are undoubtedly confounded with attitudinal elements, partly because attitudes to some extent condition behavior and partly because behavior also conditions attitudes.

Another reason to avoid direct attitudinal measures is the difficulty of placing attitudes in their proper causal order in a complex of variables.

---

[5] The unique contribution of the Combined Acquaintance Index to the explanation of the total variance in the Personal Experience Index is 14% and 10% in the case of General Beliefs about Police Abuse Index.

Are attitudes mainly a rationalization of more objectively viewed behavior or are they determinants of behavior? There is no clear evidence for one interpretation over the other. Hence the placement of attitudinal data in a model of action in any area of human concern is fraught with ambiguity.

Perhaps the best way to conceptualize the place of attitudinal measures in a study of this sort is to view the relationship between attitudes and behavioral practices as mutual reinforcement. We find ordinarily that there is a congruence between the two types of human actions. Attitudes account for the persistence of behavioral patterns because they condition future behavior, and attitudes also represent an intellectual crystallization of behavior, providing the bearer with a way of justifying his past behavior.

It will hardly come as a shock to the readers of this chapter to learn that many policemen hold quite negative views of the residents of their precincts. We saw earlier that policemen generally were among the most likely of the occupational groups studied in Chapter 4 to espouse a position of optimistic denial vis-a-vis the black population of their cities. We also saw that few policemen, especially whites, had close ties to their patrol precincts. And so on.

The policemen were given a set of stereotyped statements and asked to indicate whether they thought such statements were true of their residents of their districts. The results are shown in Table 6.7. Half of the statements are worded positively, that is, they assert that some positive quality is held by the residents, and the remainder are worded negatively. The positively worded statements are contained in the upper half of the table and the negatively worded views are shown in the lower half of the table.[6]

Positive views of the precinct residents are rejected completely by proportions of 10, 16, and 27, while being accepted completely by 35, 18, and 20%. In short a strong minority reject positive statements which indicate that the residents are honest, industrious, and "respectable (and) religious." One in five to one in three endorse such statements. This leaves the majority of the police in a position of ambivalence, partially endorsing the statements and partially rejecting the statements as applying to the residents of their precincts.

The negatively worded statements get more endorsement from the policemen. One in five claim that their "clients" do not care for law and order. One fourth claim that residents are not very careful about their

---

[6] In many attitude surveys, it has been shown that some people, either through indolence, ambivalence, or prevarication, are more likely to endorse a statement when it is worded positively than when the statement is worded negatively.

health, and one in three claim that the residents are often hostile to outsiders. About the same proportions of policemen reject these same statements untrue of their precincts, leaving between two in five and one in two in a position of ambivalence.

When we look at the differences between white and black policemen, strong contrasts appear. Black policemen are much more inclined to deny negative views of precinct residents and to endorse positive statements. (All of the differences between white and black policemen shown in Table 6.7 are statistically significant at the .001 level.)

As a corollary, white policemen hold particularly negative views. For example, only 30% endorse the statement that their "clients" are honest (as compared to 50% of black policemen).

The six statements described in Table 6.7 have been combined into an index that measures the extent to which each policemen endorses the six statements. Thus a high score can be attained by someone who endorses the negative side of all or a large proportion of the statements, while a low score is given to policemen with the opposite endorsement characteristics.

A multiple regression analysis was performed on the Negative Images Index whose results are shown in Table 6.8. The four factors—race, city, background, and community participation—together account for 17.8% of the total variation in Negative Images Index scores, the equivalent of a multiple correlation of .422. Among the single factors, city differences account uniquely for more of the variance (6.3%) than any of the others. The closest runner up is community participation (3.7%) followed by police background characteristics (2.4%) and lastly by race (0.8%).

The effects of race as a conditioner of attitudes are masked by the close relationships between race and community participation. The overlap effects are the only combination that accounts for large proportions of the total variance [particularly the overlap between race and community participation (2.9%) and the overlap variance shared by race and background (1.4%)].

Once again the findings of Table 6.8 show the importance of city differences. The average scores (converted into Z-scores) for each of the thirteen cities are shown in Figure 6.4. High average scores are attained by Detroit policemen, with police from Chicago, Newark, and St. Louis in the top third of the cities. At the opposite extreme, with low average Negative Image scores (hence more positive views of their "clients") are Philadelphia, Cincinnati, Brooklyn, Gary, and Baltimore. Most of the cities can now almost be predicted in their positions on any of the indexes. Detroit, Chicago, and Newark often share the characteristic of having police departments who are most standoffish and negative toward their

TABLE 6.7

Police) Endorsement of Positive and Negative
Interviews) Views of Ghetto Residents by Race
(Total N = 522, White N = 397, Black N = 125)

	Race of Policeman	Proportion Saying Statement is			
		Generally True	Partially True	Not True at all	DK & NA
A. Positive Views:					
"They are honest people"	White	30%	58	11	1
	Black	50	44	6	#
	Total	35%	55%	10%	1
"They are industrious people"	White	15%	52	32	2
	Black	27	60	11	2
	Total	18	53	27	2
"They are respectable, religious people"	White	17	60	19	4
	Black	29	64	3	5
	Total	20	61	16	4

TABLE 6.7 (Cont'd)

B. Negative Views:

	Race of Policeman	Proportion Saying Statement is			
		Generally True	Partially True	Not True at all	DK & NA
"These people do not care much for law and order"	White	22	46	31	1
	Black	14	40	45	1
	Total	21	44	34	1
"They don't look after their health very well"	White	29	44	20	7
	Black	14	51	27	8
	Total	26	46	22	7
"Often they are hostile to outsiders"	White	34	43	20	4
	Black	19	39	37	5
	Total	31	42	24	4

*Based on Q8: In your estimation which of these are generally true, which are partially true and which are not true at all for the people in your precinct?"

Note: All differences between white and black policemen are statistically significant beyond the .001 level (Chi-Square).

169

TABLE 6.8

Police   ) Negative Images of Ghetto Residents Scale:
Interviews) Relative Contributions of City, Race,
             Background and Community Participation (N = 522)

City *	Race	Background	Community Participation	Proportion of Total Variance Uniquely Attributable
+	0	0	0	6.3%
0	+	0	0	0.8
0	0	+	0	2.4
0	0	0	+	3.7
+	+	0	0	0.3
+	0	+	0	-0.3
+	0	0	+	-0.3
0	+	+	0	0.5
0	+	0	+	2.9
0	0	+	+	0.2
+	+	+	0	0.1
+	+	0	+	0.0
+	0	+	+	-0.1
0	+	+	+	1.4
+	+	+	+	-0.1

(In the header: COMBINATION spans City, Race, Background, Community Participation)

Proportion of total variance explained by
     all four (R^2)   = .178

                                    R   = .422

* "+" indicates the presence of the factor as an independent variable. "0"
indicates the absence of the factor as an independent variable.

"clients." As contrasts, Washington, D.C., Baltimore, and Gary police departments often show up on the side of being more sympathetic and less negative about their precinct residents.

The items which make up the Negative Images Index were characteristics of precinct residents without specifically mentioning their race. Of course, since the precincts were mostly black in composition, policemen could hardly have had the few whites in these neighborhoods in mind. Yet, the use of the racial designations produces more in the way of polarization between white and black policemen (as shown in Table 6.9), where answers to a series of questions directly focused on blacks are shown.

TABLE 6.9

Police) Perceived Threat From Blacks*
Interviews)

A. "....in terms of blacks gaining what they feel to be equality, do you feel the blacks have tried to move much too fast, too fast, too slow or has it been about right?"

Race of Policeman	Much too Fast	Too Fast	Too Slow	About Right	DK & NA
Whites (N = 125)	40%	36	3	17	5
Blacks (N = 397)	6	6	52	35	2
Total (N = 522)	32%	28	15	21	4

B. "How do you feel about...."

Race of Policeman	Very Disturbed	Slightly Disturbed	Not at all Disturbed	DK & NA
(1) "Negroes draining resources through welfare payments"				
Whites	64%	24	9	2
Blacks	31	32	33	5
Total	56%	26	15	3
(2) "Negroes taking over political power"				
Whites	13	28	58	2
Blacks	2	10	84	4
Total	10	23	64	2
(3) "Negroes moving into areas that are occupied by whites"				
Whites	28	32	37	2
Blacks	2	10	82	6
Total	22	27	47	3
(4) "Negroes socializing with whites"				
Whites	22	28	40	4
Blacks	2	6	86	6
Total	17	22	56	4

*Total N = 522, White N = 397, Black N = 125

The central theme running through the questions of Table 6.9 is the threat of competition presented by blacks. The first item is a familiar one used in Chapter 4 asking whether the respondent thinks that blacks are moving too fast or too slow in their drive for equality. The vast majority (76%) of the white policemen see blacks as moving too fast, with 40% characterizing this movement as "much too fast." In stark contrast, black policemen claim that the move toward equality is going too slow (52%) or "about right" (35%). It should be emphasized that a contrast on an attitudinal question between two groups in the same population as strong as this is very rarely seen. Most attitudinal items only weakly distinguish between social groups.

Since black policemen are usually a minority in any of the cities, the attitudinal climate in most of the police departments is one in which the drive toward equality is seen as moving too rapidly, probably closer to the "total" lines in Table 6.9.

The other items in this table refer to how disturbed the respondents are about other characteristics of blacks in their cities—blacks consume resources through welfare payments, take over political power, move into white neighborhoods, and socialize with whites. The majority of policemen are at least slightly disturbed about the amount of welfare payments to blacks; one third are concerned over blacks taking over political power; about half are worried about neighborhood racial succession; and 39% are disturbed about blacks socializing with whites.

Stark contrasts again are shown between white and black policemen. Where whites are concerned and disturbed, blacks are scarcely ruffled. Indeed, it is this contrast which provides justification for the label given to the index formed by combining responses to the four items of Table 6.9. Whites are expressing the extent to which they feel threatened by moves made by the black population (obviously blacks are hardly threatened by their own advances); hence the index formed has been called Perceived Black Threat Index.

A multiple regression analysis of scores on the Perceived Black Threat Index is presented in Table 6.10. The four clusters explain a rather high proportion of the total variation (38%), equivalent to a multiple correlation of .616. A very large proportion of the total variance is explained by race, whose unique contribution to the total variance is 20%, a little more than half (52%) of the explained variance. In addition the unique contributions of the overlap of race with other clusters is also large (e.g., the unique contribution of race and community participation is 4.8%). Obviously, whether blacks are seen as threatening depends very greatly on whether one is white or black.

City differences account uniquely for a usual 6%, while community

TABLE 6.10

Police   )   Perceived Black Threat Index:
Interviews)   Relative Contributions of City, Race
              Background and Community Participation (N = 522)

City*	Race	Combination Background	Community Participation	Proportion of Total Variance Uniquely Explained
+	0	0	0	6.0%
0	+	0	0	20.0
0	0	+	0	1.7
0	0	0	+	0.0
+	+	0	0	1.8
+	0	+	0	-0.3
+	0	0	+	0.0
0	+	+	0	3.4
0	+	0	+	4.8
0	0	+	+	0.0
+	+	+	0	0.0
+	+	0	+	-1.0
+	0	+	+	0.0
0	+	+	+	2.0
+	+	+	+	-0.5

Total Variance Explained   37.95%

R = .616

* "+" indicates the presence of the factor as an independent variable.
  "0" indicates the absence of the factor as an independent variable.

participation contribute nothing to the total variance and background factors contribute a minor 1.7%.

The distribution of average scores for the thirteen cities is shown in Figure 6.4 (as Z-scores). Chicago policemen are most threatened by blacks and Philadelphia policemen least threatened.[7] Sharing honors with Chicago are Detroit, Cincinnati, and Cleveland, while the least threatened third of the cities include Washington, D.C., Brooklyn, and Pittsburgh.

The last set of variables we consider in this section are how friendly or hostile policemen perceive their "clients" to be. As with other variables relating to how policemen relate to their patrol districts, we have sepa-

---

[7] Ironically, these two cities are among those with the highest proportions black in their police forces. Philadelphia in 1968 actually had the highest proportion black, with Chicago at least among the top half of the 15 cities in this respect.

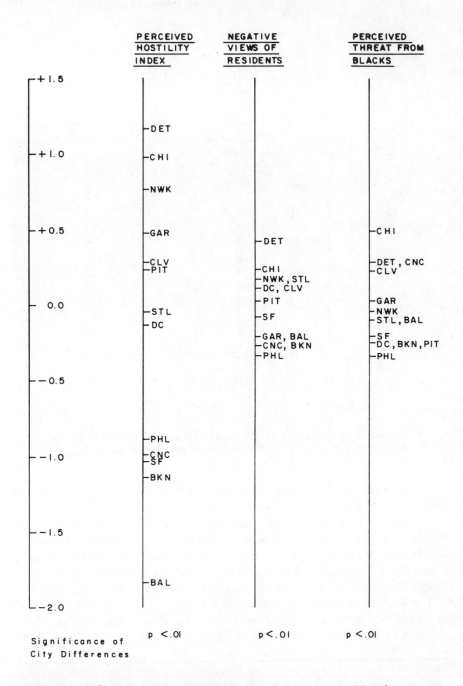

Figure 6.4 Police interviews: city averages (Z-scores) on perceived hostility. Negative views of precinct residents and perceived black threat indexes.

rated their perceptions into different categories of precinct residents. The results for eight different categories of residents are presented in Table 6.11.

Whether the perception of client hostility-friendliness is an attitude is somewhat ambiguous. Obviously, there is a "reality" to which the police are reacting: Precinct residents may be friendly and cooperative, or they may be unfriendly and obstructionist. However, the delicate problem is interpreting the hostile or friendly intent of gestures, phrases, body movements, in the course of which anyone can misread a great deal. Fortunately, it is possible to examine whether policemen are mainly reacting to objective reality or whether they are reacting mainly to stimuli located within their psyches. The contrast between white and black policemen in perceived hostility provides some useful information. Where both white and black policemen perceive much the same levels of hostility or friendliness, more likely the objective situation faced by the police generates the findings. We can make this judgment, because we can assume that black policemen are not prejudiced against members of their own race (as the results of Tables 6.9 and 6.10 substantiate).[8]

The eight categories of residents vary in the degree to which they are perceived as friendly or hostile to the police. Older persons, storekeepers, teachers, and whites are seen by the overwhelming majority of the police as "on their side," with percentages of 94, 83, 82, and 70% respectively, claiming that these groups are friendly. Oddly enough, two of these groups—storekeepers and whites—produce the only racial differences in the perception of hostility which reaches statistical significance. Black policemen are more likely to see both storekeepers and whites as "on their side" than are the white policemen.

In contrast, the resident categories "most adolescents" and "most young adults" are seen by the police as regarding policemen with indifference and hostility. Only 15% of the policemen perceive that adolescents are "on their side." In contrast, 53% perceive adolescent attitudes as hostile (regard the police as enemies) and 31% claim that adolescents display indifference to the police. Similar findings pertain to the police perceptions of young adults: 16% see young adults as friendly, 42% see them as hostile, and 41% as indifferent. Note that the differences between black and white policemen in these respects are not significant.

Policemen believe that "most blacks" regard them either with hostility

---

[8] "Prejudice" may be the wrong word and the less critical attitude of black policemen is not as obvious a finding as might first appear. Later we see that black social workers tend to be more critical of their clients than white social workers. Complex processes are operating in this issue, and we lack the necessary data to say much more about it.

TABLE 6.11

Police) Perception of Precinct Residents
Interviews } Hostility-Friendliness Toward Police
by Race* (Total N = 522, White N = 397, Black N = 125)

Group in Precinct	Race of Policemen	Proportion Who Say Police Are Regarded				Significance White-Black Differences
		As Enemies	On Their Side / Their Side	Indifferent Toward Police	DK & NA	
Residents in General	White	21%	34	41	4	.20>p>.10
	Black	17	42	36	4	
	Total	20	35	40	4	
Old Persons in Neighborhood	White	1	94	5	1	.30>p>.20
	Black	0	95	5	0	
	Total	1	94	5	#	
Most Blacks	White	32	30	36	2	.50>p>.30
	Black	27	35	34	5	
	Total	31	31	36	3	
Most Storekeepers	White	#	81	18	#	p<.01
	Black	0	90	10	#	
	Total	#	83	16	#	
Most Adolescents	White	54	16	29	1	.50>p>.30
	Black	47	13	37	3	
	Total	53	15	31	1	

TABLE 6.11 (Cont'd)

Proportion Who Say Police Are Regarded

Group in Precinct	Race of Policemen	As Enemies	On Their Side Their Side	Indifferent Toward Police	DK & NA	Significance White-Black Differences
Most Young Adults	White	45	15	39	1	
	Black	31	17	51	2	.95>p>.90
	Total	42	16	41	1	
Most Teachers	White	2	82	14	3	
	Black	0	81	15	4	.70>p>.50
	Total	1	82	14	2	
Most Whites	White	1	68	29	2	
	Black	2	77	18	2	p<.01
	Total	1	70	27	1	

*Based on Q6: "In some precincts more people regard the police almost as enemies. In others they regard the police as being essentially on their side, and in some, they are indifferent to the police. How do most people in this precinct look on the police?"

= less than 1%.

177

or indifference (31 and 36%, respectively), and only 31% see blacks as friendly or indifferent (35 and 40%, respectively) and less likely to be viewed by policemen as hostile (20%). It should be noted that these findings are quite consistent with the others in Table 6.11. "Residents in general" are made up of a mixture of blacks, young adults, adolescents, and whites (in the case of mixed precincts), and hence should be perceived as being less hostile than the young but more hostile than storekeepers. Whether the levels of perceived friendliness-hostility is viewed appropriately as a weighted average of the composition of the precincts is almost impossible to judge without more accurate data both on perceived attitudes and precinct compositions.

Given the findings of Table 6.11 we can characterize the police as serving large portions of a client population that do not see the police as their friends but regard police either with indifference or hostility. Especially with respect to the young, the police appear to view themselves as beleaguered, almost as troops occupying unfriendly enemy territory.

Using the responses to the items of Table 6.11, a Perceived Hostility Index was constructed, essentially measuring the extent to which individual policemen see themselves in hostile or friendly environments. The city distributions of average Perceived Hostility Index scores is shown in Figure 6.4. Note that the cities show a larger dispersion with respect to this index as compared with the two other indices contained in Figure 6.6. In short, police departments differ more in their perceptions of general ghetto hostility than they differ with respect to negative views of the residents or black threats. Detroit policemen believe themselves the most beleagured department, followed closely by Chicago and Newark. At the opposite end of the bar, indicating a perceived friendly environment, Baltimore's police department is by far the least beleagured department, followed, although at some distance, by Brooklyn, San Francisco, Cincinnati, and Philadelphia.[9]

A multiple regression analysis of the Perceived Hostility Index is presented in Table 6.12. The four clusters explain a little less than 17% of the total variance among policemen, equivalent to a multiple correlation of .408. City differences, as we might be led to expect from the dispersion of scores in Figure 6.4, account uniquely for more of the variance than any other factor, accounting for 7.9% (47% of the explained variance). Background factors, particularly age,[10] account for another 4.8% with

[9] It should be recalled that policemen were surveyed in Baltimore in the spring of 1968, before the April 1968 civil disorders, and in Chicago after the disorders.

[10] A more detailed analysis of this scale is contained in W. Eugene Groves and Peter H. Rossi, "Police Perceptions of a Hostile Ghetto," *Amer. Behav. Sci.*, 13 (5 and 6), 727–743 (1970).

TABLE 6.12

Police) Perceived Hostility Index: Relative
Interviews) Contributions of City, Race, Background
and Community Participation (N = 522)

City*	Race	Combination Background	Community Participation	Proportion of Total Variance Uniquely Attributable
+	0	0	0	7.9%
0	+	0	0	0.7
0	0	+	0	4.8
0	0	0	+	0.6
+	+	0	0	0.3
+	0	+	0	1.3
+	0	0	+	-0.4
0	+	+	0	0.0
0	+	0	+	1.0
0	0	+	+	0.3
+	+	+	0	0.0
+	+	0	+	-0.2
+	0	+	+	0.0
0	+	+	+	0.5
+	+	+	+	0.0

(R^2) Total Variance Explained 16.68%

R = .408

* "+" indicates the presence of the factor as an independent variable.
"0" indicates the absence of the factor as an independent variable.

insignificant amounts of variance explained by either community participation or race.

The analysis of the Perceived Hostility Index indicates that this measure should be used less as an indicator of police attitudes than as a reflection of what the police objectively perceive as characteristic of their environments. This interpretation is supported mainly by the fact that black and white policemen scarcely differ in their perceptions, and the main source of explained variation comes from city differences rather than individual characteristics.

Community Leadership and Police Behavior. In this and the previous chapter, ample evidence has been displayed that the police departments of the thirteen cities vary significantly. Among the more important differences are the reported behaviors of police vis-a-vis the citizens of the

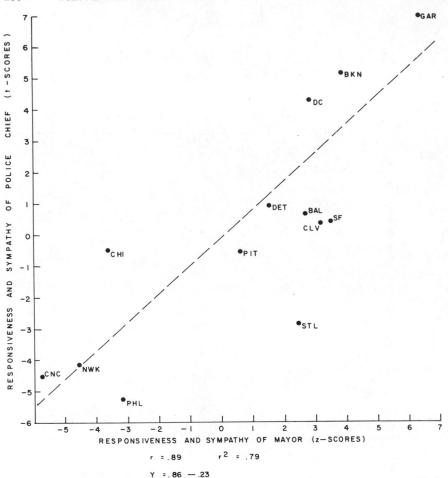

Figure 6.5 Elite interviews: ratings of mayor's sympathy and responsiveness to black civil rights movement related to sympathy and responsiveness of police chief. $r = .89$, $r^2 = .79$, $Y = .86X - .23$.

precincts they patrol. Figure 6.4 showed considerable differences in the extent to which police engage in stop-and-frisk practices, searching without warrants, breaking up loitering groups, and interrogating suspected drug users. We also showed that these differences among the police departments were reflected in residents' personal experiences with abuse at the hands of the police, a finding which substantiates the importance of police reports of their behavior on patrol.

Although there are some differences among the police departments in terms of their personnel composition, there still remains a considerable amount of variance among the cities unaccounted for by such personnel differences. In other words, some determinants of city differences do not reflect demographic aspects of police departments. It is to one of the more important sources of such differences that we turn to in this section.

In most of the cities in our sample, police departments are under the direct control of the mayor. The mayor ordinarily appoints the police chief, and in many cities a change in city administration is often accompanied by a change in the head of the police department.[11] Given the quasi-military nature of the organization of the police, it is to be expected that changes in policy initiated by the mayor's office and transmitted through the police department head will manifest themselves in changes in police behavior than would be the case for other city departments, for example, the school system.

The close connection between the mayor's office and the upper echelons of the police department is shown in Figure 6.5, where a measure of sympathy and responsiveness of mayor to the local black civil rights movement is related to the same measure for the police chiefs.[12] The relationship between the two ratings is very high ($R = .89$) suggesting that the tone of police administration may be set by the mayor's posture toward the civil rights movement. For a few of the cities, the mayor's reputation is more sympathetic than his police chief (the major example is St. Louis); and in others, the police chief's reputation is more sympathetic than the mayor (e.g., Chicago).

The data shown in Figure 6.5 are drawn from elite interviews and therefore represent the ways in which the mayor and the police chief are viewed by those local political figures to whom our interviewing team talked. The critical question is whether these public postures are translated into differences in the behavior of policemen on the beat. Table 6.13 contains data which answer this critical question. The correlations of mayor's ratings and police chief ratings with the Potentially Controversial Police Practices Index are $-.64$ and $-.57$, respectively. In short, it does make a difference how the elites interviewed regard the mayor and the chief of police, because these two officials establish policies which are translated into differences among cities in levels of controversial police practices.

Table 6.13 also contains two additional variables taken from the police interviews, the Perceived Hostility Index and the Combined Acquaint-

---

[11] In two cities, Baltimore and St. Louis, police chiefs were appointed by the governor.
[12] The measures in question are taken from elite interview ratings and are averages of ratings of each official on the following measures (see Chapter 3):

Responsiveness to demands of civil rights leaders
Accessability to civil rights leaders
Sympathy with civil rights movement

ance Index. They are presented here, because they do not show very strong relationships to the civil rights reputations of the mayors and police chiefs. The highest relevant correlation is .14, hardly indicative of any relationship worth noting. The contrast between these correlations and those involving the PCPP indicate that the mayor and police chief are affective in altering levels of occupational behavior but not in altering attitudinal sets[13] (e.g., Perceived Hostility) or in behavior which takes some time to establish (the extent of acquaintance among precinct residents).

Table 6.13 contains other information of considerable interest. First, the mayor and police chief apparently can influence police behavior, but they cannot determine it completely. The correlations involved are high enough to be regarded as indicating serious impact, but not high enough to be regarded as overwhelming determination. Second, we may note that both the Perceived Hostility Index and the Combined Acquaintance Index are related to PCPP, indicating that some part of police behavior is affected by characteristics of the police department which are independent of leadership policy. Indeed, if we compute the multiple correlation of all four variables with the Potentially Controversial Police Practices Index, the resulting value is .74, indicating that the four variables taken together account for more than half of the intercity variance in this index of police behavior.[14]

The residuals for individual cities (as computed from the multiple regression) are shown at the bottom of Table 6.13 in terms of proportions of the standard error of the estimated values of PCPP. Note that a negative residual indicates that the regression equation *overestimates* that city's level of police abuse while a positive residual indicates an *underestimation*. If we take residuals which are greater than the standard error of the estimate as indicating a large deviation, two cities stand out: Cincinnati in which the level of police abuse is underestimated and

---

[13] In addition, other attitudinal scales (discussed earlier in this chapter) show the same pattern of low correlations with PCPP. For example, the correlations of the PCPP with the "Negative Image" Scale and with the "Perceived Threat" Scale are .08 and .12, respectively.

[14] In this equation and several to follow a relatively large number of independent variables are used given the N of 13 cities. As the number of variables approaches the number of cases, the multiple correlation is artificially inflated. In the case when the number of variables is one less than the number of cases the scatter plot is completely determined ($R = 1.0$) regardless of the real association between the variables. There are several different kinds of adjustments that can be made to remove this artifact. For our data, when the N is 13 and the number of independent variables is between 4 and 7, all variance statistics should be discounted about 10%. Note that this does not alter the relative importance of each variable, but simply reduces its absolute importance.

TABLE 6.13

Elite and Police) Relationships Among Responsiveness and Sympathy
Interviews   ) Ratings of Mayor and Police Chief, Potentially
                   Controversial Police Practices Index (PCPP),
                   Perceived Hostility Index and Combined
                   Acquaintance Index [N = 13 cities]

A. Zero Order Correlations:

		Responsiveness and Sympathy Ratings of		Police Practices Index (PCPP)	Perceived Hostility Index	Combined Acquaintance Index
		Mayor (1)	Police Chief (2)	(3)	(4)	(5)
Mayor	(1)		.89	- 64	-.06	.08
Police Chief	(2)			-.57	.05	.14
PCPP Index	(3)				.39	-.34
Perceived Hostility	(4)					-.51
Combined Acquaintance Index	(5)					

B. Multiple Regression of variables 1, 2, 4 and 5 on PCPP:

$$R = .74 \quad (R^2 = .54) \quad [p < 05]$$

C. Residuals for Individual Cities:

City	Residual (Proportions of Standard Error of Estimate)
Baltimore	- .13
Brooklyn	.59
Chicago	- .10
Cincinnati	-1.30
Cleveland	- .73
Detroit	.02
Gary	.67
Newark	.002
Philadelphia	.85
Pittsburgh	- .71
St. Louis	1.74
San Francisco	- .11
Washington, D.C.	- .80

St. Louis whose level of police abuse is overestimated. It is somewhat
idle to speculate at this point why these two cities deviate from the
patterns of the total group. It is clear at any rate that other variables
affect police behavior beyond those considered in Table 6.13.

To show the strength of public officials' influence on police behavior
relative to the other variables in Table 6.13, the unique contributions of
the variables to the total explained variance in police behavior is shown

in Table 6.14. In this table we have combined the ratings of the police chief and the mayor into a single cluster of variables because of the high relationship between the two officials' ratings.

Because we are dealing with such a small number of cases, it is not wise to take the variance partitioning shown in Table 6.14 as displaying anything more than a crude indication of the relative contributions of the three clusters of variables. Small changes in the measures for two or three cities can affect markedly the correlations of Table 6.13 and in turn the distribution of variance shown in Table 6.14. In addition, the one rather large negative variance partition (for the three variable joint contribution) indicates considerable multicolinearity. Under these conditions, perhaps the firmest statement that one can make about the relationships is that *both* the ratings of the public officials and characteristics of the police departments affect the levels of police behavior.

If we take the partitioning as meaning more than that, we note that the largest unique contribution to the total explained variance in police behavior is made by the ratings of the police chief and the mayor combined. Twenty-five percent of the total variance (46% of the explained variance) is accounted for by these two ratings taken as a cluster. An additional 7% is contributed by the unique effects of the Perceived Hostility Index. The unique contribution of the overlap between Perceived Hostility and the Combined Acquaintance Index accounts for an additional 16%. The remaining amounts of explained variance is scattered through the other combinations shown in the table.

The main finding of this section is that the behavior of police departments is strongly affected by the stances mayors and police chiefs take toward the black civil rights movement. This finding can be interpreted in a variety of ways. First the public officials may place some very direct pressure upon the lower ranks of the police to behave differently toward residents of black neighborhoods. Second, the issues of police behavior raised by the black civil rights movement may lead to public officials' directing changes in police behavior which affect all the residents of the cities in question. Sensitivity to black complaints about the police lead to changes in overall public policy in the cities. In either case, we may raise the more general question of whether these intercity differences in police behavior are reflected in the ways in which residents—black and white—experience the behavior of their police departments.

Police Behavior and the Public.   Measures of personal experiences with local police were included in the Survey Research Center's sample survey of white and black residents of each of the thirteen cities. A set of items

TABLE 6.14

Elite & Police)   Potentially Controversial Police Practice Index:
Interviews   )   Relative Contributions of Mayor and Police Chief,
                  Perceived Hostility and Combined Acquaintance
                  Index [N = 13 Cities]

Mayor and Police Chief *	Combinations Perceived Hostility Index	Combined Acquaintance Index	Proportions of Variance Uniquely Attributable
+	0	0	25%
0	+	0	7
0	0	+	0
+	+	0	4
+	0	+	4
0	+	+	16
+	+	+	- 3 **

Total Variance Explained (R^2) = .54

*"+" indicates the presence of the factor as an independent variable. "0" indicates the absence of the factor as an independent variable.

**Recall, this is an artifactual result reflecting considerable multicolinearity, large zero order corrections with the dependent variable, a negative partial correlations.

asked each respondent whether they had "personally experienced," "know someone who has experienced," and "think happens in their neighborhood" incidents of the following in relation to the police:[15]

  ... the police don't come quickly when you call them for help.
  ... the police don't show respect for people or they use insulting language.
  ... the police frisk or search people without good reason.
  ... the police rough up people unnecessarily when they are arresting them or afterwards.

Three indices formed from these data were each a summation of responses to the four items above centering around the respondents' own personal experiences (Personal Experience Index), knowledge about other persons' personal experiences (Reported Experience Index), and

---

[15] The actual questions asked were as follows: "Do you think this happens to people in this neighborhood?" "Has it ever happened to you?" "Has it happened to anyone you know?"

the respondents' general beliefs about the prevalence of such incidents in their neighborhoods (General Beliefs Index). Averages for each of the cities were computed separately for black and white residents for each of the indexes.

The correlations among the indexes and between the indexes and the PCPP Index are shown in Table 6.15.[16] The relationship between each of the indexes and the PCPP Index are shown in the rectangular boxes in the table. Note that the relationships are fairly high. Both white and black respondents' levels of Reported Police Abuse are related to the police reports of their own behavior. In short, in cities where the police report that they are likely to engage in such practices, the residents black and white—are likely to report high levels of personal experiences with police abuse and failure to respond to calls for help.

In the upper left-hand triangle are contained the correlations among indices for blacks. In cities where Personal Experience levels are high the levels for Reported Experience and General Beliefs are also high. The same correlations for white residents are shown in the triangle in the lower right-hand part of the table. Much the same generalization can be made for white respondents, except that the correlations tend to be higher. Indeed, for whites it can be said that it matters very little whether one index or another is taken as a measure of the extent to which police abuse and neglect is perceived. The correlations among the indices are so high (ranging from .88 to .90) that the indices are interchangeable. Interchangeability in the same sense is not true of the indices for blacks, however. The levels of Personal Experience correlate .67 and .66, respectively, with the General Beliefs Index and the Reported Behavior Index, indicating a sharper separation between those matters for blacks.

We may also note that the PCPP is more highly correlated with white respondents' perceptions of police abuse and neglect than with blacks' perceptions. This is particularly puzzling, since the measures of PCPP refer to the behavior of police who are stationed in precincts in black areas of their cities. A possible interpretation of this finding is that when the police are ordered to ease up on such practices as "stop-and-frisk," the orders are issued in a general form and affect white residential areas

---

[16] Table 6.14 has appeared in an early analysis of these data (P. H. Rossi and R. A. Berk, "Local Political Leadership and Popular Discontent in the Ghetto," *The Annals*, September 1970) in which different values are given for the relationships among the indices for white respondents. We have been at a loss to explain how this came about other than to blame the fallibility of the authors. We apologize to those readers of the previous article who may have been led astray by the errors and their interpretations. We do believe, however, that the errors are not serious enough to vitiate completely the explanations given in the previous article.

TABLE 6.15

Police Interviews)
and Survey   ) Relationships Among Potentially Controversial Police
Interviews   ) Practices, Personal Experience, Reported Experience
                       and General Beliefs about Police Abuse Among White
                       and Black Residents of 15 Cities

		Black Respondents Experience with Police Abuse			Potentially Controversial Police Practices (PCPP)	White Respondents Experience with Police Abuse		
		Personal Exp.	Reported Experience	General Beliefs		Personal Exp.	Reported Experience	General Beliefs
		(1)	(2)	(3)	(4)	(5)	(6)	(7)
BLACKS	Personal Exp. (1)		.66	.67	.83	.59	.51	.38
	Reported Exp. (2)			.92	.55	.25	.07	-.10
	General Beliefs (3)				.51	.31	.13	-.05
	PCPP (4)					.78	.71	.55
WHITES	Personal Exp. (5)						.90	.88
	Reported Exp. (6)							.89

187

as well as black. In any event, the influence of mayor and police chiefs' sympathy and responsiveness to the black civil rights movement on police behavior is a very general one, which affects police practices with respect to both white and black residential areas.

The correlations in the upper right-hand section of Table 6.16 (outside of the boxes and triangles) describe the relationships across the indices for the two races. The highest correlation of the nine presented is that between the black and white Personal Experiences Indexes (.59). Almost all of the remaining correlations are low and two are even negative; the highest correlations are those between the black Personal Experiences Index and the three indices for white residents.

Apparently the processes of generalization from personal experiences to general assessments of the tone and character of police department behavior are different for whites as compared to blacks. For whites, a high level of Personal Experiences leads to high levels of Reported Police Abuse from persons they know and generalized beliefs that the police are abusive. Black communities maintain a degree of separation between personal experiences and generalizations about police behavior.[17]

Since our data on the police refer only to those policemen who are assigned to largely black inhabited precincts, the analysis of the links between police behavior and the responses of citizens is confined to black neighborhoods and communities. At this point we can only speculate on the linkages for whites in the thirteen cities. Indeed, from the results shown in Table 6.14, linkages may well be different, or at least differently structured.

To examine the relationships between police behavior and residents' perceptions of police behavior in greater detail, Table 6.16 presents the correlations between black perceptions and seven indices of police behavior. The police practices on patrol are represented by four separate indices, all highly interrelated. The familiar PCPP Index, of course, is the one most highly related to black perceptions of police behavior: Indeed,

---

[17] Of course, black residents report considerably higher levels on all three indices, as indicated below:

	Average Index Values		Standard Deviation	
	Blacks	Whites	Blacks	Whites
Personal Experience	288	88	83	44
Reported Experience	722	187	176	93
General Beliefs	277	96	92	26

The indices for blacks are on the average two to three times larger than those for whites.

TABLE 6.16

Police and   ) Relationships Among Police Behavior Indices and Black
Survey Interviews) Residents' Perceptions of Police Behavior N = 13 cities

| | Black Residents | | | | | Police Behavior Indices | | | | |
	Personal Exp. (1)	Reported Exp. (2)	Beliefs (3)	PCPP Ind. (4)	Comb. Acq. Ind. (5)	Eff. Ind. (6)	Imp. Ind. (7)	St. Ind. (8)	Perc. Host. Ind. (9)	Perc. Eff. Acq. Ind. (10)
Personal Experience (1)		.66	.67	.68	-.73	.72	.39	.69	.44	-.69
Reported Experience (2)			.92	.55	-.56	.33	.54	.59	.39	-.39
General Beliefs (3)				.51	-.68	.25	.55	.48	.39	-.27
PCPP Index (4)					-.42	.72	.82	.96	.49	-.62
Combined Acquaint. Index (5)						-.48	-.23	-.34	-.51	.45
Efficiency Index (6)							.19	.75	.10	-.63
Impact Index (7)								.73	.65	-.34
Street Index (8)									.39	-.65
Perceived Hostility (9)										-.52

Efficiency Index = Search Index minus proportion searched who are found to have weapons or to have committed a crime.

Impact Index = Search Index weighted by proportion who have been found to have weapons or to have committed crimes.

Street Index = Based upon combination of items relating to police behavior in public places (i.e. stop-and-frisk, breaking up loitering crowds, interrogating suspected drug users).

Effective Acquaintance Index = Combined Acquaintance Index weighted by proportion of time police spend on foot patrol.

that is why the analyses presented earlier in this chapter have used this index so frequently. Two of the indices have been formed by combining the police reported success rates in stop-and-frisk practices with the PCPP. The "Efficiency Index" expresses the extent to which PCPP practices "pay-off"; the higher the index the more likely are police patrol practices to result in the detection (according to police) of actual or potential wrongdoers. Note that the Efficiency Index is particularly strongly related (.72) to Personal Experiences with police abuse, possibly indicating that what may be efficiency in the eyes of the police may be abuse to those who are the targets of stop-and-frisk and other practices.

Another way of looking at the relationship between police behavior and popular response is to weigh the PCPP by multiplying it by the success rate, as in the Impact Index; a city gets a high score if it has both a high level of PCPP and a high success rate in such activities as stop-and-frisk. The Impact Index has a relatively high relationship to both Reported Experiences and General Beliefs about Police Abuse. It is hard to interpret what these findings mean however.

Although there is some interest in the individual correlations, it would be useful to examine the impacts of all seven indexes as a group. Unfortunately, the high multicolinearity makes this impossible. A stepwise procedure indicates that once PCPP and the acquaintance index are included, the other five scales add virtually nothing to the variance explained, and if forced into the equation, they produce serious artifacts.

Table 6.17 shows the contributions to variance explained for the three population survey indices (Personal Experience, Reported Experience, and General Beliefs about police abuse), using the acquaintance index and the PCPP as independent variables. These two measures were chosen because they typically have the highest correlations with the dependent variables, have demonstrated their utility in earlier analyses, and involve fewer manipulations of the original questionnaire items.

The total amounts of explained variance are quite high. For Personal Experience with abuse 71% of the variance is explained. Reported Experience and beliefs about police abuse have 42 and 54% explained variance. All the variance partitions are also substantial. The order of relative importance of PCPP, the acquaintance index, and their joint effect are roughly the same for Personal Experiences and Reported Experiences. The joint contribution comes out on top, followed closely by the acquaintance index and the PCPP. For the General Beliefs Index, the contribution of the PCPP drops markedly relative to the acquaintance index, suggesting the farther removed an assessment from a respondent's first-hand knowledge, the more important the style and quality of police activity.

Since we have shown previously that the behavior of police depart-

TABLE 6.17

Police & Survey) Personal Experience, Reported Experiences and
Interviews   ) General Beliefs About Police Abuse and Neglect:
                  Relative Contribution of PCPP and Police
                  Acquaintance 〔N = 13 cities〕

Independent Variables		Variance Explained on Dependent Variables		
PCPP*	Acquaintance	Personal Experiences	Reported Experiences	General Beliefs
+	0	18%	11%	8%
0	+	25%	12%	28%
+	+	28%	19%	18%

R^2 (Total Explained Variance   = .71   .42   .54

R = .84   .65   .73

* "+" indicates the presence of a factor as an independent variable
  "0" indicates the absence of a factor as an independent variable

ments is closely related to the stances taken by public officials in relation
to the black civil rights movement, it is worthwhile to see the extent to
which public officials contribute directly to the experience of police
behavior in the black communities involved. Public policy may be experienced in this area only to the extent that it is transformed into actual
police practices. In this case, we would expect that adding information
on public officials' stances to the data of this section would show that
public officials have no effect on the experiences of blacks with the police
beyond what could be accounted for by police behavior.

An alternative possibility is that the stances taken by police chiefs and
the mayor are directly perceived by the black residents of their communities and accordingly modify their interpretations of police behavior.
In other words, where the police chief and the mayor are known as sympathetic and responsive to blacks, the actions of the police department
are interpreted as more benign than if the reputations of these public
officials were to the contrary.

Data bearing on this issue are in Table 6.18, in which elite interview
ratings of the mayor and police chief have been added to variables relating to the behavior, acquaintance ranges, and attitudes of the police
departments. Table 6.18 contains a partitioning of the variance among

TABLE 6.18

Elite, Police and) Personal Experience, Reported Experience and
Survey Interviews) General Beliefs About Police Abuse and Neglect:
Relative Contributions of Public Officials and
Police Behavior: [N = 13 cities]

Combination of Independent Variables	Unique Explained Variance in		
	Personal Experiences	Reported Experiences	General Beliefs
Public Officials Alone	7 %	20.1%	23.9%
Police Behavior Alone	51.2	23.1	62.2
Jointly Public Officials and Police Behavior	26.1	31.1	- 4.4
(R^2) Total Explained Variance =	84.3%	74.3%	81.7%

Clusters are defined as follows:

Public Officials: Responsiveness and Sympathy Ratings of Police Chief
and Mayor (Elite Interviews)

Police Behavior: PCPP Index, Street Behavior Index, Combined
Acquaintance Index and Perceived Hostility Index
(Police Interviews)

cities for three dependent variables—Personal Experiences, Reported
Experiences, and General Beliefs. Two clusters of independent variables
are considered; a cluster labeled "public officials," consists of the ratings
of the sympathy and responsiveness of the police chief and the mayor,
and a second cluster entitled "police behavior" contains most of the
individual variables previously considered in this section. The unique
contributions and joint contributions of the two clusters are percentages
of the total variance in each dependent variable as explained by the two
clusters and their combination.

Although the small number of cities and moderate multicolinearity
undoubtedly make this partitioning unstable in detail, the overall patterning is probably stable. In this last respect, the major finding is that
public officials' stances have an independent effect on the apperception
of police behavior. Furthermore, this effect is greater for Reported
Experiences and General Beliefs than for Personal Experiences, as indicated by unique contributions of 20.1 and 23.9% as compared to 7%.
In short, the stances of public officials modestly and directly affect
what people claim to experience, but may alter substantially the inter-

pretation of police behavior observed or alleged in black communities. In cities whose mayors and police chiefs are reputed to be sympathetic to blacks, police behavior is seen as more benign. In cities where such officials have opposite reputations, police behavior received a less benign interpretation.

The major findings of this section point to the strong effects of police behavior and public policy relating to such behavior on the way in which the police are viewed in our cities' black neighborhoods. In this area of community life, public opinion is based partly on reality and partly on its interpretation. Stances of public officials and the acquaintance range of policemen on the line fundamentally alter the way police patroling practices are perceived. The implications of this finding are explored in greater detail later in this volume. For the time being, it is worth noting that we have uncovered one area of community life in which public policy can make a considerable difference to the way in which some municipal services are perceived as satisfactory.

Overall Satisfaction with Police Services: An Unsolved Question. As we indicated in Chapter 4, two aspects of police behavior are opposite each other. On the one hand, the more vigorous and active a police department may be, the more likely it may be to detect crime and to render protective services to citizens. On the other hand, the same high level of activity may lead to complaints of unfair treatment on the part of those who may be swept up in the nets of patrol activities vigorously set up by such police departments. Up to this point we have concentrated mainly on experiences of unfair treatment at the hands of the police. We turn now to the other side of police behavior as seen by citizens—the extent to which they are satisfied with police protection.

We are handicapped in investigating this problem because the data available are not as detailed as in the case of police abuse. Essentially we rely on the answers to a single question, asked of all respondents in the sample survey conducted by the University of Michigan, asking how satisfied each was with "police protection in his neighborhood." [18]

The proportions who replied that they were "generally satisfied" with police protection in their neighborhoods are shown in Figure 6.6, separately for black and white respondents. The range is quite considerable:

---

[18] The exact wording of this item is as follows: ". . . . how satisfied are you with some of the main services the city is supposed to provide for your neighborhood? What about . . . police protection in this neighborhood? Are you generally satisfied, somewhat dissatisfied, or very dissatisfied?"

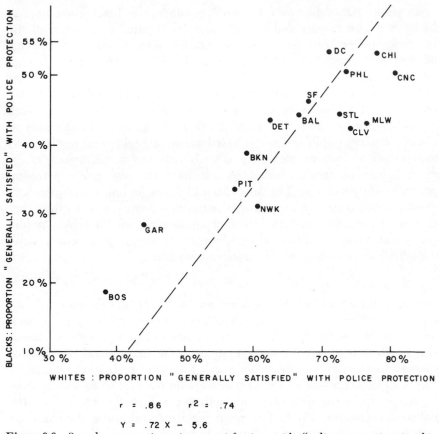

$$r = .86 \qquad r^2 = .74$$

$$Y = .72 X - 5.6$$

Figure 6.6 Sample survey interviews: satisfaction with "police protection in this neighborhood" for blacks and whites in fifteen cities. $r = .86$, $r^2 = .74$, $Y = .72X - 5.6$.

on the low side, the residents of Boston—black and white—appear to be most dissatisfied with police protection, with proportions of 18 to 38% generally satisfied. At the high extreme, black and white, and Chicagoans have majorities who are generally satisfied (53 and 78%, respectively).

Black residents generally show a lower level of satisfaction than whites: In eleven of the fifteen cities, the proportion generally satisfied are in a minority, as compared to only two out of the fifteen for whites. In no city, do blacks show a higher level of satisfaction than whites.

Yet there is a close relationship between levels of black and levels of white satisfaction. The correlation in Figure 6.6 is .86, as high a relationship as any others shown in this chapter and much higher than the correlations between black and white perceptions of police abuse. Apparently whatever leads to white satisfaction is linked to black dissatisfaction.

It cannot be said that we have been very successful in uncovering what affects the above. The measures of police behavior which have proved so successful in understanding popular perceptions of police abuse have not been very useful in understanding levels of satisfaction with police services. Table 6.19 contains some of the observed correlations computed across cities between the level of satisfaction with police services.

Several tendencies stand out in Table 6.19. First of all, measures of police behavior (e.g., the PCPP Index and the Combined Acquaintance Index) are only weakly related to satisfaction levels in the thirteen cities. However, the directions of relationship are interesting. First, the higher the level of the PCPP Index and the lower the Combined Acquaintance Index, the higher the level of satisfaction with police services. Second, higher relationships can be found with the indexes of reported police abuse. The higher the levels of reported police abuse the more satisfied are blacks with police services.

The bottom of Table 6.19 refers to variables that have not been discussed so far in this chapter. One of the four items incorporated into reported police abuse indices asked whether the police came quickly in response to calls for help. Replies to this item have been related to satisfaction in three versions: *Personal experiences* with slow services, *reports* of slow service from friends, and *general beliefs* about the slowness of the service. Note particularly that the more complaints about slowness reported by respondents as personal experiences, the more likely are residents to show a high level of satisfaction! However, the higher the level of general assessment that police are responsive to calls for help, the more likely are the black communities to be highly satisfied with police services rendered in their neighborhoods.

It is obvious in these findings that no clear interpretation can be found for levels of satisfaction with police services. The data hint somewhat that levels of satisfaction increase with the amount of aggressive activity displayed by the police and experienced by residents. It is also clear that the black communities are not responding to quickness of police response to calls alone. Beyond these speculations, we can do nothing further with these data. Obviously satisfaction with police services is a complicated matter, perhaps a balance between aggressive police actions on behalf of residents and aggressive actions which hit residents indiscriminately. If such is the case, we have to leave it to future research to unravel the exact network of connections implied.

Police Protection and Police Brutality as Local Political Issues. In the last two decades police departments have moved to the center of local political arenas—levered into that position by the increasing salience of

TABLE 6.19

Police and   ) Satisfaction with Police Service in
Survey Interviews) Neighborhood and Selected Police
                     Behavior Indices (N = 13 cities)

Correlation with Satisfaction with
Police Services in Neighborhood

	PCPP Index	.14
	Combined Acquaintance Index	-.21
Reported Police Abuse	Personal Experiences	.45
	Reported Experiences	.34
	General Beliefs	.28
Complaints about Police Responsiveness to Calls for Aid*	No Complaints Personally	-.58
	No Reported Complaints	.02
	Does not Believe Police are Unresponsive	.48

*Based on answers to items asking respondents whether they
believed the police to be slow in answering calls for help
in their neighborhoods, whether they had experienced such
slowness in response and whether they knew of anyone who had
experienced any instances of unresponsiveness.

urban crime rates and the apparent breakdown of local order in the civil
disorders of the 1960s. The specific issues are complicated and inter-
woven. In part, they arise out of the civil rights movement (conceived
broadly) whose partisans have often either flaunted local regulations in
an effort to draw attention to inequities or directly attacked police
departments as discriminatory. In part, the issues are caused by an
apparent increase in the crime rates—a matter about which the public
feels strongly. The two sources of increasing concern with the police and
criminal justice systems are interrelated, because a weakening of police

and court discretion is seen as aiding "criminal elements" in the community to ply their trades more easily, hence contributing to the rise in crime. Increased civil rights for blacks and the poor are seen as contributing to the urban problem in a direct way.

In Chapter 3 we presented measures of how salient were various issues in the fifteen cities studied. The ratings were derived from qualitative interviews with local elites and are essentially measures of how much attention, with what degree of intensity, were paid by the eiltes interviewed to these issues. The primary issues in this chapter are those involving charges of police brutality and charges that the police do not provide adequate protection to city residents.

Figure 6.7 presents the salience ratings for each of the fifteen cities, the higher the rating on a scale of 1 to 10, the more salient the issue in the elite interviews. On the average, police brutality is more salient than police protection, the means being 7.4 and 5.9, respectively. For three cities, Detroit, Newark, and Philadelphia, all of the staff members reading the interviews for those cities agreed that police brutality was at its maximum salience (10). This finding is hardly surprising for Newark and Detroit, cities just then recovering from the shocking experiences of the disorders of 1967, but somewhat surprising for Philadelphia which had enjoyed a relatively calm summer in 1967. Of course, Philadelphia's police chief enjoyed a national reputation for "toughness" and had become a controversial figure locally for championing "hard policing" policies.

The relationship between the two salience ratings in Figure 6.9 is essentially zero (.04) indicating that cities in which one issue is high in visibility are not necessarily cities in which the other is also at the center of concern. Police protection is an important issue in Cincinnati, Milwaukee, St. Louis, and San Francisco, and least important in Gary and Detroit. It is difficult to make any sense immediately out of this patterning, as it appears to respond to events which are particular to cities and not well enough known nationally.

City differences in the salience of police brutality has a well-defined structure. For example, Figure 6.8 shows the relationship for thirteen cities between the salience ratings and the PCPP Index. Note that the relationship is a fairly strong one, the correlation between the two being .61. In general cities which have a high PCPP level, police brutality is more salient. In three cities saliency ratings and the PCPP Index numbers are "out of line": Gary has a lower salience rating than its PCPP Index apparently warrants, a condition also experienced by Brooklyn. The exact opposite combination is shown in Washington, D.C., whose police brutality salience rating is much higher than the PCPP Index warrants.

Obviously, there is more to the generation of a political issue than

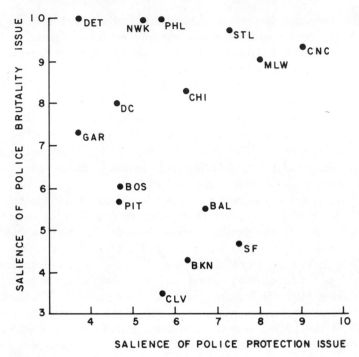

Figure 6.7 Elite interviews: salience ratings of police brutality and police protection as local issues (N = fifteen cities).

the existence of an objective condition at issue. Whether an objectively existing condition becomes an issue depends in part on the actions of political elites who raise issues in the public forums of city council, mass media, and political associations. In part, an issue may fade from the scene before its objective condition counterpart is remedied because the regime has changed and works on the objective conditions. In other words, we have frozen the process of public opinion formation and issue saliency at one particular point in time: For some cities, the issue has passed from the center of attention (e.g., Gary, whose Mayor Hatcher had just been elected) and in others the issue may be raised in salience beyond objective conditions warrant because a group among the elite is contesting the existing regime (possibly Washington, D.C.).

Indeed, there is a closer relationship between the characteristics of local political regimes and the salience of issues than between behavior indices and salience ratings, as Table 6.19 indicates. The more sympathetic and responsive to the black civil rights movement a city's mayor and police chief, the lower the rating of police brutality as a salient issue—correlations of −.76 and −.71, respectively. The indices measuring the black community's perceptions of police abuse show slightly lower

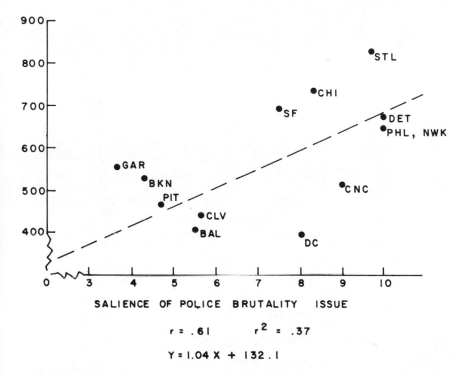

$r = .61$ $r^2 = .37$

$Y = 1.04 X + 132.1$

Figure 6.8 Elite and police interviews: PCPP Index and salience of police brutality issue. $r = +.61$, $r^2 = .37$, $Y = 1.04X + 132.1$.

relationships to police brutality salience, as do the measures of police behavior shown in the bottom of the table.

It would be tempting to make more of the differences between the top and the bottom of Table 6.19. It would be more correct, however, to point out that these relationships are of roughly the same magnitude. Given the small number of observations on which these correlations are based, it is quite conceivable that another sample of cities would show patterns in which the objective conditions would be more closely related to the salience of police brutality than sympathy and responsiveness reputations of mayors and police chiefs.

A considerably different patterning of relationships is shown for the salience ratings of police protection, shown in the right-hand column of Table 6.20. First, the correlations are much smaller, on the average, indicating that whatever sparks the appearance of this issue has not been caught in our net. Second, police protection recedes in importance as an issue where the public officials are sympathetic and responsive to the black civil rights movement, although this tendency must be regarded as very weakly apparent in our data. Police protection tends to become more

TABLE 6.20

Elite, Police) Salience of Police Brutality and Police Protection
and Survey   ) as Local Issues: Relationships to Public Officials'
Interviews   ) Sympathy Ratings, Police Behavior Indices and Survey
               Reports of Police Abuse: [N = 13 Cities]

| | | Correlations with Salience Ratings of | |
		Police Brutality Issue	Police Protection Issue
Responsiveness and Sumpathy Ratings	Mayor	-.76	-.35
	Police Chief	-.71	-.15
Reports of Experiences with Police Abuse	Personal	.61	.16
	Reported from Others	.54	-.20
	General Beliefs	.71	-.14
Police Behavior Indices	PCPP Index	.61	.18
	Street Behavior Index	.65	.15
	Combined Acquaintance Index	-.25	.37

salient as an issue in cities in which the PCPP Index and the Street Behavior Index is high, but also where the police know more of the black community in which they patrol. The patterning shown by this issue is similar to that shown by "satisfaction with police services" discussed in the last section.

The full set of correlations among the variables in Table 6.20 were not shown here because most of those correlations have appeared in previous tables in this chapter.[19] For our purposes it is mainly important to note that these interrelationships are rather high, or at least of the same magnitude of the correlations shown in the left-hand column of Table 6.20. This means that the sizes of the correlations in Table 6.20 do not indicate the relative magnitudes of the effects of each of the variables on either issue. The colinearity existing among variables makes the unraveling of the relative contribution of the variables more complicated.

---

[19] See Table 6.15.

One approach to the task of specifying relative contributions is shown in Table 6.21 where the intercity variances in the salience ratings of both issues have been partitioned into unique contributions of four of the variables shown in Table 6.20.[20] Although the R^2 for Police Brutality is statistically significant, it is just barely so at the .05 level. Obviously, the R^2 for Police Protection Salience is not significant at the usually recognized probability levels: The main justification for presenting its partitioning in Table 6.21 is to provide a contrast with the police brutality salience ratings.

The left-hand column of Table 6.21 contains the proportions of variance of Police Brutality Salience uniquely attributable to each of the combinations of the four variables involved. The degree of multicolinearity among the four variables is shown by the rather large proportion variance which are attributable to the joint influence of combinations of variables. For example, the joint contribution of police chief, Personal Experiences Index, and the PCPP Index accounts uniquely for 12.3% of the variance, the second largest proportion in that column. Combinations of pairs and triplets of variables account for more of the variance (approximately 40%) than the unique contributions of the variables taken singly. If we take this finding seriously, we are obviously dealing with a highly mutually interactive system whose parts affect each other with about equal impact.[21]

Despite the importance of combinations of variables, two of the individual variables still account uniquely for noticeably large proportions of the intercity variance in police brutality salience ratings. Particularly important is the contribution of the police chief's rating, 15.7% of the variance. The PCPP Index accounts uniquely for 7.4% of the variance, indicating that the behavior of the police contributes something on its own to the explanation of the salience of this issue.

A considerable contrast is presented by the right-hand column of Table 6.21 in which the partitioning for the police protection issue is

---

[20] We chose four variables because the small case base made it impossible to accommodate any more. Variables were chosen, one from each of the main groupings of variables.
[21] An alternative interpretation is that the variables are all restatements of a general tendency of cities to have regimes and police departments which are about equally "tough"; hence each of the variables more or less reflects this general tendency rather than separate processes, as we have interpreted them here. We believe there is more evidence for our interpretation, resting our argument largely on the fact that the data were collected from different sources; hence are most likely measuring different phenomena.

TABLE 6.21

Elite, Police and)	Salience of Police Brutality and Police
Survey Interviews)	Protection as Local Issues: Relative
	Contributions of Police Chief Ratings,
	General Beliefs about Police Abuse,
	PCPP Index, and Combined Acquaintance
	Index: [N = 13 Cities]

Combination				Proportions of Variance Uniquely Attributable	
Sympathy Police Chief *	Personal Experience w/ Police Abuse	PCPP Index	Combined Acquaintance Index	Police Brutality Salience	Police Protection Salience
+	0	0	0	15.7%	1.1%
0	+	0	0	2.2	0.9
0	0	+	0	7.4	9.9
0	0	0	+	0.7	9.6
+	+	0	0	9.5	- 0.6
+	0	+	0	9.0	3.1
+	0	0	+	3.7	2.9
0	+	+	0	1.9	- 0.7
0	+	0	+	- 0.6	13.6
0	0	+	+	- 0.6	- 3.1
+	+	+	0	12.3	0.8
+	+	0	+	- 3.7	- 2.6
+	0	+	+	- 1.1	0.5
0	+	+	+	2.7	- 4.6
+	+	+	+	5.2	- 2.8

(R^2) Total Variance Explained =   64.3%   28.0%

*"+" indicates the presence of the factor as an independent variable.
"0" indicates the absence of the factor as an independent variable.

shown. Considerably less of the total variance is explained by this set of four factors, 28% as contrasted with 64.3%. Furthermore, most of the explained variance is explained by the unique contribution of two individual variables, the PCPP Index and the Combined Acquaintance Index, 9.9 and 9.6%, respectively. The reader is warned not to take this analysis too seriously, since the relationships are low enough to ensure considerable instability in any of the proportions calculated.

Metropolitan Police: An Interpretation. This and the previous chapter have covered a great deal of ground, starting with social characteristics of police in metropolitan areas and ending with a hypothesized model of the conditions under which police departments become issues in local politics. There are several salient findings in these data, sufficiently striking as to be worthy of special comment and emphasis.

First, it is clear that the police are quite unlike most other municipal agencies. They tend to form an occupational community, and in relation to the black communities in which they patrol perceived themselves in many cities as almost an occupying force in a hostile and uncooperative environment. The police neither have a strong regard for their clients nor have a positive view of the blacks in their precincts.

Secondly, the perceptions and attitudes of the police are not as important as their practices. Blacks in the cities studied were more sensitive to police practices than they were to police attitudes. Police abuse is more a matter of the way in which police comport themselves than of the opinions they hold concerning their clients.

Third, police practices are in turn sensitive to public policy. Where the mayor and his police chief are sensitive and responsive to blacks, police behavior is more restrained and blacks feel less abused at the hands of the police.

Fourth, police abuse and police protection are quite different matters. Our data hint that convincing residents of their thorough protection by the police at the same time gives rise to complaints about police abuse. In short, the dilemma of the police and of police policy in this area is that correcting one problem (under present schemes of police operation) aggravates the other problem.

Finally, the police and their behavior are locally determined phenomena. The variation among police departments is considerable, enough to produce quite wide variations in the extent to which both blacks and whites in the cities evaluate police practices and police services.

Chapter 7

SELLING AND BUYING IN THE GHETTO

Residential neighborhoods have fewer and less prominent salient features than do the cities in which they are embedded. Indeed, for some residential neighborhoods there are few landmarks around which an image can coalesce. But, for most—especially the older neighborhoods of the inner portions of a city—landscape and architectural features are a means around which the center of the neighborhood can be formed. Churches can serve such a function as can the local schools and perhaps fire stations. More frequently, however, the centers of local neighborhoods are retail shopping areas. In older residential neighborhoods, the strips of retail stores located along main streets and the clusters of stores at main intersections are patronized most frequently by residents. Buying food, tobacco, newspapers, gasoline, drugs, and sundries; getting clothes cleaned; and buying clothes and furniture are some goals that draw people to where stores are located. As a consequence, shopping areas for many older residential areas are central places where people—especially youths—meet.

The retail shopping areas of older neighborhoods are important in a

---

This chapter is based largely on Richard Berk, "The Role of Ghetto Retail Merchants in Civil Disorders." Unpublished Ph.D. dissertation, The Johns Hopkins University, Department of Social Relations, 1970.

more basic sense as well. Retail stores are the connecting links between the producers of goods and the households in the neighborhood. A large proportion of the disposable income of a household is spent on food and the other necessities sold in local retail stores. The quality of such purchases and their cost depend in part on retailing practices of local merchants. Furthermore, shopping is not entirely an impersonal matter. For some goods, for example, appliances, the price is a matter of negotiation. Other goods, for example, clothes, have to be chosen from among a variety of styles, the selection among which is often aided by the "advice" and "guidance" of salesmen. Of course, such staples as meats and vegetables also can vary widely in quality, and a salesman or saleslady seemingly influences the purchases' choices. These services offered by retail merchants can be pleasurable when one is helped in making the "right" choice for his budget and tastes, or distressing when one is pushed into making wrong choices for one's budget or taste. Furthermore, the process of buying can be a pleasant interpersonal exchange between customers and merchants who like each other, or a tug of war between parties who suspect each other of bad intentions and shady practices.

The retail merchants located in the major ghetto areas of our large cities suffer additional disabilities which are the mirror images of disabilities experienced by their customers. The overwhelming majority of the merchants are white, adding the barrier of race to the distance that ordinarily exists between merchant and customer. Furthermore, ghetto residents are poor; thus merchandizing has to be tailored to fit low household budgets. Customers have to carefully spend their funds to their best advantage. At the same time, the physical plants of commercial buildings in older residential areas are not built to accommodate modern retail practices; hence overhead costs tend to be larger. For a variety of reasons, ghetto areas are high crime rate districts, and retail merchants are prime targets for robbery and burglary as well as pilfering and shoplifting, which add to overhead costs. Ghetto customers, in turn, may well resent the precautions taken by merchants to protect their goods—the heavy iron shutters and gates put up at night, the constant surveillance of customers by salesmen, and the suspicion directed at customers who are "just looking around."

For these and other good reasons we can anticipate that the relationships between ghetto merchants and their customers are at best uneasy and at worst verging on hostility. The retail market is not a trivial part of urban systems; hence this interface between ghettos and the larger community deserves some attention. Indeed, it is hardly an accident that the main targets of the civil disorders of the sixties were retail stores.

Therefore the attention paid to ghetto merchants in this chapter is justified. We develop a composite sociological portrait of the ghetto merchant by describing the merchants' views of doing business in the ghetto, probing into residents' reactions to merchant behavior, and finally looking at patterns of destructive activity directed toward merchants in "normal" times and under the conditions of civil disorder. We also consider the circumstances under which alleged ghetto merchant exploitation becomes an issue in race relations.

The Data. In each of the fifteen cities, thirty retail merchants whose stores were located in areas populated by blacks were selected by sampling procedures to represent within each city the typical spread of types of retail stores in residential neighborhoods. The person who was in day-to-day charge of retail practice in each store was interviewed. In most cases, this person was also the owner of the store.

The interview schedule used is reproduced in Appendix A. In addition to the questions asked of all the six types of institutional agents, the central section of the questionnaire was concerned with the merchants' views of his retail practices, the problems he saw in doing business in the ghetto, his appraisal of his customers, and his experiences with vandalism, pilfering, and looting. Thus this section of the questionnaire provides most of the basic data for this chapter.

A special effort was made in the sampling of retail establishments to obtain stores run and/or owned by blacks. A quota of one-fourth black respondents was set in each city. The effect of this quota is to over-represent black merchants in our sample, since according to our best estimates blacks compose much less than one in four of the ghetto merchants. Hence for measures related to race, our sample as a whole is more liberal toward blacks than would be a sample more representative with respect to race.

The types of stores sampled in our survey are shown in Table 7.1. It is, of course, no accident that the distribution among types resembles that to be found typically in residential neighborhoods: Groceries and supermarkets, hard and soft good stores, restaurants, and bars and barber (or beauty) shops make up more than half of the stores in the sample. We see later that, in general, the stores are small and do not have large gross incomes.

In Table 7.1 most striking are the differences between stores managed by whites and stores managed by blacks. Personal services—restaurants and barber or beauty shops—make up almost half of the black-managed stores (as compared to 20% of the white manager stores). Black managed stores are therefore smaller, more likely to be managed by a woman

TABLE 7.1

Merchants)   Distribution of Kind of Store by Race*
Interviews)

	Stores Owned or Managed by		
	Whites	Blacks	Total
Small Grocery	4.7%	9.1%	5.9%
Supermarket	5.3	2.5	4.6
Hard Goods Store	16.0	2.5	12.4
Soft Goods Store	10.7	11.6	10.9
Restaurant, Bar, Snack Shop	8.0	22.3	11.8
Jewelry Store	4.2	.8	3.3
Liquor Store	6.2	1.7	5.0
Car Dealer	4.5	0	3.3
Drug Store	3.9	.8	4.1
Novelty Store	5.3	.8	3.1
Discount, Department Store	8.3	9.9	8.7
Cigar/Newspaper Store	4.7	0	3.5
Cleaning, Pressing, Laundry	4.5	11.6	6.3
Pawn Shop	6.8	0	5.0
Gas Station	4.5	0	3.5
Barber Shop, Beauty Shop	2.4	25.6	8.5
100% =	(337)	(121)	(458)

*Since sampling was done with quotas set for kind of store, this table reflects sampling quotas, not findings.

(beauty shops contribute heavily to this sex ratio).

Who are the Merchants? The overwhelming majority of retail store merchants located in the ghetto are white, as we have indicated before. Our sample overestimates the proportion black in this group deliberately to make comparisons between the two races. The other characteristics of merchants,[1] however, are not artifacts of the sampling procedures employed and deserve some comment.

The salient socioeconomic characteristics of the ghetto merchants are shown in Table 7.2.

The majority (60%) of the merchants were migrants to the cities in which they were doing business. This proportion is considerably higher than the general proportion of migrants to be found in the same cities (40%).[2] Furthermore, merchants were much more likely than the general population to have been foreign born (14% as compared with 7% for the general population).[3]

Although the merchants are fairly well to do (see below), their educational attainment is not very high. Over one-fourth have had less than a high school education. Well over half have no more than high school education. Yet, overall, the ghetto retail merchant appears to be better educated than the population of the city that he serves. According to the 1970 census, 52% of adults over 25 years of age in Standard Metropolitan Statistical Areas over 1,000,000 in population had less than a high school diploma.

Being a ghetto merchant is not a young man or young woman's occupation. The merchant's median age falls approximately at 50 years, with slight skewing toward the younger end of the continuum. The age range spanned by merchants is very large: A few of the merchants are well above the usual retirement age of 65, and a few are below 21. On the average, however, the ghetto merchant is past the prime of middle age.

Compared to the general population of their cities, merchants are quite different in their religious preferences; 38% are Jewish, 36% Protestant, and 23% Catholic.[4] Jews appear to be far more concentrated in ghetto

---

[1] For convenience in this volume we refer to the manager-respondents as "merchants," even though some of the respondents are only the salaried managers of stores owned by others.

[2] Angus Campbell and Howard Schuman "Racial Attitudes in Fifteen American Cities," *Supplemental Studies for the National Advisory Commission on Civil Disorders*, U. S. Government Printing Office, July 1968.

[3] Campbell and Schuman, *ibid.*, report that 6% of the population in the fifteen cities were foreign born. The 1960 census data for all SMSA's estimates 7%.

[4] This finding is consistent with Herbert Gans' extrapolation from Naomi Levine's work, which shows the percentage of Harlem stores owned by Jews to be about 40%; it is a bit lower than Raines' estimate of the percentage of Jews from a sample of merchants in the Watts area of Los Angeles. Campbell and Schuman found that 60% of the population of the fifteen cities then surveyed were Protestant, 30% Catholic, and 5% Jewish. See also Herbert J. Gans, "Negro-Jewish Conflict in New York City," *Mainstream*, 4 (March 1969); Walter J. Raine, *Los Angeles Riot Study: The Ghetto Merchant Survey*, Clearinghouse, U. S. Department of Commerce, 1967.

TABLE 7.2

Merchant   ) Selected Socio-Economic Characteristics
Interviews) of Merchants
             (N = 458)

A. Origin

Born in City	Born Elsewhere in U.S.	Foreign Born
% 39.5	46.1	14.4

B. Educational Attainment

Less than High School Diploma	High School Diploma	Some College or Better	N.A.
% 26.2	32.3	41.5	.2

C. Age

Median = 50 years

D. Religion

Protestant	Catholic	Jewish
% 36.0	22.9	37.9

E. Total Family Income before Taxes

Less than $5,000	$5,000-9,999	$10,000-15,000	Above $15,000	N.A.
% 9.4	28.6	22.1	21.8	18.1

F. Race*

White	Black
73.5	26.5

*Sampling Artifact

businesses than in the general population. There are several reasons for this phenomenon. First, Jews are statistically overrepresented among retail merchants, especially older and first generation Jews, who found individual entrepreneurship one of the few means to economic advancement in a period when anti-Semitism was widespread in American society. Second, in many large cities, blacks replaced Jews in the expansion of the post World War II ghetto. Thus the heavily ghettoized areas of Brooklyn up to 20 years ago were areas in which working class Jews had made their homes. Some innercity Jewish merchants, particularly the elderly ones, run stores patronized once by Jewish clientele but now cater to their residential successors—blacks.

As one might expect, few ghetto merchants are starving; they report a median family income before taxes of $10,200. Approximately one out of five report earnings above $15,000 per year. (About 18% refused to reveal their incomes, a rate of nonresponse, which is not especially high for questions of this nature in surveys.)

The composite ghetto merchant's background may be summarized as follows: They are, by and large, middle-aged people with more income and slightly more education than the general population in their cities. In addition, they are more likely to be Jewish and to have come from foreign countries.

Of course, one may anticipate that white merchants and black merchants would be different in crucial respects. We have already seen (Table 7.1) that as merchants they run different kinds of stores.

One of the most striking differences between white and black ghetto merchants is their gender. Eighty-seven percent of white merchants are male, while only 58% of black merchants belong to this "majority group." Almost equally striking are differences in origin between white and black merchants.

As noted earlier, merchants in the aggregate were more likely to have been born outside their present city location than the general population in the fifteen cities. From Table 7.3 we can see that this difference is due almost entirely to the geographic mobility of black merchants. Eighty percent of black merchants were not born in the city in which they were doing business, while only 58% of white merchants were in-migrants. Moreover, two-thirds of black merchants came to their city from the South, compared to only 5% of white merchants.

Black merchants are slightly younger, on the average, than are white merchants; thus part of the contrast in migration patterns could stem from the age-selectivity of migration. Migration also is known to be selective for education, but this factor clearly does not account for the greater geographic mobility of black merchants.

White merchants are considerably better educated than black merchants, a difference which is especially marked in the "less than high school diploma" category. Twenty-three percent of white merchants, as compared with 36% of black merchants, failed to finish high school. (The 36% for black merchants, however, is a good deal below the 52% of the general population over 25 years of age in SMSA's over 1,000,000 in population who had less than a high school education in 1970.)

Another cultural contrast between white and black merchants is their religious affiliation. About one-half (51%) of white merchants are Jewish. One-fourth are Protestant, and about one in five (19%) is Catholic. One black merchant in the sample is Jewish; 83% are Protestant, and the remainder are Catholic.

White merchants in the ghetto find business a good deal more profitable than black merchants. Nearly twice as many white merchants earn more than $15,000 per year, and almost three times as many black merchants earn less than $5000 per year. The median income for white merchants is around $10,700. For black merchants, the median falls at

TABLE 7.3

Merchant) Selected Socio-economic Characteristics
Interviews) of Merchants by Race

A. Sex

	White (N= 337)	Black (N=121)
Male	86.6%	57.9%
Female	13.4	42.1

B. Origin

Born in City	42.0%	20.0%
Born in South	5.4	64.5
Born Elsewhere	52.6	15.5

C. Educational Attainment

Less than High School Diploma	22.6%	36.4%
High School Diploma	31.8	33.1
Some College or Better	45.1	30.6
N.A.	.6	--

D. Age

Median =	58.5 years	44.5 years

E. Religion

Protestant	18.7%	83.4%
Catholic	27.0	11.6
Jewish	51.3	.8

F. Total Family Income Before Taxes

Less than $5,000	6.6%	19.0%
5,000-9,999	26.7	29.7
10,000-15,000	26.1	18.2
15,000 and above	24.9	13.2
N.A.	14.5	19.8

$7700. The 1970 census figures for central cities show median family income for whites at $10,200, and $6800 for blacks. Allowing for inflation since 1968, white merchants in the ghetto do better than the general population in large cities. Black ghetto merchants do not do quite as well as the general population, but a good deal better than their black "brothers and sisters" in other occupations in large urban areas.

Black and white ghetto merchants are almost equally likely to own their own homes, 74% and 67% of white and black merchants, respectively.[5]

In general, a comparison of the background characteristics of black and white merchants shows the following. Black merchants are more likely to be women and less likely to be native to their present city. They represent a more geographically mobile population. The white merchants are older and better educated, and they have a higher income. Though the black merchant falls below the white merchant on most measures of socioeconomic status, he is still quite a bit above the general population of blacks. The black merchants have more education, higher incomes, and a far greater probability of owning their own homes. Both census data and the Michigan findings support this class gap between the black merchant and the general black city population.

Based upon background characteristics, it is difficult to anticipate how the black merchant may be viewed in the ghetto. On one hand, he or she could be seen as an example of a black man or woman who is "making it," and thus evoke respect from black neighbors. On the other hand, a black merchant could be seen as a person trying to place himself or herself above, or, even worse, as an exploiter of, his people. Such an evaluation could make the black merchant a target of hostility, rather than an object of respect.[6] It is likely that the black community sees the black merchant with a mixture of both attitudes and thus may not be especially more sympathetic to the black merchant than to the white merchant.

Some support for a lack of preference for black merchants over white merchants by the black population can be found in the Michigan sample survey data. The vast majority of black ghetto residents (60 to 70%) feel that there is "not much difference" between the treatment they get from white and black merchants with respect to being overcharged for goods and being treated with disrespect.[7] On another question, "How about stores in this neighborhood—do you think they should be owned and run by Negroes, or that race should not make any difference?" 80%

---

[5] The similarity in these proportions contrasts sharply with results of the Campbell-Schuman, *ibid.*, survey of the general populations in the same fifteen cities. They found that 58% of whites and 35% of blacks either owned or were buying their places of residences.

[6] Clark notes this kind of hostility reaction to "indigenous leaders" who became part of the Community Action Programs of Office of Economic Opportunity (OEO). Their credibility in the community decreased as soon as they were seen as starting to "make it." See Kenneth B. Clark and Jeannette Hopkins, *A Relevant War Against Poverty*, Harper and Row, New York, 1968.

[7] Angus Campbell and Howard Schuman, *ibid.*

say it makes no difference. Yet the positive side of the ambivalence toward black merchants appears also, for on a question asked about patronizing black-owned stores wherever possible, 70% agree. In short, the Michigan survey data suggest that white and black merchants are seen as very much alike by the ghetto community in the way they treat customers. However, all things being equal, ghetto residents would rather patronize black shops.

Doing Business in the Ghetto.   Our respondents were selected because they were the active managers of retail enterprises. Managing a retail store in the ghetto, however, is not a role that takes one out of contact with ghetto residents. Of the respondents 95% also personally wait upon customers. Indeed, this finding probably mainly reflects the fact that most of the businesses involved are small enterprises with few employees. Managing a small retail enterprise does not involve much in the way of employee supervision or elaborate paperwork.

Small size is indicated in the median number of employees—3.4 (the range is from zero to over a hundred). Fifteen percent have one employee or less, and a third have less than two employees. These findings are also quite consistent with the average gross income (total amount of business per year) of approximately 94,000 dollars.[8] Thus it seems reasonable to conclude that, although most of the stores generally are not "Mom and Pop" operations, the businesses sampled are on the whole quite small.

As we saw in Table 7.1 black and white managers are handling quite different sorts of retail enterprises. Blacks are overrepresented in smaller businesses specializing in personal services (e.g., barber shops) and/or those businesses that generally need less initial capital (and credit) to get started (e.g., snack shops). The need for a college degree in some businesses, as in the case of pharmacies, may also be a limiting factor for blacks. The most salient exception to this general hypothesis is found in the proportions of blacks that run cigar stores and newspaper stands. There is no ready answer for this exception.

Other data also suggest that blacks run smaller businesses than whites. The median number of employees in black stores is just under three, while the median number of employees for white stores is a little over four. When we consider the gross store incomes, it becomes even more obvious that blacks do indeed run smaller operations. The average gross

---

[8] Under solvent circumstances, about 10% of the gross income actually winds up in the business owner's pocket. This seems to be the general rule of thumb for small retail business.

income for white stores is approximately 111,000 dollars, compared to approximately 45,000 dollars for black managed stores.[9] This does not mean that whites automatically have a larger income, because, obviously, the costs of running a larger business is greater, but at least a large income is possible. In any case, this differential volume of business seems consistent with the finding that 18.2% of the blacks, as compared to 13.4% of the whites, said they find it very difficult to stay in business.[10]

What Merchants Do: Behavioral Measures.   The ghetto merchants in our sample deal primarily with black customers. Seventy-six percent of the merchants have clientele that are 50% or more black; 25% have clientele that are 94% or more black. (Some of the stores located in the ghetto serve a citywide clientele, as in the case of certain types of specialty stores or gas stations on main thoroughfares.)

The shopkeepers offer their customers a variety of services, besides the goods normally sold in the store. Sixty-five percent often give to local charities, 32% often give advice on personal problems, and 22% often cash payroll checks. Thus many of the merchants appear to be running relatively unbureaucratic, informal, and perhaps even friendly neighborhood stores.

Somewhat surprisingly, credit and interest on credit seem to play a relatively small role in the business operations of the stores in our sample. Only 41% extend any credit at all and only 12% (or about three in ten of those extending credit) charge for this service. This small percentage may be partly a function of the kind of stores in our sample, a large portion of which (e.g., newspaper stores, beauty shops, and supermarkets) do not normally extend credit. Of those who do charge interest on the credit, the median interest is a little over 1% a month. Unfortunately, we did not ascertain if this interest is on the total amount bought or on the unpaid balance. Yet, in either case, the rate, although high, is not at all unusual.

The two paragraphs above suggest that, at least some of the information provided by the ghetto merchant, many of the customers appear to be receiving a number of useful services from their neighborhood store. Furthermore, the fact that approximately 70% of the merchants claim that some of their customers are personal friends could indicate that the providing of "extra services" is not motivated solely by a cynical

---

[9] T-test was significant with $p < .001$. A large percentage (18%) failed to respond, however.
[10] This difference is not significant.

quest for profit.[11] Of those naming a specific number of customers that are personal friends, the median comes to 25.2 people. Some merchants, approximately 10%, say that *all* of their customers are their personal friends.

The friendships that many shopkeepers claim exist between many merchants and their customers have apparently developed largely during working hours. Only 24.9% of the merchants sampled live in the neighborhoods where they work. (The median distance from the place of work to the place of residence for those not living where they work is between 9 and 10 miles.) However, there has been a good bit of time for such relationships could develop, because the median time that our sample of businesses have been in operation in the same neighborhoods is between 10 and 11 years.[12]

Merchant-Community Relations.   On the retail level, selling is not merely a matter of buying goods wholesale, displaying them in a convenient location, and waiting for customers to come through the door. Some types of retail merchandising involve personal contacts between merchant and buyer (perhaps most obvious in the case of barber and beauty shops), but such personal contacts are also involved in dispensing drugs (and sometimes medical advice), selling clothes (and sometimes profering fashion advice), or even selling cars. A merchant may offer more than goods to his customers, accommodating to more than their consumption needs.

We can expect that the social characteristics of a merchant have some bearing on the kinds of relationships that he can build with his customers. For example, black merchants are more intimately involved generally

---

[11] We examine this issue in detail later.

[12] This distribution was heavily skewed toward the longer end, with 10% in business a year or less, and is quite consistent with a series of findings on the mortality experiences of ghetto business published in *The Impact of Urban Renewal on Small Business* by Brian J. L. Berry, Sandra J. Parsons, and Rutherford H. Platt, Center for Urban Studies, University of Chicago, 1968. Considering data involving only the most recent information, 1963–1965, the percentages of new businesses per year in their sample (in our data this would show up as those in business a year or less) ran from 10.3 to 15.6%. The fact that the 10% in our merchant sample is slightly below the bottom of the Berry distribution may be due to two factors. First, the kinds of areas from which the two studies drew their samples may not be exactly the same, our sample being from more run down neighborhoods. Second, our sample was drawn 2 years after the most recent data in the Berry sample, and the desirability of locating a business in ghetto neighborhoods may have gone down still further due to the riots and other urban problems. Thus there would be fewer new businesses in our sample.

with the black community than are white merchants. Although they have been in business in the community a far shorter period of time (median for blacks is just under 6 years, and for whites, just under 15 years), black merchants are far more likely to live in the neighborhood in which they work, 55 to 14%.[13] The median of 6 years in business for the black merchants is enough time to estabilsh personal relationships. Furthermore, black merchants are more likely to have a higher percentage of black clientele. Sixty-seven percent of the black merchants have a clientele that is over 94% black, white only 25% of the white merchants have a clientele that is over 94% black. Black merchants are also more likely to see customers as personal friends. Seventy-eight percent of the black merchants have customers that they would consider personal friends, while 10% less of the white merchants feel this way.[14] In another indication of involvement in the black community, 34% of the white merchants have no black employees as compared to only 6% of the black merchants who have no black employees.

One way in which some merchants can relate to their customers above and beyond buying and selling is by offering and performing special service for their customers. Some merchants act as bankers—cashing payroll, welfare, and personal checks for their customers. Others offer advice on personal problems. Some merchants can be more generous in extending credit than is ordinarily the case. Any merchant can make a contribution to local churches and to local charitable causes. At least some of the ghetto merchants engage in one or more of these practices, as Table 7.4 indicates.

One in five merchants often cashes checks for his customers. One in four helps his customers "fill out forms," ranging from income tax returns to employment applications. Fewer extend credit generously than one might have anticipated, but a heavy majority—two out of three—often make contributions to charity.

One might anticipate that black merchants and white merchants would differ considerably in the extent to which they proffered such services. Indeed, such is the case, as Table 7.4 indicates. Yet, black merchants are not necessarily more friendly and helpful to their customers than whites: For example, they are less likely to cash checks for their customers. In part, the effect of race upon these services is concealed, because black merchants and white merchants are running different types of stores.

Table 7.5 indicates that the offering of extra services varies by type of store. Supermarkets and grocery stores are likely to offer check cashing

---

[13] Chi square significant at <.001 level.
[14] Chi square significant at <.05 level.

TABLE 7.4

| Merchant   ) | Special Services Offered to Customers |
| Interviews) | by Ghetto Merchants: [N= 458] |

Special Service Offered to Customers		Frequency of Offering Services			
		Often	Sometimes	Never	DK,NA
Cash Payroll Checks	Total	22%	29	48	#
	Whites*	27	27	46	#
	Blacks*	10	34	54	2
Help Fill Out Forms	Total	24	31	45	#
	Whites	26	31	42	#
	Blacks	18	30	50	2
Extend Credit to People Other Stores Wouldn't Help	Total	12	21	66	1
	Whites*	11	18	70	1
	Blacks*	12	21	66	2
Contribute to Local Charities and Churches	Total	64	31	5	1
	Whites	62	33	5	1
	Blacks	69	25	4	2

N for Blacks = [121]

N for Whites = [337]

*Chi Square significant at .01 level for black-white differences.

= less than 1%.

services, but cigar stores and beauty shops are not. Since few blacks are running supermarkets but many are running beauty shops, black–white comparisons are confounded with store type.

Of course, we can expect that race is not the only personal characteristic of merchants which might lead them to offer more or less in the way of extra services. Older merchants may be more conservative in their credit practices, and better educated merchants may be more likely to give advice. The consideration of such background variables as age

TABLE 7.5

Merchant)   Special Services Offered to Customers
Interviews)   by Type of Store

Services Offered to Customers Often or Sometimes*

Type of Store	Checks Cashed	Applications Filled	Credit	Contributions to Charity	Advice on Personal Problems	Average for all Services	100%
Grocery	63	63	44	96	82	70	(27)
Supermarket	90	67	14	90	57	64	(21)
Hard Goods	53	65	46	93	63	64	(57)
Soft Goods	61	46	26	98	61	58	(50)
Rest/bar	46	44	28	100	61	56	(54)
Jewelry	60	67	46	87	73	67	(15)
Liquor	57	57	17	96	61	57	(23)
Car Dealer	47	80	47	93	67	67	(15)
Drug	86	63	47	100	100	79	(19)
Novelty	29	57	14	93	64	52	(14)
Variety/Dept. Store	48	65	36	100	67	63	(40)
Cigar	12	31	25	80	67	43	(16)
Cleaning	43	46	36	100	46	54	(29)
Pawnshop	83	65	17	96	74	67	(23)
Gas Stations	25	56	25	94	56	51	(16)
Barber/Beauty Shop	21	36	43	92	23	46	(39)

*Entries in this table are percentages who "often" or "sometimes" offer the services in question to their customers.

and educational attainment could conceivably affect the offering of services, and these need to be considered along with and apart from "race." Furthermore, "type of store" *per se* offers little in explanatory value. This variable would be far more useful if it were broken down into some underlying dimensions (e.g., cost of items for sale in the store) of more substantive interest. These and other considerations led to a series of regression analyses.

To begin with, the problem was broken into two parts. First, an analysis was done to determine how much of the variance in special services offered was "explained" by background characteristics of each merchant, and how much was "explained" by the type of store in which the merchant was located. "Kind of store" was a dummy variable, and the race, religion, education, and age background variables. The dependent variable in each run was one of the special services asked about in the questionnaire. The results are shown in Table 7.6.

Several tendencies can be discerned in Table 7.6. Store type is roughly twice as useful as merchant background characteristics in "explaining" the variation in the propensity to offer special services. The range of the ratio of background variable variance to store type variance runs from about one to one for the last item on the table, "giving advice on personal problems," to about one to three for the first item on the table, "cashing payroll checks." This pattern suggests that certain types of services are more closely tied to the nature of the business than others. Possibly the more closely a service is related to the actual running of a business, the more important is type of store as a variable. Background variables seem to have about the same size of impact regardless of the service involved.

The impacts of the joint contributions of background and store types are generally smaller than the impacts of each block of variables considered alone. In the table the primary purpose of these variances is to show that relatively little of the explained variance should be allocated jointly to the overlap between the two blocks of independent variables, and that reasonable interpretations of the impacts of background and store type can be made by looking at their "unique" covariation with the dependent variable.

Finally, the last column in the table indicates that the F-ratios for the multiple R's are all statistically significant. This is especially impressive, since type of store was entered as a dummy variable. The mean square in the numerator of the F-ratio was considerably reduced by the necessity of using what is conceptually one variable (store type) in the regression equations as fifteen dummy variables.

"Type of store" as a dummy variable is scarcely a useful variable. Ideally one would prefer to measure store impact through a few underlying dimensions. We chose two such variables—the value of items of merchandise sold in the store and the frequency with which customers need the store's goods. For example, the value of merchandise in an

TABLE 7.6

Merchant) Regression Analysis of "Special Services"
Interviews) Offered by Ghetto Merchants: [N= 458]

Amount of Variance in Special
Service Uniquely Explained by

Special Services Offered	Merchants' Background*	Type of Store	Jointly by Background and Store Type	Total Variance Explained
Cash payroll checks	.0465*	.1292*	.0588	.2345*
Help fill out forms and applications	.0463*	.0648*	.0312	.1425*
Extend credit to people others wouldn't help	.0341*	.0694*	.0093	.1128*
Make contributions to local churches and charities	.0175	.0437	.0108	.0720*
Give advice on personal problems	.0495*	.0440	.0172	.1071*

*F ratio statistically significant at <.05 level.

*Background consists of race, religion, education and age. The race of each
merchant was entered as either black or white, with "other" (four cases)
coded as black. Religion was entered as a dummy variable for each case,
either Protestant, Catholic, or Jewish. Education was entered with five
values: 1 for "less than high school", 2 for "high school graduate",
3 for "some college", 4 for "college graduate", and 5 for "professional or
graduate school". "Age" was entered as the year in which the respondent
was born. Merchants born before 1900 were coded as being born in 1900.

The dependent variable was entered with a 1 for "never" offering the service,
a 2 for "sometimes" offering the service, and a 3 for "often" offering the
service. The determination of how much variance could be attributed to
background alone, store type alone and that which could be attributed jointly
to both background and store type required three runs for each service.
The first run included both blocks of variables. The second run dropped
all of the biographical variables. And the third run replaced the background variables and dropped the store type variables. This three part
regression process is simply a version of analysis of covariance.

appliance store is high, but the frequency with which the store is patronized is low. In contrast, the average value of items in a grocery store is
low, but the frequency of shopping there is high.

Unfortunately, direct information on the value of goods and the frequency of use of the different types of stores was not directly available.
We were forced to construct measures with the limited data on hand.

To obtain a measure of the "average price" of merchandise offered in each store type, members of the research staff (four in all) independently rated each type of store on a scale of 0 to 9 according to his/her perception of the "average" price of merchandise typically sold in that store type. A high rating (9) indicated a high "average" price. The mean of the four resulting ratings was then used as the variable "Price" to be substituted for type of store. For example, car dealers were given a mean rating close to 9.[15]

The second dimension was the frequency of use by customers ("Traffic"). As with price, four raters independently rated each store type, and the mean rating was then substituted for kind of store. High ratings indicated a high amount of traffic. For example, supermarkets rated very high.[16] The dependent variables were the same as in the earlier part of the analysis—the propensity of merchants to offer various kinds of special services. One regression equation was run for each service. The results can be seen on Table 7.7.

The first five variables across the top of the table are the variables that were aggregated and analyzed for the impact of background in the paragraphs above. In other words, the effect of background, as discussed earlier, is the effect of all five of these variables as a block. This is in contrast to the last two variables in the tables, "Traffic" and "Price," which are two new variables that were introduced as *replacements* for kind of store when this more detailed data analysis (Table 7.6) was conceptualized. Thus while the first five variables in the aggregate are the whole of the effect of background, "Traffic" and "Price" explain only part of the effect of store type. In short, many effects of store type are not subsumed under "Traffic" and "Price." It is important for the reader to keep this in mind when looking at Table 7.7, because, in that table the effect of background variable is overestimated.

Up to this point we have not looked beneath the superficial labels applied to the extra services offered by merchants. Obviously, the services we have described could be more fundamentally conceptualized in a variety of different ways. Since we have no data in which our respondents explained motives for offering a given service, we can only suggest one of several possible schemes. Probably the simplest, most

---

[15] The four raters were all researchers working on this project. "Price" was conceived as "the average price of merchandise in the store." Interrater correlations were each above .85.

[16] The four raters for "traffic" were the same as for "price." The variable was conceived as the "probability that a given individual would use a particular kind of store in a given period of time." Once again interrater correlations were quite high (above .65) though not as high as for "price."

TABLE 7.7

Merchant) Merchants' Offerings of Special Services to Customers as Explained
Interviews) by Background Factors and Store Variables

Proportions of Variance in Special Services Uniquely Explained by

| | | Background Factors | | | | | Store Variables | |
		Age	Catholic	Jew	Education	Black	Traffic	Price
Cash Payroll Checks	Unique Variance	(+).001**	(+).001	(+).010	(+).024	(+).0003	(+).012	(+).006
	F ratio	0.51	0.57	5.41*	13.84*	0.17	6.26*	3.05
Help Fill Out Forms and Applications	Unique Variance	(-).002	(+).004	(+).009	(-).033	(+).004	(+).002	(+).021
	F ratio	1.07	1.78	4.98*	16.62*	2.19	0.95	10.46**
Extend Credit to People Others Wouldn't Help	Unique Variance	(+).000	(+).001	(+).003	(-).013	(+).019	(+).002	(+).015
	F ratio	0.19	0.29	1.38	6.49*	9.14*	1.10	7.23*
Contribute to Local Churches & Charities	Unique Variance	(-).003	(+).005	(+).011	(+).0003	(+).005	(+).015	(+).016
	F ratio	1.31	2.35	5.16*	0.14	2.36	7.17*	8.08*
Give Advice on Personal Problems	Unique Variance	(+).0001	(+).004	(+).013	(+).008	(+).035	(-).0005	(-).001
	F ratio	0.49	1.22	6.10*	3.66	17.29*	0.24	0.58

N=458

*Statistically significant $\leq$ .05 level.

**Signs in parentheses are the signs of the beta coefficients.

useful way to view special services is by the degree to which they are linked to immediate financial gain. For example, since cashing payroll checks is often contingent on making a purchase, this service can quickly lead to a sale. In contrast, giving personal advice does not directly or immediately increase profits, although fostering good will between customers and merchants may in the long run increase a store's volume. More idealistically, giving personal advice may not be motivated by profit at all, but simply by good will.

In Table 7.7 the special services are ranked by their likely short-run impact on sales. For the reasons just described, cashing checks heads the list. Next is helping customers fill out forms and applications. Although sometimes merchants may profit little from such assistance, at other times sales may be contingent on filling out forms (e.g., in pawn shops, for car dealers, and any time credit is formally extended). Extending credit to people whom others would not help may lead directly to sales, but altruism may be largely a factor. This service is placed in the middle of the table, because of the "good guy" motive of the service than its impact on sales being any less direct than service ranked above it. Actually, it is probably safer to group the top three services in one category called perhaps "sale inducements." The final two services of giving to churches and charities and giving personal advice seem clearly different from the first three services. If there are direct immediate links to sales, we fail to see them.

With the issues of "profit" to "altruism" in mind, we can begin summarizing from the unique effects of background variables by noting from Table 7.7 that being black makes the merchant a bit more likely to offer altruistic services. In contrast, greater education encourages the offering of sales-oriented services. Being Jewish seems to combine the effects of race and education, but is a smaller effect in absolute size. "Being Catholic" shows a pattern somewhat similar to that of "being Jewish," but the variance partitions are probably too small to have any effect. Age appears to have no impact.

The effects of the two store type variables, "Traffic" and "Price," generally have a small positive relationship to the propensity to offer special services. For the variable "Traffic," two unique contributions stand out. Stores characterized by high Traffic (e.g., supermarkets) tend to cash payroll checks and to contribute to local churches and charities.

The impacts of "Price" are in the same direction and generally greater than the "Traffic" impact on services. Stores with higher priced merchandise are more likely to extend credit, help customers fill out forms, and contribute to local churches and charities than are stores that offer cheaper products and services. Both store-type variables somewhat increase the likelihood that all services (with the exception of the most altruistic "giving advice on personal problems") would be offered. Furthermore, the total effect of store type (with store entered as a dummy variable) accounts for much more of the variance in the types of services offered than do background characteristics of merchants.[17]

Merchandising Practices. One of the major reasons for choosing retail merchants as one of the six groups of institutional agents was that exploitation by retail merchants was (and still is) a common complaint voiced by black leaders. It is alleged that ghetto merchants charge higher prices, sell shoddier goods, charge higher interest rates on credit purchases, and treat their customers with less than usual courtesy and civility. In some ideal world, where one has all the time and resources necessary at his command, he can comparison shop to contrast ghetto stores and stores located in other neighborhoods. It might also have been feasible to observe how customers were treated by salespeople and whether high-pressure sales tactics, for example, were more frequently employed by ghetto merchants.

Unfortunately, we were not in an ideal world: It was necessary to rely upon the merchants themselves for information about their merchandising practices. Direct items on questionable merchandising practices seemed out of the question: We did not think that the merchants would give us frank and candid answers, and we are also afraid that such questioning might be offensive. As a consequence, we relied on indirect indicators of questionable practices.

---

[17] It is important to keep in mind, in the discussion above of "Traffic" and "Price," that these two variables account for only a part of the variance "explained" by type of store entered as a series of dummy variables. Certain potentially interesting effects that cannot be subsumed by "Traffic" and "Price" are lost in the analysis. For example, merchants in drug stores show a strong tendency to give advice on personal problems. This effect probably has to do with the nature of the dispensing of medicine and the kinds of discussions that emerge during such sales. However, the unique characteristics of drug stores that encourage such conversations are not subsumed under "Traffic" or "Price" and are lost. Fortunately (for the sake of parsimony), the unique effects of each store not covered by "Traffic" and "Price," although fairly frequent in occurrence, are relatively small when compared to the effects of other kinds of variables. Thus it was decided not to delve into what would be a long and tedious analysis by each kind of store. In short, even though a lot of "explained" variance was thrown away when it was decided to examine the effects of kind of store through two variables rather than sixteen dummy variables, when this total amount of discarded variance is partitioned into components for each kind of store, the unique effects of each kind of store are quite small and hardly worth examining.

The indirect nature of the data presented here should not be considered sufficient reason to dismiss the analysis as trivial. We measure attitudes and business practices that undergird such controversial issues as overcharging, selling inferior goods, and disrespectful behavior toward black clients. Thus if we find that merchants show little understanding of the socioeconomic position of their ghetto customers, we can infer that their behavior toward individual customers are going to show, however indirectly, a lack of empathic understanding. Similarly, although we are not able to discuss in a direct way the extent to which larger markups are used in ghetto stores, we do ask merchants whether such practices make sense for businesses in the ghetto, measuring at the least the support of such practices among ghetto merchants.

The analysis of this section ranges over a wide set of attitudes and practices. Our net is spread wide, because we want to show the extent to which the general stance of ghetto merchants is consistent in a number of subareas. Thus we see that merchants appraisals of the general position of blacks in their cities is also reflected in their attitudes toward blacks as customers.

It is abundantly clear in Table 7.8 that black ghetto merchants are more aware of ghetto problems than are white ghetto merchants. Averaged across the seven "opportunity" areas listed in Table 7.8, a mean of 28% of the white merchants feel that blacks are less well off, while for the black ghetto merchants 61%. For each of the questions in this "awareness" series, the difference is in the same direction (whites less aware), and every chi square is significant beyond the .001 level. The largest gap appears on the question about treatment by public officials. Here only 9% of the whites feel blacks are worse off, while 53% of the blacks feel this way. A fairly large group of white merchants actually see blacks as better off in this respect. In other words, large groups of both black and white merchants lack confidence that their group is treated fairly by their public officials.

Cross-tabulations of "awareness" by kind of store yielded inconclusive results. One primary problem is that, since race is so salient a factor and race and type of store are correlated, the store effects (if any) are confounded.

A more sophisticated analysis is called for. A regression analysis for each item in the series of questions on awareness of black opportunities is presented in Table 7.9, in which the unique effects of a block of background variables and a block of store variables, as well as the "joint" or overlapping effects of both blocks, are shown.

It is immediately apparent that background variables are far more effective as predictors of awareness than store type. In every problem

TABLE 7.8

Merchant   )   Merchants' Views of Relative Standings
Interviews)   of Whites and Blacks in their Cities

Percentages Who Say Negroes are....

Standing with Respect to		Less Well off	As Well off	Better off	Don't Know	Difference (Black-White) Saying Less Well Off
Educational Opportunities*	Whites	27%	59	10	3	33.0
	Blacks	60	31	7	2	
Employment Opportunities*	Whites	41	43	13	3	31.2
	Blacks	72	20	5	3	
Treatment by Police*	Whites	17	52	19	12	42.3
	Blacks	60	28	3	9	
Housing*	Whites	59	31	6	4	22.2
	Blacks	81	13	4	1	
Treatment by Public Officials *	Whites	9	52	25	13	50.7
	Blacks	53	38	0	9	
Medical Care*	Whites	12	57	25	6	22.0
	Blacks	34	53	4	9	
Recreation Opportunities*	Whites	30	52	11	7	38.9
	Blacks	67	25	5	2	

N for Whites = 337
N for Blacks = 121

*Chi square p <.001.

area, the effects of background variables reach statistical significance while none of the store variables do. The joint effects of the two blocks also tend to be very small. The ratios of the unique contributions of background variables to store-type variables ranges from a low of about two to one to a high of about fifteen to one. These findings contrast sharply with Table 7.6 on "special services," where store-type variables were far more effective as predictors than background variables. Table 7.9 also suggests that the closer the behavior (or attitude) is related to the actual running of a business, the more salient store-type variables are in the analysis.

The blocks of variables in Table 7.9 are broken into their main com-

TABLE 7.9

Merchant) Interviews) Merchants' Awareness** of Problems Faced by Blacks in their Cities: Regression Analysis (N = 458)

Problem Area	Proportions of Total Variance in Awareness of Problem Explained Uniquely by			Proportion of Total Variance Explained
	Background of Merchants	Store Characteristic	Jointly by Both	
Educational Opportunities	.0716*	.0271	.0075	.1062*
Employment Opportunities	.0785*	.0134	.0101	.1020*
Treatment by Police	.1535*	.0185	.0331	.2051*
Housing	.0802*	.0250	.0000	.1048*
Treatment by Public Officials	.1744*	.0111	.0710*	.2565*
Medical Care	.1067*	.0353	.0132	.1552*
Recreation	.1126*	.0485	.0115	.1726*

*Significant at .05 level.

**See Table 7.7 for fuller description of dependent variable, "Awareness".

227

ponent variables in Table 7.10. Thus the block of background variables are broken down into race, religion, age, and education, and the store variables into "Price" and "Traffic." The unique contributions of each variable toward the explanation of the total variance in awareness of each of the problems faced by blacks are the entries in the table.

From Table 7.10 we see that, indeed, race is the crucial variable underlying the impact of background variables. In all cases, the signs of the relationship are positive, and the F-ratios are very large. As was suggested by Table 7.8, the question concerning treatment by public officials especially stands out as a difference white merchants from black merchants. However, unlike the findings based on Table 7.9, we discover that race is not the only statistically significant variable. Merchants with more education consistently are more aware of the problem of the black man, and six of the seven F-ratios in that column reach statistical significance. Even though the impact of education is not as large as that for race, it is quite large. Being Jewish also tends to make a merchant a bit more aware of the difficulties faced by black people. The signs of the relationships are all positive, although only two of the F-ratios are statistically significant, and the unique contributions are very small. What is surprising is that these two significant F-ratios appear for opportunities (medical care and recreational facilities) that generally have not been especially salient areas of controversy in most large urban areas. In contrast other issues, such as inequalities in treatment by police, which have been well publicized surprisingly do not achieve a large F-ratio.

Being Catholic appears to have no effect on awareness, but age does. Generally (five out of seven F-ratios), younger merchants are more aware, and the F-ratio for unequal treatment by police reaches the .05 level of significance. Also of interest is the pattern of effects for age of the merchant. The two highest F-ratios appear for unequal treatment by public officials and by police. (The only other F-ratio nearly this high is for medical care.)

The effects of Traffic and Price show the unimportance of these variables in predicting awareness. One statistically significant F-ratio is far out of line with the rest—housing—but even this salient effect does not support the importance of store-type variables.

Consistent with the racial differences on the awareness scale, we find white merchants far less sympathetic toward the civil rights movement for greater equality. Seeing blacks as not particularly less well off makes black demands for equality seem unreasonable. Thus only 8% of the white merchants see the pace at which blacks are gaining equality as too slow, while 46% of the blacks see the pace as too slow. Sixty-five

TABLE 7.10

Merchant) Interviews) Merchants' Awareness of Black Problems: Unique Contributions of Individual Background, and Store Variables (N = 458)

"Proportions of Total Variance in Awareness Uniquely Contributed by"

Problem:	Age	Background Variables			Black	Store Variables	
		Catholic	Jew	Education		Traffic	Price
Educational Opportunities	**						
Unique Variance	(−).0006	(−).0003	(+).003	(+).012	(+).043	(−).0000	(+).001
F ratio	.29	.15	1.66	5.66*	21.02*	.0000	.49
Employment Opportunities							
Unique Variance	(+).001	(+).0000	(+).002	(+).016	(+).044	(−).0000	(+).0004
F ratio	.58	.0000	1.12	7.57*	23.06*	.0000	.15
Treatment by Police							
Unique Variance	(+).010	(+).0000	(+).001	(+).015	(+).092	(−).0002	(−).0000
F ratio	5.21*	.0000	.60	8.45*	50.68*	.11	.0000
Housing							
Unique Variance	(−).0007	(−).0005	(+).004	(+).026	(+).037	(+).002	(+).009
F ratio	.341	.24	2.14	12.81*	17.83*	1.04	4.26*
Treatment by Public Officials							
Unique Variance	(−).007	(−).0002	(+).0007	(+).003	(+).115	(−).0006	(−).0000
F ratio	3.81	.12	.41	1.76	67.56*	.36	.0000
Medical Care							
Unique Variance	(+).007	(+).001	(+).009	(+).009	(+).079	(−).0003	(+).003
F ratio	3.66	.57	4.80*	4.70*	40.93*	.16	1.45
Recreation							
Unique Variance	(+).0009	(+).001	(+).008	(+).015	(+).082	(−).0000	(+).0004
F ratio	.47	.58	4.11*	8.54*	43.32*	.0000	.21

*Significant at .05 level.

**Signs in parentheses are signs of Beta coefficients.

percent of the whites feel the pace was much too fast or too fast, while only 10% of the blacks feel this way.[18]

Regression analysis of attitudes toward progress in civil rights movements is shown in Table 7.11. Although 30% of the variance is "explained," only about 2% of the variance can be uniquely attributed to the store variables, and 20% explained by background factors.

In the lower section of Table 7.11 individual variables are considered, and we see that the two background variables that account for most of the variance are education and race. Being black "explains" 11% of the variance and having a greater amount of education "explains" 2% of the variance. Both have very large F-ratios.

The interpretation that emerges is that being black and better educated makes the merchant more sympathetic to the push for black equality. Neither effect is surprising because blacks would from self-interest sup-

---

[18] Chi square for all of response categories broken by race is significant at well beyond the .001 level.

TABLE 7.11

Merchant ⎫ Sympathy for Civil Rights Movement:
Interviews ⎭ Background and Store Variables Considered (N = 458)

A.   Regression Analysis Using Blocks of Variables

Proportions of Total Variance in Sympathy for
Civil Rights Movement Explained Uniquely by

Background Variables	Store Variables	Jointly	Total Variance Explained
.2046*	.0194	.0810*	.3050*

B.   Regression Analysis Using Individual Variables

Proportions of Total Variance in Sympathy for
Civil Rights Movement Explained Uniquely by

		Background Variables			Store Variables	
Age	Catholic	Jewish	Education	Black	Traffic	Price
Unique Variance (+).0007	(-).0001	(-).001	(+).021	(+).111	(+).0009	(+).002
F ratio .44	.063	.75	13.24*	69.76*	.57	1.34

*F ratios statistically significant at .05 level.

**Signs in parentheses are the signs of the Beta coefficient.

port their movement, and more educated people who would generally tend to be more aware and more "liberal" on civil rights issues might see the need for social activism.

What is somewhat surprising is that Jewish merchants, who on earlier items seemed a bit more aware of most black problems and more likely to offer the altruistic services, are not more sympathetic to the black movement. If anything, the relationship is negative. It is difficult to interpret this finding with the limited data at hand. Obviously complex interactions of attitudes are at work. However, one possibility may be that Jewish merchants are using their own historical experience to evaluate the black push for equality. Jewish merchants may feel that members of their minority group progressed by hard work without benefit of a "movement"; thus blacks should do the same. Furthermore, the tactics used by the blacks may be seen as too far outside the law and a threat to the security of whites still living and/or working in the ghetto. The Jewish merchants may admit that things are bad for blacks in the ghetto, but they were once bad for Jews also. And Jews did not chose to resort to the style employed by militant blacks. Such an attitude of Jewish merchants might explain the data in Table 7.10 and have important implications for the awareness material presented earlier.

The items discussed so far have been concerned with rather generalized views of Negroes, hence of customers indirectly. We turn now to specific kinds of business practices, more directly relevant to the role of merchants. Three questions included in the interview schedule for merchants attempted to tap a "dollar value" dimension of business practices. The items describe three types of business practices, which, if implemented, would tend to pass on to the black consumer (or any consumer) a lesser value of goods per unit cost. It would have been better obviously if we had actually observed whether the practices outlined in the questions were, in fact, taking place. However, given the limitation of survey techniques, we have to settle for questions about attitudes toward these practices. The assumption is that there is at least some degree of correlation between the endorsement of the practices and actual behavior.

Table 7.12 gives the texts of the items used and the distributions of responses. The first business practice involves the buying of "bargain merchandise" by the merchant to keep retail prices down. Since most of the merchants in our sample are small, it is not likely that they could buy on the scale necessary to get volume discount prices. Thus for the small merchant, "bargain merchandise" could reasonably be assumed to mean the purchasing of "seconds" or spoiled goods. Thirty-six percent of the merchants endorse this practice; 21% endorse it strongly.

TABLE 7.12

| Merchant) | Merchants' Endorsement of "Dollar |
| Interviews) | Value" Business Practices: [N=458] |

Percent Who

Question	Agree Strongly	Agree Slightly	Disagree Slightly	Disagree Strongly	Don't Know and No Answer
"..merchants say the main thing to do is buy bargain merchandise so that they can keep their retail prices low enough for people to afford."	21%	15	17	40	6
"..Others feel that the best way to stay in business in a neighborhood like this is to bargain with each customer and take whatever breaks he can get."	5	7	8	76	4
"..merchants feel that in business the main thing in a neighborhood like this is to learn how to price their merchandise to cover the extra costs of poor credit risks, petty thievery and the like."	16	20	14	42	8

The second question inquires about the policy of bargaining with each customer and "taking whatever breaks you can get." Here we examine the practice of quoting unfair prices on unmarked merchandise. Twelve percent of the merchants endorse this practice; 5% endorse it strongly.

The third question asks about the practices of pricing retail goods to "cover extra costs of poor credit risks, petty thievery, and the like" that one has to face in doing business in ghetto neighborhoods. Thirty-six percent of the merchants endorse this practice, 16% strongly.

It should be emphasized that with respect to each of the items listed in Table 7.12, the majority of retail merchants disagree. Three quarters of the merchants disagree with the statement that the best way to get along is to bargain with customers. Forty percent disagree strongly that merchants should pick up bargain merchandise, and slightly more disagree strongly that they have to price their merchandise carefully to cover the extra costs of doing business in ghetto neighborhoods. In short the majority of ghetto merchants are clearly opposed to such practices in theory.

It is difficult to interpret this degree of consensus. We suspect that the merchants saw through our questions and denied any wrong doing beyond their actual practices. Of course, this is only a suspicion. The sole course open to us is to treat the answers at their face value. In addition, there is some sense in treating the variation that was manifested among merchants. Those who have endorsed such practices are still likely to support in their own establishments practices that would yield a lower dollar value to their customers.

In great contrast to the attitudes considered earlier, the three "dollar value" items showed no racial differences in response. Chi square significance levels on tables were broken by race range between approximately .60 and .10, and no consistent pattern appears in the data. Cross-tabulations by kind of store were barely more revealing than those by race. The most useful information appears from the regression analyses.

In Table 7.13 it is immediately apparent that background variables have very little effect on merchant attitudes toward customers. None of the F-ratios approach statistical significance. Store effects are generally several times as powerful as background effects, and two of the three F-ratios reach statistical significance. The joint effects are essentially zero, indicating that any interpretations from the data can be confidently based on the "unique" contributions of each block of variables.

However, only one of the F-ratios for the entire multiple regression reaches statistical significance. In short, the independent variables in these cases do not "explain" a great amount of the variance; thus interpretations based on the impacts of these independent variables are not worthy of much confidence. This is in considerable contrast to analyses presented earlier in the chapter and especially to the analyses of police attitudes and practices.

From Table 7.13 it is apparent that a relatively large proportion of variance can be accounted for by type of store when each store is a dummy variable. Type of store "explains" 5% of the variance for the item "buying bargain merchandise," and nearly 10% of the variance for "bargaining with each customer." But when type of store is replaced by "Traffic" and "Price," the usefulness of store variables decreases to about half of 1% variance "explained." This finding suggests that the store characteristics that affect business practices go beyond Price and Traffic.

TABLE 7.13

Merchant   )   Merchants' Endorsement of Practices
Interviews)   Tending to Lower Dollar Values for
              Customers: Regression Analysis   (N = 458)

| | Proportion of Total Variance Uniquely Explained by | | | |
"Dollar Value" Business Practice	Background Variables	Store Variables	Jointly by Background and Store Variable	Total Variance Explained
"buy bargain merchandise"	.0149	.0530**	.0000	.0600
"bargain with each customer"	.0146	.0981**	.0045	.1172**
"price merchandise to cover extra costs"	.0143	.0378	.0000	.0507

*See Table 8.12 for full text of items.

**F ratios significant at .05 level.

For example, bargaining with customers may only occur in certain types of stores, for example, in furniture and appliance stores but rarely in liquor or food stores.

We now turn to measures that probe how the merchants regard black customers. Table 7.14 presents answers to six items on this theme. Differences between black merchants' and white merchants' views of their black customers are large. On four of the six items, white merchants are far more likely to view black customers and black neighborhoods unfavorably. For example, 58% of the white merchants see black customers possibly passing bad checks, while only 22% of the black merchants feel this way. That almost a quarter of the black merchants agree with the statement indicates that much of the white attitude may be realistic. Nevertheless, the difference between the groups is substantially important and statistically significant beyond the .001 level (i.e., if half the white merchants feel this way, this is a large enough figure to have impact on the real world).

Despite the very striking contrast between white and black merchants, it can scarcely be said that the white merchants all hold negative images of blacks as customers. Most white merchants dissent from the view that blacks are poor credit risks, and also from the view that blacks are more apt to be cheated. The majority (three out of four) do agree that blacks

TABLE 7.4

Merchant) Merchants' Attitudes Towards Blacks as Customers,
Interviews) by Race

Statements About Blacks as Customers		Percentages Who				
		Agree Strongly	Agree Slightly	Disagree Slightly	Disagree Strongly	Don't Know and No Answer
*"Poorer credit risks, so charged higher interest"	Whites	10	16	17	44	13
	Blacks	5	5	7	73	10
"Less apt to appreciate a good bargain so more apt to be cheated"	Whites	14	18	19	44	6
	Blacks	13	15	9	54	9
*"Less likely to complain, so less likely to be treated fairly"	Whites	7	12	16	60	6
	Blacks	26	20	11	38	5
*"More apt to steal, so have to be watched especially closely"	Whites	48	24	10	15	3
	Blacks	12	16	10	54	7
"Shops in Negro areas must be especially burglar proof"	Whites	63	21	5	8	3
	Blacks	39	29	7	22	4
*"More apt to pass bad checks so best not to cash them"	Whites	37	21	12	18	12
	Blacks	8	14	19	51	7

N for Whites = 337
N for Blacks = 121

*Chi square for race differences: p < .001.

are more apt to steal and that shops in black areas must be made burglar proof (eight out of ten). Apparently the white merchant image believes that black customers are competent shoppers but possibly pilferers and burglars.[19]

The effects of background variables and store types on merchant attitudes toward black customers can be seen in Table 7.15. In the right-hand column of the table proportions of total variance are explained (R^2). All of the proportions are statistically significant. Comparing the variance contributions in each row indicates that most of this "explained" variance is due to background variables.[20] Store type and joint contributions are relatively small, and none reach statistical significance.

Table 7.16 further supports and elaborates the finding that background variables, especially race, are central to an understanding of merchant

TABLE 7.15

Merchant) Interviews)	Merchants' Attitudes Toward Blacks as Customers: Regression Analysis [N=458]			
	Proportion of Total Variance Uniquely Explained by			
Views of Blacks as Customers	Background Variables	Store Types	Jointly by Background and Store Types	Total Variance Explained
Poorer credit risks, so charged higher interest	.0665*	.0336	.0176	.1177*
More apt to steal, so have to be watched especially closely	.1432*	.0172	.0642	.2246*
Shops in Negro areas must be especially burglar proof	.0432*	.0434	.0365	.1231*
More apt to pass bad checks, so best not to cash them	.1247*	.0197	.0413	.1857*

*F ratio significant at .05 level.

---

[19] Indeed, considering the high crime rates in ghettos, it is more likely that the white merchants are expressing their correct appreciation of the situations they face, while black merchants to some degree deny that these problems exist.

[20] The pattern from left to right across the table is very similar to that of the awareness items (Table 7.10).

TABLE 7.16

Merchant) Interviews) Merchants' Attitudes Toward Blacks as Customers: Regression Analysis Using Single Variables [N=458]

Proportions of Total Variance Uniquely Explained by

Views of Blacks as Customers		Background Variables					Store Variables	
		Age	Catholic	Jew	Education	Black	Traffic	Price
Poorer credit risks, so charged higher interest	Unique Variance	(-).001	(-).0001	(-).003	(+).025	(+).018	(+).0001	(+).003
	F ratio	.54	.05	1.68	12.11*	9.08*	.05	1.78
More apt to steal, so have to be watched especially closely	Unique Variance	(-).0000	(+).003	(-).003	(+).004	(+).081	(-).0000	(+).0001
	F ratio	.0000	1.57	1.52	2.31	45.77*	.0000	.06
Shops in Negro areas must be especially burglar proof	Unique Variance	(-).0005	(+).001	(-).008	(-).0003	(+).010	(+).001	(-).001
	F ratio	.25	.65	3.93*	.15	5.17*	.64	.69
More apt to pass bad checks, so best not to cash them	Unique Variance	(+).0001	(+).009	(+).0007	(+).015	(+).086	(-).0001	(+).003
	F ratio	.05	4.98*	.37	7.92*	45.89*	.11	1.63

*F ratios significant at .05 level.

**Signs in parentheses are signs of Beta coefficients. Attitude items were coded so that a high score indicates disagreement with the item or a more favorable opinion of black customers.

attitudes toward their ghetto customers. None of the store variables ("traffic" and "price") approach statistical significance. Of the background variables, only race has F-ratios that are all statistically significant. The impact of race is obviously many times more important than any other variable. Black merchants simply are far less likely to hold unfavorable images of black customers. The impact of race becomes especially noticeable when the statements label blacks as a *more criminal* people. The items calling blacks vandals and thieves and the items accusing blacks as passing bad checks elicit especially negative reactions as compared to the item stating that blacks are poor credit risks and that saying ghetto neighborhoods are high crime areas.

The effect of higher education on merchant attitudes is similar to that of being black. Generally, the more educated the merchants, the less likely he is to speak unfavorably about blacks. However, compared to the impact of race, the impact of education, with only two statistically significant F-ratios, is rather small. Furthermore, the pattern of responses suggests that a somewhat different mechanism operates. The questions about attitudes toward black customers are "double-barreled." And although the pattern of effects for "race" probably are reactions to the statements about black *per se,* the pattern of effects for "education" may have more to do with the second part of these double-barreled questions—what should be done, given certain characteristics, about the ghetto customer. More educated merchants are much more likely to not favor those items that suggest techniques that specifically single out individual blacks and subject them to special, harsh practices. For example, the item that suggests that because blacks are poor credit risks, they should be given less credit and charged higher interest rates, receives a far more negative reaction than the next item that suggests that since blacks were more likely to shoplift and vandalize, they should be watched closely. Similarly, the items that suggest that since blacks are more likely to pass bad checks, their checks should not be cashed, receives a far more negative reaction then the item that suggests that since black neighborhoods are high crime areas, stores operating in these communities should take special precautions (e.g., burglar alarms). Perhaps more educated merchants are less likely to feel that special practices aimed at blacks are justified, or that since they sensed that these items were aimed at discerning discriminatory practices, they were not about to admit to such behavior.

To summarize the effects of a number of variables on attitudes toward black customers: It is apparent that being black is by far, the most important variable. Higher education decreases the propensity of the merchant to think unfavorably about ghetto customers, but the impact is small compared to that of being a black merchant. There are hints that other variables may have some impact; however, these variables (especially education and religion) are really of small import.

It is difficult at this point to state whether white merchants hold decidedly negative images of blacks. Certainly they deny the real and severe problems that blacks face in their cities. Yet, the attitudinal items suggest that white merchants are certainly not of one mind on the topic. It is only in contrast with black merchants that the gulf between the races shows clearly. If the crucial issue in the relationships between white merchants and their clients is the difference between these merchants and their black counterparts, then white merchants are indeed accumulating ill will. The explanation of "retaliation" for store looting and vandalism in the ghetto is thereby given some support.

However, before we accept this retaliation explanation, we look at some very direct evidence on the incidence of such acts reported to us by the merchants.

Vandalism and Merchant-Customer Relations.[21]   The fate of ghetto merchants during the civil disorders has received much attention. Indeed, at least one commentator argues that the defining characteristic of the 1960s civil disorders was that commercial establishments in ghetto areas were the main targets.[22] For many Americans, the most dramatic visual memories of the disorders in Newark, Detroit, and elsewhere are televised shots of blacks looting stores and of smoke rising from the gutted innercity commercial districts.

Although vandalism and looting of ghetto businesses reached its peak during civil disorders, ghetto businesses are frequent targets during "ordinary" times as well. The prevalence of store robberies and vandalism in the ghettos has led many merchants to take special precautions against such acts and raised insurance premiums to beyond the reach of the poorer merchants. The extent to which robbery, shoplifting, and vandalism are perceived as serious problems by the merchants in our sample can be seen in Table 7.17, as responses to the question—"As a retail merchant in this city, what are your major problems?" One out of ten of the problems cited involved vandalism and damage to their stores,

[21] This section borrows very heavily from the analysis presented in Richard A. Berk and Howard E. Aldrich, "Patterns of Vandalism During Civil Disorders as an Indicator of Selection of Targets," *Amer. Sociol. Rev.*, October 1972.

[22] E. L. Quarantelli and R. Dynes, "Looting in Civil Disorders: An Index of Social Change," in *Riots and Rebellion* L. R. Masotti (Ed.), Sage Publications, California, 1968.

TABLE 7.17

Merchant   ) Major Problems of Doing Business in
Interviews) the Ghetto

Problem Cited	Proportion of Responses Citing Problem
Shoplifting, Theft	23%
Staying Solvent	10
Vandalism	9
Customers Rude, Drunk, Disorderly	9
Quality of Employees (Late, Lazy, Dishonest)	7
People Afraid to Shop Here	7
Other	35
100% =	(622)*

*Ghetto merchants tended to cite more than one problem. The proportions
given are of all problems cited.

although the most frequently cited problem, accounting for 23% of the
responses, was shoplifting and theft.

It is clear from Table 7.17 that vandalism and theft are major problems
for ghetto merchants. Furthermore, the remaining problems cited by merchants were relations with the ghetto community around them. Indeed,
it should be abundantly clear from these findings and others presented
earlier in this chapter that ghetto merchants perceive serious problems
in their relationships to customers and their community.

The prevalence of vandalism as a serious problem, however, under-
estimates the incidence of vandalism among the merchants. Slightly more
than three in ten merchants (31%) experienced at least one incident of
vandalism during the summer of 1967. It is difficult to extrapolate from
these findings to the "ordinary" incidence of vandalism. First, we did not
specify to the merchants what period of time he should consider as
"summer." Second, only some of the cities were scenes of very serious
civil disorders during the summer of 1967. Indeed, as Table 7.18 indicates
that the proportion of merchants claiming to have been vandalized in the
summer of 1967 ranges widely from city to city, being lowest in St. Louis
(13%) and highest in Newark (52%).

TABLE 7.18

Merchant   ) Incidences of Vandalism During "Summer
Interviews) 1967" by City

City	Proportions Vandalized*	100% =
A. **Cities with Major Civil Disorders in 1967**		
Newark	52%	(29)
Detroit	50%	(30)
Boston	50%	(30)
Cincinnati	47%	(30)
Milwaukee	29%	(31)
B. **Cities with Minor Disorders in 1967 or Disorders in Previous Years**		
Cleveland	30%	(30)
Philadelphia	24%	(33)
Chicago	23%	(30)
Brooklyn	19%	(37)
San Francisco	17%	(29)
C. **Cities with No Disorders in 1967 or Earlier**		
Pittsburgh	38%	(29)
Gary	28%	(30)
Baltimore	28%	(29)
Washington, D.C.	23%	(31)
St. Louis	13%	(30)
Overall Proportion (Cities Combined)	31%	(458)

*Responses to the item, "Last summer (1967) did your store suffer damage from vandalism?"

In Table 7.18 the cities have been grouped according to the criteria by which they were selected. The first five cities were chosen because each had experienced a serious civil disorder in the summer of 1967. However, even within this group, the nature of the disorder varied. In Milwaukee, groups of blacks conducted many protest marches through the city, while in Newark and Detroit rioters managed to wrest ghetto control from the police and suspended property rights for a number of

TABLE 7.19

Merchant   ) Dollar Value and Kind of Damages
Interviews) Suffered in Vandalism*

A.   Dollar Value of Damages Inflicted:

Amount	Proportion
Less than $500	47%
$501-1000	14
$1001-3000	13
$3001-5000	9
$5001-9999	7
$10,000-15,000	3
More than $15,000	8

100% =   (101)**

MEDIAN DOLLAR VALUE = $607

B.   Kind of Damages Inflicted

Inventory	19%
Damages to Store	80
Personal Attack	1

100% =   (56)

*Response to question, asked of merchants who claimed to
have been victims of vandalism in 1967, "How much damage?"

**Note that 142 merchants claimed to have been vandalized,
41 of whom did not reply in terms of dollar damages.

days. Looting and vandalism were more extensive, obviously, in the latter cities, as compared with Milwaukee; this pattern is reflected in the merchants' responses.

Among the remaining ten cities, there is considerable variation. Some cities, for example, Pittsburgh, have vandalism incidences which are close to those rates for cities which had civil disorders in 1967. This variability in part reflects differences in definition of vandalism, in part differences in the meaning on the reference time period, and in part real differences among the cities.

The problem of definition is illustrated in Table 7.19 which shows responses to the question—"How much damage occurred?" Unfortunately, although some of the respondents answered in terms of an estimated dollar value of damage, others responded in terms of the kinds of damages inflicted. This lack of uniformity makes it difficult to use this question as an index of the severity of vandalism.

By and large the dollar amount of damage inflicted was not very large, the median being $607, with close to half of the respondents suffering less than $500 in damages. Of course, significant proportions of stores suffered very extensive damages, 8% being inflicted with more than $15,000.

It should be noted that these estimates err on the "conservative" side. Stores that went out of business after suffering vandalism could not be included in our study.[23] Indeed, the conservative bias extends to most of the analyses to be presented in this section.

The fact that only some stores have been vandalized serves to discern whether vandalism is due to the relationships between merchants and their customers or to other factors. Indeed, one may postulate that vandalism represents at least one or more of the following five processes:

---

[23] These figures can also be compared to several other studies: In a 1968 study of small businesses (A. J. Reiss, Jr. "Appendix A: Field Surveys," in *Crimes Against Small Business*, A Report of the Small Business Administration Washington, D. C., Government Printing Office, 1969) throughout the nation, 37% reported glass breakage, 21% damage to buildings, 18% damage to vehicles, 10% damage to store fixtures, and 5% damage to merchandise. In a panel study of businesses in ghetto precincts in Boston, Chicago, and Washington, D.C., Aldrich and Reiss find a vandalism incidence of 24% [H. Aldrich and A. J. Reiss "The Effects of Civil Disorders on Small Business in the Inner City," *J. Social Issues*, **26** (Winter 1970)]. Because of the differences in the definition of time period, retail businesses and such, it is difficult to compare these estimates. At least in one respect, the estimates are comparable: They are all of the same magnitude and are roughly in the same "ballpark."

1. *Vandalism for*   Stores that contain desirable goods are
   attractive merchandise: more likely to be "hit."

2. *Vandalism as*   Stores whose owners or managers employ
   retaliation: sharp business practices and/or objec-
                         tionable manners are more likely to be
                         hit.

3. *Vandalism through contact*   Stores that are frequented by many cus-
   and familiarity: tomers are more likely to be vandalized.
                         Patterns of vandalism are not very differ-
                         ent from those of shopping.

4. *Vandalism as*   Stores owned or managed by whites are
   interracial hostility: more likely to be vandalized.

5. *Vandalism as incidental*   All stores in cities that have experienced
   to civil disorders: civil disorders are about equally likely
                         to be vandalized.

These analyses are included here in part because of their intrinsic interest and in part because they cast some light on the importance of the analyses presented earlier in this chapter. The civil disorders of the 1960s have been interpreted by some as primarily carnivals in which primitive desires for property acquisition were somehow released.[24] Others have interpreted the patterns of looting and vandalism as acts of retaliation against exploitative merchants or as expressions of hostility toward white economic domination. Indeed, each of the processes listed above have been posited alone or in combination as the main generating forces underlying the high levels of vandalism during "normal" periods and during the extraordinary events of civil disorders.

Some data described earlier in this chapter can test whether any of these processes can explain why only some merchants are vandalized. In addition, we employ a panel study of small businesses in Washington, Boston, and Chicago, conducted over the period 1966 to 1968 by Albert J. Reiss and Howard Aldrich.[25] In the latter study, 432 businesses in largely black precincts were surveyed in 1966 and again in 1968, using many parallels many of our critical variables. Consequently, there is a unique opportunity for replication.

Tables 7.20 and 7.21 contain the results of several regression analyses which use whether businesses were vandalized as the dependent variable.

---

[24] See especially Edward A. Banfield, *The Unheavenly City*, Little Brown, Boston, 1970.

[25] A fuller description of the Reiss and Aldrich study is given in Reiss and Aldrich, *op. cit.*

In Table 7.20 the data are from the present study and in Table 7.21 from the Reiss–Aldrich study. It should be noted that a critical difference between the two studies lies in the time ordering of the independent and dependent variables. In the latter (Reiss–Aldrich) the independent variables were collected in 1966 and the dependent variable in 1968, while in the present study both are collected simultaneously.

In Table 7.20 six predictor variables are used to account for experiences with vandalism, and separate analyses employed by types of city (whether a civil disorder was experienced in 1967, etc.). Note that for merchants in the cities that had civil disorders in the summer of 1967, the six variables manage to "explain" 23% of the variance in vandalization, an amount which is quite comparable to the 21% for the Reiss–Aldrich study, shown in Table 7.21. Therefore, at least in riot cities, the hypothesis of random vandalism is refuted. Much less variance is accounted for in cities where there were no civil disorders in 1967, a patterning that indicates that vandalism approaches a more random patterning in "normal" times (at least for our measures), and that civil disorder vandalism may be qualitatively different from day-to-day vandalism.

The beta weights (standardized) are arranged in Table 7.20 in terms of decreasing size in the column pertaining to cities that experienced severe riots in 1967. Each of the predictor variables were included in the tables because they were reasonable tests of the processes outlined earlier in this section. (All of the beta weights in this column reach statistical significance at the .05 level, indicating that to a greater or lesser degree all of the processes have been at work.)

In Table 7.21 the beta weights also have been arranged in terms of decreasing size (absolute value). The Reiss–Aldrich data support the same conclusions: All of the processes are important in predicting vandalism.

If one reason for attacking a business is racial hostility to white ownership of ghetto businesses, we would expect race to be an important predictor of vandalism. The zero-order correlation between race and being vandalized during riots is only 0.017 in our data and 0.068 in the Reiss–Aldrich data, indicating that race can only be important when other characteristics of merchants are held constant. Black merchants are often located in high traffic stores of high exposure, tend to offer special services, and hold attitudes positively correlated with being vandalized. It is only when these effects are controlled that the effect of race is of

---

[26] We use slope rather than variance measures here because our dependent variables is dichotomous; consequently, variance measures are especially vulnerable to marginal distributions.

TABLE 7.20

Merchant) Predictors of Probability of Being
Interviews) Vandalized by Type of City

	Beta Weights Shown by 1967 Riot Status of City			
Predictor Variables*	Severe Riots	Minor or Previous Riots	Non-Riot	Relevance of Beta Weights
Price of Merchandise	.342**	-.019	.313**	Attractive Merchandise Vandalism
Merchants' Awareness of Blacks' Plight	.319**	-.078	-.148**	Contact-Familiarity/ Retaliation
Intensity of Store Use	.283**	-.047	.104	Contact-Familiarity
Merchants' Offering Special Services	.171**	.090	.115**	Retaliation
Race	.157**	.054	.081	Race Hostility
Rejection of Negative Views of Customers	-.114**	-.169**	-.059	Retaliation
R^2 =	.23**	.04	.10**	
N =	(150)	(149)	(159)	

TABLE 7.20 (Cont'd)

*Awareness - An index composed of seven items "Compared to other groups in the city of the same income and education do you think blacks are about as well off, less well off, or better off with respect to educational opportunities, housing, treatment by the police, etc." A high score indicates that the respondent was more likely to admit that blacks were less well off, and that the respondent, then, was considered more aware of objective conditions facing blacks.

Special Services - An index composed of five items which asked "Here are some services that some stores often, sometimes, or never extend to their customers. Do you... cash payroll checks, help fill out applications and other forms, make contributions to local churches and charities, give personal advice, and extend credit to people others wouldn't help." A high score indicates that the merchants offered more services.

Rejection of Negative Views of Black Customers - An index based on four items asking about blacks as customers centering around such practices as passing bad checks, shoplifting, and vandalism. The items were scored so that a high score meant a failure to endorse the items and thus a less negative view of customers.

Intensity of Store Use - This variable was defined as the probability that a given individual in the black ghetto would use a store type in a given period of time. Four raters independently rated each kind of store (zero through 10, with 10 being high) on this probability, the resulting interrater correlations being very high. The mean score based on these four ratings for each type of store was then calculated and was the score entered into the regression equation.

Price - This variable, like "traffic," was constructed after the data was collected. Four raters independently scored each store type on the average price per item of merchandise. The scores ranged from zero to 10 with 10 being high. Once again the interrater correlations were very high. As with "traffic," means were calculated for each store based on the scores of the four raters.

**p < .05, One tailed test.

247

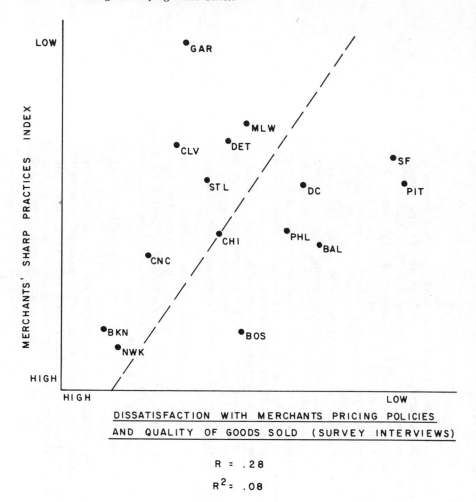

Figure 7.1   Merchant and survey interviews: Merchants' Sharp Practices Index and ghetto dissatisfaction with neighborhood stores.

some importance.[27] For riot cities in our material the beta is .157 and in the Reiss–Aldrich data, .114. White merchants do have a higher probability of being attacked. However, the beta for race in our data barely reaches the .05 level of significance and ranks fifth in magnitude among the six coefficients. In the Reiss–Aldrich data, race ranks sixth out of six coefficients. In addition, the regressions of Table 7.20 indicate that the impact of race is salient only under riot conditions. Thus the independent impact of race gives but modest support to the racial hostility interpretation, and then only during civil disorders.

The relatively small impact of race in our data may be partially an error of measurement. The racial label applied to a store was based on the race of the person in charge on the scene—the owner *or* the manager—hence may inaccurately reflect actual ownership and the public racial identity of the store.[28]

Given the small effect of "race" measured through the owner or manager of the store, we tested the racial hostility process by using another measure of a store's racial identify—proportion of employees who are white. However, when this Reiss–Aldrich variable was added to the regression equation, both the increment to explained variance and the raw regression coefficient failed to reach even the .10 level of significance[29]

Other types of intergroup hostility were also tested. Much has been said about the rise of anti-Semitism among ghetto blacks, presumably because many ghetto merchants are Jewish. No support for this contention can be found in our data, however, Jewish merchants were no more likely to be vandalized than merchants of other faiths.

Nor does absentee ownership play any role in vandalization. Absentee owned stores (largely white) were no more likely to be vandalized than other stores, once the other variables of significance were taken into account.

Vandalism for "profit" is a more important process. The higher the dollar value of merchandise sold in a store, the more likely it is to be vandalized during a riot. In our data, the beta is .342 in riot cities and .313 in nonriot cities; in Reiss–Aldrich data the beta is .222. This finding implies that vandals could be acting in part for personal gain, although the reader should not automatically assume this interpretation. It may be that more expensive items such as TV sets are valuable symbols of white society.[30]

---

[27] These correlations are all below .50 (most around .20); thus multicolinearity is not a problem.

[28] The small impact of "race" in the Reiss–Aldrich data may be a result of a similar labeling problem.

[29] In the Reiss–Aldrich material replacing the variable "race of owner or manager" with "percent white employees" yielded a smaller R square and a smaller beta coefficient for the impact of racial identity of the store. There was no measure of racial composition of employees in our own data.

[30] The pattern of effects across the three kinds of cities in our data clearly indicated that "Price" loses its importance in early-riot cities. There is at least one *Post hoc* interpretation: Since merchants in early-riot cities had already experienced a riot, mercants with large amounts of capital invested in a store (i.e., high "Price") may have decided to take special precautions to prevent vandalism in the future (e.g., hire guards and install snooping devices). This would in turn cut rates of vandalism for those stores.

The case for retaliatory vandalism is far less clear than for racial hostility and profit vandalism. Four separate approaches were attempted, and for various reasons, none of them is especially satisfying.

The first approach assumed that merchants that harbored hostile and derogatory attitude toward their customers would be likely to behave in ways that neighborhood residents would perceive as abrasive. This in turn would make such merchants likely targets for retaliation. To test this approach in our material an Index of Merchants' Attitudes Toward their Customers (IMATC) was developed. Interestingly, positive attitudes toward black customers does have a statistically significant beta in riot and early-riot cities, but interpretation is complicated by unclear causal direction: Do those merchants who have favorable attitudes toward their customers behave in less abrasive ways thus minimizing retaliatory vandalism, or do merchants who are not vandalized think more highly of their customers?

Though we cannot make as strong a case as we would like, there is some support from the Reiss–Aldrich data for the retaliatory interpretation of causal direction. Table 7.21 shows a beta of .114 for the variable "Negative Attitudes To Civil Rights," which, because of the longitudinal nature of the data, makes this cluster of attitudes clearly an independent variable. Thus at least one cluster of attitudes does seem to generate retaliation. Earlier in this chapter, we showed that merchants who feel negatively toward their customers are also likely to be those who are unsympathetic to black grievances and black demands. This argues that our predictor IMATC and Reiss–Aldrich's "Negative Attitudes To Civil Rights" are likely to be correlated and that consequently IMATC is an antecedent rather than a result of being vandalized.

A second approach assumed that offering credit to ghetto customers might create a substantial amount of antagonism. Certainly there is evidence from other studies[31] that at least some customers who are overcharged for credit have to face painful collection procedures. Also, the economically unpredictable lives of many ghetto residents probably make buying on credit an agonizing procedure even under the "fairest" of circumstances. In short, it was assumed that stores that sold merchandise on credit would be targets for hostility. However, when entered into the regression, offering credit apparently explained little variance and yielded a regression coefficient of virtually zero.

A third attempt to test the retaliation model was based on items discussed earlier that asked merchants to evaluate three business practices that, if implemented, would be likely to produce a poorer dollar value

---

[31] David L. Caplovitz, *The Poor Pay Moore*, The Free Press, New York, 1962.

for customers. Recall that the questions concerned bargaining with customers and taking whatever breaks one could get, buying "seconds," and pricing to cover the "unusual" overhead in doing business in ghetto neighborhoods. Unexpectedly, these items were useless in predicting patterns of vandalism.[32] Significant F-ratios for any of these items would have been support for the retaliation model (merchants who do not give their customers good dollar values get vandalized), but none appeared.

The fourth approach involved variables that measured the offering of "special services" (e.g., cashing payroll checks and giving personal advice). In our data, "offer special services" was originally conceived as a measure of good will. However, surprisingly, all three betas were positive, indicating that the more merchants offered special services to their customers, the *more* likely they were to be vandalized in all of the three types of cities. The largest beta was for 1967 civil disorder cities, but the beta in nonriot cities was also statistically significant. We were at first inclined to dismiss these findings as provocative but probably due to chance, until the same findings appeared in the Reiss–Aldrich prediction equation (see Tables 7.21).

Thus offering of special services is not viewed favorably by the local community. Indeed, our earlier analysis of special services suggested that a large component of business self-interest could be operating. The cashing of payroll checks is often made contingent on buying merchandise in the store; often, there is a service charge. Helping customers fill out forms and applications is often part of the sales process (for certain businessmen such as car dealers and pawn brokers), and clearly required when credit is extended. "Extending credit to people others would not help" certainly may have an altruistic component, but the extension still facilitates sales, and interest is earned on the loan. In other words, even under the most honorable of circumstances, at least three of the services can be conceptualized in part not as favors, but as ways to increase sales and profits. Consequently, customers may see these special services as manipulative devices.

The remaining two special services—contributing money to local churches and charities and giving personal advice—are more clearly altruistic, but merchant altruism also may be abrasive to innercity residents. Giving personal advice can be interpreted as a sales pitch or profit-motivated public relations. And even when giving advice on personal

---

[32] A reasonable interpretation for this finding can be seen in the results on the next section of this chapter where we present evidence that black customers are not directly aware of merchant exploitation in the sense that city levels of dissatisfaction with merchant practices are not related to these practices. There is evidence, however, that these practices may be more visible to black laders who raise merchant exploitation as a political issue in those cities where merchant practices seem to warrant such complaints.

problems is not directly linked to dollars and cents, the interpersonal processes may not be especially flattering to the recipient. Advice can be given in a most patronizing manner even when it is well-intentioned. Indeed, given the racial, class, and life style differences between retail merchants and large numbers of ghetto residents, it would take an unusually skilled diplomat to avoid "talking down" to his customers.

Effects of giving to local churches and charities may be more difficult to evaluate. Many recipients of merchant charity have little to do with the black community directly (like the Red Cross) and even when the causes are clearly tied to the neighborhood, identification of the donor is frequently problematic. Additionally, the assumption that donors are liked is subject to the same kinds of questions raised about giving advice.

Further support for this line of interpretation is provided in part by the findings in Table 7.20 concerning the effect of the variable, "awareness of blacks' plight." A straightforward expectation would lead one to predict, on the basis of the retaliation process, that the more aware merchants were of the plight of blacks in their cities, the less likely they would be to be vandalized. This expectation is borne out in cities which have not experienced civil disorders and to a lesser extent (although not statistically significant) in cities which had minor or previous-to-1967 disorders. However, the results for 1967 disorder cities are quite puzzling: The more aware were merchants in these cities, the more likely they were to be vandalized! Furthermore, their regression coefficient is the second largest in the left-hand column; thus it is a sizable effect, likely to be quite stable.

We can only offer an explanation along the same lines with respect to services: Expressing understanding may be viewed as patronizing, and possibly also as a sign of weakness. In any event, the merchants' expressed understanding of his customers' social position is a factor, albeit puzzling, that plays an important role in whether he will be vandalized during a riot.

"Awareness" may also be in part a consequence of frequent contact between merchants and customers; the Reiss–Aldrich data have one variable that relates rather directly to the amount of contact. There is a beta of $-.341$ between the estimated percentage of white customers using a store and the probability of being vandalized. In other words, stores more likely to be frequented by blacks are more likely to be attacked. Though the percentage of black customers is not a direct measure of the amount of contact between innercity residents and ghetto merchants, it is a reasonable inference that a store more heavily used by blacks (as compared to whites) will have relatively more contact with black residents and will be more familiar to blacks.[33] Stores with which potential rioters are more familiar may be selected as riot targets because (1) familiar stores will seem safer in times of danger and stress, (2) rioters who seek specific kinds of merchandise will choose stores they know well enough to systematically loot, and (3) more impulsive rioters might vandalize the first store that comes to mind.

The measure of "intensity of use" (see Table 7.20) may be similarly interpreted. Stores with a higher probability of use by customers in a given time period had a higher probability of being vandalized. Stores with high intensity of use are stores with which customers have more contact and familiarity.

Finally the Reiss–Aldrich measure of location indicates that businesses located in predominantly commercial areas are more likely to be attacked than those located in residential or mixed areas (the beta is .124). Since stores in commercial districts have frequent use, "location" is in part a measure of contact. Additionally, civil disorders, for obvious reasons, were centered on commercial streets in the ghetto, suggesting that proximity to rioting *per se* may be a factor.

The two sets of data used in this section were drawn independently; thus the Reiss–Aldrich longitudinal material may be viewed as a replication of some of the findings from the "fifteen-city" material. This is especially important, since the analyses of both sets of data are quite congruent. Not only were there no contradictions in findings, but in every case the two data sets complement each other. Consequently, our interpretations take on additional credibility. The findings can be summarized as follows.

All five types of vandalism receive some confirmation but to varying degrees. "Vandalism for profit" is probably the most convincingly demonstrated. "Racial hostility," although supported by the data, has a relatively small beta coefficient. The contact-familiarity and "retaliation" processes support may be vulnerable to alternative explanations.

Most important for understanding the position of ghetto merchants in their communities is that we are able to account for some patterns of vandalism in times of riots and to a lesser extent in times before riots. In other words, merchant behavior and the attitudes displayed toward their clients have enough impact upon customers to make some merchants more popular targets than others. In addition, civil disorders facilitate

---

[33] This would not be true if "percentage white customers" was strongly and positively related to the number of people that used the store.

somewhat different kinds of vandalism than appear in day-to-day situations.

Consumer Discontent and Merchant Exploitation as a Local Issue.   The practices of individual merchants affect their relationships with the community which surrounds them: That is the message of the last section of this chapter. We also know from Chapter 3 that exploitation by retail merchants is frequently a salient issue in local race relations. The problem of this section is to explore the links on the level of communities between the practices and attitudes of merchants, popular response to those variables, and the rise of merchant exploitation as a local issue in race relations.

In the previous chapter a rather direct linkage between public policy, police practices, and public assessments of police activities in the ghetto was easily perceived. For very obvious reasons, we can scarcely find such linkages in the area of retail merchandising. The police are a public bureaucracy that operates under the controls of the chief of police and other public officials. Retail merchants are not so directly connected with the local government, and most of the retail stores studied can only be considered bureaucratic organizations by stretching the imagination considerably. Retail merchants are individual entrepreneurs operating within the framework of public policy regulations that provide for much freedom of action in pricing and services rendered.

Given the organizational characteristics of retail merchandising, it would be surprising if there were considerable differences in merchant practices and attitudes from city to city. Indeed, although there are some differences in the levels of merchant practices and attitudes from city to city, the differences are not large enough to reach statistical significance. In short, merchants in one city are not strikingly different from those in another in their merchandising practices and their attitudes toward their customers.

Yet there is some weak evidence that those slight differences from city to city are reflected in customer dissatisfaction. In Figure 7.1 the relationship between the "Sharp Practices Index"[34] is plotted for each city and an index of consumer dissatisfaction with merchant pricing policies and the quality of goods sold in neighborhood stores (Con-

---

[34] The Sharp Practices Index consist of merchant responses to the following questions:
. . . the main thing to do is to buy bargain merchandise. . . .
. . . main thing . . . is to learn how to price merchandise to cover the extra costs of poor credit risks, petty thievery, and the like. . . .

TABLE 7.21

| Reiss-Aldrich) Predictors of Probability of |
| Three City Study) Being Vandalized in 1968 |

Predictor Variables*	Beta Weight	Relevance of Beta Weights
Proportion White Among Customer	-.341**	Contact-Familiarity
Price of Merchandise	.222**	Attractive Merchandise Vandalism
Special Services Offered to Customers	.190**	Retaliation
Commercial Street Location	.124**	Contact-Familiarity
Negative Attitudes Toward Civil Rights	.114**	Retaliation
Race of Owner - Manager	.114**	Racial Hostility

$$R^2 = .21$$

$$N = (331)$$

** $p < .05$ One tailed test.

*Proportion White Among Customers (1966) - Interviewers estimate in response to, "The customers observed at the time of the interview were..." with one of the following categories: (1) All black (coded 0% white), (2) Predominantely black, some white (25%), (3) About equal (50%), (4) Predominantly white (75%), (5) All white (100%). This was coded as an interval measure, from 000 to 100.
Customer Services (1968) - Respondents were asked if they offered a variety of services including: (1) Cashing checks for people, (2) lending or giving money to people from the neighborhood, (3) Being friendly to customers (as a method of protecting the business from crime -- a dubious "service" but one that fits in with our rather cynical view of customer services in general.) These 3 are given equal weight in the index, with a high score indicating the offering of more special services.
Commercial Street Location (1966) - Interviewer rating.
Negative Attitudes to Civil Rights (1966) - Based on responses to: "What effect do you think the Civil Rights movement has had on police work?"
Price - Same as Price Variable in Table 8.20.

Race - Same as Race variable in "Table 8.20".

sumer Dissatisfaction Index)[35] derived from surgery interviews with blacks in each of the cities is shown. Over the fifteen cities, there is some slight tendency for consumer dissatisfaction to be highest in cities in which merchants are more likely to be high on the Sharp Practices Index.

[35] The Consumer Dissatisfaction Index is composed on survey responses to the following questions:

Do you think you are unfairly overcharged for goods ... ?
Do you think you are sold spoiled or inferior goods ... ?

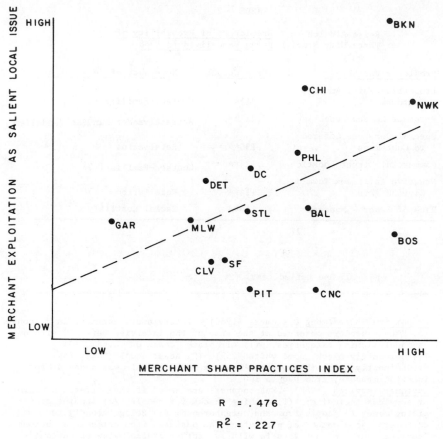

$$R = .476$$
$$R^2 = .227$$

Figure 7.2 Elite and merchant: Merchants' Sharp Practices Index and salience of merchant exploitation as local issue.

Of course, a correlation of .28, especially based on fifteen cases, is scarcely worth noticing, as it is likely to have arisen by sampling variation in circumstances when the "true" correlation is actually zero.

Quite a different story emerges, however, when we relate Merchant Sharp Practices to the Salience of Merchant Exploitation as a local issue, as in Figure 7.2. In this figure the correlation is much higher (.48), teetering on the border of statistical significance at the .05 level, which indicates that the higher level of merchants' assessment of "sharp" merchandising practices is a means of getting business done in the ghetto, the more likely is exploitation to be an issue in local politics.

These two correlations provide a clue to the links between merchant behavior and customer dissatisfaction. The linkage is through the actions of political elite who are apparently more sensitive to variations in merchant behavior than are their customers. Indeed, if we consider that it is difficult without a basis of comparison to determine whether one is being sold inferior goods or overcharged, the hypothesized linkage appears even more plausible. Because the elites are more knowledgeable about the range of prices and goods available in the larger community through their contacts with a variety of sections of the city, they may be more sensitive to the small differences that exist from city to city. We can expect them to be even more sensitive to such differences, if the black leaders present grievances and to work for their rectification. Indeed, the grievance orientation of black leaders is a prime determinant both in exploitation as an issue and in the level of consumer dissatisfaction.

Although each of the variables considered contributes weakly to the levels of consumer dissatisfaction in the fifteen cities, their joint contribution is quite high. Table 7.22 shows that it is possible to account for over 70% of the variance among cities with three clusters of variables involving a total of five separate variables. Merchant Practices, the Salience of exploitation as a local issue, and the Style of Civil Rights Movement provide a very high level of prediction of the variation from city to city in levels of consumer dissatisfaction.

The unique contribution of each of the clusters is also very high. Merchant Practices accounts for 16% of the variance: The Salience of exploitation as a Local Issue accounts for more than 21% and the Style of the Civil Rights Movement account for almost a third of the variance (32%). For all practical purposes the unique contributions of combinations of clusters are insignificant, which indicates that each cluster contributes independently to the arousal of dissatisfaction among consumers. In other words, the cities in which the levels of consumer dissatisfaction is high are also the cities in which merchant practices may be abrasive, and/or black leaders have raised exploitation as an issue, and/or in which the civil rights movement is oriented toward the correction of specific grievances. Since the latter two sources are more prominent as independent contributors to the level of dissatisfaction, it does appear that the actions of elites are more important to the arousal of consumer dissatisfaction than direct apprehension of objective conditions on the part of consumers.

Although judgments about whether one is being overcharged or sold inferior goods may be difficult matters for individual customers to assess, other aspects of merchant behavior may be felt directly more easily. A customer may be able to detect directly when a merchant treats him impolitely or disrespectfully. If such is the case and merchant behavior

TABLE 7.22

Merchant, Elite and Survey Interviews	)))	Consumer Dissatisfaction, Relative Contributions of Merchant Practices, Salience of Merchant Exploitation as an Issue, and Style of Civil Rights Movement [N = 15 Cities]

Combination

Merchant Practices **	Exploitation as Issue	Civil Rights Style	Unique Contribution to Total Variance in Consumer Dissatisfaction
+	0	0	16.2%
0	+	0	21.5
0	0	+	32.2
+	+	0	- 7.0
+	0	+	0.0
0	+	+	4.3
±	+	+	3.2

Total Variance
Explained　　70.5%

p < .01

*Merchant Practices Cluster Includes:
　　Sharp Practices Index and item on bargaining with customers

　　Civil Rights Style Cluster:　Includes ratings of Grievance Orientation
　　　and Integration Orientations of local civil rights movement (See
　　　Chapter 2 for more detailed description of these ratings).

**"+" indicates the presence of the factor as an independent variable.
　"-" indicates the absence of the factor as an independent variable.

varies between cities, then we should find that measures of merchants'
attitudes toward their customers should be more directly related to
intercity differences in customers' feelings as being treated well in their
local retail stores.

Indeed, such appears to be the case, as Figure 7.3 indicates. The
higher the proportion of merchants who agree that it is not necessary to
"treat black customers equally with whites" in a city, the more likely are
blacks to claim that they are treated often "with disrespect" in their local

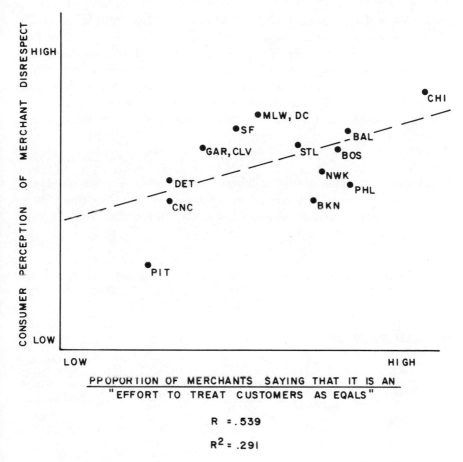

Figure 7.3 Merchant and survey interviews: merchants' attitudes and consumer perception of disrespect.

stores.[36] The correlation between the two items across cities is .539, indicating that about 29% of the variation among cities in the levels of customer complaints about treatment by merchants.

By adding another measure of merchant attitudes—the merchants' ratings of the "rudeness" of their customers—we can account for an addi-

---

[36] The exact wordings of the two items are as follows:

Merchant Interviews: Some merchants feel that since blacks many times seemingly do not care about good manners, there is no special need to make an effort to treat them as politely as whites.

Survey Interviews: In such stores (neighborhood stores) are you treated disrespectfully often, sometimes, rarely or never?

tional 28% of the variance, as Table 7.23 shows.[37] About 55% of the inter-city variance can be accounted for by the two items.

In short, customer levels of feeling abused by retail merchants are related to levels of merchants attitudes toward their customers. In cities where merchants feel that customers do not have to be treated well and where they also feel that customers treat them rudely, blacks rate their local neighborhood stores as places where they are treated disrespectfully.

Conclusion. We have dwelt at length on the characteristics of ghetto merchants because of the special connections between the retail merchandising system and local neighborhoods. Stores and local service

TABLE 7.23

Merchant and   ) Merchants' Attitudes Toward
Survey Interviews) Customers and Consumer Discontent
                   About Merchant Treatment (N = 15)

A.   Correlations:

	Not Necessary to Treat Blacks Equally	Customers are often Rude	Treated Disrespectfully in Neighborhood Stores
Treat Blacks Equally		-.28	.53
Customers Rude			.36
Treated Disrespectfully			

B.   Multiple Regression on "Treated Disrespectfully in Neighborhood Stores"

$$R = .74$$
$$R^2 = .55$$
$$p < .01$$

---

[37] Alternative items selected from the merchants' questionnaires that tap the dimensions either of merchants' attitudes toward their customers or their assessments of customers' manners would produce very much the same results as those displayed in Table 7.23. Since the items in question are all intercorrelated, we selected these two as representing one from each set of items.

organizations are systems that provide interfaces between the larger society and the local community. They function in ways that are similar to those of the police and the local schools because they are organizations which are on the scene and provide services on a local scale.

Ghetto merchants are hardly the most prosperous and most enlightened of the retailing industry. Their stores tend to be small—although perhaps not smaller than in other local neighborhoods—but their salient characteristic is the separation in social terms between the merchants and their customers. The retail merchants are not part of the ghetto. They are outsiders whose understanding of the plight of urban blacks is hardly enlightening, whose views of their customers are hardly flattering, and whose business is seen by themselves as perilously close to marginal.

Retail stores have been targets in civil disorders, but they are also subject to vandalism and thievery in ordinary times. During civil disorders, a patterning to the looting and vandalism occurs. Retail merchants who sell more expensive items and who show attitudes that are either hostile or patronizing to customers are more likely to be "hit." In calmer times, other merchant characteristics similarly pattern the incidences of vandalism and thievery, although the pattern is less pronounced.

Finally, we showed that merchant exploitation is an issue which is raised by elites rather than by mass discontent. Indeed, it appears that customer dissatisfaction rises mainly when the elites raise the issue, rather than in direct response to the practices of merchants themselves. In contrast, black customers are more directly sensitive to the ways in which merchants treat them, showing high levels of discontent in cities where merchants hold derogatory attitudes toward their customers.

Chapter 8

JOBS AND BLACKS:
Personnel Procurement Policies

Although some black residents can find employment with firms or public agencies that are located within their neighborhoods, the overwhelming majority have to find employment outside the ghetto. White collar employment is concentrated heavily in the central business district. Heavy industrial firms usually will be found on waterways and along railway lines. Lighter manufacturing is spread along major streets and sometimes in new industrial parks. To be sure, there are some firms that are located within ghetto areas, but ordinarily such firms do not provide employment opportunities to more than a fraction of blacks seeking work. Of course, in this respect, blacks are scarcely in a different position than other city residents, most of whom journey daily to and from their place of employment.

Where employment opportunities are located has important implications for blacks. Blacks have to venture out of their ghettos to locate employment. It also means that managers of employing organizations may have little direct knowledge of the conditions of life in ghetto areas,

---

This chapter is largely based on Bettye K. Eidson, *Institutional Racism: Minority Group Manpower Policies of Major Urban Employers.* Unpublished Ph.D. Dissertation, Department of Social Relations, The Johns Hopkins University, 1971.

or, for that matter, in other types of central-city poorer neighborhoods. It is quite possible that many managers' main contact with the ghetto has been through the mass media.

To study the impingement of employing organizations on the life chances of blacks, one must move one's concentration from the ghetto to the larger metropolitan area. Unlike the other institutional areas in this volume, the locations of the employers are spread throughout the metropolitan regions that include the central cities involved. The metropolitan region's major employers in the private sector are the institutions that provide potentially the largest share of employment opportunities available to ghetto residents.

Employers—public and private—define the demand of local labor markets. Their actions expressed in hiring, promotion, and dismissal patterns profoundly influence the lives of all residents. A man or woman consist of more than his or her occupation, but a large part of life chances are determined by the income derived from jobs, and the concomitant feelings of worth and self-respect that come along with employment and holding a "good job" as compared with being unemployed or holding a demeaning position. Hence the patterns of employment in a city are critical to the position of blacks.

A large metropolitan area may have literally thousands of employing organizations, including government agencies. Most of the employers are small and hire fewer than 100 employees. A relatively few large employers, however, hire a large proportion, and in some cities, a majority of workers. As a consequence, working for an employer who hires more than 100 employees is not an atypical experience.

The large employers set the tone of employment in other respects as well. The boards of civic associations tend to be dominated by the men who manage the larger corporations, banks, and stores, and the term "civic leader" ordinarily connotes someone high in the corporate structure of a large employing organization.

A reasonable account of how the institutions of a city impinges upon its inhabitants would be incomplete without some attention to employment patterns. This statement applies equally, if not greater, to urban blacks. Indeed, from many points of view, employment is *the* critical problem of the ghetto, for here unemployment rates are the highest and income levels are the lowest.

To provide some measure of employment patterns vis-a-vis blacks, we drew a sample of the major employers in the private sectors of the metropolitan areas of each of the fifteen cities. The ten largest employers were chosen, along with a sample of 20 of the next 90 largest employers in each metropolitan area, totaling 30 private firms in each city.[1] For every city, the sample[2] represents employers who hire as much as one-half of the labor force. The cooperation of employers was very high: Only three firms refused.

In each firm, the personnel manager (or equivalent position) was interviewed. We chose the personnel manager as the person in the firm management level who would be know most generally about personnel practices, and who would have more complete factual information about the proportions of black in various levels of the firm. Although we refer to our respondents throughout this chapter as "employers," it should be borne in mind that the responses were given to us by personnel managers.

The ethic of social responsibility of business was overwhelmingly endorsed by the employers. Eighty-six percent agreed with the statement that employers "have a social responsibility to make strong efforts to provide employment to blacks and other minority groups." The messages of the older and newer civic associations that have stressed opening employment opportunities to blacks have diffused widely. However, as we know, endorsing a statement of principle and putting that principle into practice, are quite separate and distinct matters.

According to the employers, the problem of black employment lies not so much with the practices of their business as in the characteristics of black workers. The overwhelming majority of employers believe that blacks are not qualified to hold any but the lowest level jobs in their firms.

Eighty-three percent stated that very few blacks are now qualified for professional or white collar jobs. Sixty-nine percent stated that few blacks are qualified for skilled level jobs. In contrast, only 23% shared this view of the qualifications of blacks for bottom-level jobs.

According to personnel officers, this set of contrasting views defines the problem of employment for blacks in their companies and in their communities. Blacks may be qualified in fact for employment on the skilled and higher levels of their firms, but if personnel officers believe that blacks are qualified, they are powerful enough to impart some social reality to their beliefs.

---

[1] In Washington, D.C., where the major employer is the federal government, the public sector was included, represented by the personnel director of the General Services Administration (GSA). Since this position is far removed from the day-to-day personnel practices of the hundreds of specific federal agencies located in that metropolitan area, it would have made more sense to sample such agencies directly rather than rely upon GSA to represent the major employer in this city. Hindsight is more intelligent than foresight!

[2] The sampling is described in greater detail in Chapter 2.

Social and Economic Characteristics of Personnel Officers. From what strategic point in the social structure do these personnel officers assess black "qualifications?" From a fairly lofty one, as it turns out.[3] All but one of the personnel officers of the major firms in these fifteen urban areas are male. All are white. Of the six occupational groups in our study, the personnel officers are the most affluent (70% with annual incomes in excess of $15,000), the best educated (40% had attended graduate or professional schools), the most likely to be Protestant (58%), and the most likely to be Republican (48%).

The personnel officers came closest to the stereotype of the "WASP establishment" of any of the occupational groups studied. The majority are white, upper-middle-class, well-educated members.

Employers and the Problems in Their Cities. In common with many other occupational groups, employers see blacks as posing some of the most serious problems facing their cities. The control of crime, the prevention of violence and other civil disorders, and release of tension in race relations generally were considered "very serious" problems by 64, 49, and 46% of the employers, respectively (Table 8.1). "Finding tax funds for municipal services" ran a close fourth at 41%, although what services employers had in mind was unspecified. Air pollution was considered very serious by a slightly larger proportion of the employers (27%) than was unemployment (21%). In contrast to the other occupational groups in this study, employers were less likely to consider each problem "very serious," with one exception—"traffic and highways" (rated very serious by 31% of the employers and 27% of the other occupational groups).

Since employers as a group rate seriously problems in their cities connected directly as indirectly to blacks, it is reasonable to inquire what employers see as the major problems facing blacks. In Table 8.2 are responses given by employers when asked to compare blacks and other groups in their cities with respect to the overall "equality of treatment." A majority of the employers see blacks in their cities as being treated as well or better than whites or as well as whites of the same social class. Personnel managers do not appear to be very sensitive to the objective positions of blacks in their communities.

Over one-third of the employers view treatment of blacks as deriving from their social class rather than from their race, and about one fourth select the opposite response—race, not class. And one-fifth, roughly, see *no* difference in the treatment that blacks receive in their cities.

---

[3] See Chapter 4 for numerical details.

TABLE 8.1

Employer   ) Problems in Their Cities Rated "Very Serious", By
Interviews) Employers and By the General Sample

Problem	Employers Only	Proportions Who Rate Problems as Very Serious
		General Sample (all Occupations Combined)
Control of Crime	64%	71%
Preventing Violence and Other Civil Disorders	49%	56%
Race Relations	46%	53%
Finding Tax Funds for Municipal Services	41%	42%
Providing Quality Education	35%	46%
Traffic and Highways	30%	26%
Air Pollution	27%	33%
Unemployment	21%	36%
Lack of Recreational Facilities	11%	31%
Corruption of Public Officials	10%	19%
100% =	[447]	[2,162]

This tendency of employers to see black problems in their cities as stemming from class rather than race may account for the pattern of differences that appear between employers and the other groups in comparing blacks and others "of the same income and education" with respect to services and resources available in their cities (Table 8.3).

The employers tend to see more local equality of black opportunity than do the other occupational groups. Nevertheless, the employers are by no means homogeneous in their perceptions. Nor are the differences in employers' perceptions of local black opportunities a simple function of the city that the employer is assessing. When the seven items in Table 8.3 are combined into an attitude scale (scored so that a score of 0 means that an employer saw blacks as "less well off" consistently and a score of 14 that he saw blacks as "better off" consistently), the result is that employers are shown to vary among cities as well as among themselves.

TABLE 8.2

Employer) Treatment Blacks Receive in Their Cities, as
Interviews) Evaluated by Employers and by the General Sample

Type of Treatment	Employers	General Sample (All Occupations Combined)
Negroes treated better than any other part of the population	6%	10%
Negroes treated equally	21	21
Negroes treated as other people of the same income	35	25
Negroes treated worse than other people of the same income	25	26
Negroes treated worse than any other part of the population	10	16
Don't know or no answer	2	2
100 percent equals	(447)	(2162)

TABLE 8.3

Employer) Employers Assessment of Availability of
Interviews) Resources to Blacks

| Resources and Services | Proportion Saying Blacks are as Well Off as Whites | |
	Employers Only	General Sample (All Occupations Combined)
Educational opportunities	57%	48%
Employment Opportunities	40%	31%
Treatment by police	56%	46%
Housing	19%	20%
Treatment by public officials	58%	48%
Medical care	59%	54%
Recreation	58%	45%
100 percent equals	(447)	(2162)

In Figure 8.1 are shown the average scores obtained by employers in each of the fifteen cities. There are considerable differences among cities: At the one extreme, employers in Washington, D.C., display the highest average score, indicating that they believe that blacks are quite well off in terms of equality of treatment in the areas discussed in Table 8.3. At the other extreme, Boston employers are least likely to think that blacks are well off. It is difficult to present a set of explanations for these intercity differences which would be convincing, without adding additional data, a task to which we attend to later on in this chapter: It is sufficient at this point to note that unlike the merchants, employers vary from city to city in their perceptions of black opportunities.

Figure 8.1 also contains the proportions of employers who claim that blacks are as well off (or better off) than whites with respect to employment opportunities, a topic on which the employers ought to be especially perceptive. The range across the cities is quite large: At the one extreme a law of 27% of employers in St. Louis claim that blacks are as well off as whites, while the other extreme view is held by Washington, D.C. employers (85%). By and large the fifteen cities are arranged in the same order on both lines (the correlation between the two is +.85).

Although city differences are quite large, there are still considerable differences among individual employers within cities as indicated by standard deviations around the mean scores. In every city some employers believe that blacks are as well off in most areas of community life while others believe quite the opposite.

Given findings which suggest that employers are hardly in agreement with the main complaints of the civil rights movement, it is all the more perplexing to find that 58% of the employers rate "major employers" in their cities as "leaders in working for equal treatment of all citizens regardless of race or color" (Table 8.4). Employers are "elected public officials like the mayor" in the forefront (74%), social workers (61%) second, themselves third, and "major retail businesses" fourth (41%).

The combined sample is much less likely to rate major employers as leaders than the employers rate themselves as leaders—29% of the general sample do so, as compared with the employers' 58%.

The variation among employers in their ratings of major firms as leaders in the drive for equality of opportunity is paralleled by the variation in the reported actions of the respondents' own firms. For example, in response to the question—"Some companies have been going out of their way lately to hire Negroes whenever possible. Is this mainly true, partially true, or not at all true of your company?"—46% of the employers

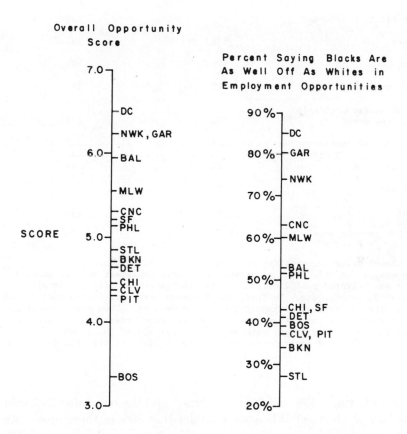

HIGH SCORE = Opportunities Perceived as More Equal for Blacks

LOW SCORE = Opportunities for Blacks Perceived as Unequal

Overall Opportunity Score

Percent Saying Blacks Are As Well Off As Whites in Employment Opportunities

[Score defined as number of areas in which Blacks as seen to have at least as good opportunities as whites.]

Figure 8.1 Employer interviews: perceived opportunities for blacks by city.

TABLE 8.4

Employer   )   Local Groups Rated as "Leaders" in the Drive for
Interviews)   Equal Treatment by Employers

Group Rated as "Leaders"	Employers Only	All Occupations Combined
Major employers	58%	29%
Major retail businesses	41%	22%
Bankers	32%	18%
Police	34%	29%
Social workers	61%	48%
Elected public officials like the mayor	74%	67%
Public school teachers	32%	33%
Homeowners	1%	6%
Landlords	2%	3%
Unions	18%	22%
100 percent equals	(447)	(2162)

Even though percentages differ substantially, there is considerable
agreement on the rank order of groups, i.e. both employers and the general
sample see "elected public officials like the mayor" as first, "social
workers" as second, etc. In fact, the Spearman rank-correlation coefficient
between the two sets of ratings turns out to be 0.88. Thus employers and
other personnel in the cities agree on the relative ordering of leadership
groups in their communities, with employers' ratings of their own
institutional sector contributing heavily to the lack of fit that does occur.

said, "mainly true," 30% said "partially true," and the remaining 24% said
it was "not at all true." When we consider that 86% of these men state
they personally feel companies in their cities have a social responsibility
to provide employment to blacks and other minority groups, it is easy to
characterize our employers as persons of complacency, who feel that they
have accomplished the fulfillment of their expressed values with respect
to discrimination, and who view the position of blacks in their communities as relatively well off.

The main question of the next few sections of this chapter are concerned with measuring the gap between value expression and behavior
in actual hiring practices of the firms involved.

Employment Practices.   In the populations of the fifteen cities surveyed, the proportion black ranged from 12 to 73% (as of 1968); for the cities combined, the mean proportion black is about 34%. Our findings indicate that is only in unskilled job categories that the proportion of blacks in the firms' employment processes corresponds to the average proportion black in the fifteen cities. The rates at which personnel officers reported their firms were receiving applications from, hiring, and retaining blacks are shown in Table 8.5.

One reason why blacks are badly underrepresented at upper skill levels can be seen immediately by comparing the top and bottom half in Table 8.5. While an average 13.2% of applicants to firms for professional and white collar jobs were blacks, this mean percentage obscures the fact that 43.3% of firms reported *no* blacks among such applicants. This pattern is repeated for skilled level employees: the mean proportion of blacks among skilled level applicants (15.2%) is a consequence, in part, of the fact that over half the firms reported no blacks at these stages in the work force formation process.

It is only when we consider the level of unskilled workers that we see large proportions of blacks hired among applicants and presently employed by the companies surveyed. Blacks are sizable minorities on this level of the work forces across the board, and, in some cities, blacks constitute a majority of the unskilled components of the work forces.

It is clear from the rates of blacks applying for positions, that one of the problems lies in the fact that few blacks apply for positions above unskilled occupations. On the average, 34% of the populations in the fifteen cities are black. If blacks were applying for positions in proportion to their contributions to the populations of their cities, their rates of applying for the two highest levels of employment would be several times greater than shown in Table 8.5.[4]

Rates of application are only one reason why blacks are underrepresented in the work forces. If we compute the relative chances of a black being hired once he has applied, as compared to that of a white, as in Table 8.6, then we can see rather dramatically that at every level of the

---

[4] The population proportions mentioned in this paragraph are for central cities, hence overstating by some degree the proportion black in the potential work forces of the firms studied. Since the firms are not restricted to the central cities as reservoirs from which to recruit, the potential work force of a firm may be the entire metropolitan area. Indeed, for certain types of workers, especially highly skilled, technical and professional occupations, a firm may be drawing typically on the human resources of a region.

TABLE 8.5

Employer)   Black Representation in Different Stages of the
Interviews)   Employment Process* Among Three Skill Levels (N = 447)

| | Mean Proportion Black | | |
	Among Recent Applicants	Among Recently Hired	In Present Labor Force
Skill Levels of Firms			
Professional and White Collar	13.2%	7.3%	5.0%
Standard Deviation	(19.1%)	(12.7%)	(10.6%)
Skilled Workers	15.2%	9.4%	11.8%
Standard Deviation	(22.0%)	(16.5%)	(20.1%)
Unskilled Workers	40.2%	29.3%	24.7%
Standard Deviation	(32.4%)	(29.4%)	(27.7%)

| | Percent Firms Reporting No Blacks | | |
	Among Recent Applicants	Among Recently Hired	In Present Labor Force
Skill Levels of Firm			
Professional and White Collar	43.3%	55.0%	33.3%
Skilled Workers	50.0%	58.1%	26.4%
Unskilled Workers	24.7%	30.2%	18.2%

*For application rates, personnel officers were asked, "Out of the last 20
people applying for work in each of the following skill groups, about how
many were Negro...?" Responses could vary between 0 and 20. In order to
transform numbers into proportions, values were multiplied by a factor of
5, and a mean was computed for the entire sample on these transformed
estimates. The same procedure was followed for hiring rates. The "current"
proportion of Negroes at each skill level was estimated directly by the
question, "What would you estimate the proportion of Negroes to be among
your employees on these three levels: (a) Professional and white collar?",
etc.

272

TABLE 8.6

Employer) Relative Chances of Blacks Being Hired
Interviews) Given Application [N = 447 Firms]

Level of Employment	Blacks' Chances of Being Hired Relative to White Chances*
Professional and White Collar	52%
Skilled Workers	66%
Unskilled Workers	86%

*Computed as follows, from Table 8.5:

Relative Chance   = $\dfrac{\dfrac{\text{Prob. Black Being Hired}}{\text{Prob. Black Applying}}}{\dfrac{\text{Prob. White Being Hired}}{\text{Prob. White Applying}}}$
Blacks to Whites

firms, blacks have a lower chance of being hired even when they present themselves for selection. On the professional and white collar level, a black has slightly better than half the chances that a white has. On the skilled level, the chances are two-thirds those of whites. The relative chances of blacks come closer to parity on the unskilled level, but even here it is lower than parity (86%).

The main task of the remainder of this chapter is to study the processes that lie behind the rates reported in Table 8.5.

Since persons have to apply before being hired and every person in a work force must at sometime have both applied and been hired, the best way to look at the three types of rates would be as intimately related to each other in a sequence of increasing commitment on the part of the firm to an individual as an employee. However, it must be borne in mind that in this study all three types of rates were measured *at the same point in time*. Thus application and hiring rates that refer to the same group of people would only apply under the condition that the number of persons applying is not much greater than the number hired. Thus if persons are applying at the rate of 100 per month, but only two persons per month are being hired, the application rate refers to a period of about a week before the time of interview while the hiring rate refers to a period extending back around 10 months.

The time reference is even more out of joint when the proportion of blacks in the firms' work forces is considered. The present work force of a company represents the net retention of employees who were hired over a period that could extend back as far as 40 years. Assuming that the average tenure of a work in an establishment is about 15 years, the proportion black in the work force of a plant was built up over a period of at least that length and possibly longer. Hence it is more logical to regard the proportion black in the work force as *temporally antecedent to the applying and hiring rates than the other way around.*

For these reasons, we consider each type of rate separately in most of the remainder of this chapter. Only a longitudinal study in which the temporal sequence can be properly laid out will permit an analysis in which the three rates can be analyzed in a causal model.

Personnel Procurement Practices.   Our first step in the analysis is to look at how the employers go about recruiting new workers to their firms. In particular we study how information about job vacancies is disseminated.

Two sets of data are relevant. First, employers were asked whether they utilized a given set of recruitment channels to advertise their job opening (Table 8.7). Second, the employers were asked which of the channels used was "most effective" in attracting applicants with the desired qualifications (Table 8.8). Table 8.7 indicates that the methods used for recruitment vary. Want ads—information available to all but the illiterate—are widely used. For both white collar (82%) and skilled level jobs (78%), newspaper ads are among the most frequently cited recruitment methods. This does not mean that want ads constitute the most *frequently used* method, only that they are a *generally used* method of advertising job openings. (Indeed, the same *caveat* must be respected in interpreting the other frequencies in the table.)

The next question is—"What is the most consistently used channel, across, rather than within, skill levels?" Where the differences in proportions of employers using a channel to recruit white collar and semiskilled or unskilled labor are small, that channel could be defined as consistently used. Conversely, where the gap is wide across skill levels, the recruitment

TABLE 8.7

Employer   ) <u>Channels of Recruitment Used</u>
Interviews) <u>[N = 447]</u>

| | Proportions of Firms Using Channels for Vacancies | | | |
Channels Used	Professional and White Collar Vacancies	Skilled Vacancies	Semi-Skilled and Unskilled Vacancies	Differences Between Cols. 1 and 3
Private Employment Services	83%	52%	31%	+ 52
Want Ads in Newspaper	82%	78%	67%	+ 15
Asking Current Employers for Referrals	73%	70%	72%	+ 1
State Employment Services	64%	65%	70%	- 6
Signs Posted Outside Plant	7%	12%	15%	- 8
Labor Unions	8%	28%	26%	-18

TABLE 8.8

Employer) <u>Effectiveness of Recruitment Channels</u>
Interviews) <u>[N = 447]</u>

| | Proportions Rating Channels Effective | | |
Channels	Professional and White Collar	Skilled	Semi-Skilled and Unskilled
Want Ads in Newspaper	33%	42%	35%
Labor Unions	0.5	9	8
State Employment Services	4	7	17
Private Employment Services	36	12	4
Asking Current Employers for Referrals	11	15	20
Signs Posted Outside Plant	0.7	0.9	2
Walk-in Applicants*	3	4	8
Recruitment at Colleges*	9	0.9	0
Don't Know or No Answer	3	4	4

275

strategy could be considered more geared to the type of employee sought, hence less consistent. To illustrate what this technicality might actually mean in the job search we could take the case of a person without a job—where should he start looking for one?

Our data indicate (Table 8.7) that if the unemployed person is not certain what skill level he should aim for, his best bet would be to ask employed people he knows about openings where they work. Asking current employees for referrals is the method most consistently used (by employers) across skill levels—a difference of 1% from the top to bottom level jobs. However, if an unemployed person aims for a white collar job, his first stop should probably be a private employment service. Private employment services represent the least consistently used source, favoring top-level technical and white collar jobs by a difference of 52%.

Referrals and private employment services—the most and the least consistently used methods by employers, respectively—have a common characteristic. Both are "filter" recruitment methods, and the information an unemployed person obtains from them will be conditioned by his access to gainfully employed acquaintances, or the extent to which he impresses the intermediary at the private employment service that he is what the client has in mind.

If a candidate has neither friends who would know of job openings nor attributes that look marketable to the agency interviewer, his next best bet, according to Table 8.7, is to answer newspaper ads or to register with his public employment service.

To see how effective employers rate these various paths to employment, we turn to Table 8.8. This table reveals that want ads are ranked first in effectiveness both for skilled labor (42%) and lower-level recruitment (35%) and are, in fact, a very close second in rank (33%) for filling white collar vacancies.

The most effective channel for top jobs is considered to be private employment services (36%, three points higher than the rating of want ads for professional and white collar category). Asking current employees for referrals would appear to increase in effectiveness as the skill level of the opening declines: 11% of the employers rank this method as "most effective" for white collar openings, with 20% so ranking it for semi-skilled or unskilled recruitment. The public employment service is not generally considered effective unless the opening is for a lower level job. Private employment services outrank the public agencies for skilled as well as for white collar recruitment: Even at the lowest skill level, we find that employers place slightly more confidence in obtaining referrals from current employees (20%) than in the public employment services (17%).

Asking employers their most effective recruitment source does not necessarily yield information about the most effective employment channel for the job-seeker. Employers may be defining "effectiveness" by the numbers of potential employees reachable by a channel, for a given cost (coverage) in relation to the result that frequency obtains (impact). But to evaluate a method accurately from the point of view of the job-seeker, we would need to know the costs of one or the other channel relative to the chances of success for those channels. Obviously, these items of information are not available in our data.

It is not clear how black application rates might be affected by employers' recruitment preferences. The effectiveness of want ads ranks high and does represent a *direct* method of recruitment. Yet, one could turn the figures in Table 8.8 around and show that 67% of employers do *not* consider want ads the most effective means of white collar recruitment, 58% do *not* consider them the most effective method for filling skilled level openings, and 65% rank other methods as more effective in the search for semi-skilled and unskilled labor.

Firms vary according to the recruitment channels that they use and rate as effective. Larger firms tend to use more passive methods; they rely more heavily on their internal labor markets and on word-of-mouth recruitment, and apparently take advantage of the large interpersonal network that their employees are tied into. There are also differences in recruitment channels used among firms according to the industry classification in which they fall, although it is difficult to summarize these findings easily.[5]

Patterns of recruitment are important because they condition the mix of applicants a firm may receive for the vacancies in its work force. Once presented with a set of applicants, however, the firm has to select and choose among candidates. Hence the evaluations that firms place upon various candidates represents another set of filters that determines the compositions of their work forces. For this reason, we now consider how firms evaluate blacks as employees. Before doing so, it is necessary to warn the reader that the evaluations that we study are those of the personnel officers of the firms. Personnel officers are undoubtedly important in the process of employee selection, especially in the initial screening of applicants and at upper skill levels. But they are by no means omnipotent. In many firms, the selection of new employees is left in the hands of first line supervisors. For top level professional and technical employees, the top manager of the firm may often make the final decisions. By studying the evaluations of personnel officers, we are using his attitudes as "proxies" for the attitudes of many other persons in the firm, a strategy

---

[5] Details of these findings are contained in Bettye K. Eidson, *op. cit.*, pp. 58–66.

that undoubtedly dilutes the importance of evaluations of blacks as employees.

Blacks are *not* valued highly as employees. This generalization comes through in a variety of ways from our data. Table 8.9, for example, shows that many of the personnel managers consider blacks to be especially "high-risk" candidates. The proportions of employers who agree ("strongly" or "slightly") with a series of statements—mostly derogatory—about what blacks would be like if one did hire them in any number. Two-thirds of the employers agreed that blacks are apt to be less well-trained than whites—"so hiring many blacks will either decrease production or increase training costs." Slightly over half agreed that blacks would upset production schedules due to their higher absenteeism rates. About one-third of the employers said they would expect increased theft and vandalism to accompany the hiring of many blacks. One-eighth agreed that the involvement of blacks in civil rights activities might predict agitation and trouble for the company that employs them in large numbers, while about one-fifth expected production costs to rise because "Negroes generally tend not to take orders and instructions as well as whites."

In sum, Table 8.9 indicates that employers as a group expect most blacks to be less well-trained and less reliable than whites. Yet all but 20% rate blacks as "trainable," if we may thus interpret the low frequency with which employers agreed that blacks take instructions poorly.

To explore what employers mean by the black "training deficit," we have compared two sets of attitude measures. The first set includes those questions about the qualifications of blacks, in general, for professional and white collar, skilled, and unskilled level jobs. Eighty-three percent of the employers felt that blacks as a group were not qualified for upper level jobs. Sixty-nine percent considered blacks as a group unqualified for skilled level jobs, and 23% saw blacks as unqualified for unskilled level jobs.[6]

The second set of questions refer to employers' specific complaints about blacks as workers (Table 8.9). In the table that follows we compare employer *general* ratings of black qualifications with their *specific* complaints about black workers. The interrelationships among the two sets of items are shown in Table 8.10.

Each set of items clusters rather well, as shown by the fact that the

---

[6] The items used were—"Other companies which have tried to go out of their way to hire Negroes have found that there were very few qualified Negroes to hire. In your experience is this statement justified in the hiring of (a) professional and white collar workers; (b) skilled workers; (c) semi-skilled and unskilled workers?"

TABLE 8.9

Employer   ) Potential Problems Associated with Hiring
Interviews) Negroes [N = 447]

	Percent who "Agree Strongly" or "Agree Slightly"
"Negroes are apt to be less well trained than whites, so hiring many Negroes will either decrease production or increase training costs"	64%
"Negroes are apt to have a higher rate of absenteeism, therefore hiring too many Negroes may upset production schedules"	53%
"Since Negro crime rates are generally higher than white crime rates, hiring many Negroes could easily lead to increased theft and vandalism in the company"	32%
"Negroes generally tend not to take orders and instructions as well as whites and, therefore to hire many of them may raise costs of production"	21%
"Since many Negroes have been involved in civil rights demonstrations and acts of civil disobedience, by hiring too many Negroes you risk bringing trouble-makers and agitators into your company "	13%

gammas within triangles are generally higher than the other gammas in the matrix. Furthermore, within the specific evaluation items, those that pertain to the "moral" characteristics of blacks cluster more strongly than the other items in that triangle. (The items in question refer to "agitation," "theft," and "absenteeism.")

The structure of Table 8.10 suggests that two scales should be constructed, one related to the *General Evaluation* of blacks as employees and the other related to the *Specific Evaluation* of the characteristics of blacks for particular levels of jobs. These two scales are used extensively in the analyses that follow.

TABLE 8.10

Employer) Inter-Relationships Among General and Specific
Interviews) Evaluations of Blacks as Workers [Gammas] (N = 447)

	SPECIFIC EVALUATIONS ITEMS (See Table 8.9 for Items)					GENERAL EVALUATION ITEMS Blacks are Unqualified for		
	Training (1)	Supervision (2)	Agitation (3)	Theft (4)	Absenteeism (5)	Professional and White Collar Jobs (6)	Skilled Jobs (7)	Semi- and Unskilled (8)
Training (1)		.40	.34	.48	.51	.49	.34	.30
Supervision (2)			.42	.46	.52	.23	.13	.15
Agitation (3)				.62	.41	.39	.08	.10
Theft (4)					.55	.37	.14	.17
Absenteeism (5)						.38	.20	.11
Professional and White Collar (6)							.91	.71
Skilled (7)								.95

Accounting for Black Application Rates. A myriad of ways in which firms differ could be related to their ability to attract (or repel) applications from potential black employees. The firms vary in size, in the industry to which they belong, in the attitudes of personnel officers, in their locations within metropolitan areas of the country, in the recruitment channels used, and so on through a large catalogue of interfirm differences.

To reduce the number of factors whose effects on recruitment practices to observe, we have grouped sets of discrete variables into clusters; each cluster contains variables that share common substantive references, as follows:

1. *Attitudes of   Containing assessments of blacks as workers,
   personnel officers:* perceived opportunities for blacks, and so on.

2. *City as context:*   Used in two forms: First as a set of categorical variables; second, as characteristics of city location (e.g., proportion black in the population).

3. *Administrative   Recruitment channels used, federal contract,
   characteristics:*   status, personnel officers assessment of reactions of employees to employment of blacks.

4. *Market   Size of firm, type of industry, relative size of
   characteristics:*   firm in city.

We hypothesize that the minority group manpower experiences of the firms is in part a consequence of control exercised at the point of entry. The occupational handicap of minority group status may turn on its implication to personnel officers of the ability of blacks, presumably culturally different, to play the game according to majority group rules.

A second consideration is that differential socialization, if seen by personnel officers as inferior for minority groups, may require special investment in training that competitive firms cannot recoup in an economic system where employees have property rights in their own training and may transfer their acquired abilities to a firm's competitor.[7] If avoidance of in-house training is a major determinant of minority manpower policies, we expect differences across sizes of firms or across types of industries (as indices of market positions) to equal or outweigh the effects of personnel officer's sentiments on rates of black incorporation. Specifically, we might expect industries with high growth rates to be

---

[7] For a good discussion of the rationality of avoidance of in-house training in labor competitive firm situations, see Gary S. Becker, *Human Capital*, National Bureau of Economic Research, New York, 1964, especially Chap. 2.

better able to afford heavy investments in employee training and more willing to make such expenditures.

Third, the implication of minority group status may be termed an information disadvantage. To the extent that firms recruit through direct advertisement techniques, this factor might be neutralized. To the extent that firms rely upon current employees or upon other "filter" channels of recruitment, black underrepresentation in the firms might be predicted by differences in recruitment channels used or by the racial distribution of current employees.

Finally, to explain intercity variation we look at the actual differences in the sizes and the qualities of the black and white labor forces. All employers within a city face the same black labor pool; hence differences in the rates at which they hire blacks might be due to personnel decisions, to methods of recruitment, and to skill needs of the firm due to market position. Across cities, the variation in the rate at which firms incorporate blacks should be sensitive to differences between the black and white labor forces or to other city differences. Holding constant the factors by which firms differ, we explore the weight that should be given to the "supply" of the firm in accounting for the rate of black economic assimilation.

These four factors have operated as clusters described above containing measures of "attitudes of firm personnel officers," "firm market characteristics," "firm administrative characteristics," and "city differences."

The strategy in the analyses in this and the next two sections of this chapter is to perform regression analyses, identifying clusters that account for significant proportions of the interfirm variance in rates of applying, hiring, and proportions in the work force. Clusters that account for significant portions of the variance are examined in detail to determine which variables included in that cluster account for the cluster's contribution to explained variance.

Explaining Black Application Rates for White Collar Jobs. Table 8.11 shows the total amount of variation in the black professional and white collar *application rate* accounted for by the clusters taken together. In addition, the separate unique contribution of each cluster to the explained variance is shown.

The clusters together account for about 17% of the total variation in the black professional and white collar application rate. When firm characteristics are held constant, "city differences" account for about 7% of the total variance. Each of the remaining clusters does not make a statistically significant contribution to the total amount of variance. However

TABLE 8.11

Employer) Black Application Rates for Professional and White
Interview) Collar Jobs: Relative Contributions of Clusters
of Firm Characteristics (N = 447)

Cluster	Zero Order Relationship of Cluster	Unique ** Contribution to Explained Variance
Attitudes of Personnel Officers	.0165	.0087
City as Context	.0704	.0677*
Administrative Characteristics	.0440	.0337
Market Characteristics	.0536	.0385

Total Unique Contribution of Four Clusters	.1677*
Sum of Unique Contributions of Each Cluster Above	.1303
Overlap Contributions	.0374

*Significant at .05 level.

**To simplify the table the small, insignificant joint contributions of
the clusters are not included.

when "city differences" are controlled, the three clusters together account for about 8% of the total variance.[8]

Although the 7% of total variance uniquely due to "city as context" is statistically significant, a very large proportion of the variation in black application rates was *not* due to the firms' city locations. Except for the possibility that some city characteristics cancel one another out, we now know that no specific city characteristic subsequently introduced will explain more than 7% of the total variation in the white collar application rate when the firm differences in the model are controlled.

The picture on the firm side is different. It is highly probable that a number of characteristics of firms, other than the ones used, could increase the amount of explained variance. With the present set, we estimate that the main "firm effect" on the black white collar application rate came through differences in the firms' market positions. Differences in attitudes of personnel officers toward blacks and differences in administrative

---

[8] This proportion is arrived at by summing the unique contributions of the variable sets that refer to firms.

characteristics of firms (as these were measured and clustered) show no significant zero-order or unique effects upon black application rate. And the unique effect of differences in the firms' market positions (4% of the total variance) is not significant by conventional (5%) standards.

Since the only cluster that uniquely contributes significantly to the dependent variable is "city as a context," it is worthwhile to substitute specific individual city characteristics to investigate which ones contribute to the explanation. Table 8.12 presents the unique contributions of five such city characteristics.[9]

Note that the combined contributions of these five characteristics fall short of the unique contribution of the "city as context" cluster of Table 8.11 (in which city has been entered as a dummy variable), indicating that some city characteristics are as yet unknown and account for about 2% of the variance beyond the five characteristics shown here.

The only city characteristic whose unique contribution is significant is "proportion black." The greater the proportion of blacks in a city, the more likely are blacks to apply for jobs on the professional and white collar levels of the firms under study. It is difficult to place a precise interpretation on this finding. It may mean that applications approach a random process in which the higher the proportion of persons with a given characteristic in a population, the more likely are such persons to show up on lists of applicants. It may also mean that the higher the proportion of blacks in a city's population, the more likely are employers to accede to black demands for greater employment opportunities. At this point it is not possible to decide between either of these interpretations: We return to this question later in this chapter.

Black Application Rates for Skilled Jobs. On the average, about 15% of the firms' recent skilled level applicants were reported to be black, and approximately one-half of the firms reported no blacks among their recent

---

[9] Defined as follows:

School segregation:	Proportion of black children who are attending schools with 90 to 100% black students.
Black-white educational differences:	The spread in years of education between the median years of educational attainment for black and white adults in each city.
Business community efforts:	Ratings from elite interviews of the effort made by the business community to ameliorate the position of blacks in the city.
Unemployment rate:	Bureau of Labor Statistics estimates of total proportion of unemployment in city, average for 1967–68.
Proportion black:	Estimates proportion black in population of city as of 1966.

TABLE 8.12

Employer) Application Rates for Professional and White Collar
Interview) Jobs: Unique Contributions of City Characteristics,
Holding Other Clusters Constant

City Characteristic	Zero Order Contribution (R^2)	Unique Contribution
School Segregation	.0239	.0007
Black-White Educational Differences	.0000	.0011
Unemployment Rate	.0021	.0000
Business Community Efforts	.0013	.0020
Proportion Black in City	.0358	.0164*

Unique Contribution of City Cluster	.0445*
Sum of Unique Contributions of Each City Variable	.0202
Overlap Contribution of Characteristics	.0243

skilled level applicants. Although black were applying, in the aggregate, at very similar rates for the firms' white collar and skilled level jobs (13 and 15%, respectively), in Table 8.13 we may observe that the set of explaining clusters accounts for a considerably higher proportion of the total variation in the black skilled level application rate, 27%.[10]

In terms of their unique contributions, "city as context" and the combined contributions of the other three clusters are about equally useful predictors of the rates at which blacks were applying for the firms' skilled level jobs. At the skilled level compared to white collar jobs, the predictive value of both "city" and individual "firm" clusters increases in absolute terms. "City" (as a dummy variable) uniquely accounted for

---

[10] The only modification is that three of the predictor variables were measured originally for each skill level. Appropriate measures on these variables were substituted in the model, as we moved down the skill ladder. Specifically, personnel officers were asked which recruitment channels their firms used to obtain professional, white collar, skilled, and unskilled level workers. Also, personnel officers were asked their opinion of the reaction of current employees to the inclusion of black co-workers, at each of the three skill levels. Similarly, personnel officers rated recruitment channels according to their "effectiveness" at each skill level. In the regression equation, measures on each of these three variables are skill-specific.

TABLE 8.13

Employer)	Black Application Rates for Skilled Level Jobs:
Interviews)	Relative Contributions of Clusters of Firm
	Characteristics (N = 447)

Cluster	Zero Order Relationship of Cluster	Unique Contribution to Explained Variance
Attitudes of Personnel Officers	.0370*	.0369*
City as Context	.1655*	.1249*
Administrative Characteristics	.0700*	.0494*
Market Characteristics	.0320	.0231

Total Unique Contribution of Four Clusters	.2702*
Sum of Unique Contributions of Each Cluster Above	.2343
Overlap Contributions	.0359

*Significant at .05 level.

only 7% of the total variation in the black *white collar* application rate, as compared with 12% on the *skilled worker* level. We find also that contributions on the "firm" side have increased proportionately.

The statistically significant effects of characteristics of firms are associated with the administrative and attitudinal clusters. Approximately 5% of the total variation in the black skilled application rate is associated uniquely with administrative differences among firms. We see in Table 8.14 that 3% of the total variance is taken up solely by differences in the recruitment channels firms used to obtain their skilled level workers. If we push the data a bit harder (probably too hard), we can evaluate the recruitment channels individually. A statistically significant, although small, contrast appears between firms that used and those that did not use private employment services for skilled level recruitment.

Private employment services originally were conceived of as a "filter" recruitment device that would negatively affect black access to job openings. If we take the details of the findings seriously, as the skilled level application stage, the opposite interpretation is suggested. The sign of the partial correlation between "use" of private services and the rate of black application to skilled jobs is positive. Furthermore, firms that used private employment services for skilled level recruitment reported about

TABLE 8.14

Employer)   Black Application Rates for Skilled Jobs: Unique
Interviews)   Contributions of Characteristics of Firms**

		Unique Contribution
I.	**Administrative Characteristics**	
A.	Recruitment channels used	.0307*
	1. State employment agencies	0
	2. Private Employment agencies	.0088*
	3. Want ads	.0030
	4. Labor unions	0
	5. Other employees	.0063
B.	Recruitment channels considered most effective	.0049
C.	Federal contract status	0
D.	Union contract status	.0006
E.	Reaction of current employees	.0008
II.	**Attitudes of Personnel Officers**	
A.	Assessment of general qualifications	.0021
B.	Assessment of specific task performance capabilities	.0004
C.	Index scale based upon scales A and B	.0101*
D.	Perceived employment opportunities	.0029
E.	Personal reactions to black competition	.0102*

*Significant at .05 level.

**Computed holding city characteristics and market characteristics constant.

30% more blacks among their recent applicants than firms which did not use this "filter" technique.[11]

Before we turn to the unique effects of components in the attitudinal variable set, we state for the record that we have found no measurable

---

[11] Firms using private employment services report 18.5% black among skilled job applicants as compared to 11.8% among nonusers.

effects on the black skilled application rate of the following: the Federal contract status of the firm, the union contract status of the firm, the personnel officers' preferences among recruitment channels, and the personnel officers' perceptions of the reactions of current skilled level workers to the inclusion of blacks.

The "reaction of current employees" that affects a black's chances of being among the firms' recent skilled level applicants turns out to be the reaction of the personnel officer himself. Personnel officers' own views of the likelihood of viable job competition from blacks uniquely account for 1% of the total variation in rates at which blacks were applying for the firms skilled level jobs. Firms with personnel officers who said it was either "possible" or "likely" a black would replace them if they left their present job counted 30% more blacks among their recent skilled level applicants than among applicants in firms whose personnel officers denied the possibility of replacement by a black. This finding deserves some comment.

One reasonable interpretation is as follows: To deny that blacks may conceivably take over one's position in the firm may be to deny that blacks have the competence to do so. Hence the prediction that a black may take over one's position may express a conviction that there are blacks with the potential of developing the requisite skills to perform the task of the personnel officer in the firm. In short, to admit that blacks may be competition is to admit that blacks may be competent; hence this item reflects the prejudices of the personnel officer, albeit in an unexpected way.

Finally, we see in Table 8.14, that the personnal officers' assessments of blacks as workers contributes to skilled worker application rates. Although the two scales individually did not reach an appropriate significance level, when combined[12] the assessment scales account for about 1% of the total variance.

"City as context" accounts uniquely for about 12% of the total variation in the black skilled level application rate (Table 8.13). When we control for "firm differences" and substitute five characteristics in place of city as a dummy variable, as in Table 8.15, the combination of city characteristics as a set account uniquely for about 7% of the total variation in this rate.

The city characteristic that is the best predictor of the black skilled application rate is simply the size of the local black labor pool. "Pro-

---

[12] The scores on each scale were dichotomized into "high" and "low" and combined to make a new three point scale, in which a respondent received a point for being high on either scale.

TABLE 8.15

Employer   ) Black Application Rates for Skilled Jobs: Unique
Interviews) Contributions of City Characteristics (Holding
Firm Characteristics Constant) (N = 447)

City Characteristic	Zero Order Relationship of Characteristic	Unique Contribution
School Segregation	.0458*	.0012
Black White Educational Differences	.0003	.0037
Unemployment Rate	.0119*	.0007
Business Community Efforts	.0026	.0029
Proportion Black	.0750*	.0230*
Total Unique Contribution of Combined City Characteristics Above		.0663*
Sum of Unique Contribution of Each City Variable		.0315
Overlap Among City Characteristics		.0348

*Significant at .05 level.

portion black" accounts uniquely for about 2% of the total variation. Independently of other variables in the model, the degree of school segregation, black white differences in educational attainment, the tightness of the local labor market, and the efforts of the business community have no statistically significant effects on rates at which blacks apply for skilled level jobs.

Explaining Black Application Rates for Unskilled Jobs. In 1968, blacks were best represented in our major firms at the bottom of the skill ladder. About 25% of the firms' "current" *unskilled* employees were reported to be black, as compared with proportion of 34% black in the fifteen cities sampled.

Because more firms reported at least some black participation at each stage of the unskilled employment process than in upper skill ranks, we have literally more variation to explain. In addition the black distribution at the bottom of the skill ladder is at once less skewed and more reflective of the average black population proportion in the fifteen urban areas. These distributional characteristics of firm application rates may be the main reason that our linear regression model is *twice* as useful in predicting the black *unskilled* application rate as in predicting variation in their application rate at the professional and white collar level, as Table 8.16 shows. The four clusters together account for 35% of the total variation. However over half of the explained variation is due uniquely to differences associated with city locations. The unique effects of the remaining three clusters that refer to firm characteristics sum to about 10% of the total explained variation.

The "attitude" cluster is statistically significant at the zero-order level, but its effect is not different from zero (above the .10 significance level) when the other variables in the model are held constant.

Both the "administrative" and "market" variable sets account uniquely for significant amounts of the total variation in the black unskilled application rate. At the zero-order level, 11% of the total variation in black unskilled application rates is associated with "administrative" differences. This effect reduces to 5% when the other independent variables are controlled. Since the most serious casualty among the four variable sets

TABLE 8.16

Employer   )   Black Application Rates for Unskilled Jobs:
Interviews)   Relative Contributions of Clusters of Firm
              Characteristics and City as Context   (N = 447)

Cluster	Zero Order Relationship of Cluster	Unique Contribution to Explained Variance
Attitudes of Personnel Officers	.0560*	.0171
City as Context	.2244*	.1718*
Administrative Characteristics	.1103*	.0490*
Market Characteristics	.0565*	.0329*
Total Contribution of Four Clusters		.3511*
Sum of Unique Contribution of Each Cluster Above		.2708
Overlap Contributions		.0803

*Significant at .05 level.

is the effect of "attitudinal" differences (when other variables are held constant), it seems reasonable to infer that personnel officers' attitudes and administrative methods of firms had an overlapping effect upon unskilled application rates.

Table 8.17 shows the result when the "city-as-context" cluster is held constant and specific characteristics of the "firm" are evaluated for their

TABLE 8.17

Employer) Black Application Rates for Unskilled Jobs:
Interviews) Relative Contributions of Firm Characteristics
Holding "City as a Context" Constant

			Unique Contribution
I.	Market Characteristics		
	A.	Type of industry	.0250
	B.	Absolute number of employees	.0080*
	C.	Relative size of firm among firms within the city	.0018
II.	Administrative Characteristics		
	A.	Recruitment channels used	.0282
		a. State employment agencies	.0022
		b. Private employment agencies	.0123*
		c. Want ads	.0011
		d. Labor unions	.0018
		e. Other employees	.0036
	B.	Recruitment channels considered most effective	.0067
	C.	Federal contract status	.0052
	D.	Union contract status	.0051
	E.	Reaction of current employees	.0010
III.	Attitudes of Personnel Officers		
	A.	Assessment of general qualifications	.0045
	B.	Assessment of specific task performance capabilities	.0056
	C.	Index scale based upon scales A and B	.0027
	D.	Perceived employment opportunities	.0071*
	E.	Personal reactions to black competition	.0033

*Significant at .05 level.

unique contributions. Each of the three "firm" clusters contains one statistically significant component that affected the rate at which blacks applied for unskilled jobs. (Note, however, that the unique contributions are very small.)

In the "attitude" set, the statistically significant component is personnel officers' perceptions of local black job opportunities, an item included in the model on the assumption that personnel officers who felt blacks suffered local job discrimination might make stronger efforts in their own firms to assure equal opportunity employment than personnel officers who did not.

However if we take a unique contribution of .007 seriously, the finding is just the reverse of our expectations. Firms whose personnel officers said blacks in their city were "better off" with respect to local employment opportunities received about 25% more applications from blacks for unskilled jobs than firms whose personnel officers thought blacks either experienced no job discrimination or had opportunities equal to others of the same social class.

This unanticipated result may mean that the proportion of blacks in a firms' unskilled applicants influenced the personnel officer's perception of local black job access: The more blacks applying to a firm, the more likely the personnel officer would believe that blacks had "better" local employment opportunities than "others of the same income and education." Yet it is only for the firms' bottom level jobs that we detect an effect of personnel officers' perceptions of black job opportunities. Our tentative conclusion is that some personnel officers felt blacks had equal job access because their firms were handing out more than a "fair share" of the firms' unskilled level application forms to blacks—"fair share" defined as a proportion corresponding to the relative size of the firm's local black–white labor pool.

What type of firms were receiving more than the average proportion of black applications for unskilled jobs? Large firms, for one. Of the three components of the "market" variable set, only the absolute size of the firm had a statistically significant effect on the level of black representation among unskilled applicants. About 1% of the total variation in the black unskilled application rate was due to variation in the firms size of employees. The larger the number of employees in the firm, the more likely were blacks to be among the firm's unskilled applicants.

The positive effect on black unskilled application rates of variation in absolute firm size could be the result of two equally plausible processes. First, firms with large numbers of employees may be the most visible firms in a city because of the sheer size of their local operation. Second, physical visibility may be a magnet attracting unskilled labor in general and black unskilled laborers, in particular.

A qualitatively different explanation for the "absolute size" effect rests on the implications of the complexity of friendship networks in large organizations for the dissemination of job information to blacks. To the extent that unskilled job vacancy information is communicated through friendship networks, the more blacks employed at the unskilled level of a firm, the greater the probability that information would be disseminated (*via* racially homogeneous networks) to potential black applicants. And the larger the firm in absolute terms, the *more* black friendship contacts at the unskilled level even if the relative black proportion were equivalent in larger and smaller firms.

Of the two explanations of the "absolute size" effect—physical visibility and friendship networks—the latter appears more plausible for the following reasons. Firm size was measured in two ways—by a firm's absolute number of employees and by its number of employees relative to other firms in the city. "Relative size" is a simple two-category classification of firms, according to whether the firm was one of the city's top ten or one of the 20 of the next largest 90 firms in the city. Both absolute size and relative size refer to the number of employees in the firm, but the first measure is of the size range across all cities sampled, while the second measure groups firms relative to other firms within the city. If the sheer physical visibility of the firm influenced the rate of black application to unskilled jobs, we would expect the top ten firms in a city to be the most visible from the perspective of the local black labor pool; hence receive the most applications from blacks when absolute size is held constant.

These are all large firms, obviously, and none would be "invisible" to the local labor market. Yet we find no effect of relative firm size on the rate of black application to the firms' unskilled jobs. Since the effect of "size" is associated uniquely with variation in the firms' absolute number of employees, we postulate that size positively influenced the black unskilled application rate not through firm visibility but rather by the mechanism of friendship networks.

Approximately 5% of the total variation in the black unskilled application rate was associated uniquely with the cluster "administrative characteristics." As we saw in Table 8.17 neither union or Federal contract statuses of firms, nor the personnel officers' preferences among recruitment channels, nor the personnel officers' perceptions of reactions to blacks of current unskilled employees had significant effects on the black unskilled application rate. However about 3% of the total variation in this rate was due uniquely to the different methods whereby firms obtained their unskilled workers. When we try to evaluate the unique effects of the specific channels of recruitment, we find a statistically significant contrast between firms that used and did not use private employment services to recruit their unskilled workers. About 1% of the total variation in the black unskilled application rate is due uniquely to the *higher* proportions of black applications received by firms that used private employment services.

In Table 8.16, the "city as context" cluster accounted for 17% of the total variation. When we substitute five city characteristics in place of "city" as a dummy variable, the characteristics in combination account for 10% of the total variation in the black unskilled application rate, as shown in Table 8.18.

About one-half of the combined effects of the five city characteristics cannot be separated. The degree of school segregation, the level of unemployment, and the size of the local black labor pool are each statistically significant (.01 level) when other variables in the model are uncontrolled. When evaluated for their unique contributions, only the effects of the unemployment rate and the proportion of blacks in the city are different from zero at or above the 5% significance level.

Variation in the size of the firms' local black labor pool accounts uniquely for about 4% of the total variation in the rate at which blacks were applying for the firms' unskilled jobs. The impact of the size of the

TABLE 8.18

Employer) Black Application Rates for Unskilled Jobs:
Interviews) Relative Contributions of City Characteristics
Holding Firm Characteristics Constant (N = 447)

City Characteristics	Zero Order Contributions	Unique Contributions
School Segregation	.0725	0.0
Black-White Educational Differences	.0006	.0007
Unemployment Rate	.0267	.0078
Business Community Efforts	.0008	.0000
Proportion Black in City	.1045	.044

Total Unique Contribution of Combined City Cluster	.1010
Sum of Unique Contributions of Each City Variable	.0534
Overlap Effects of City Characteristics	.0476

black labor pool on unskilled applications is at least twice as great as for any of the white collar and skilled level employment rates.

An additional 1% of the variance can be attributed uniquely to differences in the tightness of the firms' labor markets. Variation in the cities' 1967 to 1968 (averaged) level of unemployment is negatively associated at the 5% significance level with the rate of black application to the firm's skilled jobs. The higher the level of unemployment in a city, the lower the probability that blacks would be represented among the major firms' unskilled applicants. Neither black–white educational differences, nor the degree of school segregation, nor the efforts of the local business community to upgrade blacks were associated uniquely with variation in rates at which blacks were applying for unskilled jobs.

It is abundantly clear that "city as a context" is the major factor that we can point to in our data which differentiates consistently between firms who have high proportions of blacks applying for positions at all occupational levels and firms who report low proportions of black applicants. Furthermore, the lower the occupational level being studied, the more important the characteristics of cities in explaining variables. Of course, these findings do not mean that firms in cities with large proportions of blacks are less discriminatory. Rather the findings are consistent with a wide range of discrimination differences among firms and even among cities. For example, it may be that firms in cities with high proportions of blacks hire proportionately fewer blacks, so that for blacks the probability of being hired in such a city is less than in cities with lower proportion black.

Conclusion. In this chapter we focused mainly on the ways in which major employers recruited new employees and on the variations among firms in the rates at which they were attracting blacks to apply for positions within the firms. Three main findings stand out. First, we "explained" the application rates for unskilled workers better than for either skilled or professional and white collar workers. Second, for each level of the firms' work forces, city differences account for from 7 to 15% of the total variation in application rates, a reflection in large part of the sensitivity of these rates to the relative size of the black labor forces in the cities. Third, personnel officers' attitudes did not amount to much as an explanatory variable. Where the characteristics of the firm made a difference, usually some more objective characteristic of the firm was involved.

Chapter 9

JOBS AND BLACKS:
Hiring, Incorporation Practices,
and Black Community Reactions
to Private Sector Employment Practices

Filing an application is obviously an important step in getting a job, but
the critical step is getting hired. We now pursue the process of employment through this step. As we saw in Chapter 8 (see Table 8.6), the
probability of a black being hired, given application, was, on the average, lower than that of whites. On every level of the firms studied,
whites had a better chance than blacks of being placed on the payroll.
Of course, there was considerable variation among firms: some hired
none of the blacks who presented themselves for employment, while
other firms gave blacks chances equal to, or greater than, those of whites.
It is this variation from firm to firm that we explain in this chapter. The
form of the analyses are similar to that of the last chapter: Multiple
regression techniques identify how much variation can be accounted for
by four clusters of factors—"city as a context," "administrative characteristics," "market characteristics," and "attitudes of personal officers."

This chapter is largely based on Bettye K. Eidson, *Institutional Racism: Minority
Group Manpower Politics of Major Urban Employers*. Unpublished Ph.D. Dissertation, Department of Social Relations, The Johns Hopkins University, 1971.

Explaining Hiring Rates for Blacks in White Collar Jobs. Turning first to professional and white collar jobs of the firms, in Table 9.1 it can be seen that the four clusters account for about the same proportion (18%) of the total variation in hiring rates as they are accounted for in application. But the source of this explained variance shifts markedly from "supply" to "demand" factors, for characteristics of the firms are more important as predictors than is "city as a context."

Differences in attitudes of personnel officers toward blacks and in market positions of the firms far outweighed effects of "city" and firm administrative characteristics at the point of hiring.

In Table 9.2 we look within the two important clusters to see how their individual components contributed to the amount of variance explained. The effect that "market characteristics" had upon hiring rates for white collar jobs is almost entirely the result of industry differences, a variable that accounts for about 5% of the variation in hiring rates. An equivalent amount of the total variation is associated with differences in personnel officers' views of the qualifications of blacks "in general." And about 1% of the variance is accounted for by the personnel officers' per-

TABLE 9.1

Employer) Black Hiring Rates for Professional and White Collar
Interviews) Jobs: Relative Contributions of Clusters of Firm
Characteristics (N = 447)

Cluster	Zero Order Relationship of Cluster	Unique Contribution to Explained Variance
Attitudes of Personnel Officers	.0611**	.0531**
City as Context	.0411	.0415
Administrative Characteristics	.0370	.0223
Market Characteristics	.0622**	.0550**

Total Unique Contribution of Four Clusters	.1851
Sum of Unique Contributions of Each Cluster Above	.1719
Overlap Contribution	.0132

*Significant at .05 level.

**Significant at .01 level.

TABLE 9.2

Employer   ) Black Hiring Rates for Professional and White Collar
Interviews) Jobs: Relative Contributions of Firm Characteristics,
             Holding "City as Context" Constant

		Unique Contribution
I.	Market Characteristics	
	A. Type of industry	.0494*
	B. Absolute number of employees	.0006
	C. Relative size of firm among firms within the city	.0010
II.	Attitudes of Personnel Officers	
	A. Assessment of general qualifications	.0417*
	B. Assessment of specific task performance capabilities	.0038
	C. Index scale based upon scales A and B	0.0
	D. Perceived employment opportunities	.0047
	E. Personal reactions to black competition	.0088*

*Significant at .05 level.

sonal sense of competition from blacks. We look at each of these effects in turn.

Although the analysis is too detailed to show here, an examination of industry categories indicates that the effects of this cluster result mainly from the relatively good showings of service and printing industry firms.[1]

The General Qualifications Scale with a unique contribution of .04 is the statistically important component in the cluster of personnel officers' attitudes. Items in this scale refer to the personnel officers' global impressions of how qualified blacks in general are for professional and white collar, skilled, and unskilled level jobs. If we assume that personnel officers' attitudes are causal factors, it is hardly surprising that personnel officers holding low opinions of blacks as qualified workers hire few blacks on the professional and white collar levels of their firms. In the typical firm, personnel officers probably have more to do directly with hiring decisions on this level of the firm than on any other level.

---

[1] Bettye K. Eidson, op. cit.

The attitudes of the personnel manager may also be a consequence, not a cause, of hiring rates. Lacking longitudinal data it is hard to make a compelling case one way or the other, and it is possible that firms in which few blacks are hired generate a self-fulfilling prophesy. The fact that few blacks are hired is taken as evidence that blacks are not qualified. Similar interpretative problems exist for the finding that the more a personnel officer believes that he may be replaced by a black, the more likely the firm is to hire blacks. Though the unique contribution is rather small (.009), "reactions to black competition" contradicts our expectations (Table 9.2). It appears that by endorsing this statement, personnel officers are endorsing the obverse of the General Evaluation Scale—namely that blacks are qualified to hold positions as personnel officers, and if blacks are in their firms on their level, it seems likely to personnel officers that a black may be their replacement. What started out to be an item measuring negative affect, may measure a combination of fact and affect. Indeed, the causal direction may go from hiring rates to attitudes of the personnel manager.

Explaining Hiring Rates of Blacks in Skilled Jobs.   We turn now to hiring rates on the skilled worker level. On the average, 15% of the last 20 applicants to the firms' skilled level jobs were black; but blacks constitute only 9% of the last persons hired. In Table 9.3, we find that at the skilled worker level, the four clusters account for 30% of the variance among firms, considerably more than in the case of hiring for white collar jobs (18%).

Among the four clusters, "city as context" has both the highest zero order relationship and the highest unique contribution, indicating that there are significant city-to-city differences in black hiring rates for skilled workers.

Among the firm characteristic clusters, "administrative characteristic" uniquely accounts for more of the variance among firms, with "attitudes of personnel officers" next, and "market characteristics" of least importance.

Table 9.4 examines the effects of the specific variables that go into each of the firm characteristic clusters. Among "market characteristic" variables, only industry reaches statistical significance in its unique contribution. Examining specific industries, we found that blacks were especially likely to be hired in retail trade service and contract construction, with correspondingly depressed hiring rates in manufacturing industries and in finance.[2]

---

[2] For details see Bettye K. Eidson, *op. cit.*

TABLE 9.3

Employer   .) Black Hiring Rates for Skilled Workers Relative
Interviews,) Contributions of Clusters of Firm Characteristics   (N = 447)

Cluster	Zero Order Relationship of Cluster	Unique Contribution to Explained Variance
Attitudes of Personnel Officers	.0665*	.0487*
City as Context	.1485*	.1040*
Administrative Characteristics	.0891*	.0638*
Market Characteristics	.0363	.0379*

Total Unique Contribution of Four Clusters	.2971*
Sum of Unique Contributions of Each Cluster Above	.2550
Overlap Contribution	.0421

*Significant at .05 level.

The main effect that the administration has on a black's chances of being hired for a skilled job comes through differences in recruitment channels that firms used to obtain their skilled workers. With respect to specific recruitment channels, the only statistically significant contrast was between firms which did and firms that did not use want ads in newspapers to communicate their skilled level vacancies.

We may recall that firms using want ads to recruit at the skilled level did not differ in their black application rates from firms that did not. However, if a firm used want ads to announce its skilled level openings, it was more likely to hire those blacks who did apply.

The question that goes begging is *why* blacks were not more likely to have applied to firms that used want ads for skilled level recruitment. One blatantly *ad hoc* hypothesis is that some firms may provide cues in their advertisements as to whether they welcome applications from blacks.

The third firm characteristic of importance was the personnel officer's sense of personal competition from blacks. Denial that blacks could present a competitive threat reduced the probability that a black would be among the last 20 persons hired for skilled level jobs in the personnel officer's firm. This finding parallels the results obtained when hiring

TABLE 9.4

Employer   ) Black Hiring Rates for Skilled Jobs: Relative
Interviews) Contributions of Firm Characteristics Holding
            "City as Context" Constant

			Unique Contribution
I.	Market Characteristics		
	A.	Type of industry	.0360*
	B.	Absolute number of employees	.0003
	C.	Relative size of firm among firms within the city	.0001
II.	Administrative Characteristics		
	A.	Recruitment channels used	.0395*
		1. State employment agencies	.0014
		2. Private employment agencies	.0067
		3. Want ads	.0102*
		4. Labor unions	.0048
		5. Other employees	.0043
	B.	Recruitment channels considered most effective	.0104
	C.	Federal contract status	.0001
	D.	Union contract status	0.0
	E.	Reaction of current employees	.0021
III.	Attitudes of Personnel Officers		
	A.	Assessment of general qualifications	.0003
	B.	Assessment of specific task performance capabilities	.0001
	C.	Index scale based upon scales A and B	.0040
	D.	Perceived employment opportunities	.0060
	E.	Personal reactions to black competition	.0171*

*Significant at .05 level.

rates for professional and white collar jobs were considered, and presents the same interpretative problems.

A familiar story emerges when we consider specific city characteristics as in Table 9.5. The five specific city characteristics of this table take up 5% of the total variation and about 3% of the total variation is accounted for by proportion black. The other four characteristics—the degree of

TABLE   9.5

Employer   ) Proximation Black Hired on Skilled Worker Level:
Interviews) Relative Contributions of Specific City
              Characteristics (N = 447)

City Characteristics	Zero Order Effects	Unique Contributions
School Segregation	.0233*	.0002
Black-white Educational Differences	.0001	.0028
Unemployment Rate	.0076	.0001
Business Community Efforts	.0012	.0016
Proportion Black	.0706**	.0297*

Total Unique Effects Combined Five City Characteristics	.0524*
Sum of Unique Contributions of Five Characteristics	.0344
Overlap Among City Characteristics	.0180

*Significant at .05 level.

school segregation, the black–white education differential, the tightness of the local labor market, and the organized efforts of the city's business community—have no statistically significant unique effect on the rate at which blacks were hired for skilled level jobs.

If the only information that we had on firms was the size of their local black labor pools, we could account (at the zero-order level) for 7% of the total variance in rates at which blacks were being hired for their skilled level jobs.

In summary, at the point of hiring the main unique effects are associated with differences in recruitment channels that firms used to obtain skilled workers (e.g., the positive effect of using want ads), with differences in personnel officers' attitudes (particularly, the depressing effect of personnel officers' denial of the possibility of job competition from blacks), and with differences in the proportion black in the firm's local labor pool.

We found that industry differences uniquely account for about 4% of the total variation in rates at which blacks were being hired for skilled level jobs. We found that service and retail trade firms—the growth sector of our economy—were the statistically significant sources of the overall effect of the component, "industry differences."

In general, this is the pattern observed at the professional and white collar level. Blacks appear to become "qualified" for both white collar and skilled level jobs when the industry is generating large numbers of new openings. If the skill differences between blacks and whites in the firm's local labor pool were the critical determinants of their relative rates of incorporation, firms in primary and fabricated metal industries should have been hiring far fewer blacks than were firms in textile and garment industries, for these industry contrasts are stark with respect to the proportion of their workers who are skilled craftsmen.

Explaining Hiring Rates of Blacks for Unskilled Jobs. Turning now to hiring rates on the level of unskilled jobs, we find that the four clusters account for even more of the variance (34%) (see Table 9.6). Uniquely "city as context" is associated with 17% of the total variation. However, unlike the upper skill ranks, we find now that "supply" differences outweigh "demand" differences in their effects on rates at which blacks were being hired.

At the zero-order level, the effect of each of the variable sets that refer to firms is statistically significant, but only the contribution of "administrative" characteristics is significant when the other clusters are held constant.

TABLE 9.6

Employer   )   Black Hiring Rates for Unskilled Jobs: Relative
Interviews)   Contributions of Clusters of Firm Characteristics (N = 447)

Cluster	Zero Order Relationship of Cluster	Unique Contribution to Explained Variance
Attitudes of Personnel Officers	.0648*	.0154
City as Context	.2197**	.1657**
Administrative Characteristics	.0989**	.0447*
Market Characteristics	.0530*	.0296

Total Unique Contribution for Four Clusters	= .3385*
Sum of Unique Contributions of Each Cluster Above	= .2554
Overlap Contribution	= .0831

*Significant at .05 level.

Table 9.7 shows the partitioning of "firm" effects on the black unskilled hiring rate, controlling for "city differences." We see in this table that components of both the "market" and "administrative" variable sets had greater and significant unique effects on the hiring rate, and that differences in personnel officers' attitudes did not.

Industry differences affected neither the rates at which blacks were

TABLE 9.7

Employer)	Black Hiring Rates for Unskilled Jobs: Relative
Interviews)	Contributions of Firm Characteristics Holding
	"City as a Context" Constant

	Unique Contribution
I. Market Characteristics	
A. Type of industry	.0157
B. Absolute number of employees	.0079*
C. Relative size of firm among firms within the city	.0082*
II. Administrative Characteristics	
A. Recruitment channels used	.0289*
1. State employment agencies	.0013
2. Private employment agencies	.0079
3. Want ads	.0002
5. Other employees	.0068*
B. Recruitment channels considered most effective	.0093
C. Federal contract status	.0010
D. Union contract status	.0011
E. Reaction of current employees	.0023
III. Attitudes of Personnel Officers	
A. Assessment of general qualifications	.0039
B. Assessment of specific task performance capabilities	.0024
C. Index scale based upon scales A and B	.0002
D. Perceived employment opportunities	.0048
E. Personal reactions to black competition	.0004

*Significant at .05 level.

applying nor the rates at which they were being hired at the unskilled level. The "market" effect is a result of the two size components in that set. We find that both the firm's absolute number of employees *and* its relative size among firms in its city affected the rate at which blacks were being hired for unskilled jobs. The first size effect is positive; the second size effect negative. The larger the firm, the more likely were blacks to be among those recently hired for unskilled jobs. But if the firm was one of its city's "top ten," it was less likely to be hiring blacks for unskilled jobs than were the city's smaller firms.

Variations in the unskilled hiring rates was also associated uniquely with differences in recruitment channels firms used to obtain their unskilled workers. We saw in Chapter 8 that firms which used private employment services to recruit unskilled labor received more applications from blacks than did firms that did not. Now it also appears that firms using private employment services also hired more blacks for these openings than did firms that recruited their unskilled labor by other means.

At the unskilled level, the cluster "city as context" uniquely accounted for 17% of the total variation in recent black hiring rates. The five city characteristics substituted in place of the original city scoring (as in Table 9.8) account for 7% of the total variation.

TABLE 9.8

Employer   ) Black Hiring Rates for Unskilled Jobs: Relative
Interviews) Contributions of City Characteristics Holding
              Firm Characteristics Constant (N = 447)

City Characteristic	Zero Order	Unique Contribution
School Segregation	.0131*	.0009
Black-white Educational Differences	.0035	.0003
Unemployment Rate	.0000	.0000
Business Community Efforts	.0000	.0007
Proportion Black in City	.0888*	.0422*

Total Unique Effects of City Characteristics Above Combined	.0666*
Sum of Each Unique Effect of Characteristics Above	.0441
Overlap Among City Characteristics	.0225

*Significant at .05 level.

Four percent of the total variation in the rates at which blacks were being hired for unskilled jobs was uniquely due to variation in the size of the firms' local black labor pool. Black–white educational differences, the tightness of the local labor market, the degree of school segregation, and the organized efforts of the local business community had no significant unique effects upon the rates at which blacks were being hired for the firms' bottom level jobs. The strong effect of the proportion of blacks on the hiring rates of the firms is less understandable than is the effect of this city characteristic on application rates. The more blacks in a city, the more apply to firms for positions, but the more that apply, the greater the likelihood of being hired. It appears that firms lose their discriminatory tendencies as the stream of applications from blacks enlarges.

Blacks in the Current Work Force. The end result of the processes described above produces in each firm a work force containing a mix that varies in the proportion of workers who are black. The current work force composition of a firm in a very real sense represents the cumulative effects of the application streams and hiring decisions of the past.

In this section the four clusters predict the current racial composition of the firms under study. There are several alternative expectations: If the clusters account for the current composition with the same patterning as shown by the analyses of application rates and hiring rates, such findings would be consistent with an interpretation of the current work force racial mixture as having been generated in the past by much the same processes in application and hiring that are currently in effect. In contrast, if the patterns are quite different, then it is quite likely that current processes are different from those in the past. Given the efforts that have been made by public and private agencies to improve the employment position of blacks over the past decade or so, it is not likely that the current work force, representing the application streams and hiring decisions of possibly several decades, will be sensitive to the same factors as current application and hiring rates.

Blacks in White Collar Work Forces. Turning first to the current racial composition of professional and white collar employees, the four clusters account for slightly less of the total variation in the *current distribution* of blacks among white collar employees than they do in the rates at which blacks were *applying* and being *hired* for these types of openings. In addition, the variation that is accounted for is spread much more evenly among city and firm characteristics (Table 9.9).

TABLE 9.9

Employer   ) Current Racial Composition of Professional and
Interviews) White Collar Employees: Relative Contributions
             of Clusters of Firm Characteristics (N = 447)

Cluster	Zero Order Relationship of Cluster	Unique Contribution to Explained Variance
Attitudes of Personnel Officers	.0302	.0155
City as Context	.0607*	.0482
Administrative Characteristics	.0452	.0248
Market Characteristics	.0619*	.0403

Total Unique Contribution of Four Clusters	= .1568*
Sum of Unique Contributions of Each Cluster Above	= .1208
Overlap Contribution	= .0300

*Significant at .05 level.

The four clusters account for about 16% of the total variance. At the zero-order level, the variance associated with "city as context" and with firm "market characteristics" are both statistically significant, but the unique contribution of each of these sets is significant only at the 10% level.

Only one of the characteristics of the firm had a unique contribution which reached statistical significance—type of industry.[3] In this connection, retail and service establishments were the two industrial groups that showed a significant high proportion of blacks employed at the white collar level.

In Table 9.9, the "city as context" cluster accounted for about 6% of the total variance in the current distribution of blacks among the firms' white collar employees. Five specific city characteristics (see Table 9.10) account for only 2% of the total variation, an amount not statistically significant. When we partition this variance into the unique effects of the five city characteristics, we find that the only significant effect comes from the variation in the size of the firms' black labor pool.

---

[3] For detailed findings, see Bettye K. Eidson, *op. cit.*

TABLE 9.10

Employer) Black Proportions of Professional and White Collar
Interviews) in Firms' Work Forces: Relative Contributions of
Specific City Characteristics (N =447)

City Characteristic	Zero Order Effects	Unique Contribution
School Segregation	.0015	.0012
Black-white Educational Differences	.0024	.0000
Unemployment Rate	.0010	.0000
Business Community Efforts	.0000	.0003
Proportion Black in City	.0211*	.0162*

Total Combined Unique Effect of Five
Characteristics   = .0220

Sum of Unique Contributions   = .0177

Overlap Contribution   = .0043

*Significant at .05 level.

The best two predictors found of the proportion black among a firm's white collar employees are the size of the firm's black labor pool and the firm's industrial classification. Industry differences account for twice as much of the total variation (uniquely) as do differences in the size of the black labor pool.

Blacks Among Skilled Work Forces.   At the skilled level the four clusters are associated with 17% of the total variation in the percent black among skilled employees. As usual, city differences account for the largest amount (80%) of interfirm differences.

Of the three clusters that refer to firm differences, only the administrative characteristics set had a statistically significant effect on the black current distribution among firms' skilled level employees. Attitudinal and market differences among firms accounted for insignificant amounts of the total variation associated with the full model.

The significant "firm" effect comes through administrative differences among firms: We can account for 3% of the total variation in the black current skilled distribution simply by knowing which recruitment channel the personnel officer rates as "most effective" in bringing the type of skilled worker sought by his firm.

It turns out that firms whose personnel officers considered site-specific methods to be the "most effective" skilled recruitment channel reported the highest proportion of blacks among their skilled level employees. Companies that preferred to recruit skilled level workers by disseminating job information among their workers reported that higher proportions of their skilled workers were black.

The finding that personnel officers' preferences for internal recruitment at the skilled level enhanced the rate of black employment is open to several interpretations. One would expect on the basis of common sense that a preference of firms for internal recruitment would reinforce black underrepresentation, following the assumption that most workers who received job information at level of the firm would be white and, that once received, job information would be disseminated through racially homogeneous friendship networks. Thus personnel officers' preferences for internal recruitment enhanced, rather than depressed, the level of black representation; one possible reason for this could be that firms who preferred this method have employed historically more blacks than firms which preferred other methods for skilled level recruitment. This interpretation reaches a good deal: only if we had information on the black skilled level distribution for some years before 1968 could we test for a feedback effect of past black employment on "current" black employment in these same firms.

The substantive meaning of personnel officers' preferences among recruitment channels is worth a bit of laboring. For when we next examine the effects of specific city characteristics on the black distribution among skilled employees, we discover that personnel officers' recruitment channel preferences outweighed the unique effects of *any* of the five city characteristics (including the size of the local black labor pool).

As we saw in Table 9.11 approximately 8% of the total variation in black representation among the firms' "current" skilled level employees was associated uniquely with "city as a context." In Table 9.12 where we consider the five specific city characteristics, the set combined accounts for about 3% of the total variation in this rate, with 2% of the total variation uniquely due to variation in the sizes of the cities' black labor force. At the zero-order level, the range in the proportion black in the fifteen cities accounts for about 3% of the total variation in the black skilled employment rate.[4]

---

[4] For the recent "skilled" hiring rate, 7% of the variance was associated with the proportion black in the city. It would appear that firms were responding more to the relative sizes of their black labor pools in their recent practices (e.g., last 20 skilled applicants and last 20 skilled hired) than in the practices contributing to the cumulative (1968) black skilled employment distribution.

TABLE 9.11

Employer   ) Proportion Black Among Skilled Workers: Relative
Interviews) Contributions of Clusters of Firm Characteristics (N = 447)

Cluster	Zero Order Relationship of Cluster	Unique Contribution to Explained Variance
Attitudes of Personnel Officers	.0149	.0181
City as Context	.0793*	.0643*
Administrative Characteristics	.0620*	.0574*
Market Characteristics	.0309	.0225

Total Unique Contribution of Four Clusters	= .1725*
Sum of Unique Contributions of Each Cluster Above	= .1623
Overlap Contribution	= .0102

*Significant at .05 level.

TABLE 9.12

Employer   ) Proportion Black on Skilled Level of Current Work
Interviews) Forces: Relative Contributions of Specific City
           Characteristics (N = 447)

City Characteristics	Zero Order Effects	Unique Contributions
School Segregation	.0060	.0008
Black-White Educational Differences	.0012	.0003
Unemployment Rate	.0002	.0005
Business Community Efforts	.0068	.0047
Proportion Black in City	.0304*	.0190*

Total Unique Effect of Combined Five Characteristics	.0319*
Sum of Unique City Contributions	.0253
Overlap Among City Characteristics	.0060

*Significant at .05 level.

The main finding at the skilled level is that the four clusters in the model appear to have more bearing on current black job chances than was true in the past, judging from the relative amounts of variation accounted for in skilled application, hiring, and "current" employment rates. The variation in recent skilled employment patterns—black representation among the last 20 persons hired for skilled jobs—was much better predicted than the current black skilled distribution by an identical set of independent variables. In short, there is some evidence that employment practices have changed and that the firms are more sensitive to the sizes of the local black communities.

Blacks Among Unskilled Work Forces. The four clusters account for 26% of the variance in the "current" distribution of blacks among the firms' unskilled employees (Table 9.13.)

In contrast to the skilled level results, we find that "city as context" heavily outweighed the effects of "firm difference" in accounting for the "current black distribution." Indeed the main reason that more of the total variance is accounted for in the unskilled black distribution (26%) is that the firms' city context had greater impact on the firms' racial composition at the bottom of the skill ladder.

TABLE 9.13

Employer   ) Black Proportions Unskilled in Current Work Forces:
Interviews) Relative Contributions of Clusters of Firm
            Characteristics (N = 447)

Cluster	Zero Order Relationship of Cluster	Unique Contribution to Explained Variance
Attitudes of Personnel Officers	.0525*	.0156
City as Context	.1727*	.1344*
Administrative Characteristics	.0453	.0183
Market Characteristics	.0618*	.0431*

Total Unique Contribution of Four Clusters	.2638*
Sum of Unique Contributions of Each Cluster Above	.2114
Overlap Contribution	.0524

*Significant at .05 level.

In Table 9.13 we may see that 13% of the total variation in the "current" proportion black among unskilled employees was associated uniquely with "city as context." Of the three variable sets referring to firm characteristics, only "market characteristics" had a statistically significant unique effect. As sets, neither "attitudinal" nor "administrative" differences among firms were significant.

Virtually all of the "market" effect was associated with the rates at which different industries were employing blacks in unskilled jobs. We find that service industry firms were more likely than other industry types to employ blacks in their unskilled jobs.

"City as context" accounted uniquely for about 13% of the total variation in the black unskilled employment rate. As a set, five specific city characteristics, when substituted in the model, take up about 9% of the total variation when "firm differences" are held constant (see Table 9.14).

For each of the eight black employment stages we have reviewed thus far, the size of the local black labor pool was the best single "city" predictor of the level of black participation. The "current" distribution at the unskilled level is no exception: uniquely, "proportion black in city" accounts for 4% of the total variation.

TABLE 9.14

Employer   ) Proportion Black on Unskilled Level of Work Forces:
Interviews) Relative Contributions of Five Specific City
             Characteristics

City Characteristic	Zero Order Effects	Unique Contribution
School Segregation	.0533*	.0001
Black-White Educational Differences	.0000	.0039
Unemployment Rate	.0202*	.0065
Business Community Efforts	.0020	.0008
Proportion Black in City	.1025*	.0432*

Total Unique Contribution of a City Characteristic as a Set	.0874*
Sum of Unique Contributions of Each Characteristic	.0545
Overlap Among City Characteristics	.0329

*Significant at .05 level.

Institutional Racism: Past and Present. The result of the analysis of the last section of this chapter are summarized in reduced form in Table 9.15 where the proportions of the total amounts of variance in application, rates, hiring rates and the current racial composition of the work forces are shown. It is clear that the four clusters of variables do not account for the same amounts of variance across skill levels (rows) or across different points in the employment process (columns). There is a tendency for the four clusters to be more effective in accounting for processes that affect the unskilled components of work forces, and there is a tendency for the clusters to be more effective in predicting the hiring rates than in predicting either rates of application or the current racial composition of the work force.

These findings suggest two generalizations. First, the application streams and/or the hiring decisions were likely to have differed in the past from current patterns. This generalization is suggested by the fact that the four clusters are more efficient in predicting recent patterns of applications streams and hiring rates than in predicting the existing racial composition of the work force.

Second, because the employment processes involving unskilled workers are more sensitive to the four clusters than are those involving higher levels of the firms, we can assume that different processes are at work on the three levels of the firms. Remembering the effects of each cluster, we may recall that characteristics of the firms play more of a role on the higher skill levels than on the lower, suggesting that more care is spent

TABLE 9.15

Employer   ) Summary of Effects of Four Clusters on Application
Interviews) Streams, Hiring Rates, and Racial Compositions of
Work Forces by Skill Levels   (N = 447)

Proportions of Variance Explained in Percent Black

Skill Level	Among Last 20 Applicants	Among Last 20 Hired	Among Current Work Force	Mean Correlation
Professional and White Collar	.17	.18	.16	.17
Skilled Workers	.27	.30	.17	.27
Unskilled Workers	.35	.34	.26	.32
Mean Correlation	.26	.27	.20	

on the selection of white collar and skilled workers than on unskilled workers.

These generalizations are supported only weakly by the data presented. The differences between the three points in the employment process are not dramatic, nor are the effects of firm characteristics very strong.

Current Work Force Composition as a Determinant of Application and Hiring Rates. Another mode of approaching the problem of the measurement of change in employment practices is to take advantage of the fact that we have a measure of the past employment behavior of each of the firms in the study. The racial composition of the work forces provides an indicator of the reception of blacks in the work force over the years past.

The racial composition of the work force should be a good predictor of the application rates of blacks if applications are affected strongly by the informal networks into which a firm's work force are tied. The composition should also be a good predictor of a firm's hiring rates, if firms reject blacks when they rate blacks as "high risk" employees and have little experience with black employees.

If the "current" racial composition in the firm is the best predictor of the rate of black application at each skill level, we would infer that blacks operate under a structural information disadvantage. Initial underrepresentation of blacks within firms would act through time despite policies of organizational goodwill toward blacks and the absence of overt discrimination.

If the racial composition of the work force were the best predictor of the *rate* at which blacks were being hired at each skill level, we would infer that a different type of institutional racism is operative. It would seem that the firm's evaluation of blacks as "high risk" candidates was more critical than any information disadvantage arising from minority group membership.

If the racial composition were the best predictor of *both* the black application rate and the rate at which blacks were being hired, we would infer that both the information disadvantage mechanism was at work and that firms change their evaluation of blacks as workers after they have had some experience with blacks in their work forces.

Table 9.16 contains the results of regression analyses of hiring and application rates of firms with the proportion black in the work forces of the firms added to the four clusters used earlier in this chapter. The last column of the table shows the additional amounts of variance accounted for (both in absolute and relative terms) by the addition of the new variable.

TABLE 9.16

Employer) Black Application and Hiring Rates: Relative
Interviews) Contributions of Four Clusters and Proportion
Black in Current Work Force

Rate Being Explained	Unique Contributions of Characteristic of Firms					Proportion Variance Explained	Additional** Variance Explained by % Black in Work Force
	Personnel Officers' Attitudes	City as Context	Administrative	Market	% Black in Work Force		
Professional and White Collar Applicants	.01	.04	.03	.03	.09	.26*	.0877 (52%)
Professional and White Collar Hiring	.04*	.02	.02	.04*	.14*	.32*	.1402 (76%)
Skilled Applicants	.02*	.08*	.05*	.02	.06*	.33*	.0633 (23%)
Skilled Hiring	.04	.07*	.06*	.04*	.06*	.36*	.0626 (21%)
Unskilled Applicants	.02	.11*	.04*	.02	.08*	.43*	.0805 (23%)
Unskilled Hiring	.01	.10*	.04*	.02	.11*	.45*	.1082 (32%)

*Significant at .05 level.

**Identical to unique contributions except for rounding.

The last column of Table 9.16 shows clearly that significant improvements in the amount of variance accounted for occurs for every one of the rates considered, ranging from a 76% improvement for the hiring rates of professional and white collar employees to a low of 21% for the hiring rates of skilled workers.

Furthermore, as we can see from the column containing the unique contributions of the new variable, in every case the unique contributions are significant beyond the .05 level. In short, the proportion of blacks hired in the past can predict the proportions applying and being hired in the present, independent of the other factors which contribute to the variances in these rates.

When we examine specific rows of Table 9.16, several important findings emerge:

The best single predictor of the rate at which blacks were applying for firms' professional and white collar jobs was clearly the proportion of blacks currently employed in the firms' white collar jobs at the time of the survey.

Though the differences in impact are small, variation in the black skilled application rate was best predicted in the modified model by "city as context," with the unique effects of the "current" black distribution and of "administrative differences" approximately equal. The black unskilled application rate was best predicted by "city as context." Yet at the unskilled level, of all "firm" characteristics, the information on the "current" unskilled black distribution is the best single predictor of rate at which blacks were applying—within cities—for the firms' unskilled jobs.

With the original four clusters alone, our best predictors of the rate at which blacks were being hired for white collar jobs were industry differences and personnel officers' negative expectations of black qualifications. The unique effects of these variables were reduced only slightly by controlling for the "current" level of black representation among the firms' white collar employees. But the best single predictor of the rate at which the firm was hiring blacks was the rate at which blacks were currently employed by the firm in white collar jobs. Fourteen percent of the total variation in recent hiring of 61 blacks for the firms' white collar jobs was due uniquely to the existing rate of black white collar incorporation in the firm. In contrast, differences in personnel officers' attitudes toward blacks accounted uniquely for 4% of the total variation in black white collar hiring. *If one could use only a single variable to predict which firms were hiring blacks for their professional and white collar jobs, our data indicate that question should be—"What proportion of your current professional and white collar employees are black?" Far less useful would be—"What proportion of your city's population is black?" or "How well educated are blacks in your city?"*

The substantive implication of the strong effect of past black incorporation on the rate of recent black incorporation seems to be that blacks are considered "high risk" candidates mainly when the firm had not previously taken chances on blacks as employees. If the firm had incorporated blacks earlier, the probability that a black would be among the last 20 persons hired for its professional and white collar jobs was greatly increased.

The effect of the social composition of the current skilled workers on the rate at which blacks were being hired for skilled level jobs was weaker than the effect observed for white collar hiring. Six percent of the total variation was associated uniquely with variation in the existing distribution of blacks among the firms' current employees. "City as context" outweighed this compositional effect, and differences in administrative characteristics of firms were as useful predictors of the rate at which blacks were being hired for skilled jobs as was the firms' current distribution of blacks among skilled level employees.

At the unskilled level we find that "city as context" accounted uniquely for 10% of the total variation in recent black hiring, while the proportion black among unskilled employees accounted uniquely for 11% of variation in this rate. Without the new variable, uniquely "city as context" previously accounted for 17% of the variation in rates at which blacks were being hired for unskilled jobs. Holding constant the "current" black distribution among firms' unskilled employees reduced this effect to 10%. The unique effects of "attitudinal," "administrative," and "market" differences among firms were barely affected by the introduction of the firms' "current" unskilled black employment rate as a predictor of the rate at which blacks were being hired for unskilled jobs. The reduction of the "city" effect comes probably from the correlation between the "current" black unskilled rate in a city's firms and the size of the city's black labor pool. To put it differently, the "current" black distribution was more reflective at the unskilled level of the size of city's black population than was the case for upper skill ranks; therefore, controlling for this "current" distribution absorbs some of the original effect of "supply" factors on rates of black unskilled incorporation. If the "current" black distribution at white collar and skilled levels had better reflected the size of the black community, we would have observed this same result for the upper skill ranks.

Two general conclusions flow from the analyses presented in this section: First, it is quite clear that the proportion black in the labor force markedly affects the racial composition of the stream of applicants on each of the skill levels of the firms, especially on the professional and white collar levels. Second, experience with black employees improves the probability that black applicants will be hired, independent of the firms' personnel officer's evaluation of blacks as employees. Of course, this last finding may mainly reflect the fact that actual hiring decisions are in the hands of other officers of the firm; thus the personnel officer's personal predilections may mainly affect the persons he hires directly.

These findings substantiate a circular process in which the racial compositions of business firms perpetuate themselves over time, regardless of the "good" (or "bad") intentions of management. Workers in largely segregated plants are usually replaced by persons of matching rather than contrasting race. Firms that have hired few blacks in the past are not likely to be hiring blacks in the present because they attract few black applicants and because they shy away from "high" risk employment decisions if they have not had any previous experiences with the outcome of such decisions.[5]

Popular Black Experiences with Employment Discrimination. We have seen that employers vary considerably in the extent to which they hire blacks for positions on three broadly defined skilled levels of the firm. Employers' practices are sensitive to the proportion black in their local

---

[5] The empirical results indicate that work organizations reproduce themselves racially over time. The argument in this chapter is that the relationship between minority group application rates and the rates at which minority groups are currently represented is reciprocal. An alternate explanation is that, for historical reasons, some firms had black employees and others did not. Hence any association between application and current employment rates is due to factors exogeneous to firms as they now exist. This argument is plausible and cannot be refuted with the present data set. However, an empirical strategy that would discredit the "feedback" explanation (in favor of the "inertia" explanation) would require the linking of past hiring practices *both* to historical factors and to current practices of organizations. The problem is the same as addressed by Arthur Stinchcombe ("Social Structure and Organizations," in *Handbook of Organizations*, James G. March (Ed.), Rand McNally, Chicago, 1965, p. 167):

It is considerably more difficult to explain why many types of organizations retain structural peculiarities after their foundation without falling into tautologous statements about "tradition," "vested interests," or "folkways" not being changeable by formal regulation. The problem is to specify who it is that carries "tradition" and why they carry it, whose "interests" become "vested," under what conditions, by what devices, whose "folkways" cannot be changed by regulation, and why. This problem is at the very center of sociological theory. Unfortunately, we are not much closer to an answer to the problem now than we were in Sumner's day.

With respect to the structure of employment opportunities for minority groups, the problem of persistance of organizational forms may have profound policy implications as well as theoretical ones. The data in this chapter yield results that are more provocative than definitive, but they do suggest that it will be at least as fruitful to search for mechanisms by which social cleavages are institutionalized at the level of organizations as at the level of individuals.

labor pools but not to the educational level of blacks either in an absolute sense or relative to the white labor pool. How much of this variance in employment practice is a function of the labor market factors and how much it is a function of intentional or unintentional discriminatory practices is hard to discern.

If discrimination is difficult for the analyst to discern on the level of employer hiring practices, it may be even more difficult for blacks to personally perceive in their attempts to enter the labor market. The United State's race relations problems have been with us for so long that we have developed an elaborate rhetoric of avoidance of direct expression of race prejudice. The avoidance in this case can take two forms: On the one hand, as we have seen, from the analysis of employer hiring practices, that blacks avoid placing themselves in positions that would lead them to experience discrimination directly. Thus firms that have no blacks on their work forces are not likely to get black applicants. The second form of avoidance is that employers in presenting reasons for not considering or hiring applicants avoid telling the applicant directly that he is not being hired because of his race. There are many "legitimate" reasons for not considering or hiring a person: "There are no job vacancies at present," or "experience is necessary," or the qualifications of the applicant may not be "sufficient."

As a consequence of these patterns of avoidance of direct confrontation, we can expect that there will be a rather loose fit between the general pattern of employment practices in a community and the perception of discrimination on the part of blacks. It may be useful to contrast the employment area with that of police abuse: If the police arrest a person unfairly or harass one's neighbors to an undue extent, discrimination is felt in a very direct way. In contrast, if one is turned down for a job or for a promotion, he may not be as certain that he has been treated unfairly.

These expectations can be tested using the surveys of blacks conducted by the Survey Research Center. A series of questions were to obtain black personal experiences with job discrimination and black citizens beliefs about the prevalence of employment discrimination in each of the fifteen cities.[6] Using these items, two indexes were constructed: (1)

---

[6] The relevant questionnaire items were as follows:

In general, do you think many, some or just a few Negroes in (City) miss out on jobs today because of their race?

Do you think you were ever refused a job mainly because of your race?

Once on a job were you ever *not* promoted because of race?

Do you think many, some or just a few in (City) miss out on promotions today because of race?

Experienced Job Discrimination, which measures the extent to which individual blacks claimed to have had direct personal experience with discrimination in either hiring or promotion; and (2) *Perceived Job Discrimination,* which measures the extent to which individuals believe in the prevalence of job discrimination in their cities. In Figure 9.1 are shown the distribution of city scores on these indices along with the proportion of skilled workers who are black and a rating from the elite interviews of the salience of discrimination in private employment as an issue.

The fifteen cities are distributed in different fashions on each of the indices displayed in Figure 9.1, indicating, a loose fit between the actual proportions of black workers (as indexed by the proportion black skilled workers in the work forces of the companies we studied)[7] and the indices of experienced discrimination. The perception of discrimination provides an even poorer fit: Indeed a case can be made that the black populations of each of the cities do not vary very much one from the other, each claiming in their cities about the same amount of perceived discrimination.

This looseness of fit is shown more precisely in Table 9.17 in which the correlations among a selected number of indices are displayed. Although the city scores of *direct experiences* with employment discrimination are fairly strongly related to both the proportions black among unskilled and skilled workers in the work forces, the indices of perceived discrimination are very weakly related to work force measures.

Turning to the salience of employment in the private sector as a local issue, the salience ratings (index of Salience of Discrimination) seem particularly strongly related to the proportions of workers who are black rather than to the extent of personal experiences with discrimination or the perceived level of discrimination.

The pattern of relationships shown in Table 9.17 suggests that the experience of discrimination and especially the perception of discrimination are related to the activities of elites as well as the actual employment practices of major firms in the fifteen cities. The stances taken by the

---

[7] The proportion black in the current skilled labor forces of the firms is used in Figure 9.1, mainly because this rate turns out in later analyses to be the one most sensitively related to the experience and perception of employment discrimination on the part of the black populations of the fifteen cities. This greater sensitivity may mainly reflect the fact that for blacks the critical point in social mobility at the present time is shifting from unskilled to skilled occupations. Thus it may be easy for blacks to get unskilled jobs (indeed, we saw earlier in this and the previous chapter, that the firms are likely to hire blacks at the unskilled level the more blacks there are in the local labor markets) but to move into the ranks of skilled labor means coming up against more barriers.

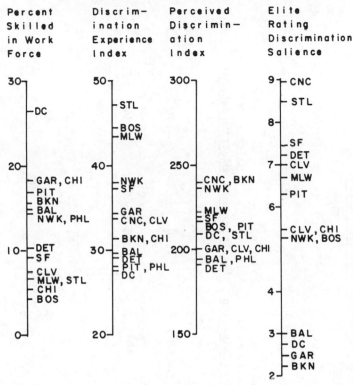

| Percent Skilled in Work Force | Discrimination Experience Index | Perceived Discrimination Index | Elite Rating Discrimination Salience |

Figure 9.1 Discrimination Experience Index, Perceived Discrimination Index, Salience Rating, and percent of skilled workers who are black.

leaders of the business community, the mayor, and the labor unions may affect both the levels of experience and the perception of discrimination. In addition, one may also take into account the "style" of the local civil rights movement: If civil rights leaders emphasize the theme of integration and register complaints concerning the incorporation of blacks into the labor force, then the perception of discrimination may be especially strong.

Table 9.18 presents the results of analyses assessing the unique contributions among city variation in the Indexes of Experienced and Perceived Discrimination and to the Salience of Discrimination of the proportions black in the skilled and unskilled levels of the work forces of the firms studied, the "sympathy and responsiveness of the mayor," business community, and labor unions, and the Integration Orientation of the local civil rights movement. Note that while these analyses have been successful in accounting for statistically significant amounts of variance with respect to the Index of Experienced Discrimination and the Index of Perceived Discrimination, the total amount of variance explained for

TABLE 9.17

Employer, Elite and Survey Interviews) Correlations Among City Means on Selected Indices of Discrimination [N = 15]

	% Black Skilled Workers (1)	% Black Unskilled Workers (2)	Index of Experienced Discrimination (3)	Index of Perceived Discrimination (4)	Salience of Discrimination (5)
% Black Skilled (1)		.80	-.69	-.30	-.70
% Black Unskilled (2)			-.50	-.16	-.54
Index of Exp. Discrim. (3)				.41	.35
Index of Perceived Discrim. (4)					.20
Salience of Discrim. (5)					

the Salience of Discrimination Index fell short of conventional (.05) levels of significance.

In the first column of Table 9.18 the intercity variance in the Index of Experienced Discrimination is decomposed into those portions that can be uniquely attributed to each of the three clusters and their combinations. Work force measures account uniquely for 12% of the variance but almost as much (11%) can be accounted for uniquely by the style of the local civil rights movement. An additional 7% of the variance can be allocated uniquely to measures of the sympathy of the mayor, business community and labor unions to the civil rights movement. Larger proportions of the explained variance are accounted for by combinations of the three measures; for example, 18% of the variance is accounted for uniquely by the overlap between work force measures and the community factors, 14% by the overlap between work force measures and the style of the civil rights movement, and an additional 17% by the overlap between community factors and the style of the civil rights movement.

It appears that a community's level of experienced discrimination is as much a function of local community political atmosphere as it is a function of patterns of employment of blacks in the major firms in the community. Indeed, the experience of employment discrimination functions very much the same as experience with merchant exploitation. In other words, a black community is especially sensitive to maltreatment in the private sector job market when and if the local political scene is insensitive to the plight of blacks in that respect. It should be noted at this point that the direction of causality is not clear from this analysis: It may well be that the experience of discrimination leads to increased political leadership sensitivity to black demands. But it may well also be the case that the lack of sensitivity on the part of political elites arouses a special sensitivity on the part of blacks to employment discrimination in personal encounters with employing firms.

Turning now to the Index of Perceived Discrimination, as in the second column of Table 9.18, we can see that this index is particularly sensitive to community factors. About 75% of the total intercity variance in the Index of Perceived Discrimination can be accounted for by these three clusters of factors, but most of that amount (64%) is uniquely accounted for by community factors. Additional proportions (17 and 12%, respectively) are accounted uniquely by work force measures and civil rights style, with the combinations of factors accounting for artifactual negative amounts of variance. Although negative amounts of variance make the details suspect, it does appear quite clear that the levels of perceived discrimination in the cities are more closely related to community factors than to any other measured factor. In short, black communities

TABLE 9.18

Relative Contributions of Community Elites, Proportion Black in
Skilled Occupations and Style of Civil Rights Movement to
Experienced Discrimination, Perceived Discrimination and
Salience of Discrimination (N = 15 cities)

(Elite, Survey, and Employer Interviews)

| Clusters* | | | Proportion of Variance Uniquely Attributed | | |
Work Force Measures	Community Factors	Civil Rights Style	Index of Experienced Discrimination	Index of Perceived Discrimination	Salience of Employment Discrimination
+	0	0	12%	17%	27%
0	+	0	7	64	20
0	0	+	11	12	0
+	+	0	18	- 5	18
+	0	+	14	- 9	2
0	+	+	17	-10	0
+	+	+	0.5	8	2
Total Explained Variance (R^2) =			83% **	75% **	68% **
P =			<.01	<.05	<.10

324

*Measures included in each cluster are as follows:

"Work Force" includes percent black on skilled and unskilled levels of the firms studied.

"Community Factors" include elite interview ratings of the Responsiveness and Sympathy of the Mayor, Business Community and Labor Unions.

"Civil Rights Style" is elite interview ratings of the "Integration Orientation" of the local civil rights movement (see Chapter 5).

**Due to the large number of independent variables, these R^2's must be discounted about 10%.

believe that discrimination is endemic when local political, business, and labor elites do not evidence sympathy for the aims of the civil rights movement.

The Salience of Employment Discrimination as a local issue has still another pattern. Most of the explained variance can be allocated almost evenly among work force measures, community factors, and the overlap ment is an issue in local affairs appears to be a function both of the between these two clusters. Whether discrimination in private employ- "objective" circumstances and the local political atmosphere.

Summary.   This and the previous chapter have mainly been concerned with explaining interfirm variations in the proportion of blacks on various skill levels of the firms and in the rates at which blacks were applying for and being hired for jobs on those levels. Although different processes were apparently at work in the treatment of blacks at the white collar and professional level, at the skilled worker level, and at the unskilled level in the firms, certain broad tendencies were at work in every case. First it was apparent that there was considerable intercity variation among firms, which went beyond the specific industries involved. Firms in cities with high proportions of blacks hired more blacks on every level of the firm. Second, firms that had already hired blacks were more likely to get applications from blacks and to hire blacks from among applicants.

Differences among skill levels were also apparent. The hiring of white collar workers was more affected by the beliefs of personnel officers about blacks, partly because hiring white collar employees was more directly the concern of personnel officers and partly because on the white collar level socioemotional factors played a role in judging the qualifications of a potential employee. It was on the unskilled level of the firms that labor market characteristics made the most difference: The more blacks available in the labor market, the greater the proportion of blacks on this level of the firm.

In the last section of the chapter we showed that the experience of discrimination on the job market and the belief that discrimination was widespread was a function both of the objective facts about the incorporation of blacks into the work forces of major firms and the general political atmosphere of city civil rights movements. In cities where the proportion black among work forces was high and where the mayor and business community expressed sympathy for the civil rights movement, both the perception of generalized discrimination and the salience of discrimination as a local issue were low. In cities where either of these two factors were absent, blacks were more likely to feel discriminated against personally and to believe that discrimination was rampant in the local labor market.

Chapter 10

EDUCATION AND TEACHERS
IN THE GHETTO

In today's times public education enjoys the dubious distinction of being a prominent issue in local urban affairs. It seems that the school systems in our central cities are under attack from almost all sides. On the one hand, a frequent criticism of the schools is that their "quality" has been declining over the past few decades: Schools are unable to serve well those students who want adequate preparation for further academic work in our colleges and universities. On the other hand, the schools are blamed for an uneven quality, doing well enough with the children of the middle class but failing to serve the needs of black residents. Schools are also criticized for using up increasingly larger proportions of the tax dollar without showing a corresponding increase in the quality of services rendered. All sides criticize the schools for allegedly cumbersome bureaucracies above the classroom level. Movements are under way to decentralize urban school systems and put more control in the hands of neighborhood school boards, a move not regarded with much favor by either school administrators or large segments of urban residents.

As a consequence of being at the center of controversies, public education in our large cities is changing. New modes of financing public education have been developed, and the state and federal governments con-

---

This chapter is based partially on a draft written by David Boesel.

tribute larger shares. The traditional schools have been supplemented by preschool programs and post-high-school training. Curricula have undergone almost constant revision in an effort to improve the learning of students. Scores of books have appeared proposing new educational forms or a return to some previous "more effective" mode. The federal government has experimented with contracting out teaching to private firms to employ the profit motive to improve teaching. The federal government is also about to launch an experiment in providing parents with vouchers to "purchase" education, in the hope that increased competition among schools, private and public, will provide incentives for the schools to improve their performance.

At the core of the current controversies over public education is an acknowledgement that public education in the ghetto areas of our major central cities is falling far short of what is desired optimally. There may be disagreement as to why this is the case, but there is remarkable agreement that achievement levels are low, school attendance poor, discipline lax, school plants inferior, and teaching assignments in such schools avoided.

Although public school controversies have been featured prominently in the mass media, it is not clear whether the controversies have penetrated deeply into the general urban population. To be sure, there are circumstances in which the general public participates widely in expressing grievances against their schools. Over the past few years, school bond issues have had higher and higher probabilities of being turned down in referenda. The bussing of black and white children to achieve racial balances in schools often brings out crowds of irate parents. New York City's decentralization plans have boiled over into controversy leading to a city-wide teachers' strike. Yet despite these instances of direct mass involvement in school controversies, the general tenor of the population has been one in which public education in general has been criticized but particular schools and school systems have enjoyed considerable approval.

It is significant that schools were infrequent targets of vandalism and looting during the civil disorders of the 1960s. To be sure, some school buildings were burnt down, but these fires usually spread from fires in other locations. There are several reasons why schools were not direct targets in the civil disorders, including their location and the fact that the looting of schools would produce little in the way of consumer goods, but another important reason is that the schools were apparently not seen as symbolic representatives of the oppressive institutions of the larger society.

In this chapter we look upon the schools serving the ghettoes of our fifteen cities as institutions which are delivering services to households in those areas. The services are personal, in the sense that education involves the interaction between teachers and youngsters. The services are delivered locally—every neighborhood has an elementary school and everyone of the cities in our sample has junior high schools serving several neighborhoods and larger high schools whose attendance areas may include more than the ghettoes under study.

In any effort to study the delivery of public education, classroom teachers and their first line supervisors (principals and assistant principals) are obviously subjects of study. Children come into contact with the school system in the classroom. Parents experience the school system most directly through the experiences of their children and their own contacts with teachers and local school administrators. Adults who do not have children currently in the schools have more indirect contact with the schools, either through their own children who have gone to local schools in the past or through friends and neighbors who have children currently in the schools. In many cases, the adults have at one time been students themselves in local schools and may have impressions still of what the schools were like.

Because teachers and first line supervisors constitute the school–community interface, our study of the school system concentrates on this level. In each of the fifteen cities, 20 teachers and first line supervisors in elementary, junior high, and senior high schools serving ghetto areas were interviewed. The first line supervisors constitute one fifth of the sample in each city (four persons) and were chosen from among principals and assistant principals in ghetto schools. In our sample, we fixed the proportion black at 50%, setting quotas to that effect in each of the cities. A total of 299 teachers and administrators were interviewed.

Social Characteristics of Ghetto Teachers.   In Chapter 4 the six occupational groups included in this study were contrasted. The educators stood out as having a unique profile. In some respects, they resembled the employers and retail merchants because they were reasonably well-to-do and had a median family income of approximately $13,000.[1] They resemble the personnel officers as they are highly educated, two thirds having had formal education beyond the bachelor's degree. It is at this point that the resemblance between educators and other institutional agents

---

[1] While this figure includes earnings of spouses and other persons in the educator's families, it also reflects the fact that teachers are better paid on the average than are policemen and social workers.

breakdown, since the educators show themselves to be almost the most liberal occupational group in the study.

Only about one in ten consider themselves to be Republicans, the Democratic Party claiming the allegiance of almost half. The remaining "independents" admit to leaning mainly in the direction of the Democrats. Their political and social views, especially on the questions of race, are liberal, as both their racial composition and party affiliation would lead one to suspect. Educators are much more inclined than are the general group of respondents in this study to claim that blacks are subject to racial discrimination. They also see that blacks making less progress in the last 5 years: Only 12% say that blacks are a "lot better off" now, compared to 27% of the institutional agents considered as a group. Furthermore, they are twice as likely (52 as compared to 27%) to claim that blacks were moving too slowly in their drive for equality.

Similarly on other measures the educators show that they hold an image of their city as beset by the problems arising out of poor race relations and poverty. They are much less likely than all of the other institutional agents (save social workers) to manifest a pattern of optimistic denial. Educators see their cities as in deep trouble, with race relations at the core of the problems. Furthermore, their views of the problems of blacks are generally more sympathetic to the civil rights movement.[2]

Table 10.1 summarizes the social characteristics of black and white teachers along with selected measures of "liberalism–conservatism" on race relations issues.

Assessments of Ghetto Schools and Education.   Although the educators acknowledge that blacks in their cities were not receiving the best quality educational services (see Table 10.1), their views of their own particular schools were not as negative. When asked what were the problems faced by their schools, they more frequently commented on deficiencies in the communities in which they served than on deficiencies in their own schools (see Table 10.2). Almost two thirds of the teachers cite "lack of community support" as one of the main problems facing their schools. In contrast only one in five gave reasons related to teacher qualities[3] and only one in four cited problems arising from the curriculum

---

[2] The majority of teachers—black and white—however have not been members of any "civil rights" groups, with only one in five claiming any activity in the period between 1966 and 1968.

[3] These reasons mainly complained about the number of teachers and low salaries paid to teachers, and not about the qualifications or motivations of teachers.

Table 10.1
Selected Social Characteristics and
Community Attitudes of Educators
(N = 299)

(Educator Interviews)

A. Race:

    White 51%   Black   49% (Note: Sampling Artifact)

B. Sex:

    Male 43%   Female 57%

C. Age:

    Median Age = 40.5 years

D. Educational Attainment:

Less than College graduation	1%
College graduation	31%
College plus post graduate work	68%

E. Place of Birth:

Born in City	44%
Born elsewhere	56%

F. Household Income:

    Median household income = $13,500

G. Major Problems Facing City Cited:

Race Relations	49%
Poverty	52
Housing	52
Public Education	43

H. Assessment of "How well blacks are treated in (City)"

Better than any other group	1%.
As well as any other group	4%
As well as any group of same income	22%
Worse than any other group of same income	44%
Worse than any other group	24%

I. Perceived Pace of Civil Rights Movement:

Blacks moving much too fast toward equality	7%
Blacks moving too fast	15%
Pace is about right	22%
Blacks are moving too slow	52%

Table 10.2
Major Problems Facing Schools in Black
Communities

(Educator Interviews)

Problems Cited*	Whites	Blacks	Total
Teachers (qualifications, shortage, etc.)	19%	21%	20%
Students (discipline, qualifications, ability, etc.)	36	26	31
Curriculum	30	19	24
Community Support	69	60	65
Finances and Plant	16	11	14
Race Relations	4	7	5
All Other	2	3	2
100% =	[152]**	[147]	[299]

*Responses to question "As you see it, what are the major
problems that face your school as it tries to fulfill its
educational mission in this neighborhood?.

**Includes one respondent who is an "Oriental."

and classroom organization.[4] Thirty-one percent saw the students as presenting problems for their schools (mainly student lack of motivation and low ability levels). In short, the main problems of their schools were seen as lying outside the schools in the nature of community support for education and in the kinds of students the schools had to work with.[5]

Note that white and black educators are not very far apart in their assessment of problems facing their particular schools. Indeed as we see throughout most of this chapter, the perspectives of race are different but less important on most issues than are the professional perspectives that arise from common training and shared job problems.

The information in Table 10.2 was obtained in response to an "open-ended" question, which presumably measured the salience of problems as well as their prevalence. Educators were free to respond in terms of their schools or in terms of the conditions facing their schools and arising out of either the city or the local community. To focus their attention more specifically upon the schools themselves, educators were asked a series of specific questions, starting with an item asking for an "overall quality" rating of their school and then going through seven specific features, (Table 10.3).

The average ratings received by each of the school qualities are shown in the last column of Table 10.3 .Since a response "average" was given the arbitrary value of 3 (on a scale from 5 to 1), it can be easily seen that the averages cluster closely about the view that their school is close to the "average" for their city. If anything, the ratings are slightly above average, the highest ratings being achieved by "quality of teaching staff" and the "availability of textbooks" (3.36 and 3.31, respectively). Only with respect to physical plant (2.88) and the "availability of extra curricular activities" (2.93) are their schools below average, but not very far below even in those cases. Apparently, public education in their cities is suffering, but their particular schools are not much better or worse than the average school in their system.

The perspectives of race lead black teachers to think less of their particular schools than do their white fellow teachers. In each of the particular qualities, black teachers give lower ratings than whites, although in only five of the seven qualities do race differences reach statistical significance. Black teachers, as compared to their white fellows, consider their schools to be relatively inferior with respect to "overall quality," "ade-

---

[4] A large proportion of these complaints (more than half) concerned the overly large sizes of classes in their schools.

[5] Governor Lester Maddox of Georgia is reputed to have said in response to a criticism of the Georgia prison system that the prison system could only be improved when "we get a better class of prisoners."

Table 10.3
Ratings of School Qualities by Race
(Educator Interviews)
(Black N = 147, White N = 152)

School Attribute		Superior	Above Average	Rating Average	Below Average	Inferior	DK&NA	Overall Average ** (Both races)
*Overall Quality	Wh	13%	21	40	16	6	3	
	Bls	3	17	58	15	4	3	3.10
Physical Plant	Wh	13	16	33	18	18	1	
	Bls	5	17	31	29	15	3	2.88
*Supplies	Wh	14	32	39	9	4	1	
	Bls	5	22	49	15	5	3	3.25
*Text Books	Wh	17	22	47	6	5	2	
	Bls	7	24	50	14	1	3	3.31
*Quality of Teachers	Wh	12	36	34	13	1	3	
	Bls	3	35	46	10	1	5	3.36

TABLE 10.3 (Cont'd)

School Attribute	Superior	Above Average	Rating Average	Below Average	Inferior	DK&NA	Overall Average** (Both races)
Extra-Curricular Activities Wh	5	22	38	22	9	3	
Bls	4	25	35	20	11	3	2.93
Counseling & Guidance Whs	11	31	37	11	7	3	
Bls	3	25	37	18	11	5	3.10
*Library Whs	13	35	31	13	5	2	
Bls	6	24	42	16	8	4	3.21

*Difference between the races is significant at the .05 level

**Average computed by giving values of 5, 4, 3, 2, and 1 to response categories with "superior" equal to 5 and average equal to 3.

335

quacy of supplies," "availability of textbooks," "quality of teaching staff," and "library facilities for students."

Although differences among the fifteen cities in the sample are significant statistically,[6] such differences are not very large, as Figure 10.1 shows. The average ratings of the schools with respect to "overall quality" ranges from 2.4 for San Francisco to 3.6 for Detroit and Pittsburgh. Most of the cities cluster close together on the five point scale of overall quality. Similarly in rating the "quality of the teaching staff," Boston's educators give themselves a very high average rating of 4.1 and Newark's teachers believe themselves to be slightly below average, as represented by a rating of 2.9.

In an attempt to account for variation among teachers and administrators in their perceptions of their schools' quality, a regression analysis

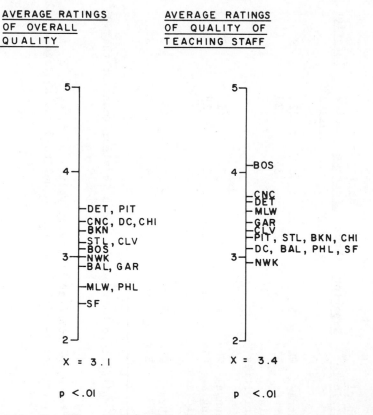

Figure 10.1   City differences in "overall quality" of schools and "quality of teaching staff" (educator interviews).

---

[6] As computed by a one-way analysis of variance.

was attempted, using the ratings of "overall school quality" as a dependent variable. Using as independent variables the ratings of specific school qualities (as shown in Table 10.3), selected background characteristics, cities, and race, the analysis accounted for better than 43% of the variance in school teacher perception of "overall quality." (See Table 10.4).

The decomposition of the total variance shown in Table 10.4 indicates

Table 10.4
Contributions of Ratings of Specific School Qualities, City Differences, Background Characteristics and Race to Ratings of Overall School Quality (N = 299)

Cluster Combinations: Specific School Qualities	Cities	Back-Ground	Race	Proportion of Variance In School Quality Uniquely Attributable
+	0	0	0	.275*
0	+	0	0	.095*
0	0	+	0	.013
0	0	0	+	.000
+	+	0	0	.019
+	0	+	0	.013
+	0	0	+	.010
0	+	+	0	.002
0	+	0	+	.001
0	0	+	+	.001
All Other Combinations				.006

Total Explained Variance $(R)^2$ =.434*

R =.659

"Specific School Qualities" Cluster includes all items in table 10.3 (with the exception of "overall school quality"

"Background Characteristics" Cluster include, age, educational attainment, income and administrative position

*Significant at .05 level or better

that specific quality ratings account uniquely for most of the explained variance, 27.5%. A significant 9.5% is accounted for by intercity differences. Only a minor amount is accounted for uniquely by teacher background characteristics, and nothing in the way of unique variance is accounted for by race. Small amounts of variance are accounted for by combinations of clusters, but none of the combinations' contributions reach statistical significance.

In judging the overall quality of their particular schools, educators apparently react largely to the specific qualities of their own schools.[7] In addition there are city differences: In some cities, ghetto schools are rated relatively better than in other systems. Older teachers and administrators take a slightly more charitable view of their schools, but the differences between the races are reflected almost entirely by the fact that blacks rate some school qualities lower than do whites.

Since the educators say they like their jobs, it is not surprising that about two thirds indicate that they would prefer to keep their present positions as long as they continue teaching. This preference for their present assignments is not likely to be due to self-selection, since the average time in their present positions is quite low (the median is 4 years).

In summary, teachers and administrators in ghetto schools apparently exempt their own particular schools from their general criticisms of public education. While they believe public education is in trouble, their own schools are "average" or a little better than the typical school in their system. This may mean that the troubles of the schools are seen as external to the school system, residing in a lack of support for public education in the surrounding community, or that all the schools in the system are in about equal amounts of trouble. It does mean that the teachers and administrators do not see very much difference between ghetto schools and the other schools in the systems in question. Younger school teachers and black teachers tend to disagree, however, and claim that the ghetto schools are less well off in quality than the average school in their systems.

Job Satisfaction. If the portraits presented in the mass media had any validity, then the two ghetto service workers that seeth with discontent

---

[7] Of course, an alternative explanation is that the ratings of specific qualities are affected by the general ratings of "overall qualities"; hence the amount of variance explained by these specific qualities represents more the "halo effect" than real differences among the schools being rated. There is no way with our data that we can test for the existence of a "halo effect."

are police and teachers. The attention given to trials of teaching in the "blackboard jungle" leave the impression of beleaguered teachers eager to jump at the chance to teach in the suburbs or shift to some less hazardous occupation. Even putting journalistic hyperbole aside, little in the conventional wisdom about ghetto schools would lead one to anticipate the results shown in Table 10.5.

Almost two thirds of the teachers and administrators consider themselves to be "very satisfied" with their positions in general. Only 11% express any degree of dissatisfaction, and of those only 2% are very dissatisfied. Even when asked about specific aspects of their jobs, in most respects the ghetto school teachers express satisfaction. Only minorities express dissatisfaction: 25% with their salaries; 34% with "working conditions in general"; 33% with their teaching loads; and 39% with their "communities." The last column of Table 10.5 contains the average of the responses to these questions, assuming a score of 4 for "very satisfied" and a score of 1 for "very dissatisfied" with the intermediate responses given 3, and 2. Teachers are most satisfied with the "community." As to be expected, most of the averages are above 3.00, indicating a position somewhere between "somewhat staisfied" and "very satisfied."

Black and white teachers are not far apart on most of the items. Black teachers tend to be more dissatisfied with their salaries and their teaching loads, but on all the other items, the differences between black and white teachers do not reach statistical significance.[8]

Nor are there striking differences among the fifteen cities, as shown in Figure 10.2. In all cities, the average amount of satisfaction with "position in general" and "salary" is safely on the "satisfied side." Milwaukee teachers are relatively more dissatisfied than those in Cincinnati, but the differences between cities[9] in satisfaction with "position in general" barely reaches statistical significance at the .05 level. There is more variation among cities in satisfaction with salary (significance reaches the .01 level), but only the extreme cities are far enough apart on this measure to be worthy of note. On this measure, Newark teachers are the most dissatisfied, while those from Milwaukee are the most satisfied. Indeed, the correlation between the two sets of scores is close to zero

---

[8] Black teachers report more dissatisfaction with their salaries despite higher "household incomes" ($13,800 versus $13,048). This discrepancy, however, may only reflect that black teachers may be more likely to come from two income households, concealing in household income figures the fact that their salaries from teaching may be lower in fact than that of their white counterparts. Unfortunately we did not ask for salaries.

[9] Computed by one way analysis of variance.

Table 10.5

Educators' Satisfaction with Jobs and

Specific Aspects of Jobs (N = 299)

(Educators Interviews)

Aspect of Position	Very Satisfied	Somewhat Satisfied	Somewhat Dissatisfied	Very Dissatisfied	DK&NA	Average**
Position In General	62%	27	9	2	0	3.49
*Salary	34%	42	19	6	0	3.06
Colleagues	48%	38	12	2	0	3.32
Supervisors	56%	27	13	4	2	3.41
Working Conditions In General	27%	38	25	9	0	2.81
*Teaching Load	33%	30	22	12	3	2.86
Pupils	37%	43	16	3	2	3.18
Community	17%	40	28	11	3	2.74
Flexibility Permitted In Classroom	57%	27	10	3	3	3.42

*Differences between black and white teachers significant at .05 level.

**Computed by giving scores of 4 through 1 to "Very Satisfied" through "Very dissatisfied".

340

(−.04), indicating that at least on the level of city averages, satisafction in general is unrelated to satisfaction with salaries.

Regression analyses of "satisfaction with position in general" and "satisfaction with working conditions" are shown in Table 10.6. In addition to the usual clusters expressing city differences, background characteristics, and race, we have added a cluster containing responses about satisfaction with particular aspects of positions (ommiting, of course, the dependent variables in question). These two dependent variables

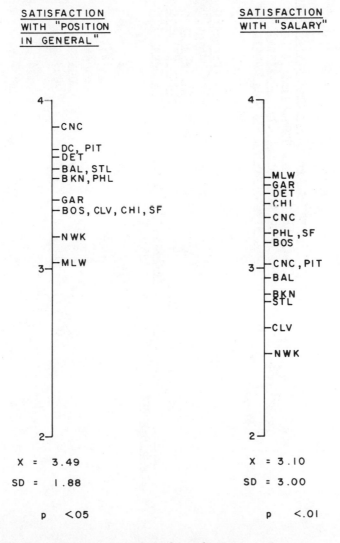

Figure 10.2 City differences in teacher job satisfaction.

Table 10.6

Contributions of Specific Job Satisfactions,
City Differences, Background Factors
and Race to Overall Job Satisfaction
and Satisfaction with Working Conditions

(N = 299)

Specific Job Aspects*	Cluster City	Cluster Background	Cluster Race	Proportion of Variance Uniquely Attributable Satisfaction With "Position In General"	Proportion of Variance Uniquely Attributable Satisfaction with "Working Conditions"
+	0	0	0	.201***	.305***
0	+	0	0	.050***	.045***
0	0	+	0	.006	.036
0	0	0	+	.007	.001
+	+	0	0	.029	.024
+	0	+	0	.017	.046
+	0	0	+	-.003	-.001
0	+	+	0	-.002	.014
0	+	0	+	-.001	-.001
0	0	+	+	.000	.000

Table 10.6 (Cont'd)

Specific Job Aspects*	Cluster City	Background	Race	Satisfaction With "Position In General"	Satisfaction with "Working Conditions"
				Proportion of Variance Uniquely Attributable	
+	+	+	0	.006	.002
+	+	0	+	.001	.001
+	0	+	+	.002	.001
0	+	+	+	.000	-.015
+	+	+	+	.000	.000

Total Variance Explained $(R)^2$ = .313*** .458***

R = .516*** .677***

---

* Specific Job Aspects Cluster includes all the items in table 10.5 except the dependent variables. In addition for the analysis of "working conditions", the dependent variable of "satisfaction with position in general" has been removed.

** Background factors include, sex, age, income, administrative position, and educational attainment.

*** Significant at .05 or better.

343

were chosen because in the one case the variable comes closest to expressing the individual's overall assessment of his "position" and in the other case, expressing satisfaction with the conditions of work, hopefully independent of overall job satisfaction. The four clusters account for rather high proportions of the total variation among teachers, 31% in the case of satisfaction with "position in general" and 46% in the case of satisfaction with "working conditions."

Most of the task of explaining both indexes of job satisfaction was shouldered by responses to questions about specific aspects of their positions. Most of the differences among teachers revolve about their perceptions of how good their jobs are in rather specific respects—satisfaction with salaries, teaching loads, the local communities, and such. It is difficult to determine whether these are "objective" differences among teachers, in the sense that most teachers in the same schools would agree with the teachers on their assessments or whether the ratings reflect "objective" conditions; these findings suggest that differences among individual schools are most important in determining whether an individual teacher is satisfied with his position and working conditions.

Differences among school systems account uniquely only for modest amounts of the variance, 5 and 4.5%. Even smaller amounts of variance are taken up by background factors and race. For all practical purposes, satisfaction with "position in general" is scarcely affected by race and background. Working conditions are more strongly affected by individual differences represented by background factors, which accounts for 3.6% of the variance in satisfaction with working conditions.

In summary, it appears that teachers' job satisfaction levels are sensitive to the specific features of their particular positions. Unlike the police and welfare workers, intercity differences are not of much importance. Being a teacher in one ghetto is similar to being a teacher in another, with room for considerable variation from one school to another within a school system.

Relations With Parents. The ghetto teachers not only like their jobs and think that their schools are about average, but they also report good relations with their pupils' parents. Close to 80% say that they have very little difficulty communicating with parents. An even larger proportion (85%) claim that parents treat them with respect; and 82% say that parents see the teachers as "mostly on their side" (See Table 10.7). Obviously parent–teacher relations in the fifteen cities appear cordial— at least that is the consensus among teachers. The consensus is shared by white and black teachers, the differences between the two races in responses to these questions being statistically negligible.

Table 10.7
Teachers' Perceived Relationships with Parents
(N = 299)

A. Difficulty in Communicating With Parents:

	Percent
Very little Difficulty	80%
Some Difficulty	18
A great deal of difficulty	1
Don't know and no answer	2

B. How Parents Treat Teachers:

Mostly with respect	86%
Mostly Indifference	12
Mostly hostility or contempt	1
Don't know and no answer	1

C. Parent's Views of Teachers:

Mostly on Their side	82%
Mostly as adversaries	9
Don't know and no answer	9

D. Perceived White-Black Differences in Parental Concern for Education
and Welfare of Children:

Black Parents more concerned than whites	20%*
White parents more concerned than blacks	20%*
Both have the same concern	57%*
Don't know and no answer	3%

E. Median Proportion of Parents Met:

White Teachers	21.6*
Black Teachers	45.1*

F. Number of Homes of Pupils Visited:

	None	Only a few	Quite a few	DK&NA
White teachers*	52%	42	7	0
Black teachers*	35%	42	22	1
Total	44%	42	14	1

* Differences between white and black teachers significant at .01 level.

345

Agreement between black and white teachers breaks down, however, when we consider the last three items in Table 10.7 (labelled *D*, *E*, and *F*). Although a majority (57%) of the teachers see no difference between white and black parents in the amount of concern they show for the education and welfare of their children, one in five think that blacks show more concern than whites, and another one in five think the opposite. Black teachers are prone to claim a superior level of concern for black parents, and white teachers a superiority for white parents.

When it comes to meeting parents and visiting pupils' homes, black–white differences persist. Although on-the-average, teachers have met a median percentage of 30% of the parents of their pupils, black teachers claim to have met a median of 45%, as compared to 22% for white teachers. Forty-four percent of the teachers have never visited any of their pupils' homes, and an additional 42% have visited "only a few." Black teachers claim to have visited more pupils' homes than do white teachers. Although it is not quite clear what are the numerical equivalents of "quite a few," 22% of the black teachers (as compared with 7% of the whites) have claimed to visit that many homes.

Variations among the fifteen cities in contacts with parents are shown in Figure 10.3. Although the range of differences among the cities is large, the cities cluster to a degree that intercity differences in the average percentage of parents met are barely significant at the .05 level, and the city percentages of teachers who have visited *any* pupils' homes does not achieve statistical significance. At the one extreme, teachers in Cincinnati claim to have met more than 60% of their pupils' parents, while Newark teachers claim to have met a little more than 25%. Visiting pupils' homes appears to be more prevalent in Brooklyn where 65% of the teachers claimed to have visited at least some of their pupils homes, in contrast to the teachers in Philadelphia where only 25% of whom have done any home visiting.

The two variables displayed in Figure 10.3 are negatively related ($r = -.37$) across cities. In other words, in cities in which the teachers claim to have met a large percentage of their pupils' parents are also cities in which fewer teachers claim to have visited any homes. It is difficult to provide a reasonable interpretation of this inverse relationship. Indeed, all that it may reflect is that the teachers vary very little from city to city on each variable; hence this negative relationship may be a statistical artifact.

The results of a multiple regression analysis of teacher responses to these two measures of teacher–parent contact are shown in Table 10.8. Only modest amounts (18 and 19%) of the variance in parent–teacher contacts could be accounted for background factors and city differences. In explaining teacher differences in the proportion of parents met, back-

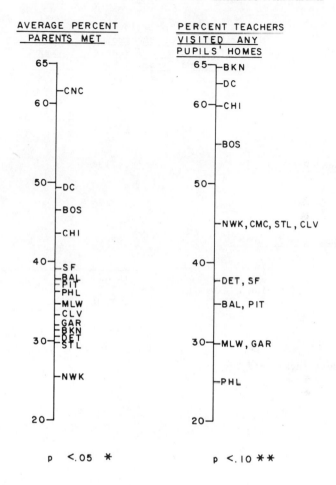

AVERAGE PERCENT
PARENTS MET

PERCENT TEACHERS
VISITED ANY
PUPILS' HOMES

p <.05 *

p <.10 **

* As computed in a one way ANOVA
** As computed in a chi = square test

Figure 10.3 City differences in average proportion parents met in homes of pupils visited by teachers.

ground factors accounted for almost 8% of the variance and city differences a little more than 8%. Among the background factors, only two (race and sex) reached statistical significance: Blacks and women were likely to have met larger proportions of their pupils' parents than were whites or men.

In accounting for teacher differences in visiting homes, background

Table 10.8
Contributions of Background, and City
Differences to Teachers' knowing
Parents and Visiting Pupils' Homes
(N = 299)

Clusters	Percentage Parents Met	Visiting Pupils' Homes
Background Factors	.0793*	.1249*
City Differences	.0819*	.0620
Joint Background and City	.0208	.0121
Total Variance Explained $(R)^2$ =	.1820*	.1990*
R =	.427*	.446*
Individual Background Factors		
Race	.0168*	.0122*
Sex	.0170*	.0120*

*Statistically significant at .05 level.

factors played a larger role. Twelve percent of the variance was explained uniquely by background factors, and only 6% by city differences (not statistically significant at .05). Among individual background factors two stand out—race and sex. Men and blacks are more likely to have visited their pupils' homes.

Teachers in the ghetto schools apparently see parents as friendly and supportive. The teachers have met one out of three parents and a large majority have visited at least some homes. Whatever problems ghetto education may have, according to the teachers, they do not lie in tense or hostile relationships to parents.

Teachers' Assessment of Community Influence. If there is anything about which the educators express reservations, it is the communities in which their schools are located. When asked about the problems faced by their schools, close to two thirds (see Table 10.2) cited "lack of community support" as a major problem. Thirty-nine percent indicated that they were dissatisfied with "the community" in response to a series of questions about specific aspects of their jobs (see Table 10.5), and registered more dissatisfaction with this aspect of their jobs than with any other.

The community generally comes in for a good deal of the blame for the difficulties that the schools experience in educating their pupils. More than half (56%) agree to the proposition that "many communities provide such a terrible environment that education doesn't do much good in the end," and 23% agree "strongly" to that proposition (see Table 10.9). The distracting influences of the community counteract the good intentions of parents according to more than four out of five of the educators. Yet, it is not hostility to public education on the part of the city's residents that causes the trouble: Only 21% endorse the proposition that "most of the people in the average community are hostile to the efforts of the city to educate the children."

The implications of these findings are that the educators endorse a "theory" of environmental causation of the difficulties faced by public education efforts. The problem lies not in the parents—apparently they are characterized as having good will and attitudes that are supportive of the efforts of the teachers and the schools. Nor does the problem lie in the implacable hostility of the general community. Yet influences are at work that have their roots in the local community and make it difficult for teachers to achieve their ends and for students to learn.

At least some of the educators endorse the idea that part of the problem lies in the locus of control over the school system. Forty-five percent agree to the proposition that more community control would lead to a more responsive school system. An ever greater proportion would like to see more participation by parents in the role of subprofessionals. All told, the responses to these two items (see Table 10.9) indicate that more community involvement would benefit the schools, especially if that involvement would not change the professional role of the teacher.[10]

Using items B1 and B2, an index was formed to express the extent to which each teacher favored a theory that "bad environment" causes pupils to fail to learn in the schools. Although the combination of background

---

[10] Differences between white and black teachers on any of the items of Table 10.3 were not statistically significant.

Table 10.9
Educators' Assessment of The Schools'
Communities and Community Factors in General
(N = 299)

A. Satisfaction With School Community: (See also table 10.5)

Very Satisfied	Somewhat Satisfied	Somewhat Dissatisfied	Very Dissatisfied	DK& NA	Average
17%	40	28	11	3	2.74

B. Teachers' Assessment of Community Influences in General:

	Proportion Agreeing to Statement
1. "Many Communities Provide such a terrible environment for the pupils that education does not do much good in the end"	56%
2. "Most Parents try to help their children get a good education, but far too many other influences distract the pupils"	81%
3. "Most of the people in the average community are hostile to the efforts of the city to educate the children"	21%

C. Teachers' Acceptance of More Community Control:

	Proportion Agreeing to Statement
1. "If the average community were given more voice in running the school, it would better meet the needs of the pupils"	45%
2. "Some schools are trying to give the parents and other community residents more control over running the school in their neighborhoods even sometimes letting the parents come into the class rooms to help with teaching and other work as subprofessionals"	73%

factors and city differences accounted for 14% of the variance[11] (see Table 10.10), neither cluster was statistically significant in the amount of variance that it uniquely explained. In short, the differences between teachers in terms of school systems and in terms of the usual cluster of

---

[11] Barely significant at the .05 level.

TABLE 10.10

Contributions of Background Factors and City Differences to
Educators' Assessment of Community Influences*

Cluster	Proportions of Variance Uniquely Attributable
Background	.0057
City	.0704
Background and City Together	.117
Total Variance Explained (R^2) =	.1378**
Significant Background Factors Age	.0137**

---

*Index composed of Agreement-Disagreement to the following statements: "Many communities provide such a terrible environment for the pupils that education does not do much good in the end." And, "Most parents try to help their children get a good education, but far too many other influences distract the pupils."

**Significant at the .05 level.

individual characteristics were not large enough to reach statistical significance. Age is the only one of the individual background characteristics to reach the .05 level. Older teachers took a more charitable view of local communities, denying the importance of community factors in educational failures.

Teachers' Assessment of Pupils.   To round out the educators' views of ghetto education and its problems, we turn now to their assessments of the pupils in their schools. Table 10.11 contains the results from a number of items tapping teacher attitudes toward students. By and large, the teachers (80%) are "satisfied" with their pupils.

Table 10.11
Educators' Assessments of Pupils
(N = 299)

A. Satisfaction with Pupils:

Very Satisfied	Somewhat Satisfied	Somewhat Dissatisfied	Very Dissatisfied	DK& NA	Average
37%	43	16	3	2	3.18

B. Assessment of Pupil Educability:

	Mainly True	Partially True	Not True	DK& NA
1. "In you view is it true in your school that..." "The pupils are uneducable and that teachers can do little more than maintain discipline?"	1%	14	85	0
*2. "The pupils can be taught only by the most skillful teachers who can arouse their interest"	31%	40	28	1
*3. "Pupils come into the school with an interest in learning but their preparation is so poor that they are hard to help?"	26%	56	18	0
*4. "These are ordinary pupils with just about average interest in schooling and with average ability?"	26%	41	33	1
*5. "Almost any teacher can teach these pupils successfully if he or she puts his mind to it and works hard at it?"	43%	25	31	1
*6. "The pupils are above average in ability but are interested only in some things"	4%	27	67	2
*7. "The pupils are above average in ability and interest and are generally cooperative with teachers"	8%	31	60	1

C. Teachers "Getting along with pupils"

1. "How many pupils do you like and get along well with?"

All	Most	Some	Few	DK&NA
46%	52	1	0	1

*2. "Do most of the pupils here regard most of the teachers?"

mostly as friends	65%
mostly as adversaries	8
mostly indifferent	23
DK&NA	1

* Differences between whites and blacks are significant at least at .05 level.

The overwhelming majority (85%) reject the idea that their pupils are "uneducable." Almost the same proportion (82%) subscribe to some degree to the proposition that pupil "preparation is so poor that they are hard to help." These two views, taken together, further support the interpretation that the educators subscribe to a "theory" that environmental deprivation adds to difficulties of education in the ghetto.

The remainder of the items in Table 10.11 add further to this interpretation. A majority of teachers subscribe to the view that through the application of their best efforts and skills, they can successfully teach ghetto students. In addition, the teachers consider the students to be "ordinary" students and reject the idea that they are above average in ability.

On six out of the ten items in Table 10.11, black teachers present a more sympathetic view of the pupils than do their white colleagues. Black teachers see pupils as more friendly, more frequently as "ordinary," and even "above average" in ability, and they believe that teaching efforts are more likely to be successful.

The unanimity among educators in their views of pupils can be discerned in the small amount of variance among teachers that can be explained by the usual clusters of city differences and background characteristics. As Table 10.12 indicates, the two clusters account for a very modest 15% of the variation among teachers, a proportion that barely reaches statistical significance at the .05 level. Neither of the two clusters accounts uniquely for significant amounts of the variance. In fact, the only single factor that accounts for a significant amount of variance is race: Black teachers espouse an even more sympathetic view of ghetto school pupils than do the teachers as a group.

An Overview of Teacher Assessments. The analyses presented in the last several sections of this chapter have not led us very far toward understanding differences among teachers in their assessments of parents, local communities, and their pupils. The amounts of variance explained by background factors and city differences have been very modest, between 12 and 20%—statistically significant but not very impressive. Indeed, the major findings of these sections concern the strong degree of consensus among teachers, transcending differences among cities and among teachers of varying backgrounds.

Several specific conclusions emerge from these analyses. First, large city differences do not exist in the attitudes held by teachers. On most of the variables discussed so far the differences among cities either failed to reach statistical significance or just barely qualified at the

Table 10.12
Contributions of Background Factors and
City Differences to Assessment of
Students in Ghetto Schools**
(N = 299)

	Proportion of Variance Uniquely Attributable
Background Factors	.0719
City Differences	.0599
Background Factors Jointly with City Differences	.0215
Proportion variance explained (R^2) =	.1533*
Specific Background Factor	
Of Race	.0300*

* Significant at .05 level.

** Dependent variable are scores for teachers combining responses to questions B1, B5, and B7 in table 10.

.05 level.[12] In short teachers have more in common across cities than any of the other occupational groups interviewed.

[12] Obviously part of the reason for the lack of statistical significance lies in the small number of interviews per city. City differences have to be considerably larger for the educators than for the employers to reach statistical significance. That this is not the entire explanation can be seen in the next chapter where city differences among social welfare workers are usually statistically significant even though the number of social welfare workers interviewed in each city is the same as for teachers.

Second, few differences among teachers relate to conventional individual characteristics. While black teachers often enough espoused a more sympathetic view of their schools, communities and students, most of the other characteristics—age, sex, and position within the school system—were only rarely related to the assessments being studied.

Third, the impressions received from the teachers goes at variance with general impressions of ghetto public education. According to many observers—expert and amateur—ghetto school children are difficult to deal with, school conditions are not good, and parents are difficult to communicate with. The fact that the educators assert to the contrary can mean a variety of things: the most uncharitable interpretation is that educators are intelligent enough to know what is a "proper" response and gave us "good" answers that demonstrate their liberal acceptance of their clients as just "ordinary" children who along with their parents were victims, if anything, of their environments. It may also mean that conventional wisdom does not reflect the truth about ghetto schools. Because of educators' intimate contact, they have provided us with more accurate and reliable assessments. Still a third possibility is that educators are telling us the truth *as they see it:* The quality of their perception is strained through their isolated positions in the ghetto communities. Like the policemen and the merchants whose daily workday lives bring them into contact with the community but who are cut off from intimate contact by the barriers imposed by race and role, the teachers see the world about them as filtered through their liberal ideology. Ghetto children are ordinary children because race does not matter. Ghetto parents are eager and interested because race does not matter. If anything is wrong, it is "the community" that is at fault in not sufficiently preparing pupils for the tasks of learning in the schools.

Unfortunately, there are no ways we can discern whether one or another alternative explanation for the views of teachers is the best "fit." There are compelling arguments for each: Teachers do know what are the "official norms" of the society concerning race differences. Also journalistic hyperbole has exaggerated the plight of the ghetto schools. Furthermore, ghetto teachers are isolated by the professional roles they play. Perhaps all three combine in a synergistic fashion to produce the generalizations we have drawn from the data discussed in the last three sections of this chapter.

Citizen Satisfaction With Schools. Although the teachers in ghetto schools appear to be believe that their schools are "average," without much in the way of variation from city to city, the black and white citizens of the fifteen cities apparently hold different assessments of their schools. In figure 10.4, city values for citizen satisfaction, compared from data[13] collected by the Survey Research Center, are presented. The two

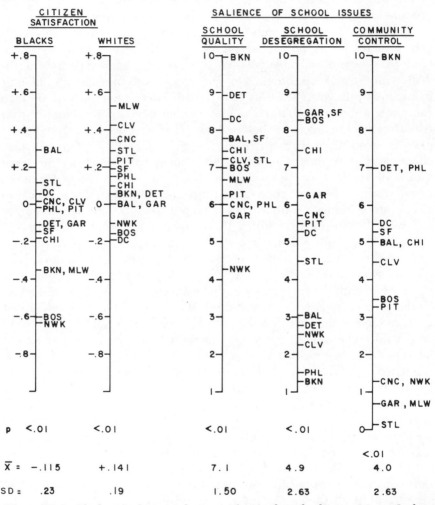

Figure 10.4 Black and white satisfaction with schools and salience ratings of educational issues (elite and sample survey interviews).

---

[13] Based upon the following item in the SRC survey:

What about the quality of public schools in this neighborhood—Are you generally satisfied, somewhat dissatisfied, or very dissatisfied?

The index shown in Figure 10.4 was computed by giving the values $+1$, -1, and -2 to the three responses categories.

graps on the left of the figure, respectively, show how satisfied black and white citizens are with the "quality of the public schools" in their neighborhoods. A positive value indicates an average in which satisfaction predominates; a negative value indicates an average level of predominant dissatisfaction.

On the whole, blacks in the average city are dissatisfied, with only three of the fifteen cities showing average levels on the satisfied side. White citizens show exactly the opposite: only three out of the fifteen cities have averages which are on the dissatisfied side. As one might expect, there is a slight positive relationship between the white and black averages for the fifteen cities (+ .36), indicating that although white citizens are generally more satisfied than their black counterparts, in cities where whites are relatively dissatisfied, blacks also are dissatisfied. There are many exceptions to this tendency: For example, black Baltimoreans are the most satisfied of any of the ghetto groups, but white Baltimoreans rate their city far down in the list. Similarly Milwaukee whites are the most satisfied in all of the cities, but Milwaukee blacks are among the most dissatisfied of all the black groups.

The remaining three graphs in Figure 10.4 are derived from our elite interviews. These are ratings of the salience of three education-related issues derived from the remarks recorded in the elite interviews. The "quality" of the public schools is a visible issue in most of the fifteen cities. In some cities, Brooklyn, Detroit, and Washington, "school quality" is a very salient issue, while in Newark, it does not seem to be very important. School desegregation has a lower profile; although it is high in Gary, San Francisco, and Boston, it is scarcely a concern in the six cities clustered at the bottom of the scale. Even less salient is the issue of community control over local schools, an obviously warm topic in Brooklyn but of minor consequence in most of the other cities.

Whether an issue is salient seems scarcely related to "grass roots" satisfaction or dissatisfaction with the public schools, as the correlations in Table 10.13 show. Black satisfaction with their neighborhood schools is related + .16 to the salience of school quality as an issue, and white satisfaction is completely unrelated to this issue ($r = 0.0$). Also citizen satisfaction does not relate at all significantly to the salience of the other two educational issues. Apparently the processes that give rise to satisfaction–dissatisfaction on the level of ordinary citizens are different from those that lead an issue to become salient in this area. Furthermore, grass roots sentiment is divorced from the issues that are of some concern on the level of decision-making in the community.

Levels of grass roots satisfaction are related to characteristics of the school systems involved, however, as Table 10.14 shows. Black satisfaction

Table 10.13'
Correlations Among Levels of School
Satisfaction and Salience
of Educations Issues
(N = 15 cities)

		Citizen Satisfaction with Schools			Salience of School Issues	
		Blacks	Whites	Quality	Desegregation	Community Control
Satis-faction	Blacks		.36	.16	-.19	-.01
	Whites			.00	.12	-.25
Issue Salience	Quality				-.14	.72
	Desegregation					-.46
	Community Control					

increases with the proportion of blacks in the population, with the extent of segregation in the school system, and with the level of job satisfaction claimed by educators; it is especially closely related (.77) to the perception of equal employment opportunities for blacks in teaching. Somewhat less related are measures pertaining to the political system—the responsiveness of the mayor or the school board to the demands of the civil rights movement, and the rate of rejection by the selective service for educational disabilities.[14]

In short, it looks as if black citizens are particularly pleased with their local schools where blacks are segregated[15] in the schools and when the teachers like their jobs, and also where the school system is seen as an equal opportunity employer of black teachers. Whites like the schools under opposite circumstances but with different weights given to the factors involved: They like the schools when there are fewer blacks in the city's population, *and* when the schools are segregated; whites are

---

[14] For some of the variables, the causal direction might go from citizen satisfaction, not vice versa. For example, when citizens are more satisfied with schools, they may get along with teachers better; teachers are more satisfied.

[15] The index of segregation employed is the proportion of black children attending schools, in which 90% or more of the children are black.

Table 10.14
Selected Correlates of Citizen
Levels of Satisfaction with Schools
(N = 15 cities)

Variable	Citizen Satisfaction with Schools	
	Blacks	Whites
Proportion Black Population	.40	−.42
Segregation Index	.58	.15
Responsiveness of Mayor	.33	−.30
Responsiveness of School Board	.20	−.30
Educators Jobs Satisfaction	.62	−.06
Selective Service Intelligence Test Rejection Rate	.18	−.57
Perceived Employment Opportunities for Blacks as Teachers in Schools	.77	−.07

also unhappy when the selective service intelligence test rejection rate is high, but are not especially sensitive to how happy ghetto educators may be with their jobs.[16] All of the correlations involving black levels of satisfaction (left-hand column) are positive. Six of the seven involving white levels of satisfaction are negative. In short, the conditions that lead to high levels of satisfaction among blacks are the circumstances that produce the opposite tendency among whites.[17]

Roughly the same pattern of white and black reactions to the perceived quality of their neighborhood schools can also be seen in Table 10.15.

---

[16] Obviously, it may be the case that whites would be more responsive to how teachers and administrators in their neighborhood schools assess their jobs.

[17] The reader may recall that findings with respect to the police were quite different. Blacks and white levels of experience with police abuse were more highly related (and positive) and whites reacted to the police department in much the same fashion as blacks.

Table 10.15
Contributions of Political Sector,
Educators' Attitudes and Demographic Factors
to Citizen Satisfaction With Local Schools
(N = 15)

Cluster*			Proportions of Variance Uniquely Attributable	
Political Sector	Educators Attitudes	Demographic Factors	Blacks	Whites
+	0	0	.08	.15
0	+	0	.37	.34
0	0	+	.42	.51
+	+	0	.05	-.04
+	0	+	-.04	.17
0	+	+	-.06	-.22
+	+	+	.02	-.06
		Total Variance Explained (R^2) =	.85**	.85**

*Compositions of Clusters are as follows:

Political Sector: Elite Interview ratings of "sympathy-
responsiveness" of Mayor, School
Superintendent and School Board

Teachers Attitudes: Educators' ratings of satisfaction with
job and with community

Demographic Factors: Schools segregation index, proportion in city
who are turned down by selective service
on educational deficiency grounds

*Significant at .05

In this table we show the unique contributions of three clusters of factors to levels of white and black satisfaction with the quality of their schools. Eighty-five percent of the variance can be accounted for in the case of each race, indicating that variation from city to city in satisfaction with schools is highly structured. The unique contribution of demographic factors (school segregation and the proportion who are rejected by the selective service) is the largest entry in both columns, accounting for 42 and 51%, respectively, of black and white satisfaction. Educators' attitudes (job and community satisfaction) account for another 37 and

34%, with the sympathy-responsiveness of school officials and the mayor accounting for a smaller 5 and 15%. The unique contributions of combinations of clusters show an erratic pattern, the negative values indicating that the stability of the unique contributions is probably quite low. A properly conservative interpretation of this table is that the three clusters account for much of the variation from city to city, but the allocation of accounted for variance among the three clusters is probably not very stable.

It should be noted that although the three clusters account for the same amount of variance for levels of black and for levels of white satisfaction, the *direction* of the clusters' influence is reversed In short, whites are more dissatisfied when the political sector is sympathetic to the civil rights movement, when the ghetto educators dislike their jobs, and when there is a heavy selective service rejection rate and a highly segregated school system. Black levels of satisfaction are sensitive to the converse state of affairs.

In Table 10.13 we saw that whether certain educational issues were salient in a city's political life was related only to a negligible and erratic

Table 10.16
Selected Correlates of Salience of
Educational Issues
(N = 15 cities)

	Salience Ratings of		
Variable	School Quality	School Desegregation	Community Control
Sympathy-responsiveness of School Board	.265	-.482	.705
Progressiveness of School System*	.517	-.527	.837
Index of Segregation	-.115	-.094	-.286
Selective Service Rejection Rate	.379	-.444	.627
Educators Job Satisfaction	.307	-.297	.241
Proportion Black in City Population	-.083	-.415	-.054

*Ratings of school system's reputation for being forward looking and innovative as discerned from elite interviews.

extent to levels of black or white citizens' satisfaction with their schools. We can therefore expect that the correlates of issue salience will be different as well. Indeed, Table 10.16 indicates that such is the case. The salience ratings of all three issues—school quality, desegregation, and community control—are all more sensitive to characteristics of the cities' political system. However, the strongest correlate of each of the issues is a rating derived from the elite interviews of the school system's reputation for progressiveness and innovation. The higher the reputation of a school system in that respect, the more likely are school quality and community control to be issues and the less likely is school desegregation to be an issue.

In many ways, this finding is something of a mystery. One might expect that the less innovative a school system, the more likely that questions about its quality will be raised in the political arena. Our findings, of course, are just the opposite. Indeed, one interpretation may be that school systems innovate and move in progressive directions in response to criticisms that their quality is low. Or an alternative interpretation is that a progressive and innovative school system constantly raises the issue of quality. Even more puzzling, however, is the very high positive correlation (.837) between progressivism and the issue of community control. The more progressive the school system, the more likely is the issue of local community control over the schools to be raised. Perhaps the most likely interpretation is that it is precisely in those school systems in which school quality and community control is being debated that the school system develops the reputation of being progressive and innovative: In short, it may be the raising and consideration of these issues that lead to or enhance the reputation of the school system.

Note that school desegregation as an issue is negatively related to all of the variables in Table 10.16. Where there are few blacks in a city (e.g., Boston and San Francisco), the school board is not likely to develop a reputation of friendliness to the civil rights movement, nor is the system likely to develop a reputation for progressiveness. In such cities, the major issue is that of school desegregation. Under this interpretation the issue of school desegregation is seen as one raised primarily where the black ghettoes are small and where the school system is not particularly sensitive to civil rights movement demands.

Although each of the correlations in Table 10.16 are relatively large, the overlap among variables is so great that it is difficult to obtain meaningful multiple regression analyses from these data. The firmest statement that we can make is that the salience of educational issues in a city is more related to the politics of education than to a response to either the objective conditions in the school system or levels of mass dissatisfaction with the schools.[18]

Summary. The teachers and school administrators are among the most "liberal" of the institutional agents interviewed in this study. They are aware of the disadvantaged positions of blacks in their city and are among the most sympathetic of all groups to the goals of the broadly defined civil rights movement. Despite the considerable criticism leveled at ghetto schools, however, educators are not very critical of either education in general or their schools in particular. Also they like their jobs and think that their schools are at least average or above.

The educators see the "community" as the source of the educational problems faced by their schools. The "community" in that sense does not include either their pupils or the parents of their pupils toward whom they show at least attitudes of approval and acceptance. Apparently influences emanate from the community which impede learning and hinder the operations of their schools, perhaps lodged in the peer group "subcultures" of their students.

Citizen satisfaction with their schools seems related only negligibly to the attitudes displayed by teachers. Blacks like their schools when the schools are segregated and when teachers like their jobs. Whites prefer the obverse conditions.

Finally, the educational issues that are salient in a community are more a function of the politics of education than of characteristics of either educators or of levels of mass satisfaction with the schools.

---

[18] For example, step-wise multiple regressions were computed using the issue salience ratings as dependent variables with the following results:

		First Step		Second Step		Third Step	
Dependent Variable	Variable	Variance %	Variable	Variance %	Variable	Variance %	Total Variance Explained
School quality	Salience community control	52*	School board response	12	Black satisfaction	8	71*
Desegregation	Progressivism	28*	Job satisfaction	3			31
Community control	Progressivism	70*	School quality salience	11*	School segregation index	6*	88*

*Indicates significance at .05 level.

Chapter 11

WELFARE WORKERS AND THE GHETTO

The present welfare system in the United States has apparently few defenders. Criticism is directed at the system from all sides. Almost everyone agrees that there is something wrong with the welfare system. The clients complain that payments are below subsistence levels and that the inevitable means test is dehumanizing. Local public officials worry about the tax burden involved. Moralists on the right deplore the subsidization of the slothful and indolent, while their counterparts on the left see the welfare system as a means for buying off the discontented. No one apparently wants the welfare system as it stands, but there is scarcely any agreement on what would be an appreciable improvement or reasonable replacement.

If the legislation presently under consideration in congress is any indicator, it is clear that the welfare system will be changed. At minimum, the burden of support will be shifted more to federal government. At maximum, there is a chance that the system will be replaced by a family allowance plan or by an income maintenance system. Within the next few years, changes will be made which may shift considerably both the sources of support for public welfare and the principles under which such support is extended to those in need.

The welfare system is a complicated combination of a number of different schemes. Some of the welfare programs scarcely cause any controversy. Old age assistance that provides payments to the aged who do not have other sources of support does not cause much concern. Nor does the plan that provides support payments to the blind. The heart of the controversy over welfare centers around General Assistance (GA) programs and Aid to Families with Dependent Children (AFDC). It is with respect to these programs that one may suspect that recipients malinger, and clients prove dissatisfied with the low levels of support received.

AFDC and GA are widely perceived to be programs whose clients are largely black. Indeed, for many of the major metropolitan areas with large black ghettoes, that is the case. For the country as a whole, however, white clients outnumber blacks, even though rates of participation for blacks are higher than for whites. The high black participation rates are partly responsible for the controversial character of "welfare," especially in the large metropolitan centers. Hence it is particularly appropriate to look at the politics of the welfare systems within each of the metropolitan centers in our study.

As with the other local municipal systems, our concern will center on "institutional agents," in this instance, case workers' in local welfare departments.[1] In addition, interviews with elites in each city asked about the welfare department, and in many cities we interviewed the officials responsible for the administration of welfare programs. SRC interviews conducted with black and white citizens in each city, included several questions about public welfare, including the welfare status of the household in which the interviewing was being conducted.

Welfare workers interviewed in this study were selected from among those who dealt mainly with black clients, ordinarily within welfare department offices with jurisdiction over largely black neighborhoods in each city. Quotas were set of 20 interviews per city, half to be with white case workers and half with blacks. All told, 307 interviews were conducted, the quotas being exceeded in several cities.

Social Characteristics of Case Workers.   As we saw in Chapter 4, case workers in contrast to all the institutional agent groups were younger, geographically more mobile, and more liberal in ideology. They were also most likely to be female. Table 11.1 recapitulates some of those earlier findings.

---

[1] Although in most cities, the administration of public welfare is a city function, in some the welfare program is directly administered by the state (e.g., Pennsylvania), or by the county in which the city is located (e.g., Cook County for Chicago or Lake County for Gary, Indiana). In such cases we sampled case workers from within the suborganization that had jurisdiction over the city in question.

Table 11.1
Selected Social Characteristics of
Social Workers
(N = 307)

A. Race:

White: 49.5%   Black: 51.2%   Other: 0.3%   (Sampling
                                                      Artifact)

B. Sex:

Male: 36.8%   Female: 63.2%

C. Age:

	Median Age
Whites	28
Blacks	34

D. Educational Attainment:

High School Graduation	Some College	College Graduation	College Plus Post-Grad	NA
1.3%	10.1	61.6	26.7	.3

E. Household Income:

Median = $9,286

F. Place of Birth:

Born in city 32.6%

G. Political Preference in National Elections:

Democrats	Republicans	Independent Democrats	Independent Republicans	Independents
51.1%	7.2%	20.8%	4.6%	14.0%

Almost two thirds of the social workers were women. The median age was low—32 for the entire sample, 28 for whites, and 34 for blacks. As one can anticipate from the educational requirements for case workers in most welfare agencies, the vast majority (88%) are college graduates, with more than a quarter (27%) having taken some courses beyond the bachelor's degree.

Although among the better educated of the institutional agents, welfare workers' household incomes are not high. The median household income is $9286, much lower than teachers or personnel officers with whom they compare in educational attainment, and not much higher than policemen, whose educational level is much lower.

Of all the institutional agent groups, the case workers are the most

likely to be migrants to their cities, two thirds having been born elsewhere. Nor are case workers likely to own their own homes, a characteristic which reflects both their youth and mobility.

The impression left by this catalogue of social characteristics is that
case workers are a highly transient group. The typical white case worker
is a woman college graduate who is not far from completing her BA and
has just recently married or is about to get married. Case work for her
is a way station on the road to other statuses. For blacks, case work
appears to be more likely to constitute an occupational career line: black
case workers are older, having been in their positions a longer period of
time, and manifest more signs of "settling in."

Both black and white case workers are different from their clients in
striking ways. In educational attainment and in income case workers are
clearly upper middle class, while welfare clients are close to the bottom
of the social heap. The gap in class and status, however, is not reflected
in a lack of sympathy on the part of social workers. Of all the institutional
groups, they are most likely to believe that blacks are badly off and are
the most sympathetic to the aspirations of the civil rights movement.

The Problems of Big City Welfare Departments. Case workers see their
major problems as stemming from within welfare departments rather
than as located in the general community or as being in the nature of
their clients. (See Table 11.2) Almost half (48%) of the case workers
cited "agency policy" as one of the major problems facing them. White
case workers were particularly critical of their agencies in this respect
(61%) as compared to blacks (37%). Other agency criticisms that received significant levels of citation include "case load" (19%), "lack of
funds" (11%), and poor training (6%).

Problems having their roots outside their agencies include "social disorganization" in their client populations (24%), unemployment, and
housing conditions (10% and 17% respectively). Black case workers are
more likely to cite such problems than whites. Inadequate public understanding attains a rather low level of mention (15%). But the most
surprisingly low level is achieved by "discrimination," cited by only 1%
of the case workers.

All told, case workers present an interesting contrast to the educators
discussed in the preceding chapter. Educators liked the school system
and their schools, reserving their complaints about problems facing public education to conditions within which the school system had to operate.
There was nothing wrong with the schools: the problems stemmed from
the lack of support received by the schools from their communities and

Table 11.2

MAJOR PROBLEMS FACING WELFARE WORKERS

Problem: Percent Citing Among:

		Whites	Blacks	Total
A.	Within Agency Problems			
	Agency policy, redtape	61%	37%	48%
	Case load	22	9	19
	Lack of funds	11	11	11
	Low salaries	3	1	2
	Poor training	9	2	6
B.	Outside Agency Problems			
	Poor public understanding	21	8	15
	Unemployment	7	12	10
	Housing Conditions	13	21	17
	Social Disorganization	22	27	24
	Discrimination against Blacks		1	1
	Blacks' need to use self help	8	6	7
	Municipal services needed	13	14	14
C.	Other			
	100% =	(153)*	(154)	(307)

Note: Percentages add up to more than 100% since respondents
       could give more than one response.

* Includes one Oriental.

in the social conditions which impede their pupils' preparation and learning. Social workers, in contrast, see their problems stemming from within
their agencies: organizational loyalty among social workers does not
appear to be very strong, especially among white case workers who are
apparently less likely to regard case work as a long-term commitment.

When asked about specific conditions within their agencies, the case
workers generally were critical of their agencies on all of the items asked.
In Table 11.3 are shown the proportions of case workers who thought
that certain problems were serious ones for their agencies. In every one
of the seven items, a majority of the case workers thought the problem
deserved at least a "somewhat serious" rating.

Table 11.3

Specific Complaints Registered About
Their Welfare Agencies by
Case Workers (N = 307)

Complaint	Very Serious	Seriousness of Problem: Somewhat Serious	Not Serious	DK& NA
Lack of money for clients	52%	29	18	2
Lack of time*	55%	28	17	0
Poor Supervision from top management of agency	22%	28	50	1
Hampering rules and regulations	40%	38	20	1
Lack of cooperation from city government	16%	33	47	4
Agency Disorganization*	30%	36	33	0
Lack of Agency Enthusiasm	24%	35	42	0

*Differences between whites and blacks significant at 05 level.

Particularly serious agency problems were seen to be "lack of time" (55% rating this problem as "very serious"), "lack of funds for clients" (52%), and "hampering rules and regulations" (40%). Of lesser concern were matters such as "supervision," "amount of cooperation from city government," "agency disorganization," and lack of "agency enthusiasm." In short, the most serious problems of the case workers were ones that hampered their ability to carry out their tasks—not being able to allocate more money to clients and not having enough time to spend with clients.

On most of the items, black and white case workers agreed on how serious the problems were. However, white case workers were significantly more concerned with "lack of time," and more complained about "agency disorganization" than did their black counterparts. Again black case workers showed more contentment with their jobs than did their white counterparts.

Welfare agencies are creatures of local government, operating within a framework of federal and state legislation. Sufficient looseness in this framework allows for considerable intercity variation, as the graphs in Figure 11.1 indicate. The proportions within each city of caseworkers who rate a problem as "very serious" range very widely. For example, at the one extreme, 85% of Philadelphia's case workers claim that they are

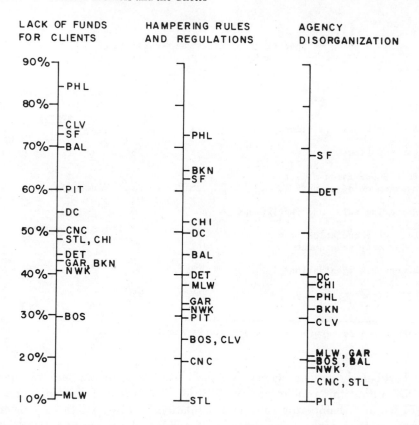

Figure 11.1 City differences in case workers' complaints about their agencies.

hampered by lack of funds for their clients: In contrast, only 12% of Milwaukee's case workers register this complaint. The same is true with the other two complaints shown in Figure 11.1 The range of city variation in case worker complaints about their agencies is as great or greater than the range of variation among police in the fifteen cities.

Indeed, the regression analyses involving city differences and the background factors as independent variables with each of the specific complaints as dependent variables shows that, with only one exception, city differences account uniquely for statistically significant amounts of variance; in four of the five remaining cases, city differences uniquely account for more of the variance than background characteristics of the case workers. (These findings are shown on Table 11.4.)

City differences uniquely account for about 10% of the variance in case worker complaints about their agencies, the main exception being "lack of time." This means that a large component is allocatable to the

Table 11.4

Contributions of City and Background
Differences to Case Workers
Complaints about their
Agencies (N = 307)

	Proportions of Variance Uniquely Attributable to:			
Agency Complaint	City Differences	Background Differences**	Jointly	Total Variance Explained
Lack of Funds	.11*	.07*	.03	.22*
Lack of Time	.02	.05*	.00	.07
Hampering Rules	.08*	.06*	.03	.18*
Cooperation from City	.07*	.06*	.05	.18*
Agency Disorganization	.10*	.13*	.02	.25*
Lack of Agency Enthusiasm	.11*	.07*	.01	.19*

* Statistically significant at .05 level or better.

** Background factors include race, age, religious affiliation, educational attainment and sex.

specific agency in which the case worker works.[2] Background differences among case workers account uniquely on the average for less variance, about 7%. The joint effects of city and background average out to about 2%, never reaching statistical significance.

Taken together, as in the last column of Table 11.4, city differences and background factors together account for about 20% of the variance in complaints about welfare agencies, statistically significant amounts in the case of every complaint, except in that of "lack of time."

Among the background variables, only one—age—appears often enough as statistically significant in the regression analyses to be worthy of mention. Younger social workers are more likely to be critical of their agencies than are older case workers. Indeed, the racial differences which we pointed to in Table 11.3 are no longer significant once age is taken into account; thus it was the lower age levels of white case workers that accounted for their higher levels of criticism of their agencies. This finding, incidentally, bolsters the interpretation offered earlier in this chapter that black case workers are more likely to look upon welfare work as a long-term commitment than are their white counterparts.

What Case Workers Do.   Our sampling instructions were to obtain case workers whose case loads were largely black. How successfully this was accomplished can be seen in Table 11.5: 84% of the persons interviewed were case workers, 12% were supervisors, and the remaining 4% were engaged in other types of social work, primarily counseling and psychiatric social work. Two out of three of the respondents had case loads which contained 75% or more black, with a clear majority (55%) having case loads which were more than 90% black.[3]

The case load of the typical welfare worker is around 100 individuals,[4] but the range is very large, running from 20 to 500 persons. Case workers claim to meet their clients at least once a week, the typical time spent with each case being 30 minutes. These meetings take place in clients'

---

[2] Although city differences are not identical with agency differences, we have interpreted the intercity differences in this context to refer largely to agency differences. This may be somewhat in error. For example, if city differences refer mainly to the inability of the agency to meet the needs of the poor in each city, needs which vary from city to city, then the city differences are not due to the agencies involved but to the interaction between agencies and the welfare problem of the cities involved.

[3] The low proportions of blacks in case loads were encountered mainly in cities where there were small black populations (e.g. Milwaukee, San Francisco, and Boston).

[4] See footnote to Table 11.5.

Table 11.5

Job Activities of Case Workers
(N = 307)

A. Job Classification:

Case Work	Other Social Work	Supervising
84%	4%	12%

B. Number of Clients Served:*

Less Than 100	100-199	200-299	300 or More	None (Includes Supervisors)
28%	19	17	15	19

C. Number of Times per Week Clients Seen:

Once or Less	Twice or More	Supervisor or Never
77%	4%	19

D. Time Spent with Clients on Visits:

30 mins. or less	31-45 mins.	46- 60 mins.	60 mins. or more	Supervisors or NOne
20	24	31	10	15

E. Proportion of Visits that Take Place in HOme or Neighborhood:

90% or More	75% to 89%	Less Than 75%	No Visits or Supervisors
45%	16%	25%	14%

F. Proportions of Clients who Are Black:

Less Than 75%	75% to 89%	90% or More	Supervisors or No Clients
19%	11%	55%	15%

---

* Case workers were asked how many people they served. It is difficult
to translate these figures into "cases" which would ordinarily involve
households containing several individuals. In addition, it is probably
the case that some of the case workers gave replies in terms of cases
rather than individuals.

homes or neighborhoods. Welfare case work is a service that is apparently delivered frequently, if not intensively, and within the ghetto either in the home or in neighborhood welfare offices.

These data on case work activities are difficult to calibrate. If one regards social work as services designed to help households through counselling and similar aid, the contacts appear to be fleeting and superficial, as case loads are higher than such aims might ideally call for. However, if one believes that case work in a welfare agency ought to mainly provide needy households with adequate monetary allowances, these data may describe a situation in which the visits of case workers may be more frequent and lengthy than necessary. Obviously, welfare departments try to do both: Visits with clients, whether in the welfare office or in the home, are designed to gauge the extent of fiscal need and to aid the household to attain an independent status.

The data of Table 11.5 do indicate that case workers have considerable first-hand acquaintance with the black ghettoes of their cities. They ply their trade in black neighborhoods and visit clients' homes. More than any of the other institutional agents, they appear to have more extensive and intimate contact with ghetto residents, especially those in financial distress.

Attitudes Toward Clients. In registering complaints about their jobs, case workers are more critical of their agencies than of anything else about their jobs (see Tables 11.1 and 11.2) The difficulties presented by the problems of social disorganization and poverty also come in for a share of complaints. Almost conspicuous is the absence of criticisms directed at clients: A few case workers (7%) felt that clients should do more to help themselves, but this viewpoint was decidedly a minority one.

Yet case workers do have some critical comments to make about clients when questioned directly on that score, as we may note in Table 11.6. Apparently such complaints are not as salient as are the defects in the welfare system. Or case workers may be too liberal ideologically to express spontaneously such criticisms. Whatever the explanation, the data in Table 11.6 indicate that sizable minorities endorse statements critical of clients, and majorities say it is at least partly true that clients do not do enough to improve themselves.

Statements referring to blacks get less critical endorsement than do statements about clients in general—suggesting that answers are at least partially ideologically tinged. Most surprising, however, are the differences between black and white case workers: Blacks tend to be more

Table 11.6

Case Workers' Attitudes Toward
Their Clients

		Proportions Endorsing Statement As:			
Attitudinal Statement		Mostly True	Somewhat True	Not True	DK& NA
Clients do not do enough to improve themselves."*	W	15%	68	21	0
	B	31%	51	16	1
"Black Clients are harder to reach."	W	16%	30	53	2
	B	14%	25	59	2
It is harder to get resources for black clients."*	W	20%	18	61	1
	B	25%	33	41	1
Clients Take services for granted."	W	33%	36	30	1
	B	36%	40	23	1
Black Clients are especially arrogant".*	W	4%	17	79	0
	B	10%	14	64	1

(N for whites = 152)
(N for blacks = 154)

Differences between white and black social workers significant at
.05

critical than whites. Blacks are more likely to endorse the statement that clients do not help themselves enough and that black clients are especially arrogant.

Inspection of responses to these statements in terms of individual cities indicates that there are wide variations from city to city, expressing again the possibility that welfare agencies differ significantly from place to place. The racial differences in Table 11.6 plus the city differences indicate that a more sophisticated analysis of these data is called for. Accordingly, multiple regression analyses were undertaken of the responses to each of the statements of Table 11.6 with objective of discerning the unique contributions of city differences and background factors. The results are shown on Table 11.7.

Table 11.7

Contributions of City Differences and Background
Factors to Attitudes Toward Clients

(N = 307)

Dependent Variable	Proportions of Variance Uniquely Attributable to:			
	City Differences	Background Factors	Joint Effects	Total Variance Explained
"Clients do not do enough to improve themselves".	.125*	.034	.013	.171*
"Black clients are harder to reach."	.089*	.029	.015	.132*
"Harder to get resources for black clients".	.101*	.057*	0.0	.152*
"Clients take services for granted."	.085*	.020	.012	.118*
"Black Clients are especially arrogant."	.120*	.019	.001	.140*

* Significant at .05 level.

City differences and background factors together explain in each case statistically significant amounts of the total variance, ranging from a low of 12% ($R = .343$) to a high of 17% ($R = .414$). Looking at the unique contributions, it can be seen that in each case, city differences have a statistically significant unique contribution and that these contributions overshadow those of background factors. In other words, there is more variation from city to city than there is among case workers according to their race, religion, sex, age, and educational attainment. The joint or overlap unique contributions are all small and statistically not significant: Background and city differences operate independently.[5]

The unique contributions of background factors taken as a cluster are only significant in connection with the statement—"It is harder to get resources for black clients. In all the other statements the unique contributions of this cluster do not reach statistical significance. If we examine individual background factors, race turns out to be significant in three of the five statements (the same ones in which racial differences turned out to be significant in Table 11.6), and sex contributes significantly to the statement that sources are harder to get for blacks.[6]

For all of the three statements in which race has an important unique effect, black social workers are more likely to be critical of clients than are their white counterparts. This finding is open to a variety of interpretations: We suggested earlier that white case workers may be constrained by their liberal ideologies. It is also the case that black social workers are more attached to their jobs and less critical of their agencies, hence perhaps for those reasons more critical of clients. It may also be the case that black social workers, many of whom are socially mobile, look on their brothers in the ghetto with some embarrassment and, express this embarrassment through criticism.

The Professional Values of Case Workers. The welfare workers we studied show a remarkable amount of agreement on how they should carry out their professional roles, as Table 11.8 indicates. To begin with, case workers endorse both a detached, objective view and also an involved sympathetic view in dealing with their clients; 62% prefer to mix both sympathy and detachment in about equal proportions.

---

[5] Of course, this is not so much a finding as a reflection of sampling design, since equal numbers of blacks and whites were set within each city sampling quotas. To the extent that other background factors (e.g., age and sex) are related to race the city samples tend to be identical with respect to such race related background factors.
[6] Women social workers are more likely to endorse this statement.

Table 11.8

Selected Measures of Case Workers'
Professional Values
(N = 307)

A. Objective Versus Sympathetic Approaches:

"... is it better to remain detached from clients in order to remain
objective, or is it better to try to put yourself in your client's
shoes in order to become sympathetic with his situation?

Largely objective	30%
About Equal	62
Largely subjective	8

B. Training Versus Financial Aid:

"Is the essence of social work to teach the poor the best way to
live or is the essence to help give the poor the means to live
as they choose?

Mostly teach	13%
Equally teach and gives means	64
Mostly give means to live	23

C. Motivation as Contingency for Financial Aid:

"Should aid to people living below the poverty level be made contingent on their showing a real desire to improve themselves or
should aid be given to all that need it?"

Aid only to those who show some effort	3%
Aid only to those who show some motivation	9
Aid to most except flagrant loafers	26
Aid to all	61
Do not know and no answer	1

D. Red Tape Versus Flexibility:

"Are rules and regulations present that you .. feel you must follow
in all cases.. or do you feel it is best to ignore rules and regulations when it seems warranted by circumstances?"

Usually follow rules	47%
Generally make dicisions on circumstances	52
Do not know and no answer	1

Similarly the case workers reject both the idea that they mainly are to teach the poor how to live properly and that they should be mainly concerned with providing financial aid; a majority (74%) prefer to mix these two modes somewhat equally.

Furthermore, most of the case workers do not believe that aid should be made contingent on clients' showing some motivation or effort to help themselves; a majority (61%) believe that aid should be given to all who need it.

A break in the consensus among case workers comes with the question of adhering to department rules and regulations; 47% believe that the rules and regulations should be followed in all cases and 52% that it is better to ignore red tape when circumstances apparently warrant doing so.

In short, the majority of the case workers subscribe to an ideology which states that case workers should neither be coolly detached nor warmly engaged, that aid and instruction are equally important, and that aid should be made contingent on need.

Given the degree of consensus, it is not at all surprising that these beliefs are not systematically and strongly related to either city differences or to background factors, as Table 11.9 shows. The multiple regression analyses shown there indicates a smaller amount of the variance accounted for by city differences and background factors together. Indeed, the analysis of the first item (detachment versus sympathy in dealing with clients) does not reach statistical significance. Furthermore, only two of the four unique variances accounted for by city differences reach statistical significance, indicating important city or welfare agency differences in the extent to which "aid to all" and "flexibility" in the application of department rules are adhered to as philosophies of case work.

In only one of the items (flexibility), do background factors contribute a significant amount of unique variance. In this connection it is age that is the significant background factor. Younger case workers are more apt to be flexible than are their older coworkers.

A Summary of Big City Case Workers. Welfare workers are young, inclined to use their jobs as way stations either to marriage or to some other career. They are also liberal and are not hostile to their clients or blame them for their situation. Rather the problems of welfare departments seem to them to be located more in the agency itself than in the clients whom they serve. Case workers also adopt a professional philosophy which is neither patronizing nor profligate.

Table 11.9

Contributions of City Differences, Background
Factors to Case Workers' Professional
Values

(N = 307)

| | | Unique Variance Attributable to: | | TOTAL |
Professional Value	City Diff-erences	Background Factors	Jointly	Variance Explained
Detachment versus sympathy	.051	.001	.020	.061
Teaching versus Financial Aid	.0584	.025	.019	.102*
Contingent Aid versus Aid based on Need	.128*	.014	.023	.165*
Rules versus Flexibility	.082*	.047*	.004	.134*

* Significant at .05 level.

Black social workers are more inclined to be career welfare workers and to be less critical of their agencies but more critical of their clients.

Finally, it is clear that there are less differences among social workers than there are among welfare departments. In almost every case, city differences overshadow differences among social workers related to their age, sex, race, educational attainment, or religion.

Popular Reactions to Welfare. In each of the previous chapters, it was possible to relate the activities of a particular institutional area to measures of popular reactions to that area. Unfortunately, we are not able to present a completely parallel analysis with respect to public welfare. The SRC questionnaire did ask respondents to react to the welfare system, but the question was only asked of welfare recipients, only a small proportion within each city. The popular reactions dealt with then are those of persons who were currently receiving some part of their income from welfare payments.[7]

The question asked of persons who acknowledged receiving welfare payments was as follows:

Are you generally satisfied, somewhat dissatisfied or very dissatisfied with the way you are treated by welfare workers or officials?

On the face of it, the question deals more with the treatment by welfare workers than it does with payments or their adequacy. It may well be for this reason that the correlation between levels of dissatisfaction and average welfare payments received[8] in each city was so low (+.24).

Replies to this question were formed into an index by weighting "very dissatisfied" response -2, "somewhat dissatisfied" response -1, and "generally satisfied" with $+1$.

The distribution of average scores given in each city is shown in Figure 11.2 as are levels of approval given by each city's black respondents

---

[7] Unfortunately we do not know in what programs respondents were enrolled when they did acknowledge welfare payments. Nor can we have very much confidence that welfare income was very accurately measured: In some cities the proportions who did not answer this question was as large or larger than the proportions who acknowledged receipt of "Welfare payments."

[8] As reported in *Welfare in Review*, 1968.

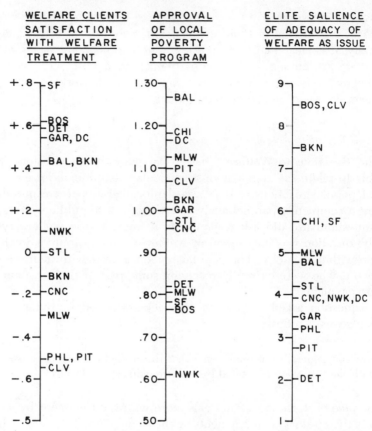

Figure 11.2 City differences in satisfaction with welfare index, approval of poverty program, and elite ratings of salience of the adequacy of welfare payments as issue.

to the local poverty programs[9] and ratings from interviews with elites on the salience of the adequacy of welfare as an issue in each city's political arena. The item asking about approval of the poverty program primarily shows that welfare clients' satisfaction with welfare department treatment is not merely a part of a general level of approval for anti-poverty efforts.

Welfare clients are most satisfied with treatment in San Francisco and

---

[9] Averaging responses given to the following question:

In general, do you think the anti-poverty program is doing a good job, a fair job, or a poor job?

Responses were given weights of +2, +1, and −1, and averaged over the respondents in each city.

least satisfied in Cleveland, with the average city having welfare clients who are slightly on the satisfied side.

There are considerably higher levels of approval for the poverty program, but the cities show a considerably different distribution. Baltimore's blacks give the poverty program[10] the highest level of approval, while Newark's blacks are just barely on the positive side. The correlation between welfare clients' satisfaction levels and levels of approval of the poverty program is essentially zero (actually −.03), which indicates that the two indices are unrelated on the level of cities.

The adequacy of welfare as a salient issue shows a much closer relationship to the index of welfare client satisfaction. Cities in which clients are dissatisfied tend also to be cities in which welfare is an issue. The correlation between the two is +.43, not high enough to reach statistical significance, but, given the small number of cases on which the welfare client index numbers are based, the correlation is probably an underestimate of the true relationship.

In the left-hand column of Table 11.10, some of the more interesting and significant correlates of city levels of welfare client satisfaction are shown. Several surprises appear. First, the case load of the welfare workers has the highest relationship to welfare client satisfaction, but in an unexpected direction; the smaller the case load in a city, the *more dissatisfied* the clients. It should be noted that this relationship is the strongest (.66) in the entire table. Apparently, the more cases a welfare worker has, the less time he or she can spend with clients, and the happier are clients with the treatment they receive at the hands of the welfare departments.

Two additional correlations reach statistical significance at the .05 level —the agency's reputation for competence, a rating derived from elite interviews, and the proportion of the black sample who are receiving welfare payments. The more competent the agency, the more satisfied are its clients. And the higher the proportion of blacks in the SRC samples who are receiving welfare payments, the higher the level of dissatisfaction with treatment at the hands of welfare officials.

A composite measure of case worker complaints about welfare agencies almost reaches statistical significance (.45), hence deserves some attention. The more complaints registered by the case workers, the higher the

---

[10] The items employed in the SCR interviews did not specifically ask about the *local* poverty program, although the intercity variation leads one to suspect that respondents had mainly local programs in mind.

[11] Formed by averaging the responses to each of the seven items shown in Table 11.3 within each city's contingent of welfare workers.

Table 11.10

Selected Correlates of Welfare Clients'
Satisfaction with Treatment
By Welfare Department, Approval
of Poverty Program, and Salience of
Welfare as a Local Issue
(N = 15 cities)

Variables	Correlation with Index of Welfare Client Satisfaction	Index of Approval of Poverty Program	Salience of Welfare Adequacy as Issue
A. Case Worker Measures:			
Case load less than 200 persons	-66	-.04	+.17
More than two weeks to get new clients on rolls	-.39	-.43	+.44
Index of Complaints About Agency*	+.45	+.06	+.05
Index of Complaints about Clients*	-.17	+.10	-.07

TABLE 11.10 (Cont'd)

Variables	Correlation with Index of Welfare Client Satisfaction	Index of Approval of Welfare Poverty Program	Salience of Welfare Adequacy as Issue
B. Welfare Officials (Elite Interviews)			
Sympathy and Responsiveness of Welfare Officials	+.37	+.55	+.15
Agency Reputation for Competence	+.53	+.08	-.01
C. Demographic Measures:			
Proportion Black in Population	+.03	+.29	+.27
Proportion Black on Welfare (SRC Data)	-.58	-.11	-.36
D. Welfare Payments:			
Statutory monthly payments per case	-.03	-.10	-.23

* Indices formed by summing proportions making strongest complaints within each city across the items in Tables 11.3 and 11.6.

level of satisfaction registered by welfare clients. This finding is consistent with the one described earlier in which clients are most satisfied when they see little of the case workers: This finding indicates that they are most satisfied when case workers are critical of their welfare agencies.

Complaints about clients show little relationship to client satisfaction, although the sign of the correlation indicates that there is a slight tendency for clients to be more satisfied with agencies whose workers do not register many complaints about clients.

The middle column of Table 11.10 shows the correlations of the same variables with the approval of poverty programs. The pattern of correlations is somewhat different in this case. For example, the highest relationship is shown between poverty program approval and the elite interview derived ratings of the sympathy and responsiveness of welfare officials to the black civil rights movement. Another high (although not statistically significant) relationship is between poverty program approval and the length of time it takes to get a new family on the welfare rolls. The remaining correlations in the middle column are small and hardly significant. In short, approval of the poverty program seems to be more a response to political climate.

The right-hand column of Table 11.10 relates to elite interview derived ratings of the salience of welfare. Correlations in this column are small, with none reaching statistical significance. The most that can be said is that the longer it takes on the average to get a client on the welfare rolls, the more welfare will be an issue.

Using the variables shown in Table 11.10 as independent variables a step-wise, multiple regression was run with levels of welfare client satisfaction as the dependent variable. Three of the variables accounted for 83% of the variance in city levels of welfare client satisfaction, with regression coefficients as shown in Table 11.11. Each of the variables, as it was entered, explained significant proportions of the variance. In short, welfare clients in a city express high levels of satisfaction with their treatment at the hands of welfare workers and officials when case loads are heavy, when there are few blacks on welfare, and when the welfare department has a high reputation of competence among elites.

Two of the variables—case load and welfare department reputation—are quite understandable. It is more difficult to interpret the strong and independent effect of the proportion of blacks who are receiving welfare payments, especially since this variable operates independently both of the proportion of blacks in the city and of such measures as the unemployment rate of the city. Perhaps the higher the proportion of blacks on welfare, the more likely clients are to know one another, and to share

TABLE 11.11

Step-wise Multiple Regression on Index of Welfare Clients
City Levels of Satisfaction with Treatment of Welfare Department
(N = 15 cities)

Variable	Unstandardized Regression Coefficient	T-Value	Additional Variance Explained
Case Load	- .7533	-1.83	.44*
Welfare Department Reputation of Competence	1.916	4.69	.23*
% Blacks on Welfare (SRC Data)	-4.546	-3.19	.16*
	Total Variance Explained =		.83*
	R = .91*		

*Significant at .01 level.

and thereby magnify their grievances. Under this interpretation, company brings misery.

Quite a different pattern of relationships is found when we consider the determinants of approval of the poverty program, as in Table 11.12. Approval of the poverty program can be explained to a considerable lesser degree (only 42% of the city differences variance could be accounted for). The two variables which emerged from the step-wise regression analysis were ratings from elite interviews of the reputation of welfare officials as being sympathetic and responsive to black civil rights movement and the proportion black employed as skilled workers in the work forces of major employers. The poverty program achieves approval where welfare officials are seen as sympathetic and where blacks constitute relatively large proportions of the skilled work force in major local firms,[12] a sensitive indicator of employment discrimination.

It was not possible to account for statistically significant amounts of the city differences variance in the salience of welfare as an issue. As one may note from the correlation in Table 11.10, none of the relationships with variables considered (and others which were tried out) reached

---

[12] As measured in interviews with the personnel officers of a sample of each city's largest firms. See Chapter 9 for a fuller explanation of this variable.

TABLE 11.12

Step-wise Multiple Regression on Index of
Poverty Program Approval City Levels
(N = 15 cities)

Independent Variable	Unstandardized Regression Coefficient	T-Value	Additional Variance Explained
Sympathy-Responsiveness of Welfare Officials	.473	1.82	.30*
Proportion Black Among Skilled Workers** employed by Major Employers	1.146	1.61	.12

Total Variance Explained = .42*

R = .537

---

*Statistically significant at .05 level.

**See Chapter 9 for detailed explanation of this variable.

statistical significance. The salience of the welfare issue is somewhat sensitive to how long it takes to *get placed on the welfare roles* ($r = +.44$) which fails to reach statistical significance at the .05 level. Adding additional variables to this highest correlation, as in step-wise procedure, does not add enough additional explained variance for the multiple correlation to reach anywhere near statistical respectability. At this point we can only say that the welfare issue salience is weakly sensitive to some characteristics of welfare service and to certain demographic variables, but this sensitivity is not strong enough to register reliably.

Summary.   In contrast to the other institutional areas studied in previous chapters, the welfare system of a city has a direct impact on a relatively small proportion of the population. In each of the fifteen cities, less than 18% of the black households were receiving welfare payments, and in the typical average city, the proportion was closer to 8%. In contrast, every household has to deal with merchants and employers, and most have some contact with the police. Our slight coverage of this institution makes it difficult to discern reliably its effects on blacks in the ghetto using sampling designs of the kind used in this study. Ideally, one would want to have special samples of households who are presently receiving welfare payments and possibly of those who have ever received such payments.

For this reason, the results presented in this chapter should be viewed as a pilot model rather than as a production run: That is to say, this chapter illustrates themes and modes of analysis, but the specific findings cannot be taken as more than highly suggestive.

This caveat applies particularly to the analysis of welfare client dissatisfaction with treatment at the hands of the welfare department. It is less applicable to the description of case workers and their activities. The institutional agent groups are more liberal in contrast to any of the occupations studied. Welfare workers are young, well educated, and hardly devoted to their occupations and to the agency that employs them. Their jobs, while bringing them into intimate contact with ghetto problems, provides them scarce opportunities for traditional social work, a mixed blessing since so few have had special training to play that role. Case work in our cities, as other investigators have shown, is essentially paper shuffling and administering of the means test. Thus welfare clients are most happy when case workers can spend little time with them.

Some of the troubles that plague our current welfare system are illustrated in the findings of this chapter. The system is administered at the delivery level by persons who are given little time and who have inadequate preparation for the tasks involved. The welfare system operates on principles that are demeaning to recipients, as reflected in the apparent satisfaction of clients when they have little to do with case workers.

Chapter 12

SOURCES IN TRUST
IN THE LOCAL COMMUNITY

The data and analysis presented so far have been concerned with the ways in which specific sectors of each urban place were affected by the nature of its local political regime, and how such sectors, in turn, affected levels of satisfaction within their black ghettoes. We now consider how these sectors are related to one another, and, perhaps more important, how those levels relating to specific sectors affect overall levels of contentment or dissatisfaction in the urban areas involved.

A community is a somewhat amorphous social phenomenon. It can serve as the context in which specific activities take place, hence constitute mainly a background of physical structures and institutions with a foreground occupied with more immediately salient activities, such as raising a family, earning a living, obtaining recreation, and meeting people. This view of a community is one in which the overall organization of a city is less salient than are specific institutions that aid or hinder the pursuit of specific objectives by households and individuals. Thus a resident is not likely to be either satisfied or dissatisfied with New York City, for example, but rather satisfied or dissatisfied with his particular job, his family life, and so on. This model of community satisfaction is one which would lead us to expect that all cities will look very much alike when we consider measures of overall satisfaction with living in the specific localities in question.

An alternative model is one in which the complaints and satisfactions with specific areas of life are generalized to an overall level of satisfaction with the community as a whole. Thus an individual who is finding it hard to get employment may see the police as harassing him and his neighbors and will develop a negative assessment of the city in which he is living, while a person enjoying the opposite set of conditions will be more satisfied with his community.

Another way of posing the questions raised by the apparent contrast between these two models is to ask whether the findings of the previous chapters in this monograph imply anything about the way in which individuals feel about their cities. Of course, one of the major problems is in defining a city, social psychologically. We could ask for some global assessment and leave it to the individual to define a "city." Or we could isolate some aspect of cities generally seen as a symbol of representing the city. In this chapter we have used both modes. The first section of the chapter is concerned with the effect of residents' satisfactions with their life upon their assessment of the major. Later sections are concerned with an assessment of the accessibility of city officials and with a more generalized assessment of political efficacy.

We have chosen to focus on the mayor and city government because these are central institutions in any community.[1] Symbolically, the mayor's office both represents the city—it is the mayor who greets important visitors—and, as the local chief executive, the mayor often sets the tone of local municipal administrations, as we have seen in some of the previous chapters. The accessibility and responsiveness of city government provides a measure of the extent to which individuals feel that the official organs of city government are attentive to and responsive to their needs.

Figures 12.1 and 12.2 show the reactions of respondents in each city according to race to the three basic questions with which this chapter deals. The two lines on the left half of Figure 12.1 refer to the answers given by black and white respondents to the SRC's questionnaire item worded as follows:

---

[1] Ideally, we would have liked to have had some global measures as well but there were none avaialble to us in the SRC questionnaires administered to samples of white and black residents in each of the fifteen cities. To some extent the analysis presented in this chapter is a fragment of a larger analysis of the relationship between citizens and their communities. But this larger and more complete investigation will have to be postponed to some future day, when research will be specifically designed to cast some empirical light on this topic.

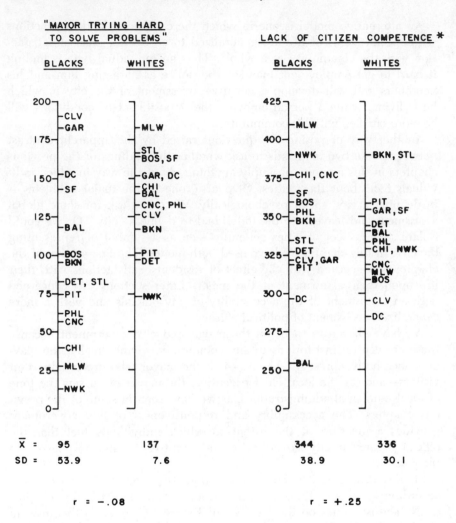

"MAYOR TRYING HARD
TO SOLVE PROBLEMS"

LACK OF CITIZEN COMPETENCE *

	BLACKS	WHITES		BLACKS	WHITES
X̄ =	95	137		344	336
SD =	53.9	7.6		38.9	30.1

r = −.08   r = +.25

*NOTE: A **High** score indicates **low** levels of competence.

Figure 12.1   City means for blacks and whites on views of mayor and citizen competence indexes.

Do you think the mayor of (CITY) is trying as hard as he can to solve the major problems of the city or that he is not doing all he could to solve these problems?

Responses were recorded as "Trying as hard as he can; Trying fairly hard; Not trying hard at all." The index numbers shown in Figure 12.1 were computed by weighting each of the responses, respectively +200,

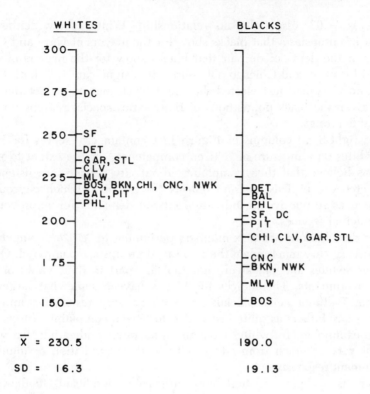

Figure 12.2 Average personal efficacy scores by city for whites and blacks. High score is high personal efficacy.

+100, and −100, and summing up the respondents in each city. An index number of 200 indicates that all respondents in a city thought that the mayor was "trying as hard as he can" while an index number of 100 indicates that the average respondent thought that the mayor was only "trying fairly hard." Of course, the latter score also indicates that a rather large proportion thought that the mayor was trying "not hard at all."

Note that by and large white respondents thought that the mayors were trying harder than did black respondents, the average city index being 137 for the former and 95 for the latter. Even more striking, however, are the differences in the distributions for whites and blacks. First, black populations vary more in their appraisals of their mayors, the standard deviation for the average ratings being 53.9 as compared with 7.6 for whites. Second, it looks as if white and black residents were referring to entirely different officials: The correlation between white and black scores is $-.08$, essentially no relationship. Whites show neither the height of enthusiasm that blacks show for the mayors of Gary and Cleveland, nor the depth of despair that blacks show for the mayors of Newark, Milwaukee, and Chicago. Of course, it is significant that both Cleveland and Gary had just elected their first black mayors, a fact that may have given the black populations of those cities special reasons for their favorable ratings.

The right-hand columns of Figure 12.1 contain city scores for blacks and whites on a measure of "citizen competence," or the extent to which citizens believe that their complaints about city services are listened to and acted upon.[2] This measure reflects the extent to which city officials are seen as responsive to individual citizen demands for improvements in municipal services.

The distributions of index numbers pertaining to "citizen competence" do not vary very much when the two racial groups are compared. On the average, whites and blacks are not too far apart in their views of their city governments. The indices for blacks have a somewhat larger dispersion; Baltimore city officials are seen as very responsive and Milwaukee city fathers as quite insensitive to citizen complaints. In contrast, the index numbers for whites have a smaller range, indicating that whites do not vary as much from city to city in their estimation of municipal government responsiveness.

There is a slight, although not statistically significant, tendency for blacks and whites to agree ($r = .25$) on the responsiveness of their cities. Visual inspection of the two distributions indicates that the low relationship may be mostly a function of the fact that for blacks several cities stand out as either very responsive (Baltimore and Washington, D.C.) or very unresponsive (Milwaukee and Newark), while for white populations most of the cities are clustered close together, with only Brooklyn and St. Louis receiving low grades on responsiveness.

Figure 12.2 contains the city means by race for a variable which is ordinarily thought of as more a measure of a personality characteristic than a political variable. The Index of Personal Efficacy is built up out of a

---

[2] The items used in the Index of Citizen Competence are as follows:

If you have a serious complaint about poor service by the city, do you think you can get city officials to do something about it if you call them?

Have you ever called a city official with a complaint about poor service?

The index is a simple count of positive answers to the two questions. The index numbers shown in Figure 12.1 are averages computed such that a high score indicates a *lack* of feelings of competence.

series of items which, in effect, ask respondents how much control they feel they can exercise over their fate.[3] Whether the index is a good measure of very general tendencies is difficult to judge without more intimate knowledge of how the index behaves statistically at the level of individual respondents. The evidence shown in Figure 12.2, however, does cast some doubt upon such a view of the index by virtue of the fact that within each racial group city means do vary considerably.[4]

Perhaps the most outstanding feature of the distributions shown in Figure 12.2 is the lack of overlap between the two racial groups. Blacks have a much lower level of "personal efficacy" in most every city, as expressed in the rather large differences between the grand means shown at the bottom of figure 12.2: The grand mean for whites is 230.5 as compared to 190.0 for blacks.

These racial differences are quite understandable in the light of well known differences between the life situations of blacks and of whites. It is objectively "more difficult to plan ahead" for blacks than it is for whites, especially when employment patterns of low skilled workers are more erratic, income more variable, the incidence of illness greater, and so on. In each city, the lower levels of personal efficacy to be found in the black subcommunity is understandable in terms of these differences in the objective situations faced by blacks and whites.

What is difficult to explain are the differences among cities in the mean scores for both blacks and whites. Furthermore, the city mean

---

[3] The items in question are:

Have you usually felt pretty sure that your life would work out the way you want it to, or have there been times when you haven't been sure about it?

Do you think it is better to plan your life a good way ahead or would you say life is too much a matter of luck to plan ahead very far?

When you do plan ahead, do you usually carry out things the way you expected, or do things usually come up to make you change your plans?

Some people feel they can run their lives pretty much the way they want to: Others feel the problems of life are sometimes too big for them. Which one are you like?

The index sums for each individual respondent the number of "efficacious" responses. The city values shown in Figure 12.2 are averages computed separately for each racial group.

[4] Of course, the intercity variation in means may be a function of the differentials among cities in the compositions of their white and black population components. Thus the intercity variation may be reflecting, for example, differences in the levels of educational attainment or some other factor that directly affects the measures of personal efficacy on an individual level. Analyses of variance testing this interpretation were run with results indicating that inter-city differences were statistically significant when background characteristics of respondents were taken into account.

scores for blacks are slightly ($r = .25$) related to those for whites, indicating that there are possibly local conditions which affect blacks and whites alike.

The correlations among city means for the three variables are shown separately for black and white citizens in Table 12.1. These correlations express the extent to which the city means of the three measures vary together within each racial group and between the two racial groups. The two sets of coefficients marked off within the triangles are those among the three measures within whites (the upper left-hand triangle) and those among blacks (lower right-hand triangle). The remaining coefficients are among measures for whites as compared with those for blacks.

Several salient findings are displayed in Table 12.1. First, black city means tend to be more highly interrelated than do the same measures for whites. The correlations in the lower right-hand triangle are considerably larger than those in the upper left-hand triangle. Particularly highly related are ratings of the mayor for "trying hard" and citizen competence

TABLE 12.1

Correlations Among City Means of Citizen
Trust and Confidence

(N = 15 cities)

		WHITE RESPONDENTS			BLACK RESPONDENTS		
		Mayor Trying Hard (1)	Citizen Compet-ence* (2)	Personal Efficacy (3)	Mayor Trying Hard (4)	Citizen Compete-nce* (5)	Personal Efficacy (6)
W H I T E S	Mayor (1)		+.10	−.29	.25	−.10	−.19
	Citizen Compet.* (2)			+.20	+.09	−.08	−.14
	Pers. Eff. (3)				.48	+.20	.25
B L A C K S	Mayor (4)					+.62	.32
	Citizen Compet.* (5)						+.68
	Pers. Eff. (2)						

*Note: "Citizen Competence" has been defined in this table and
subsequent tables such that high scores indicate high
levels of citizen competence.

(.62), indicating that in cities where the mayor is viewed as a "good guy" by black residents, such residents also show high levels of citizen competence. A slightly higher relationship (.68) is shown between the city means in personal efficacy and citizen competence. City ratings of the mayor and personal efficacy levels are not as high (.32).

The correlations for whites show a considerable contrast. None of the correlation coefficients in the upper left-hand triangle reach statistical significance, indicating that the city levels on each of the three measures are essentially independent of each other. Black residents and white residents tend to show city levels which are quite independent of each other, as the correlations in the upper right-hand corner of Table 12.1 indicate.

The results so far indicate that although these three variables are sensitive to locality, the measures for blacks appear to be especially so. Black city means tend to vary more from city to city and the city means tend to co-vary with each other. Cities in which the blacks think highly of the efforts made by their mayors are also cities in which blacks have high levels of competence and personal efficacy. In short it does look as if the specific political regime makes a difference for blacks, but not as much (or not at all) for whites.

Urban Mayors and Their Constituencies. The political regime of an urban place consists of the set of policy makers who determine the course of local political policy and who administer local municipal institutions. For a large urban political subdivision, the full set may contain a relatively large number of specific positions and incumbents, including the mayor, city council, school board, appointed officials heading up various departments, and perhaps public corporations (e.g., The Port of New York Authority) if such exist. Among these policy makers, the mayor turns out to be of paramount importance both in the policy making sense and in a symbolic sense. The mayor's office has considerable appointive power, as well as, in many cases, the power to introduce or to veto local legislation. More important, symbolically, is the prominence given to the Mayor's office by the mass media. The mayors of our largest cities often become national figures (e.g., John Lindsay of New York and Richard Daley of Chicago) to whom attention is given in an area which extends far beyond the boundaries of their cities. The mayor is seen as the person who can speak in the name of the city on important ceremonial occasions and on behalf of the city in conducting business with state and federal authorities.

The importance of the mayor's office is sufficient to justify paying special attention to the way in which his constituencies view him. Constitu-

ency views of the mayor have importance to the continuance of a particular political regime: A replacement of a mayor may mean a considerable
shakeup in the higher levels of the appointed municipal officials. These
views also represent the presence or absence of confidence in the local
regime.

The main question we want to raise concerns what the determinants of
confidence in the mayor and implicitly in his regime are. The indicators
we employ are the city averages of answers to the item on the SRC's
questionnaire which asks whether individual respondents thought the
mayor was trying hard or not. Although one would ideally like to have
an index which would be composed of a variety of measures, unfortunately we have to be content with just one measure.[5]

We are especially interested in the ways in which the actions of institutional agents affect attachment to the local political regime. Hence we
are concerned with the impact of police practices, educational policies,
and the like, on constituency views of their mayors. Table 12.2 presents a
selected set of such measures and their relationships (separately for
black and white constituencies) to the average levels of approval of the
mayors' efforts. Some of the indices presented in Table 12.2 have not
appeared in any previous chapters, since they pertain to areas of urban
life for which we have no corresponding data from either elite interviews or from our surveys of institutional agents (e.g., The Index of
Perceived Housing Discrimination).

For blacks in the fifteen cities, their average ratings of their mayors as
"trying hard" are most closely related to ratings obtained from elite
interviews on how sympathetic the mayor is toward the black civil rights
movement. And the more sympathetic the mayor is the more likely he is
to receive a high rating as trying hard. Indeed, the relationship is so
high (.83) that there is scarcely any point to examining the other relationships in the table, since it is unlikely that the other relationships, no
matter how high in their own right, can contribute anything more to our
understanding of the ratings achieved by the mayors.

The remaining correlations in the left-hand column are all much
smaller than are the eilte ratings of mayor's sympathy. Indeed only two
of the correlations, "belief in the existence of police abuse" and "police

---

[5] For example, one may have obtained ratings of other decision-making positions or
bodies, (e.g., the city council and school board), or considered other aspects of role
performance besides "trying hard," (e.g. achieving results and paying attention to
the needs of citizens). Of course, it is not at all clear that a multiitem index of support for the local political regime would be appreciably different in results from the
one item already used.

TABLE 12.2

City Level Correlates of "Mayor Trying Hard:
Blacks and Whites (N = 15 cities)

	Correlation with "Mayor Trying Hard" Ratings Among --	
Variables	Black Citizens	White Citizens

A. Population Survey Data:

Neighborhood Services Dissatisfaction* Index	-.26	-.39
Belief in Existence of Police Abuse	-.53	.34
Dissatisfaction with Neighborhood Stores	.00	.30
Belief in Housing Discrimination Against Blacks	-.28	Not applicable
Personal Experiences with Job Discrimination	-.35	Not applicable

B. Data from Institutional Agents

Proportion Black Reported in Skilled Work forces of Employers	.14	-.05
Police Reports of Potentially** Abrasive Police Practices	-.58	.18
Educators' Reports of Job Satisfaction**	.19	Not applicable

C. Elite Survey Ratings:

Composite Ratings of Mayor's Sympathy for Civil Rights Movement	.83	-.10
Composite Ratings of Business Community's Sympathy for Civil Rights Movement	.46	-.04

---

*Neighborhood dissatisfaction index is composed of answers to five items asking respondents how satisfied they were with "neighborhood public schools", "neighborhood parks and playgrounds", "neighborhood facilities for teenagers", "sports and recreaction", "neighborhood police protection", and "neighborhood garbage collection".

Belief in Housing Discrimination against Blacks is composed of answers to two items: "Do you think there are many, some or just a few places in (CITY) where you (your family) could not rent or buy a house because of racial discrimination?"; and, "On the whole, do you think many, some or just a few Negroes in (CITY) miss out on good housing because of race?"

The other indices in this table are defined in earlier chapters that pertain directly to the area being studied.

**These may show low correlations with white ratings in part because they measure activities in black neighborhoods.

reports of potentially abrasive police practices," reach statistical significance. In short, it is the reputation of the mayor which plays the major role in the level of acceptance achieved by mayors among blacks.

The importantance of the reputation of the mayor can be seen by the fact that if we add just one more variable to the reputation of the mayor, namely his race, we can increase the correlation significantly. The multiple correlation between the average level of rating of the mayor "trying hard" and the elite ratings and a dummy variable expressing the race of the mayor is .92. A mayor gets a high rating among blacks if he has a strong reputation of being sympathetic to black demands and an additional rating if he is black.[6]

The correlations in the second column of Table 12.2 pertaining to whites shows quite a different pattern. With one exception the relationships are all lower and sometimes reversed in sign. Thus the composite rating of the mayor sympathy with black civil rights movement correlates −.10 for whites, as compared with .83 for blacks. Even though blacks and whites agree[7] on whether the police force engages in abusive practices, the correlation of this index with the rating of the mayor is .34 for whites and −.53 for blacks. In short, whites are more likely to rate a mayor as trying hard in cities where there is widespread belief (among whites) that the police engage in abusive practices—a pattern that is exactly opposite for blacks.

Indeed, the measures most related to the feeling of whites that the the mayor is trying hard are those which measure the levels of satisfaction in each city with city services, police practices, and neighborhood stores.[8] None of the correlations are very high, however, and may therefore not be appreciably different from zero. In short whether a mayor is seen as trying hard by whites is left a mystery.

A mayor's standing among his black constituents is largely a matter of his reputation as sympathetic or antipathetic to the needs of blacks. In part, this reputation can be enhanced if he himself is black, as our data indicate. In part, the reputation rests on his performance, particularly in areas of city life that have a direct and immediate impact on life in the

---

[6] The resulting regression equation is as follows:

$$Y = -2.5 + .13X_1 + 18.7X_2$$

where Y = the mean score of a city on "mayor trying hard"

      X_1 = the elite rating of the mayor's sympathy for the civil rights movement

      X_2 = a dummy variable which takes the value 1 when the mayor is black

[7] See Chapter 6 for more detail on this relationship.

[8] The multiple correlation of these three ratings on the rating of mayor trying hard for whites is .56, a value which is considerably below statistical significance.

ghetto, as, for example, in the behavior of local police. In part, his reputation is built upon his relationships to black leaders, as the ratings from
our elite interviews indicate.

Of course the critical question is whether performance and "image"
are separable. Is it possible for a mayor to do nothing concrete for his
black constituents except keep his door open for black leaders to come
through? Or, on the contrary, is a reputation built upon performance
accompanied by sympathetic statements and an open-door policy? Our
data cannot answer these questions since the relationships among the
relevant variable are too high to allow for more than a suggestive untan-
gling of the threads of causation. Since the correlation between the
mayor's reputation among elites and his reputation as trying hard among
the mass is so high, we suspect that "image" plays the more important
role.[9]

Levels of Citizen Competence. The Index of Citizen Competence can
measure citizens' relationships to municipal agencies. A high level for a
city indicates that citizens believe that their requests to agencies will
be honored and that their experiences with such requests bear out such
beliefs. Although there is a fairly strong tendency for the Index of Citizen
Competence to vary with opinions on the mayor's "trying hard," especially for black citizens ($r = .62$), the relationship is low enough to be
regarded as a separate issue.

Table 12.3 presents the relationships between a number of city level
variables and the Index of Citizen Competence. Although most of the
same variables are used as in Table 12.2, the pattern of relationships is
quite different: Among black citizens the Index of Citizen Competence
is much more sensitive (the correlations are higher) to city differences
with respect to measures of satisfaction with municipal services, housing
discrimination, job discrimination, and so on. Indeed, as one would
expect, whether black constituents feel that their requests addressed to
municipal agencies would be honored is closely related to their feelings
about how well such agencies deliver services to them. Particularly important in this respect are relationships to the police. Where there are
widespread beliefs that police behave badly toward blacks, there are

---

[9] It should be noted that the three black mayors (Washington, of D.C., Hatcher
of Gary, and Stokes of Cleveland) had been in office only short periods of time at
the time of the surveys (Spring 1968). The higher regard for black mayors necessarily has to be based more on expectation than performance since not enough time
had elapsed for the latter to occur.

TABLE 12.3

City Level Correlates of Citizen Competence Index for Blacks and Whites
(N = 15 cities)

Variables	Correlations with Levels of Citizen Competence Among	
	Black Citizens	White Citizens
A. Population Survey Data:		
Neighborhood Services Dissatisfaction Index	-.34	+.05
Belief in Existence of Police Abuse	-.77	-.29
Dissatisfaction with Neighborhood Stores	-.41	-.24
Belief in Housing Discrimination Against Blacks	-.40	Not Applicable
Personal Experiences with Job Discrimination	-.54	Not Applicable
"Mayor Trying Hard"	+.62	+.10
B. Data from Institutional Agents:		
Proportion Black Reported in Skilled Work Forces of Employers	+.41	+.05
Police Reports of Potentially Abrasive* Police Practices	-.64	-.22
Educators Reports of Job Satisfaction*	+.58	-.21
C. Elite Survey Ratings:		
Composite Ratings of Mayor's Sympathy for Civil Rights Movement	+.74	-.17
Composite Ratings of Business Community's Sympathy for Civil Rights Movement	+.61	+.09

*These may show low correlations with white attitudes in part because they measure activities in black neighborhoods.

low levels of citizen competence ($r = -.77$), and reports from police about their practices are also related in the same way ($r = -.64$) to levels of citizen competence.

Quite a different pattern emerges with respect to the white citizens of the fifteen cities, as shown in the right-hand column of Table 12.3. Here none of the measures are related to levels of white citizen competence highly enough to reach statistical significance. The signs of the correlations are in consonance with those for blacks, especially those dealing with the police. Apparently, the white citizens in the fifteen cities are responding to some other dimensions of city life, unmeasured in this particular survey, or perhaps reflecting individual differences unrelated to their cities in their ratings.

The stronger structure for black constituents can be seen more dramatically in Table 12.4 where a series of multiple correlations are shown. There we find that three indices of ratings of municipal services correlate jointly .90 with levels of citizen competence. In short, if one knows how much confidence black citizens collectively have in their police, in their own ability to get jobs without discrimination and in the honesty of their neighborhood stores, he can predict how much confidence blacks have collectively in the responsiveness of local municipal agencies. That this relationship is not independent of either elites or actual practices can be seen in the other two high multiple correlations in Table 12.4. The proportion of blacks in the skilled labor forces of the companies studied, the level of job satisfaction shown by public school educators, and the police reports of potentially abrasive police practices together correlate .74 with city levels of black citizen competence. An equally

TABLE 12.4

Regression Analyses of City Levels of Citizen Competence
(N = 15 cities)

Variables	Multiple Correlations with Index of Citizen Competence	
	R =	p =
A. For Black Citizens:		
Beliefs in Hiring Discrimination, Belief in Police Abuse, and Dissatisfaction with Neighborhood and Stores	.90	< .01
Proportion Black in Skilled Work Force of Companies, Educator's Job Satisfaction, and Police Report of Abrasive Practices	.74	< .05
Elite Ratings of Mayor's Sympathy and Sympathy of Business Community	.75	< .01
B. For White Citizens:		
Neighborhood Services Dissatisfaction, Belief in Police Abuse, and Dissatisfaction with Neighborhood Stores	.35	> .05

high correlation (.75) can also be seen to hold between elite ratings of the mayor and the business community and citizen competence.

Note that the multiple correlation shown at the bottom of Table 12.4 using three measures of white citizens satisfactions with services fall far short ($R = .35$) of statistical significance.

Within the black constituencies of the fifteen cities, whether blacks show a high or low degree of confidence that their requests for municipal services will be met depends on how good the services are to begin with and how responsive and sympathetic the political and civic elites appear to be to black demands. In cities whose mayors and civic elites have reputations of being sympathetic and where local institutions are believed to provide good services, the ghettos show high levels of confidence that things can be done.

As in the case of the rating of the mayor "trying hard," it is difficult to sort out one correlate from another: We cannot be sure from the evidence presented here whether the reputation of the mayor counts more than the actions of the municipal agencies. All we can be sure of is that the black ghettoes respond to both.

Personal Efficacy. The Index of Personal Efficacy is some degrees removed from the political sphere of life. The items that go into this index call for rather general ratings from individuals concerning the predictability of their environment and the likelihood that their goals will be realized. An "efficacious" individual is one who can count on the world around him and who expects that his efforts to get somewhere will pay off. The area of life involved, however, is not specified. It may be the job market, the housing market, or intimate interpersonal transactions.

For these reasons we might expect that the differences among cities in respect to the level of "personal efficacy" to be slighter than in the case of the previous two variables discussed in detail in this chapter, and that, furthermore, data on the cities will not show strong correlations with city levels of personal efficacy. These expectations are only partially fulfilled: As we noted earlier, for both blacks and whites, there is less variation from city to city in levels of personal efficacy (Figure 12.2 as compared to Figure 12.1). In the second respect, however, black levels of personal efficacy appear to be related to certain types of city characteristics, as Table 12.5 shows.

For black constituencies, the more satisfied blacks are with neighborhood services ($-.51$), with neighborhood stores ($-.66$), and with housing and hiring ($-.42$, $-.44$), the higher the levels of personal

TABLE 12.5

City Level Correlates of "Personal Efficacy"
for Black and White Citizens
(N = 15 cities)

Variables	Correlations with Levels of "Personal Efficacy" Among	
	Black Citizens	White Citizens
A. Population Survey Data:		
Neighborhood Services Dissatisfaction Index	-.51	-.31
Belief in Existence of Police Abuse	-.40	0.00
Dissatisfaction with Neighborhood Stores	-.66	-.29
Belief in Housing Discrimination Against Blacks	-.42	Not Applicable
Personal Experiences with Job Discrimination	-.44	Not Applicable
Mayor Trying Hard	+.32	.30
Citizen Competence Index	+.68	- 20
B. Data from Institutional Agents:		
Proportion Black Reported in Skilled Work Forces of Employers	.41	.30
Police Reports of Potentially Abrasive Police Practices	-.30	-.24
Educators Reports of Job Satisfaction	.55	Not Applicable
C. Elite Survey Ratings:		
Composite Ratings of Mayor's Sympathy for Civil Rights Movement	.40	.32
Composite Ratings of Business Community's Sympathy for Civil Rights Movement	.67	.18

efficacy. Similarly strong relationships are shown with the other variables in the table, indicating that levels of personal efficacy vary with actual hiring conditions, police reports of abrasive police, and elite interview derived ratings of the mayor's and civic elite's sympathy for black civil rights.

Table 12.6 contains the results of multiple regression analyses of some

TABLE 12.6

Regression Analyses of City Levels of Personal
Efficacy Among Black Citizens

(N = 15 cities)

Variables	Multiple Correlations with Index of Personal Efficacy	
	R =	p =
Dissatisfaction with Neighborhood Stores, Belief in Housing Discrimination and Belief in Hiring Discrimination	.87	< .01
Elite Ratings of Mayor's Sympathy and Business Community Sympathy for Black Civil Rights Movement	.69	< .05
Proportion Black in Skilled Work Forces of Companies Sampled, Police Reports of Abrasive Police Practices and Jobs Satisfaction of Educators	.64	> .05

of the city-level determinants of personal efficacy in the ghettoes of the fifteen cities. Widespread levels of belief in housing, hiring, and merchandising discrimination correlate jointly quite highly (.87) with city levels of personal efficacy. The two elite interview ratings (sympathy of the mayor and of the business community) are less highly related (.69) and objective measures from interviews with institutional agents (proportion of blacks in work forces of major firms, police reports of abrasive practices, and job satisfaction levels of educators) correlate even less highly (.64), the latter not reaching statistical significance.

Returning to Table 12.5, we find that none of these measures correlate to any appreciable extent with personal efficacy levels of the white citizens in the fifteen cities. Obviously, white personal efficacy levels are unrelated to at least these measures of city differences.

In the analysis of this section, there is some suggestion that levels of personal efficacy are tied closely with the direct experiences of blacks in neighborhood stores and in the housing and labor markets. This has important implications, not only for the issues raised in this monograph, but also for a variety of psychological characterizations of the poor. Weaving through the literature on the "culture of poverty" is the notion that people at the bottom of the society (including criminals and juvenile delinquents) suffer from a fundamental inability to postpone gratification. The cause of this malady is rarely specified in detail and in many analyses its genesis is not even considered problematic. Whatever the cause, the inability to postpone immediate rewards is considered given and is presented as a stable psychological weakness that not only lasts the lifetime of an individual, but also is transmitted from generation to generation. Our data are not consistent with such a view and indeed may contradict it. If a sense of personal control of one's environment, a psychological attribute highly correlated with so-called hedonism, is sensitive to differences in the delivery of city services, questions are raised about this "culture of poverty" theory. Rather than being a victim of a devilitating culture, the poor may be victims of very real societal inequities. It is these inequities, not culture, that generate feelings of helplessness and apathy. And helpless people are not about to plan for a future over which they have no control and which provides few promises for long run satisfactions.

Conclusions. The data presented in this chapter provide ample documentation for the generalization that the black constituencies in our major urban central cities are sensitive in a general way to the institutional areas studied in previous chapters. Black citizens' levels of confidence in the mayor differ by city as do blacks' confidence in their own abilities to "get things done" and finally in their sense of being able to plan ahead in the world. Even more important than these differences is the fact that the political apparatus of the city, including its elected officials and low level functionaries, can affect these levels through their actions vis a vis black citizens.

Of course, it is not entirely clear what precise mechanisms link together the reputation of the mayor among elites with the sense of citizen competence displayed by the average black citizen, for example. The links are apparently manifold: In part, the local mass media pay considerable attention to the doings and sayings of mayors and of other local notables. In part, because the level of services received by blacks is considerably lower than whites (and perhaps their needs for such services are higher), blacks are apparently more sensitive than are whites to variations from place to place in those services.[10] Finally, a lot apparently depends on how blacks evaluate the quality of those services, especially those which impinge directly upon them in an evaluative way. Thus discrimination in employment, housing, and police treatment are especially important.

The sensitivity of black levels of confidence in local government and of personal efficacy to differences among the fifteen cities show that at

---

[10] In addition, it may also be the case that services actually delivered to blacks are more variable from city to city than are comparable services delivered to whites.

this juncture in history the local political community is much more important to blacks than to whites. It may be symbolically important to blacks to have one of their race as mayor, but it is also important that every mayor make efforts to improve the position of blacks vis a vis local municipal institutions. With the data on hand, we can only speculate as to the reasons for this sensitivity. Obviously the location choices for blacks play some role: If you can not move from the central city because of discrimination and low income levels, then what goes on in the central city's mayor's office is more salient. Also more of the total real income of blacks may be provided by municipal services. In other words, if you are poor and black, it is more important that the public schools be of reasonable quality, that the police treat you with respect and provide protection and aid, and so on, because you have little discretionary income to provide such services from alternative sources or to compensate in other ways for their absence.

Chapter 13

AN OVERVIEW

Regardless of the many side excursions, the main route followed in this book emphasized the nature of differences among the fifteen major metropolitan areas in our sample. We were particularly concerned with the variability generated by major institutional complexes within each city as experienced by the black residents. The route has taken the reader through several points of interest: We have examined the structure and function of the civic and political elites in each city, paying particular attention to the mayor's office. We have also looked closely at the social origins and ideological stances of institutional agents, persons who are responsible for the delivery of certain types of services to black ghetto residents. The main attractions, however, were the analyses of the impact upon blacks of five institutional sectors—police department, major employers, retail merchants, school system, and local welfare department.

The side excursions along the main road largely involved topics specific to each of the institutional sectors. For example, in studying the ghetto retail merchants, we examined patterning of vandalism of retail enterprises. Or in the case of the police and educators, we delved into sources of job satisfaction. These analyses were presented because we felt that some knowledge of the internal functionings of these groups was important both to understand their impact upon their clients, customers, or employees, but also to give deserved attention to these critical occupational groups.

The details presented in each of the chapters could easily distract both the authors and the reader from apprehending the main themes suggested by the data. The purpose of this chapter is to provide an overview of our long journey, and emphasize highlights and generalize about the findings. We also suggest some policy implications based on the interactions between the findings and our ideological predilections.

Obviously, no overview can substitute for a careful reading of the book itself. We are all too aware of the tenuous support for many of our findings, and that about many points readers may draw different, and perhaps more valid, generalizations. We encourage readers to examine critically the generalizations of this chapter in the light of their own perspectives and the data presented earlier.

Do Major Cities Differ?   Conventional wisdom and urban "romanticism" would lead one to expect that our country's major cities would differ from each other in ways that went beyond their physical structure. The ambience of New York is reputed to be different from that of San Francisco; as are the climate, topography, and life style. However, both conventional wisdom and romanticism are concerned mainly with the experiences of visitors and of more affluent residents. The view from Nob Hill and the view from Murray Hill are different, but neither would be similar to those enjoyed by the majority of residents in San Francisco and New York.

Conventional wisdom and romanticism may well be correct about some city differences. The critical question in this volume is whether there are differences in major institutional sectors and in the experiences of ordinary residents. Indeed, since the "ordinary residents" with whom we would mainly be concerned were black residents of local ghettoes, our discussions have reflected issues that are not especially salient in typical "top down" perspectives.

Nothing seems more firmly established in our findings than that there *are* critical differences among cities on each of the three levels we studied. These differences survived all our attempts to explain them away through the demographic compositions and predominant economic mixes in the cities. More specifically, political and civic elites played roles that varied with their locations. For example, nothing seems further apart than the superordinate role played by Mayor Daley in Chicago and the insignificance of the mayor's office in Cincinnati. Similarly, business and financial elites were important in the decision-making in some cities and not in others. In short, it was possible to discern styles in governance in each city that were more or less a unique mix of superordinate and subordinate elements.

It was not possible to determine definitely the sources of these city differences at elite levels. There are some patterns that seem obvious: For example, the impotence of the mayor's office in Cincinnati can be ascribed with some confidence to the effectiveness of the council-manager system. But the low potency of the mayor's office in Detroit cannot be as easily linked to nonpartisan local politics, since we also know that Chicago officially is nonpartisan. The best we can say on this score is that the idiosyncracies of history play a role, along with formal political structures and the strengths of local political alignments.

Nor can we say very much about the stability over time of the patterns among elites found in 1968. Of course, Mayor Daley is still very much with us, but the mayors of many of the other cities have been replaced, possibly by persons with different styles and amounts of power. In 1968, the constellations of local political alignments were also different. Black leaders in many cities enjoyed considerable attention, largely due to the whites' fears that the summer of 1968 would be long and "hot."

When we consider the level of institutional agents, we can more easily generalize about the stability of the patterns. The differences among cities' institutional areas for which there are no central controlling bodies, such as retail merchandising and major employing organizations, are especially likely to persist and change slowly in response to long-term trends. The behavior of those institutional sectors that are closely tied into the political regimes, such as police departments, change as political regimes change. For example, because we are particularly close to the scene in Baltimore, we know that its police department has changed since 1968, in response to a variety of other changes in that city.

We have less to say about the stability of welfare and school systems where smaller intercity differences were discerned in our data. Both institutions enjoy ordinarily a certain degree of autonomy from local political regimes; the school systems are usually governed by separate legislative bodies (school boards) and the welfare departments are closely tied into state and federal government. The implications for stability are not clear partially because the services they provide are not easily monitored and regulated.

Finally, when studying the level of black community responses to local institutions and their trust in local regimes, we saw that black citizens are sensitive to intercity differences. In cities such as Milwaukee and Newark blacks had little confidence that their interests were considered and that local institutions treated them with ordinary levels of respect and courtesy. At the other extreme, the black communities of Washington, D.C., and Gary, Indiana were buoyed by confidence in their black and employees.

Of course, the responses of black citizens are subject to the same his- mayors, and apparently enjoyed satisfactory roles as customers, clients, toricity as is the categorization of political regimes. The measures we took are bound to the early spring of 1968: Much may have (and probably has) taken place since that time to change the ordering of cities and the levels of confidence displayed by black communities.

The existence of differences among the fifteen cities on each of the levels studied has several important implications. First, cities are not helplessly steered by the massive trends in the larger society. A city can do much to provide a much more satisfactory environment for its citi- zens. This ability may be especially important for its less advantaged citizens who may be more dependent on local institutions.

Second, some of our findings cause considerable doubt about previous notions about the fixed psychological characteristics of poor blacks. In particular, we found that such variables as "personal efficacy" and "citi- zen competence" show enough variability from city to city to question whether these variables reflect personality characteristics. One may antici- pate that other so-called personality variables, especially those that are supposed to make up the "culture of poverty," show a similar degree of sensitivity to environmental differences.

Finally, these findings point the way to an important line of policy- related research. The data indicate that there is much to be learned from the existing variation among cities about how to deliver services properly. Cities do vary, presumably in a lawful manner, and the future study of this variation may tell us much about how to organize services to maxi- mize delivery of the quality of service desired.

Does Intercity Variation Make a Difference?   The differences discerned among our fifteen cities are also important because the variations are related across levels of data. Thus a mayor's being regarded as either a lovable (or damnable) figurehead or a critical determinant of the quality of city life may depend on whether mayoralty styles are reflected in the services delivered by municipal institutions and the way these services are assessed by city residents.

Here again, our data are quite unequivocal. There are strong and law- ful kinds of relationships across the three levels of data in our study. Thus the stances taken by mayors are reflected in police behavior that impinges on innercity residents. Similarly, the employment practices of major employers are partially responsive to the political climates of the cities and are certainly reflected in the experienced levels of discrimination among black citizens.

For two of the institutional sectors—retail merchandising and public education—the direct appreciation of quality of services is not as important as are the reactions of black leaders. In these two areas we found that variations in service have a more direct impact upon black leaders who in turn raise questions about these areas and turn them into political issues.

In any event, it is clear that complaints are related to reality. The experiences and attitudes of citizens mirror specific city differences in the behaviors manifested by institutional sectors. In some cases, the complaints need to be articulated by black elites; and in other cases, the complaints are registered directly by black rank-and-file without direction from above. That complaints are anchored in reality gives lie to public relations approaches to municipal administration and politics. Superficial appearances may produce a favorable reception initially, but our findings indicate that in the long-run performance counts.

Black and White Citizens' Responses.   Our data are rich in black community responses to the fifteen cities, and relatively skimpy in white citizens' responses. Indeed, for most of the analyses, we had very little to say about white responses because our interviews with institutional agents focused so narrowly on those agents whose clients or customers were mainly black. Only major employers also dealt with whites, although even here our interviews with personnel officers concentrated primarily on the employment opportunities extended to black citizens.

What little evidence we have of white responses to city differences show white citizens to be less sensitive to these differences. Thus whites do not show either the heights of adulation nor the depths of despair that blacks showed in their regard for city mayors. Nor did whites show as much difference from city to city in their feelings of competence in dealing with local public officials. It is, of course, difficult to make very strong statements about these fragmentary findings. They suggest that blacks are especially dependent on local variations, possibly because their options about where to live are fewer because of income and discrimination. After all, if a white does not like Mayor Daley he can move out to Oak Lane or Evanston, but Chicago's blacks have fewer options and less income to indulge those options.

It may also be the case that whites would be more sensitive to aspects of city life that are slighted in our surveys. For example, there is some hint in the data of Chapter 12 that whites pay more attention to less fundamental neighborhood municipal services—street lighting, public library, and such. Transportation, recreation, and sanitation all may be more important issues to whites in part because their more basic needs are satisfied.

In any event, there is no reason to believe that white citizens are qualitatively different in their ability to react to city differences. Both groups are probably sensitive to the variance between cities of those municipal services deemed important. There is enough evidence in our fragmentary findings to make it worthwhile to extend our studies to white citizen responses to the local institutional practices.

It would be most gratifying to the authors if the line of research started with this book would be taken up in further work that extended both the topics and the populations studied. Thus it is clear that we have not exhausted the critical institutional areas of urban places. Two conspicuous gaps in this monograph concern the institutions of the housing market and of medical care. The varied subgroups of an urban population also ought to be studied: We can anticipate considerable variability in sensitivities to city differences depending on socioeconomic level, life cycle, ethnicity, and sublocation within the city. It may well be the case that in studying blacks we have "inadvertently" picked the group most sensitive to local variation, but this remains a point yet to be proven.

A Note on Methodology. Much of the value of this book lies in its methodology. We believe it to be the first urban research that is both comparative and structural. It is comparative in the sense of studying the differences among a relatively extensive set of large urban centers. Of course, there have been many moments in the course of analyzing these data when we have been profoundly frustrated by comparing only fifteen cities. Yet, it is important to note that there have been no previous studies in which as many as fifteen (or even three) have been studied comparatively using similar data.

The research is structural in the sense that the data come from three distinct levels in the social structure of each city's major institutional sectors. This special and unusual character of these data imparts to our study its ability to unravel the nexus between the functioning of central institutions in the political sphere, the outlying agents who deliver services, and the citizens who serve as clients, customers, or employees.

The comparative and structural aspects of the study provide other benefits besides the illumination of the dynamics of city politics. Recall that our sampling procedures for elites and delivery system personnel have many weaknesses, ranging from nonprobability selection procedures to likely bias in the kinds of respondents made available. Without the ability to compare patterns within and across cities, much of the data would have been next to useless. We are not arguing that our sampling techniques are desirable, but that the overall research design salvaged otherwise problematic materials. That seems such an important lesson that one might almost say our sampling liabilities have been turned into assets.

Similarly, our decision midway into the study to transform our qualitative elite interviews into sets of quantitative variables may be deemed a provocative methodological technique. We are not suggesting that this approach is necessarily the best way to gather information from city influentials, but we are also not conceding that structural questionnaires with precoded responses would have produced better data in this instance. At the very least, our coding of the qualitative materials may illustrate a useful fall-back position when more standard data gathering techniques are inapplicable.

The statistical methods used to analyze the data are not as unusual as is the nature of the data themselves. The multivariate analysis techniques are perhaps somewhat more sophisticated than was common a decade ago, but they are widely used in much empirical work in sociology and political science today. Probably more interesting than our use of various statistical procedures is our all too frequent misuse of them. Despite sampling problems, significance tests were often applied. In some cases we presented analyses where multicolinearity should have suggested more prudence. Occasionally, we pushed the number of variables that could be simultaneously considered with a case base of fifteen beyond what is commonly acceptable. These and other questionable procedures were not undertaken casually, but with the calculated gamble that if carefully scrutinized, important substantive insights might be forthcoming. It is clear that many cookbook recipes have been altered: We hope the cake is still eatable.

Finally there are many points at which we have strained the analysis up to the limits of credibility. We have done so because we felt that the illustration of the ways in which these unique data could be used was important. The proper study of sociology and political science is the examination of structural relationships. To illustrate how data of this kind could be used to study important elements of social structural within cities seemed at times to be more important than precision or prudence.

Some Political Implications.   If any overall message comes through in our analysis, it is that behavior is more important than are attitudes. We have seen that institutional agents may deliver services in a way that quite contradicts their ideological stances, in either direction. Thus the most liberal of all groups—social workers—receive highest rating from poor blacks when they stay away from their clients. And the least liberal of all groups—the police—can function in a way that is more satisfying to their clients when their superiors order proper behavior toward blacks.

There are also hints that public relations may not be as important as performance. While it is true that a mayor who shows his sympathies toward the civil rights movement gets more votes of confidence than one who does not, a well-performing delivery system can also either augment or detract considerably from such a public image. Local politics is not simply image making, a finding that pleases our rationalist biases considerably.

Another important political implication of our findings is that local political systems are responsive. It is in cities with high proportions of blacks in the electorate that mayors and other public officials are particularly responsive to blacks. It is also the case that militancy enhances rather than detracts from political influence. Indeed, the lesson is quite clear: Make noise, organize yourselves, and make demands. It also helps to have an articulate and perceptive elite. Where black leaders were alert to the faults in local social systems and articulated the faults into political issues, the public officials and civil elites appear to have responded.

Finally, it must be said that we have found no city in which there was clear political equality between whites and blacks. There was variation from place to place in the extent to which blacks received a hearing at the decision-making tables, but there is nothing in our data to suggest that for blacks chances for employment, freedom from police harassment, treatment at the hands of the public school system, or service by welfare agencies were the equal of comparable chances for whites. We have seen how the gap may be narrowed, but in 1968, the gap was still to be closed.

Appendix A

INTERVIEW SCHEDULES

CORE QUESTIONNAIRE

AUDITS & SURVEYS, INC.   #5338
One Park Avenue
New York, N.Y. 10016   March 1968

CIVIL DISORDER STUDY

Card 1
5-1

6-

RESPONDENT'S NAME: _____   INTERVIEWER'S NAME: _____

RESPONDENT'S ADDRESS: _____   INTERVIEWER'S NUMBER ☐ ☐ ☐ ☐ ☐
                                                                7- 8- 9- 10- 11-
CITY _____ STATE _____   DATE OF INTERVIEW: _____

RESPONDENT'S TELEPHONE NUMBER: _____   PLACE OF INTERVIEW: _____

RESPONDENT'S POSITION: _____   (IF AN ESTABLISHMENT)

RACE OF RESPONDENT: WHITE ☐   12-1   NAME OF FIRM: _____

                    NEGRO ☐   -2   ADDRESS OF FIRM: _____

                    OTHER (SPECIFY) -3   _____

SEX OF RESPONDENT: MALE ☐ 13-1
                     FEMALE ☐   -2

Hello, I'm from Audits & Surveys. We are conducting a study on behalf of a group of social scientists at Johns Hopkins University of local communities in urban areas throughout the country. We are especially interested in the experiences and opinions of persons like yourself whose job involves working with people in the city as a whole or with local neighborhoods. As you answer the following questions, please try to keep in mind that this is for scientific purposes only. No one in the city will see your answers. What you tell us is strictly confidential.

DO NOT WRITE IN THIS BOX

Validated by:

Date:

   Phone Call ☐

   Post Card ☐

14-   15-   16-

157

Now I am going to ask you a series of questions about the city in which you work. As before, all that is said will remain strictly confidential.

1. Every city faces problems nowadays. What do you see as the two or three major problems facing your city?

_____ 17–
_____ 18–
_____ 19–
_____ 20–
_____ 21–
_____ 22–
_____ 23–

2. Thinking back over the last few years and the problems your city has had to face, what have been the major improvements?

_____ 24–
_____ 25–
_____ 26–
_____ 27
_____ 28–
_____ 29–
_____ 30–

3. I am going to read a list of problems which face some cities in this country today. In your view, how serious is each of the problems in your city? That is, do you feel that (TYPE OF PROBLEM) is very serious, somewhat serious, slightly serious, or not at all serious? (CHECK APPROPRIATE BOX FOR EACH PROBLEM LISTED)

	Very Serious	Somewhat Serious	Slightly Serious	Not Serious	DK
a) Control of crime...........................	☐ 31–1	☐ –2	☐ –3	☐ –4	☐ –6
b) Unemployment.............................	☐ 32–1	☐ –2	☐ –3	☐ –4	☐ –6
c) Air pollution.................................	☐ 33–1	☐ –2	☐ –3	☐ –4	☐ –6
d) Race relations..............................	☐ 34–1	☐ –2	☐ –3	☐ –4	☐ –6
e) Providing quality education..........	☐ 35–1	☐ –2	☐ –3	☐ –4	☐ –6
f) Finding tax funds for municipal services......................................	☐ 36–1	☐ –2	☐ –3	☐ –4	☐ –6
g) Traffic and highways....................	☐ 37–1	☐ –2	☐ –3	☐ –4	☐ –6
h) Preventing violence and other civil disorder.......................................	☐ 38–1	☐ –2	☐ –3	☐ –4	☐ –6
i) Lack of recreation facilities..........	☐ 39–1	☐ –2	☐ –3	☐ –4	☐ –6
j) Corruption of public officials.........	☐ 40–1	☐ –2	☐ –3	☐ –4	☐ –6

158

4. Compared to other cities of the same size, how well do you think __(CITY)__ is doing in meeting the problems it faces? Do you think it is doing much better than average, about average, or less than average?

> Much better than average......... ☐ 41–1
> About average.......................... ☐ –2
> Less than average.................... ☐ –3
> Don't know............................... ☐ –6

Now I have a few questions concerning some of the social problems of urban life. I'll start with some questions about Negroes here.

5. In your opinion, how well are Negroes treated in __(CITY)__ ? Do you feel they are . . .
   (READ STATEMENTS BELOW AND CHECK APPROPRIATE BOX)

. . . Treated better than any other part of the population?....................................... ☐ 42–1

. . . Treated equally?... ☐ –2

. . . Treated as other people of the same income?... ☐ –3

. . . Treated worse than other people of the same income?.. ☐ –4

. . . Treated worse than any other part of the population?... ☐ –5

    Don't know.. ☐ –6

6. Compared to other groups in the city of the same income and education, do you think Negroes are about as well off, less well off, or better off with respect to . . .
   (READ STATEMENTS BELOW AND CHECK APPROPRIATE BOX)

	As Well Off	Less Well Off	Better Off	DK
a) . . . Educational opportunities?......................	☐ 43–1	☐ –2	☐ –3	☐ –6
b) . . . Employment opportunities?......................	☐ 44–1	☐ –2	☐ –3	☐ –6
c) . . . Treatment by the police?..........................	☐ 45–1	☐ –2	☐ –3	☐ –6
d) . . . Housing?...	☐ 46–1	☐ –2	☐ –3	☐ –6
e) . . . Treatment by public officials?...................	☐ 47–1	☐ –2	☐ –3	☐ –6
f) . . . Medical care?...	☐ 48–1	☐ –2	☐ –3	☐ –6
g) . . . Recreation?...	☐ 49–1	☐ –2	☐ –3	☐ –6

159

7. Compared to about five years ago, would you consider Negroes in this city . . .
(READ STATEMENTS BELOW AND CHECK APPROPRIATE BOX)

    . . . A lot better off?................................ ☐ 50–1

    . . . Generally better off?........................ ☐   –2

    . . . Generally worse off?......................... ☐   –3

    . . . About the same?.............................. ☐   –4

    Don't know...................................... ☐   –6

8. As you see it, how does the average White person in this city view Negroes? Here are some statements which I will read to you. Please tell me whether the statement fits the situation of White attitudes towards Negroes as you see them. Is the statement completely true, mostly true, somewhat true or not true at all?
(READ STATEMENTS AND CHECK APPROPRIATE BOX)

	Completely True	Mostly True	Somewhat True	Not True	DK
a) Most Whites would like to see Negroes get an even break, but few have the time to worry much about it..	☐ 51–1	☐ –2	☐ –3	☐ –4	☐ –6
b) Most Whites are deeply prejudiced against Negroes but are afraid to show it out in the open.................	☐ 52–1	☐ –2	☐ –3	☐ –4	☐ –6
c) Most Whites are for giving Negroes a fair deal and generally back up these beliefs..................................	☐ 53 1	☐ –2	☐ –3	☐ –4	☐ –6
d) Most Whites are prejudiced and given the opportunity would send the Negroes back to the South......	☐ 54–1	☐ –2	☐ –3	☐ –4	☐ –6
e) Most Whites are not prejudiced, but they do not feel comfortable with Negroes in most situations...	☐ 55–1	☐ –2	☐ –3	☐ –4	☐ –6

160

9. As you see it, how does the average Negro person <u>in this city</u> view White people? Here are some statements which I will read to you. Please tell me whether the statement fits the situation of Negro attitudes towards Whites as you see them. Is the statement completely true, mostly true, somewhat true or not true at all? (READ STATEMENTS BELOW AND CHECK APPROPRIATE BOX)

	Completely True	Mostly True	Somewhat True	Not True	DK
a) Most Negroes feel friendly towards Whites but don't know how to show it...................................	☐ 56–1	☐ –2	☐ –3	☐ –4	☐ –6
b) Most Negroes feel friendly towards Whites and generally back up these feelings.........................	☐ 57–1	☐ –2	☐ –3	☐ –4	☐ –6
c) Most Negroes dislike Whites intensely but are afraid to show it...	☐ 58–1	☐ –2	☐ –3	☐ –4	☐ –6
d) Most Negroes hate Whites and given the opportunity would seek revenge.......................................	☐ 59–1	☐ –2	☐ –3	☐ –4	☐ –6
e) Most Negroes dislike Whites and, given the opportunity, Negroes would live by themselves and not have anything to do with whites...	☐ 60–1	☐ –2	☐ –3	☐ –4	☐ –6
f) Most Negroes feel friendly towards Whites but do not feel comfortable with Whites in most situations..	☐ 61–1	☐ –2	☐ –3	☐ –4	☐ –6

10. In every city there are groups that are leaders in working for equal treatment for all citizens regardless of race or color. Other groups are less apt to be concerned with this. How about various groups in this city? Are the <u>(GROUP)</u> leaders, in the matter of equal treatment for all, <u>active</u> in this area but not necessarily leaders; <u>indifferent</u> to the problem—in other words, don't particularly care one way or another; or are they <u>dragging their feet on it</u>? (CHECK THE APPROPRIATE BOX FOR EACH GROUP LISTED BELOW)

	Leaders	Active But Not Leaders	Don't Care One Way or the Other	Drag Their Feet	DK
a) Major employers..........................	☐ 62–1	☐ –2	☐ –3	☐ –4	☐ –6
b) Major retail businesses...............	☐ 63–1	☐ –2	☐ –3	☐ –4	☐ –6
c) Bankers......................................	☐ 64–1	☐ –2	☐ –3	☐ –4	☐ –6
d) The police...................................	☐ 65–1	☐ –2	☐ –3	☐ –4	☐ –6
e) Social Workers.............................	☐ 66–1	☐ –2	☐ –3	☐ –4	☐ –6
f) Elected public officials like the Mayor...	☐ 67–1	☐ –2	☐ –3	☐ –4	☐ –6
g) Teachers in public school............	☐ 68–1	☐ –2	☐ –3	☐ –4	☐ –6
h) Homeowners...............................	☐ 69–1	☐ –2	☐ –3	☐ –4	☐ –6
i) Landlords...................................	☐ 70–1	☐ –2	☐ –3	☐ –4	☐ –6
j) Unions..	☐ 71–1	☐ –2	☐ –3	☐ –4	☐ –6

11. Now, in terms of Negroes gaining what they feel to be equality, do you feel the Negroes have tried to move much too fast, too fast, too slow, or has it been about right?

Much too fast...................... □ 72–1   About right.. □ –4

Too fast................................ □ –2   Don't know.. □ –6

Too slow.............................. □ –3

Card 2
5–2

12a. Many <u>Whites</u> are greatly disturbed by things they see happening in and around the Negro community in cities across the country. How about this city? How disturbed do you think <u>most Whites</u> are about <u>(INSERT EACH ITEM LISTED BELOW)</u> – very disturbed, slightly disturbed or not disturbed at all? (CHECK BELOW FOR EACH ITEM LISTED)

b. Many <u>Negroes</u> are greatly disturbed by things they see happening in and around the community in cities across the country. How about this city? How disturbed do you think <u>most Negroes</u> are about <u>(INSERT EACH ITEM LISTED BELOW)</u> – very disturbed, slightly disturbed or not disturbed at all? (CHECK BELOW FOR EACH ITEM LISTED)

c. How do <u>you</u> feel about the matter of <u>(INSERT EACH ITEM LISTED BELOW)</u> – are <u>you</u> very disturbed, slightly disturbed, or aren't you disturbed at all about it? (CHECK BELOW FOR EACH ITEM LISTED)

	Q. 12a Most Whites				Q. 12b Most Negroes				Q. 12c Respondent's Opinion			
	Very Disturbed	Slightly Disturbed	Not Disturbed	Don't know	Very Disturbed	Slightly Disturbed	Not Disturbed	Don't know	Very Disturbed	Slightly Disturbed	Not Disturbed	Don't know
a) The amount of individual crime (theft, murder, etc.).....................	□ 6–1	□ –2	□ –3	□ –6	□ 7–1	□ –2	□ –3	□ –6	□ 8–1	□ –2	□ –3	□ –6
b) Mass violence (riots and mass disorders)...........	□ 9–1	□ –2	□ –3	□ –6	□ 10–1	□ –2	□ –3	□ –6	□ 11–1	□ –2	□ –3	□ –6
c) Increased competition for blue collar jobs (unskilled and semi-skilled)................	□ 12–1	□ –2	□ –3	□ –6	□ 13–1	□ –2	□ –3	□ –6	□ 14–1	□ –2	□ –3	□ –6
d) Draining resources through welfare payments..................	□ 15–1	□ –2	□ –3	□ –6	□ 16–1	□ –2	□ –3	□ –6	□ 17–1	□ –2	□ –3	□ –6
e) Negroes taking over political power................	□ 18–1	□ –2	□ –3	□ –6	□ 19–1	□ –2	□ –3	□ –6	□ 20–1	□ –2	□ –3	□ –6
f) Negroes moving into areas that, until recently, were occupied only by Whites................	□ 21–1	□ –2	□ –3	□ –6	□ 22–1	□ –2	□ –3	□ –6	□ 23–1	□ –2	□ –3	□ –6
g) Negroes socializing with Whites................	□ 24–1	□ –2	□ –3	□ –6	□ 25–1	□ –2	□ –3	□ –6	□ 26–1	□ –2	□ –3	□ –6
h) Increased competition for professional and white collar positions......	□ 27–1	□ –2	□ –3	□ –6	□ 28–1	□ –2	□ –3	□ –6	□ 29–5	□ –2	□ –3	□ –6

(ASK ONLY IN DETROIT, NEWARK, BOSTON AND MILWAUKEE:)

(ASK IN ALL OTHER CITIES:)

13. Were the mass disturbances or disorders in this city last summer serious enough to be called riots or rebellions?

Yes ☐ 30-1

No ☐ -2

13. Were there any mass disturbances or disorders in this city last summer serious enough to be called riots or rebellions?

Yes ☐ 31-1

No ☐ -2

14. Were there any other mass disturbances or disorders in this city last summer that were serious but not large enough to be called a riot or rebellion?

Yes ☐ 32-1   No ☐ -2

(IF "NO" TO Q.13 AND Q.14, SKIP TO Q.18. ASK ALL OTHERS Q.15.)

15. As you see it, what were the main reasons for the disturbances in your city?

33–
34–
35–
36–
37–
38–
39–

16a. Was there any way that the disturbances could have been prevented?

Yes ☐ 40-1 (ASK Q.16b)

No ☐ -2 (SKIP TO Q.17a)

b. (IF "YES" TO Q.16a:) How could they have been prevented?

41–
42–
43–
44–
45–
46–
47–

163

424

17a. Now that the disturbances are over, what do you think have been some of their consequences? For example, has anything been done to meet the Negro complaints and grievances?

Yes ☐ 48–1   No ☐ –2   Don't know ☐ –6

b. Have White attitudes changed towards Negroes to be more favorable, less favorable, or remained much the same as before the riot?

More favorable......... ☐ 49–1   About the same ☐ –3

Less favorable......... ☐   –2   Don't know........ ☐ –6

c. Have Negro attitudes changed towards Whites to be more favorable, less favorable, or remained about the same?

More favorable......... ☐ 50–1   About the same ☐ –3

Less favorable......... ☐   –2   Don't know........ ☐ –6

d. How about the police? Have they changed in their attitudes towards Negroes to be more favorable, less favorable, or much the same?

More favorable......... ☐ 51–1   About the same ☐ –3

Less favorable......... ☐   –2   Don't know........ ☐ –6
                                          (SKIP TO Q.21)

18. (IF "NO" TO Q.14, ASK:) In your view, what are the major reasons for civil disturbances and riots in cities that have had them?

	52–
	53–
	54–
	55–
	56–
	57–
	58–

19. How likely is it that a riot could occur here in (CITY)—is it . . .

. . . Extremely likely?............... ☐ 59–1

. . . Somewhat likely?............... ☐   –2 } (ASK Q.20)

. . . Possible but not likely?....... ☐   –3

. . . Not at all likely?................. ☐   –4 } (SKIP TO Q.21)

      Don't know....................... ☐   –6

20. (IF "EXTREMELY LIKELY", "SOMEWHAT LIKELY", OR "POSSIBLE BUT NOT LIKELY" IN Q.19, ASK:) Why do you suppose a riot did not occur here in (CITY) last summer?

	60–
	61–
	62–
	63–
	64–
	65–
	66–

164

21. (ASK EVERYONE)
One view of the riots is that they occur because Negroes feel that their complaints are not being paid sufficient attention by local authorities. In your view is this . . . (READ STATEMENTS AND CHECK APPROPRIATE BOX)

> The main reason?... ☐ 67–1
>
> Largely true but not the only reason?............... ☐　–2
>
> True but not a major reason?........................... ☐　–3
>
> Not true at all?... ☐　–4

22. Another view of the riots is that they are mainly the result of the criminal element in the Negro ghetto getting out of hand and taking advantage of minor incidents to provide opportunities for looting? In your view—for your city—is this . . . (READ STATEMENTS AND CHECK APPROPRIATE BOX)

> The main reason?... ☐ 68–1
>
> Largely true but not the only reason?............... ☐　–2
>
> True but not a major reason?........................... ☐　–3
>
> Not true at all?... ☐　–4

23. Still another view of the riots sees them mainly as the result of the agitation of Negro nationalists or other militants who are taking advantage of the grievances of the Negro population to create the conditions for a rebellion. Is this . . . (READ STATEMENTS AND CHECK APPROPRIATE BOX)

> The main reason?... ☐ 69–1
>
> Largely true but not the only reason?............... ☐　–2
>
> True but not a major reason?........................... ☐　–3
>
> Not true at all?... ☐　–4

24. Another view has it that the riots are political actions designed to obtain concessions and changes from local authorities. Do you feel this is . . . (READ STATEMENTS AND CHECK APPROPRIATE BOX)

> The main reason?... ☐ 70–1
>
> Largely true but not the only reason?............... ☐　–2
>
> True but not a major reason?........................... ☐　–3
>
> Not true at all?... ☐　–4

25. Another view sees the riots mainly provoked by police brutality in handling arrests and other problems in the Negro community. In your view is this . . . (READ STATEMENTS AND CHECK APPROPRIATE BOX)

> The main reason?... ☐ 71–1
>
> Largely true but not the only reason?............... ☐　–2
>
> True but not a major reason?........................... ☐　–3
>
> Not true at all?... ☐　–4

165

426

26. Yet another view sees most Negroes as basically violent, with little respect for the laws and mores of our society. Riots occurred mainly because authorities generally have been too permissive. Do you feel this is . . . (READ STATEMENTS AND CHECK APPROPRIATE BOX)

The main reason?.. ☐ 72–1

Largely true but not the only reason?............... ☐ –2

True but not a major reason?............................ ☐ –3

Not true at all?... ☐ –4

27. Cities differ in the way in which they approach their problems. Here are some statements that have been made about different cities. For this city, please tell me whether each statement is completely true, mostly true, somewhat true, or not true. (CHECK APPROPRIATE BOX FOR EACH STATEMENT LISTED)

	Completely True	Mostly True	Somewhat True	Not True	DK
a) The political leaders of our city are imaginative and are always coming up with new ideas on how to meet the city's problems.........	☐ 73–1	☐ –2	☐ –3	☐ –4	☐ –6
b) This is a city which has always been among the last to try new ideas like urban renewal, educational reforms, and so on.............	☐ 74–1	☐ –2	☐ –3	☐ –4	☐ –6
c) One of the good things about this city's government is the tremendous cooperation various agencies give to each other.................	☐ 75–1	☐ –2	☐ –3	☐ –4	☐ –6
d) The rank and file city employee here tries his best to do his job, but he gets little support from his superiors.....................................	☐ 76–1	☐ –2	☐ –3	☐ –4	☐ –6
e) No matter how imaginative our city officials may be, the rank and file public employees just plug away doing things the same way anyhow......................................	☐ 77–1	☐ –2	☐ –3	☐ –4	☐ –6
f) The average citizen can always find someone in the city government who is willing to help him solve his problem.......................	☐ 78–1	☐ –2	☐ –3	☐ –4	☐ –6

166

Card 5
5–5

Now I want to ask you some questions concerning your own background.

1a. Were you born here in (CITY)?

Yes ☐ 6–1 (SKIP TO Q.2)
No ☐ –2 (ASK Q.1b & c)

7–

b. (IF "NO" TO Q.1a, ASK:) How old were you when you moved here? _____ 8–

9–

c. (IF "NO" TO Q.1a, ASK:) Where did you come from? _____ 10–

11–

2. In what year were you born? _____ 12–

3. How many years of formal education did you complete? (READ EDUCATION GROUPS BELOW AND CHECK APPROPRIATE BOX)

Less than high school (1–11 years)................................. ☐ 13–1
High school graduate (12 years).................................... ☐ –2
Some college (1–3 years)... ☐ –3
College graduate (4 years)... ☐ –4
Professional or graduate school (more than 4 years)...... ☐ –5

4a. In <u>national</u> elections, do you mainly consider yourself a . . .

Democrat............. ☐ 14–1 (SKIP TO Q.5a)
Republican........... ☐ –2 (SKIP TO Q.5a)
Independent......... ☐ –3 (ASK Q.4b)

b. (IF "INDEPENDENT" IN Q.4a, ASK:) As an Independent, do you mainly lean towards the Democrats or the Republicans in the candidates you support?

Democrats............. ☐ 15–1
Republicans......... ☐ –2
Neither................ ☐ –3

5a. In <u>local</u> elections, do you mainly consider yourself a . . .

Democrat............. ☐ 16–1 (SKIP TO Q.6a)
Republican........... ☐ –2 (SKIP TO Q.6a)
Independent......... ☐ –3 (ASK Q.5b)

b. (IF "INDEPENDENT" IN Q.5a, ASK:) As an Independent, do you mainly lean towards the Democrats or the Republicans in the candidates you support?

Democrats............. ☐ 17–1
Republicans......... ☐ –2
Neither................ ☐ –3

167

6a. Do you belong to any unions, professional associations, social clubs, civic groups or other organizations?

        No ☐ 18–1 (SKIP TO Q.7)
        Yes ☐   –2 (ASK Q.6b)

b. (IF "YES" TO Q.6a, ASK:) What are they? _____

19–
20–
21–
22–
23–
24–
25–

7. Have you been active with any civil rights groups in the past 2 years?

        No ☐ 26–1
        Yes ☐   –2

8. If you were to change your present work—taking a new job or moving your business elsewhere— how likely would it be that a Negro (White) (WHICHEVER IS OPPOSITE THE RESPONDENT) would take you place here, considering the number of people around here who have some of your skills and resources? Would it be . . . (READ STATEMENTS BELOW AND CHECK APPROPRIATE BOX)

        Very likely?........................... ☐ 27–1

        Somewhat likely?................ ☐   –2

        Possible but not likely?........ ☐   –3

        Not at all likely?................. ☐   –4

        Don't know?........................ ☐   –6

9. To what religious denomination do you belong?

        Protestant........................... ☐ 28–1

        Catholic.............................. ☐   –2

        Jewish................................ ☐   –3

        Other (SPECIFY)_____   –4

10. Do you own or rent your home or apartment?

        Own............... ☐ 29–1

        Rent.............. ☐   –2

168

11. Would you please tell me into which income group your total family yearly income falls? (READ INCOME GROUPS LISTED AND CHECK APPROPRIATE BOX)

Under $5,000..................... ☐ 30-1

$5,000 to $7,499.................... ☐   -2

$7,500 to $9,999.................. ☐   -3

$10,000 to $12,499.............. ☐   -4

$12,500 to $15,000.............. ☐   -5

Over $15,000...................... ☐ 31-1

Finally, I would like to ask you a question or two on the recent report submitted to President Johnson by the Commission on Civil Disorders?

12. Are you aware of the recent announcement of the findings and recommendations of President Johnson's Commission on Civil Disorders?

Yes ☐ 32-1 (ASK Q.13a & b)

No ☐   -2 (TERMINATE INTERVIEW)

DK ☐   -6 (TERMINATE INTERVIEW)

13a. (IF "YES" TO Q.12, ASK:) In general, do you agree or disagree with the statements of the Commission?

Agree................... ☐ 33-1

Disagree.............. ☐   -2

DK...................... ☐   -6

b. Do you think the report from the Commission will ever have much of an effect on the day-to-day lives of people in this city?

Yes ☐ 34-1 (ASK Q.14a)

No ☐   -2 (SKIP TO Q.14b)

169

14a. (IF "YES" TO Q.13b, ASK:) How soon? That is, . . . (READ STATEMENTS)

. . . In less than 6 months?...................................... ☐ 35–1

. . . In 6 months to 1 year?.................................... ☐ –2

. . . More than 1 year – and up to 5 years?.............. ☐ –3

. . . Longer than 5 years?...................................... ☐ –4

Don't know.. ☐ –6

b. (IF "NO" TO Q.13b, ASK:) How true are each of the following reasons for your anticipating that the report will have no effect on the day-to-day lives of people in this city – largely true, partially true, or not true at all? (READ EACH STATEMENT AND CHECK APPROPRIATE BOX)

	Largely True	Partially True	Not True At All	Don't Know
1) Lack of practical suggestions in the report...	☐ 36–1	☐ –2	☐ –3	☐ –6
2) White public opinion which will not support the findings and recommendations of the Commission..	☐ 37–1	☐ –2	☐ –3	☐ –6
3) Local politicians who will not act on the recommendations of the Commission...........	☐ 38–1	☐ –2	☐ –3	☐ –6
4) Federal politicians who will not act on the recommendations of the Commission...........	☐ 39–1	☐ –2	☐ –3	☐ –6
5) Lack of Government funds to implement the recommendations of the report....................	☐ 40–1	☐ –2	☐ –3	☐ –6

Thank you very much. You have been most helpful.

LENGTH OF INTERVIEW: _____ Minutes

POLICE

The police force always plays an important role in any community. This is the main reason why we are interested in determining the policemen's views on local community problems.

1. To begin with, what do you see as the major problems you face in doing your job here in your precinct?

_____

_____

2a. Compared to assignments in other precincts of the city, how do you regard this particular assignment? That is, do you feel that the work is harder, about the same, or easier here than in other precincts of the city?

             Harder........................... □ 13–1

             Easier............................. □   –2

             About the same.............. □   –3

b. Is the work safer, isn't there any difference, or is it more hazardous here than elsewhere in in the city?

             Safer.............................. □ 14–1

             No difference................... □   –2

             More hazardous............... □   –3

3. How is the job of being a policeman in this city? Are you very satisfied, somewhat satisfied, somewhat dissatisfied, or very dissatisfied with this kind of work?

             Very satisfied........................... □ 15–1

             Somewhat satisfied.................. □   –2

             Somewhat dissatisfied.............. □   –3

             Very dissatisfied .... □   –4

             Don't know.............................. □   –6

4. Would you prefer working in this precinct for several more years (maybe even permanently), would you prefer some other assignment in this city, or doesn't it matter to you where you work?

             Prefer the present assignment............... □ 16–1

             Prefer another assignment.................... □   –2

             Doesn't matter...................................... □   –3

171

5. How much respect does the average resident of this precinct have for the police . . . a great deal of respect, some respect, neither respect nor contempt, some contempt, or a great deal of contempt for the police?

Great deal of respect........................... ☐ 17–1

Some respect..................................... ☐ –2

Neither respect nor contempt.............. ☐ –3

Some contempt................................... ☐ –4

A great deal of contempt.................... ☐ –5

Don't know....................................... ☐ –6

6. In some precincts most people regard the police almost as enemies. In others, they regard the police as being essentialy on their side, and in some, they are indifferent toward the police. How do most people in this precinct look on the police. . . . (READ STATEMENTS BELOW AND CHECK APPROPRIATE BOX)

	Police Regarded as Enemies	Police Regarded As On Their Side	Indifferent Towards Police	DK
. . . In general?....................................	☐ 18–1	☐ –2	☐ –3	☐ –6
. . . How about most old persons in the neighborhood?................................	☐ 19–1	☐ –2	☐ –3	☐ –6
. . . Most Negroes?..............................	☐ 20–1	☐ –2	☐ –3	☐ –6
. . . Most storekeepers?........................	☐ 21–1	☐ –2	☐ –3	☐ –6
. . . Most adolescents?.........................	☐ 22–1	☐ –2	☐ –3	☐ –6
. . . Most young adults?........................	☐ 23–1	☐ –2	☐ –3	☐ –6
. . . Most teachers?.............................	☐ 24–1	☐ –2	☐ –3	☐ –6
. . . Most Whites?................................	☐ 25–1	☐ –2	☐ –3	☐ –0

7a. Looking back over the last three or four years, have the attitudes of Negroes towards the police changed here in this city?

No ☐ 26–1 (SKIP TO Q.8)

Yes ☐ –2 (ASK Q.7b)

b. (IF "YES" TO Q.7a, ASK:) Are Negroes more likely or less likely to regard the police as enemies?

More likely........................... ☐ 27–1

Less likely........................... ☐ –2

Don't know........................... ☐ –6

172

433

8. I will read to you some comments and criticisms that have been used to describe the people in various neighborhoods in this city. In your estimation, which of these are generally true, which are partially true, and which are not true at all for the people in your precinct? (READ STATEMENTS BELOW AND CHECK APPROPRIATE BOX)

	Generally True	Partially True	Not True At All	DK
a) These people do not care very much for law and order	☐ 28–1	☐ –2	☐ –3	☐ –6
b) They are honest people	☐ 29–1	☐ –2	☐ –3	☐ –6
c) They don't look after their health very well	☐ 30–1	☐ –2	☐ –3	☐ –6
d) They are industrious people	☐ 31–1	☐ –2	☐ –3	☐ –6
e) Often they are hostile to outsiders	☐ 32–1	☐ –2	☐ –3	☐ –6
f) They are respectable, religious people	☐ 33–1	☐ –2	☐ –3	☐ –6

9. Since the problems differ from precinct to precinct in this city, some of the practices of the police department will naturally differ somewhat. In your precinct, are policemen called upon frequently, sometimes, seldom, or never to . . . (READ EACH STATEMENT BELOW AND CHECK APPROPRIATE BOX)

	Frequently	Sometimes	Seldom	Never
. . . Intervene in domestic quarrels?	☐ 34–1	☐ –2	☐ –3	☐ –4
. . . Search with a warrant?	☐ 35–1	☐ –2	☐ –3	☐ –4
. . . Search on suspicion but without a warrant?	☐ 36–1	☐ –2	☐ –3	☐ –4
. . . Stop and frisk suspicious people?	☐ 37–1	☐ –2	☐ –3	☐ –4
. . . Break up loitering groups?	☐ 38–1	☐ –2	☐ –3	☐ –4
. . . Interrogate suspected drug users?	☐ 39–1	☐ –2	☐ –3	☐ –4

10a. Of every ten people you stop to question and frisk, about how many actually turn out to be carrying something on them that might have led to a crime or some sort of trouble (knife, gun, etc.)?

_____ Out of ten   40–   Don't know ☐ 41–6

b. Of every ten people you stop to question and frisk, about how many actually turn out to be criminals you are looking for, or people engaged in illegal activity, such as carrying marijuana or stolen goods?

_____ Out of ten   42–   Don't know ☐ 43–6

173

11. A police officer should be in control of situations with people he suspects are criminals or are otherwise dangerous. Which way do you think is it best to deal with someone you stop on the street for questioning or frisking? That is, should you . . . (READ STATEMENTS BELOW AND CHECK APPROPRIATE BOX)

   . . . Deal aggressively and authoritatively from the start so that the suspect knows who is in control... □ 44-1

OR

   . . . Deal firmly from the start, but be polite until a hostile move is made by the suspect?.. □   -2

12. When you stop people to question and frisk them, which of the following four statements best describes their usual reaction? Are they . . . (READ STATEMENTS BELOW AND CHECK APPROPRIATE BOX)

   . . . Willing to give you any information you want without any hesitancy about being frisked?... □ 45-1

   . . . Willing to give you information, but don't like being frisked................................... □   -2

   . . . Unwilling to respond to you adequately, but finally do under threats or pressure?.. □   -3

   . . . Unwilling to respond and physically resist your efforts to get information and if you were to search them, they would injure you or escape if not restrained?.............. □   -4

   Don't know.. □   -6

13. Some claim that all people are reasonable if you show enough patience and respect in working with them. Others say that people respect only force and power—obeying the law out of fear of punishment. In your job, do you find that . . . (READ STATEMENTS BELOW AND CHECK APPROPRIATE BOX)

   . . . People generally respond in the end to reason and respect and very few respond only to power and force?.. □ 46-1

   . . . Some people respond to reason and respect; others respond only to power and force?.. □   -2

   . . . Very few people respond to reason and respect. Most people respond primarily to power and force?.. □   -3

   Don't know.. □   -6

174

14a. A number of agencies have tried to work with gangs to turn them into constructive activities. In your experience, are these agencies making the policeman's job easier in the long run, are they making law enforcement efforts more difficult, or are they making no difference at all?

Making policeman's job easier in long run............... ☐ 47-1

Making law enforcement more difficult..................... ☐   -2

Making no difference.. ☐   -3

Don't know... ☐   -6

b. How about the efforts of welfare workers to help the people living in the poor neighborhoods? Do they make your job easier, more difficult, or don't they make any difference at all?

Easier......................... ☐ 48-1

More difficult............... ☐   -2

No difference............... ☐   -3

Don't know.................. ☐   -6

c. How about poverty program workers (Headstart, VISTA, Community Action Agency, etc.) Do they . . . (READ STATEMENTS BELOW AND CHECK APPROPRIATE BOX)

. . . Make your job easier?............................ ☐ 49-1

. . . Make your job more difficult?.................. ☐   -2

. . . Not make any difference at all?............... ☐   -3

Don't know... ☐   -6

d. How about organizers from SNCC, CORE, NAACP, and from various poverty and/or rights groups? Do they . . . (READ STATEMENTS BELOW AND CHECK APPROPRIATE BOX)

. . . Make your job easier?............................ ☐ 50-1

. . . Make your job more difficult?.................. ☐   -2

. . . Not make any difference at all?............... ☐   -3

Don't know... ☐   -6

175

15. In some neighborhoods a policeman has little time to worry about being absolutely certain before he picks up someone on suspicion. Some of these people, whether really guilty, or whether the victim of a genuine mistake, will complain to your superiors, to a city councilman, or to other authorities. In this precenct, do policemen have to worry about getting into trouble because of their mistakes and complaints more or less than in most other precincts of the city, or isn't there any difference between precincts at all?

Worry more about it here in this precinct than in most others.................... ☐ 51–1

Worry more about it in most other precincts than in this precinct............... ☐ –2

Doesn't make any difference at all.. ☐ –3

Don't know.. ☐ –6

16. In many communities, the control of crime and the enforcement of the law is hampered by many factors not under the control of the policeman. In your opinion, how serious are the following problems in your own job? Do you consider it very serious, somewhat serious, or not at all serious that . . . (READ EACH STATEMENT AND CHECK APPROPRIATE BOX)

	Very Serious	Somewhat Serious	Not at All Serious
a) . . . The residents do not cooperate very well in your efforts to control them?...	☐ 52–1	☐ –2	☐ –3
b) . . . The laws and court decisions about evidence and treatment of suspects prevent adequate investigations and convictions in order to control crime?........	☐ 53–1	☐ –2	☐ –3
c) . . . The police department does not have enough resources—men, cars, facilities, etc.—to do a good job in controlling crime?...	☐ 54–1	☐ –2	☐ –3
d) . . . Other city agencies do not have adequate resources to eliminate the social and economic conditions that breed crime?...	☐ 55–1	☐ –2	☐ –3

Now I would like to ask you some questions about your activities on the job.

17. How long have you been a policeman? _____ Years 56–
                                                   57–

18. What shift do you generally work—that is, is it the early morning, day, or evening shift?

Early morning............... ☐ 58–1

Day.............................. ☐ –2

Evening........................ ☐ –3

176

19a. Do you have a regular beat, do you have a desk job at this precinct, or do you do both?

Has regular beat............... ☐ 59-1 (ASK Q.19b)

Has desk job.................... ☐   -2 (SKIP TO Q.22)

Has both..:........................ ☐   -3 (ASK Q.19b)

b. How many months have you been on your present beat?   _____ Months 60–
                                                                                                       61–

20. Do you generally patrol by yourself, or with a partner?

By yourself.................... ☐ 62-1

With a partner............... ☐   -2

21a. Do you ever patrol with an officer who is a . . . (IF RESPONDENT IS WHITE, INSERT THE WORD "NEGRO" ☐. IF HE IS NEGRO, INSERT THE WORD "WHITE" ☐ AND CHECK HERE)

No ☐ 63-1 (SKIP TO Q.22)

Yes ☐   -2 (ASK Q.21b)

b. (IF "YES" TO Q.21a, ASK:) Do you travel with this officer most of the time, sometimes, or just once in a while?

Most of the time............... ☐ 64-1

Sometimes...................... ☐   -2

Once in a while................ ☐   -3

22. About what percentage of your work day is spent in a car, how much on foot in the community and how much in the station or other office of the area, and how much on other things? (RECORD PERCENTAGES BELOW)

	Percentage	
In a car...	_____	65– 66–
On foot in the community..................	_____	67– 68–
In the station or other office...............	_____	69– 70–
Other (SPECIFY)..............................	_____	71– 72–
Other (SPECIFY)..............................	_____	73– 74–
TOTAL	100%	

177

23. In some precincts it is more difficult than in others to get to know people. In your precinct, for example, about how many people among _____(GROUP)_____ do you know well enough to speak with whenever you see them? (WHEN NUMBER IS OBTAINED, CHECK THE APPROPRIATE BOX FOR THAT GROUP)

	None	1-5	6-10	11-25	26-50	51-100	101 Plus	DK·
a) Shop owners, managers, clerks............................	☐ 6-1	☐ -2	☐ -3	☐ -4	☐ -5	☐ 7-1	☐ -2	☐ -6
b) Important adult leaders in the neighborhoods.....	☐ 8-1	☐ -2	☐ -3	☐ -4	☐ -5	☐ 9-1	☐ -2	☐ -6
c) Residents in general......	☐ 10-1	☐ -2	☐ -3	☐ -4	☐ -5	☐ 11-1	☐ -2	☐ -6
d) Important teenage and youth leaders................	☐ 12-1	☐ -2	☐ -3	☐ -4	☐ -5	☐ 13-1	☐ -2	☐ -6
e) People from various government and private agencies who also work in the neighborhoods. For example, welfare, religious and utilities people...........................	☐ 14-1	☐ -2	☐ -3	☐ -4	☐ -5	☐ 15-1	☐ -2	☐ -6
f) The continual troublemakers..........................	☐ 16-1	☐ -2	☐ -3	☐ -4	☐ -5	☐ 17-1	☐ -2	☐ -6
g) Organizers of unlawful activities like crime syndicates, numbers rackets, drug pushing people.......	☐ 18-1	☐ -2	☐ -3	☐ -4	☐ -5	☐ 19-1	☐ -2	☐ -6

24. Is the crime rate in the neighborhood where you work . . . (READ STATEMENTS BELOW AND CHECK APPROPRIATE BOX)

. . . Among the highest in the city?...................................... ☐ 20-1

. . . Higher than average for this city?................................ ☐ -2

. . . About average for the city?... ☐ -3

. . . Below average for the city?... ☐ -4

. . . Very low compared to other parts of the city?............... ☐ -5

Don't know.. ☐ -6

25a. How would you characterize the composition of the neighborhood where you patrol or supervise? Is the neighborhood mostly, partly, very little residential in composition, or isn't it residential at all?

Mostly residential...................... ☐ 21-1

Partly residential...................... ☐ -2

Very little residential............... ☐ -3

Not residential at all................ ☐ -4

439

b. Are the non-residential parts of this neighborhood primarily retail or manufacturing establishments, or does it comprise some other types or segments?

Primarily retail.............................. ☐ 22–1

Primarily manufacturing............... ☐ –2

Other (SPECIFY)_____ ☐ –3

26. Some of the complaints often heard about policemen are listed below. Whether they are justified or not, can you tell me if you often, sometimes, seldom or never hear these complaints? (READ EACH STATEMENT BELOW AND CHECK APPROPRIATE BOX)

	Often	Some- times	Seldom	Never	DK
a) Policemen are physically brutal to people in the streets.............	☐ 23–1	☐ –2	☐ –3	☐ –4	☐ –6
b) They are corrupt and take bribes from those with money..	☐ 24–1	☐ –2	☐ –3	☐ –4	☐ –6
c) Policemen are generally hostile to the residents.................	☐ 25–1	☐ –2	☐ –3	☐ –4	☐ –6
d) They do not understand the problems of the residents........	☐ 26–1	☐ –2	☐ –3	☐ –4	☐ –6
e) They give too many tickets and do not help the residents..........	☐ 27–1	☐ –2	☐ –3	☐ –4	☐ –6
f) Policemen do not adequately prevent crime because they are not tough enough....................	☐ 28–1	☐ –2	☐ –3	☐ –4	☐ –6

27. Have you had any special training in riot control and prevention since you joined the police force?

Yes........................... ☐ 29–1

No....................... ☐   –2

Don't know............... ☐   –6

28a. Have you had any special training in general human relations, psychology, counseling, etc., since you joined the police force?

Yes........................... ☐ 30–1 (ASK Q.28b)

No........................... ☐   –2 (SKIP TO Q.29)

Don't know............... ☐   –6

b. (IF "YES" TO Q.28a, ASK:) In what areas? (SPECIFY) _____

_____

_____

31–
32–
33–
34–
35–
36–
37–

29. Do you live in the same area of the city in which you work most frequently?

Yes........................... ☐ 38–1

No........................... ☐   –2

179

440

30. Do any of your relatives live in the neighborhood in which you generally work?

Yes ☐ 39–1   No ☐ –2

31a. Do you have friends in the neighborhood where you work that you see socially when you are off duty?

Yes ☐ 40–1 (ASK Q.31b)   No ☐ –2 (SKIP TO Q.32a)

b. Do you see these people a lot, or just some of the time?

A lot... ☐ 41–1

Just some of the time............... ☐   –2

32a. Do you ever attend meetings of organizations in the neighborhood where you work?

Yes ☐ 42–1 (ASK Q.32b)   No ☐ –2 (SKIP TO Q.33)

b. Do you attend these meetings often, sometimes, or only seldom?

Often..................... ☐ 43–1

Sometimes............... ☐   –2

Seldom.................... ☐   –3

33. Each job has its advantages and disadvantages. Consider several aspects of your particular job as a policeman, compared to other jobs in this city. Are you generally very satisfied, somewhat satisfied, somewhat dissatisfied or very dissatisfied with how this job is treating you with respect to pay, for example?

	Very Satisfied	Somewhat Satisfied	Somewhat Dis-satisfied	Very Dis-satisfied	Don't Know
a) Pay...	☐ 44–1	☐ –2	☐ –3	☐ –4	☐ –6
b) How about working conditions?..............................	☐ 45–1	☐ –2	☐ –3	☐ –4	☐ –6
c) What about the other policemen with whom you have to work?..........................	☐ 46–1	☐ –2	☐ –3	☐ –4	☐ –6
d) How about the physical danger you often face?..............	☐ 47–1	☐ –2	☐ –3	☐ –4	☐ –6
e) The respect you get from citizens?....................................	☐ 48–1	☐ –2	☐ –3	☐ –4	☐ –6
f) The flexibility you have in doing your job?.........................	☐ 49–1	☐ –2	☐ –3	☐ –4	☐ –6
g) Your supervisors?.....................	☐ 50–1	☐ –2	☐ –3	☐ –4	☐ –6
h) What about the resources and facilities you have available to help you do your job?.............	☐ 51–1	☐ –2	☐ –3	☐ –4	☐ –6

180

EDUCATORS

In many neighborhoods, the schools are the largest local community institutions and the teachers and the professionals within these institutions generally know more about what goes on in the community than any other group.

1. How is it here in this neighborhood—do you feel that the school you are teaching in is a major force in the community?

    Yes ☐ 6–1

    No ☐ –2

2. As you see it, what are the major problems that face your school as it tries to fulfill its educational mission in this neighborhood?_____

    _____

    _____

3. What are the main strengths of this neighborhood which help the school to reach its educational objectives?_____

    _____

    _____

7–
8–
9–
10–
11–
12–
13–
14–
15–
16–
17–
18–
19–
20–

4. I am going to read you some statements that have been made about pupils in schools like this in other cities. In your view, is it mainly true for your school, partially true, or not true at all that . . . (READ EACH STATEMENT BELOW AND CHECK APPROPRIATE BOX)

	Mainly True	Partially True	Not True	Don't Know
a) . . . The pupils are uneducable and that teachers can do little more than maintain discipline?	☐ 21–1	☐ –2	☐ –3	☐ –6
b) . . . The pupils can be taught only by the most skillful of teachers who can arouse their interest?	☐ 22–1	☐ –2	☐ –3	☐ –6
c) . . . Pupils come into school with an interest in learning, but their preparation is so poor that they are hard to help?	☐ 23–1	☐ –2	☐ –3	☐ –6
d) . . . These are ordinary pupils with just about average interest in schooling and with average ability?	☐ 24–1	☐ –2	☐ –3	☐ –6
e) . . . Almost any teacher can teach these pupils successfully if he or she puts his mind to it and works hard at it?	☐ 25–1	☐ –2	☐ –3	☐ –6

181

442

f) . . . The pupils are above average in ability, but
are interested only in some things?............ ☐ 26-1   ☐ -2   ☐ -3   ☐ -6

g) . . . The pupils are above average in ability and
interest, and are generally cooperative
with teachers?.. ☐ 27-1   ☐ -2   ☐ -3   ☐ -6

5. Children often have personal and emotional problems at home or with other students in the
school that have a direct effect on the child's performance in school. Do you feel that it is your
job to teach only the subject matter, and that emotional problems should be resolved outside
the classroom by parents or psychologists; or, on the other hand, do you feel that a teacher
must pay particularly close attention to the pupils' emotional development because it is directly related to the learning process?

A teacher's job is to teach only the subject matter... ☐ 28-1

A teacher must pay close attention to emotional development of pupils........... ☐   -2

Neither.. ☐   -3

Don't know... ☐   -6

6. Compared to White parents of about the same economic status, are Negro parents more or
less concerned for the education and welfare of their children? In other words, do you feel
that . . . (READ STATEMENTS BELOW AND CHECK APPROPRIATE BOX)

. . . Negro parents are generally more concerned than Whites?..................... ☐ 29 1

. . . Negro parents are generally less concerned than White?........................ ☐   -2

. . . Both have about the same concern?... ☐   -3

Don't know... ☐   -6

*In some schools teachers have a great deal of contact with the parents of their pupils and in others
there is very little.*

30-
7a. Approximately, what proportion of your pupils' parents have you met?_____ Percent
31-

b. Have you visited any of your pupils' homes?

Yes ☐ 32-1 (ASK Q.7c)

No ☐   -2 (SKIP TO Q.7d)

c. (IF "YES" TO Q.7b, ASK:) Have you visited only a few or quite a few of your pupils' homes?

Only a few............................. ☐ 33-1 (ASK Q.7d)

Quite a few............................ ☐   -2 (ASK Q.7d)

d. About what percentage of your pupils' parents are members of the PTA?

_____ Percent 34-
35-

182

443

8. In talking with parents of your pupils, do you usually find that you have very little difficulty, some difficulty, or a great deal of difficulty in communicating with them?

Very little difficulty................................... □ 36–1

Some difficulty....................................... □ –2

A great deal of difficulty....................... □ –3

Don't know... □ –6

9. In some schools, the parents treat teachers with a great deal of respect, in other schools parents treat teachers with indifference, and in still others with hostility or contempt. How is it in this shcool?

Mostly respect....................................... □ 37–1

Mostly indifference............................... □ –2

Mostly hostility or contempt.................. □ –3

Don't know... □ –6

10. In Your opinion, do the parents mainly think of the teachers as "on their side" or as adversaries in this school?

Mostly on their side.............................. □ 38–1

Mostly as adversaries........................... □ –2

Don't know... □ –6

11. Do most of the pupils here regard most of their teachers mainly as friends, mainly as adversaries, or do you feel that they are mostly indifferent?

Mostly as friends.................................. □ 39–1

Mostly as adversaries........................... □ –2

Mostly indifferent................................. □ –3

Don't know... □ –6

12. Compared to the average school in this city, would you rate this particular school as superior, above average, average, below average or inferior to the other schools on . . . (READ EACH ITEM BELOW AND CHECK APPROPRIATE BOX)

	Superior	Above Average	Average	Below Average	Inferior	Don't Know
a) . . . Overall quality?...	□ 40–1	□ –2	□ –3	□ –4	□ –5	□ –6
b) . . . Adequacy of physical plant?............	□ 41–1	□ –2	□ –3	□ –4	□ –5	□ –6
c) . . . Adequacy of supplies?..................	□ 42–1	□ –2	□ –3	□ –4	□ –5	□ –6
d) . . . Textbooks?..........	□ 43–1	□ –2	□ –3	□ –4	□ –5	□ –6
e) . . . Quality of teaching staff?.............	□ 44–1	□ –2	□ –3	□ –4	□ –5	□ –6
f) . . . Extra curricular activities?............	□ 45–1	□ –2	□ –3	□ –4	□ –5	□ –6
g) . . . Counseling and guidance?............	□ 46–1	□ –2	□ –3	□ –4	□ –5	□ –6
h) . . . Library for students?.................	□ 47–1	□ –2	□ –3	□ –4	□ –5	□ –6

183

13. What do you think about the role of the community, generally, as it relates to the schools? Do you strongly agree, slightly agree, slightly disagree or strongly disagree that . . . (READ STATEMENTS BELOW AND CHECK APPROPRIATE BOX)

	Strongly Agree	Slightly Agree	Slightly Disagree	Strongly Disagree	Don't Know
a) . . . Many communities provide such a terrible environment for the pupils that education doesn't do much good in the end?	☐ 48–1	☐ –2	☐ –3	☐ –4	☐ –6
b) . . . If the average community was given more voice in running the school, it would better meet the needs of the pupils?	☐ 49–1	☐ –2	☐ –3	☐ –4	☐ –6
c) . . . Most of the people in the average community are hostile to the efforts of the city to educate the children?	☐ 50–1	☐ –2	☐ –3	☐ –4	☐ –6
d) . . . Most parents try to help their children get a good education but far too many other influences distract the pupils?	☐ 51–1	☐ –2	☐ –3	☐ –4	☐ –6

14. Some schools are trying to give the parents and other community residents more control over running the school in their neighborhoods, even sometimes letting parents come into the classroom to help with the teaching and other work as sub-professionals. Do you strongly agree, slightly agree, slightly disagree or strongly disagree that this might be a good policy in general?

Strongly agree...................................... ☐ 52 1

Slightly agree.. ☐ –2

Slightly disagree.................................... ☐ –3

Strongly disagree.................................. ☐ –4

Don't know.. ☐ –6

Now I would like to ask you questions about yourself:

15. How long have you been teaching in this school? _____ Years 53–
          54–

16. How long have you been teaching altogether? _____ Years 55–
          56–

184

17. Do you look upon your teaching position as a permanent career choice, a temporary career while you wait for or work for a better position, or do you look upon it as a career which you can take up when you want to, but to which you are not particularly committed?

Permanent career choice.. ☐ 57-1

Temporary career... ☐ -2

Something you can take up when you want to............... ☐ -3

Don't know... ☐ -6

18. How about your position as teacher in this school—is it an assignment you want to have as long as you are teaching, or would you prefer to have some other teaching assignment?

Hold as long as I am teaching............... ☐ 58-1

Prefer some other assignment.............. ☐ -2

Don't know.. ☐ -6

19. With respect to this particular teaching position, are you very satisfied, somewhat satisfied, somewhat dissatisfied or very dissatisfied with . . . (READ EACH STATEMENT AND CHECK APPROPRIATE BOX BELOW)

	Very Satisfied	Somewhat Satisfied	Somewhat Dis-satisfied	Very Dis-satisfied	Don't Know
a) . . . The position in general?.......	☐ 59-1	☐ -2	☐ -3	☐ -4	☐ -6
b) . . . Its salary?.............................	☐ 60-1	☐ -2	☐ -3	☐ -4	☐ -6
c) . . . Your colleagues?...................	☐ 61-1	☐ -2	☐ -3	☐ -4	☐ -6
d) . . . Your supervisors?.................	☐ 62-1	☐ -2	☐ -3	☐ -4	☐ -6
e) . . . Your working conditions in general?...............................	☐ 63-1	☐ -2	☐ -3	☐ -4	☐ -6
f) . . . The teaching load?...............	☐ 64-1	☐ -2	☐ -3	☐ -4	☐ -6
g) . . . The pupils?...........................	☐ 65-1	☐ -2	☐ -3	☐ -4	☐ -6
h) . . . The community?...................	☐ 66-1	☐ -2	☐ -3	☐ -4	☐ -6
i) . . . The flexibility permitted in the classroom?.....................	☐ 67-1	☐ -2	☐ -3	☐ -4	☐ -6

20. Has your professional training included . . . (READ EACH STATEMENT AND CHECK APPROPRIATE BOX)

	Yes	No
a) . . . Special training for work with culturally deprived youngsters?.........	☐ 68-1	☐ -2
b) . . . Training in working with slow learners?..	☐ 69-1	☐ -2
c) . . . Training for work with exceptionally bright students?.....................	☐ 70-1	☐ -2
d) . . . Training in working with special emotional problems of students?......	☐ 71-1	☐ -2

185

21. Do you live in the same area of the city in which most of your pupils live?

        Yes ☐ 72–1

        No ☐   –2

22. Do you think, generally speaking, that people can control what happens, or are they controlled largely by forces they cannot fully understand or affect? That is, do you feel that people . . . . (READ STATEMENTS BELOW AND CHECK APPROPRIATE BOX)

        a) . . . Largely can control what happens?...................... ☐ 73–1

        b) . . . Can somewhat control what happens?................. ☐   –2

        c) . . . Can control very little of what happens?.............. ☐   –3

        d) . . . Can't control what happens at all?....................... ☐   –4

        Don't know.. ☐   –6

23. Would you say that, in general, you like and get along well with all, most, some or only a few of your pupils?

        All.................. ☐ 74–1

        Most.............. ☐   –2

        Some............. ☐   –3

        Few............... ☐   –4

        Don't know..... ☐   –6

                                                                                              Card 4   5–4

24a. In your estimation, is your school teaching pupils what they are interested in learning or doing, or are most pupils much more interested in other things that are not considered in the classroom?

        Teaching what pupils are interested in ☐ 6–1 (SKIP TO Q.25a)

        Pupils more interested in other things ☐   –2 (ASK Q.24b)

  b. (IF "PUPILS MORE INTERESTED IN OTHER THINGS", ASK:) What kinds of things are pupils more concerned about these days?_____

                                                  7–

                                                  8–

                                                  9–

                                                 10–

                                                 11–

                                                 12–

                                                 13–

25a. Is there any opportunity for teachers in your school to help with programs that are designed to give assistance outside the school system to young people in the neighborhood (Community Action Agencies, Tutorial projects, etc.)?

        No ☐ 14– (SKIP TO Q.26a)

        Yes ☐   –2 (ASK Q.25b)

  b. (IF "YES" TO Q.25a, ASK:) Does your school encourage teachers to become involved in these activities?

        No ☐ 15–1

        Yes ☐   –2

186

447

SOCIAL WORKERS

I would first like to ask you some questions about your job.

1. As a social worker in this city, what are your major problems?_____ 6–
   7–
_____ 8–
   9–
_____ 10–
   11–
_____ 12–

2. What is your case load – in other words, how many people do you work with or serve?

   13–
   _____ People 14–
   15–

3. What percentage of your clients are Negro?

   16–
   _____ Percent 17–

4. On the average, how often do you visit with each client or group? 18–
   19–
   _____ Times per week 20–
   21–
   _____ Times per month 22–
   Other (SPECIFY): 23–
   _____ Per _____ 24–

5. On the average, about how long do you spend with each client or group that you visit –
   what is the length of your call?

   _____ Hours 25–
   26–

6. About what percentage of your contacts with clients are in the clients home or in his
   neighborhood?

   _____ Percent of total 27–
   28–

7. What is the time lag between referral and action?

   ___ Days $\begin{array}{l}29–\\30–\end{array}$ ___ Weeks $\begin{array}{l}31–\\32–\end{array}$ ___ Months $\begin{array}{l}33–\\34–\end{array}$

8. Is it very difficult, slightly difficult or easy for a potential client to gain the services of
   your agency?

   Very difficult..................... ☐ 35–1

   Slightly difficult................ ☐ –2

   Easy................................. ☐ –3

   Don't know........................ ☐ –6 187

448

9. About what percent of your working time do you spend in your office?... _____ Percent   36–
                                                                                                 37–

10. About what percent of your working time do you spend in the field?... _____ Percent   38–
                                                                                                  39–

100   Percent

11. Following is a list of complaints one often hears in talking to social workers. Please tell me whether each statement that I read is a very serious, somewhat serious, or not at all serious drawback to your doing your job. (READ EACH STATEMENT AND CHECK APPROPRIATE BOX)

	Very Serious	Somewhat Serious	Not Serious	Don't Know
a) Lack of money for clients............................	☐ 40–1	☐ –2	☐ –3	☐ –6
b) Lack of time..	☐ 41–1	☐ –2	☐ –3	☐ –6
c) Poor supervision from top management of agency..	☐ 42–1	☐ –2	☐ –3	☐ –6
d) Hampering rules and regulations..................	☐ 43–1	☐ –2	☐ –3	☐ –6
e) Lack of cooperation from city government...	☐ 44–1	☐ –2	☐ –3	☐ –6
f) Agency disorganization...............................	☐ 45–1	☐ –2	☐ –3	☐ –6
g) Lack of agency enthusiasm...........................	☐ 46–1	☐ –2	☐ –3	☐ –6

12. There are groups in every city that get better and quicker service from agencies than others. Please indicate which of the following groups in your area tend to get better treatment than most, which get average treatment, and which get the poorer treatment. (READ EACH GROUP BELOW AND CHECK APPROPRIATE BOX)

	Better Treatment	Average Treatment	Poorer Treatment	Don't Know
a) Aged persons...	☐ 47–1	☐ –2	☐ –3	☐ –6
b) Teenagers..	☐ 48–1	☐ –2	☐ –3	☐ –6
c) Urban Negroes...	☐ 49–1	☐ –2	☐ –3	☐ –6
d) Middle class people......................................	☐ 50–1	☐ –2	☐ –3	☐ –6
e) Mentally ill people..	☐ 51–1	☐ –2	☐ –3	☐ –6
f) Juvenile delinquents.....................................	☐ 52–1	☐ –2	☐ –3	☐ –6
g) Working class Whites....................................	☐ 53–1	☐ –2	☐ –3	☐ –6

188

13. In your experience, how true is each of the following complaints that are often heard from social workers about the clients they serve? Is it mostly true, partially true, or not true at all that (STATEMENT)? (READ STATEMENTS BELOW AND CHECK APPROPRIATE BOX)

	Mostly True	Partially True	Not True	Don't Know
a) Clients in general don't do enough to improve themselves?....................................	☐ 54–1	☐ –2	☐ –3	☐ –6
b) Negro clients are generally harder to reach?...	☐ 55–1	☐ –2	☐ –3	☐ –6
c) It is more difficult to get resources for Negro clients?...	☐ 56–1	☐ –2	☐ –3	☐ –6
d) Clients in general tend to take your services for granted?..	☐ 57–1	☐ –2	☐ –3	☐ –6
e) Negro clients are often especially arrogant?...	☐ 58–1	☐ –2	☐ –3	☐ –6

Now I am going to ask you a series of questions about your approach to your job. Each question will be phrased in such a way as to present two opposing sides on the same issue. Please indicate with which side you tend to agree.

14. As a social worker, is it better to remain detached from clients in order to remain objective, or is it better to try to put yourself in your client's shoes in order to become sympathetic with his situation? In other words, do you feel it is better for a social worker to be largely objective, largely subjective, or about equal in these matters?

Largely objective .... ☐ 59–1

About equal............................. ☐   –2

Largely subjective.................... ☐   –3

Don't know.............................. ☐   –6

15. Is the essence of social work to teach the poor the best way to live, or is the essence to help give the poor the means to live as they choose? In other words, is it best to mostly teach, to mostly give means to live, or about equal amounts of both?

Mostly teach............................. ☐ 60–1

Give equal amounts of both....... ☐   –2

Mostly give means to live.......... ☐   –3

Don't know............................... ☐   –6

189

450

16. Should aid to people living below the poverty level be made contingent on their showing a real desire to improve themselves, or should aid be given to all that need it, no matter what their apparent level of motivation? Putting it another way, should aid be given only to those who make a real effort to help themselves; only to those who show at least some effort to help themselves; to everyone who needs help except the most flagrant loafers, or should aid be given to all who need it regardless of their efforts to help themselves?

Aid only to those who make a real effort......:... ☐ 61-1

Aid only to those who show some motivation... ☐ -2

Aid to most, except flagrant loafers................. ☐ -3

Aid to all... ☐ -4

Don't know... ☐ -6

17. Are there rules and regulations that you, as a social worker, feel you must follow in all cases, regardless of the client, or do you feel it is best to ignore rules and regulations when it seems such is warranted by circumstances?

Usually obey.. ☐ 62-1

Generally make decisions largely on circumstances ☐   -2

Don't know.. ☐   -6

Now, about people in general.

18. Do you feel most people are basically good and only get into trouble when under great stress, or do you feel that most people are essentially out for themselves alone and must be carefully socialized and controlled in order to keep society functioning? Putting it a bit differently, all in all, are most people basically good; only somewhat good, only somewhat bad, or are most people basically bad?

Basically good................... ☐ 63-1

Somewhat good................. ☐   -2

Somewhat bad.................. ☐   -3

Basically bad.................... ☐   -4

Don't know....................... ☐   -6

190

19. Do you believe that people can <u>largely</u> control what happens to them, control <u>somewhat</u> these things or people can do <u>very little</u> to control what happens to them?

Largely can control............... ☐ 64–1

Control somewhat................. ☐ –2

Control very little................ ☐ –3

Don't know........................... ☐ –6

Now, I would like to ask you some questions about attitudes towards Negroes that specifically relate to social work, as some social workers sometimes find it hard to work with Negro clients.

20. With regard to your clients do you feel:

a) Negroes are more difficult to reason with than Whites?

Yes...................................... ☐ 65–1

No.. ☐ –2

Don't know........................... ☐ –6

b) Negroes are, overall, more difficult to work with than Whites?

Yes...................................... ☐ 66–1

No.. ☐ –2

Don't know........................... ☐ –6

c) Negroes are more apt to cheat on the system?

Yes...................................... ☐ 67–1

No.. ☐ –2

Don't know........................... ☐ –6

d) Do you feel less safe walking through Negro neighborhoods than White ones?

Yes...................................... ☐ 68–1

No.. ☐ –3

Don't know........................... ☐ –6

e) Are you less optimistic about the outcome of Negro cases than White cases?

Yes...................................... ☐ 69–1

No.. ☐ –2

Don't know........................... ☐ –6

191

452

f) Do you pay less attention to Negro cases than to White ones?

Yes ☐ 6-1   No ☐ -2   Don't know ☐ -6

g) Is your manner less relaxed when working with Negroes?

Yes ☐ 7-1   No ☐ -2   Don't know ☐ -6

21. What is the major function of this agency? That is, does it do mainly case work, group work, community organization, or does it do something else?

Case work................................. ☐ 8-1

Group work................................ ☐ -2

Community organization............. ☐ -3

Other (SPECIFY)_____ ☐ -4

22. Does your <u>agency</u> work with . . . (READ LIST AND CHECK AS MANY AS NECESSARY BELOW)

23. How about you—which of these do <u>you</u> work with? (READ LIST AND CHECK AS MANY AS NECESSARY BELOW)

	Q.22 Agency Works With		Q.23 Respondent Works With	
a) Infants?..	☐ -1	9–	☐ -1	10–
b) Youths?..	☐ -2	11–	☐ -2	12–
c) Adolescents?..................................	☐ -3	13–	☐ -3	14–
d) Adults?..	☐ -4	15–	☐ -4	16–
e) Aged?..	☐ -5	17–	☐ -5	18–

24. Which of the following best characterize your job? (CHECK ONE UNLESS RESPONDENT HAS TWO SEPARATE JOBS.) Do you, for the most part, do . . .

. . . Case work (welfare, medical, adoption, neglect, legal aid, school, etc.)?... ☐ -1   19–

. . . Counselling (marriage, jobs, school, birth control, etc.)?........................ ☐ -2   20–

. . . Psychiatric social work?... ☐ -3

. . . Recreation work?.. ☐ -4

. . . Group work (senior citizens, gangs, etc.)?.. ☐ -5

. . . Community organization work?.. ☐ -1   21–

. . . Jack-of-all trades work (like CAA counselor or detached youth worker)?... ☐ -2   22–

192

453

EMPLOYERS

As part of our survey of local communities throughout the country, we are interested in the way in which companies view their local labor market.

We are mainly interested in interviewing persons who have charge of setting employment policy or in actually hiring employees. We were told that your position involves such duties.

1. First of all, in what ways are you involved in this company's employment policies and practices?

6–
7–
8–
9–
10–
11–
12–

INTERVIEWER: IF RESPONDENT GIVES REPLY WHICH SHOWS THAT HE DOES NOT EITHER SET POLICY, PARTICIPATE IN THE SETTING OF POLICY, OR ADMINISTER EMPLOYMENT FOR THIS COMPANY, TERMINATE INTERVIEW. HOWEVER, BEFORE LEAVING GET THE NAME OF THE PERSON WHO HAS THIS RESPONSIBILITY AND OBTAIN AN INTERVIEW FROM HIM.

2. As an employer in this city, what are your major problems?

13–
14–
15–
16–
17–
18–
19–

3. How many employees does your company have here in (CITY)?

_____ Employees

20–
21–
22–
23–
24–

4a. Does your company have any contracts with labor unions covering employees in this city?

No ☐ 25–1

Yes ☐ –2

193

5. I would like you to consider three classes of employees: Professional and white collar workers; skilled workers; and semi- and unskilled workers.

How does your company usually go about getting new workers in each of these three categories? I will read you a list of ways used by companies and I want you to tell me whether this is a means which is employed by your company.

a. (1) First, let us consider <u>professional and white collar</u> employees. In order to get new employees of this type do you use . . .

	Yes	No	Most effective (CHECK ONE)
. . . Want ads in newspapers?	☐ 26-1	☐ -2	☐ 32-1
. . . Labor unions?	☐ 27-1	☐ -2	☐ -2
. . . State employment services?	☐ 28-1	☐ -2	☐ -3
. . . Private employment services?	☐ 29-1	☐ -2	☐ -4
. . . The system of asking other employees to get referrals?	☐ 30-1	☐ -2	☐ 33-1
. . . Signs posted outside of the plant?	☐ 31-1	☐ -2	☐ -2

(2) Now which <u>one</u> of the means your company uses is most effective? (CHECK ABOVE)

b. (1) Now let us consider <u>skilled</u> workers. To get new employees in this group do you use . . .

	Yes	No	Most effective (CHECK ONE)
. . . Want ads in newspapers?	☐ 34-1	☐ -2	☐ 40-1
. . . Labor unions?	☐ 35-1	☐ -2	☐ -2
. . . State employment services?	☐ 36-1	☐ -2	☐ -3
. . . Private employment services?	☐ 37-1	☐ -2	☐ -4
. . . The system of asking other employees to get referrals?	☐ 38-1	☐ -2	☐ 41-1
. . . Signs posted outside of the plant?	☐ 39-1	☐ -2	☐ -2

(2) Now which <u>one</u> of the means is most effective? (CHECK ABOVE)

c. (1) Finally, how do you go about getting <u>semi-skilled and unskilled</u> workers? Do you use . . .

	Yes	No	Most effective (CHECK ONE)
. . . Want ads in newspapers?	☐ 42-1	☐ -2	☐ 48-1
. . . Labor unions?	☐ 43-1	☐ -2	☐ -2
. . . State employment services?	☐ 44-1	☐ -2	☐ -3
. . . Private employment services?	☐ 45-1	☐ -2	☐ -4
. . . The system of asking other employees to get referrals?	☐ 46-1	☐ -2	☐ 49-1
. . . Signs posted outside of the plant?	☐ 47-1	☐ -2	☐ -2

(2) Now which <u>one</u> of the means is most effective? (CHECK ABOVE)

194

6. In choosing new employees from among applicants, what do you usually regard as important? That is, for <u>white collar workers and professional employees</u> do you consider (<u>INSERT ITEMS LISTED BELOW</u>) as very important, somewhat important or not important at all?

	Very Important	Somewhat Important	Not at all Important
a) Previous experience	☐ 50–1	☐ –2	☐ –3
b) Recommendations	☐ 51–1	☐ –2	☐ –3
c) Performance on tests of ability	☐ 52–1	☐ –2	☐ –3
d) Age	☐ 53–1	☐ –2	☐ –3

Now for <u>unskilled workers,</u> do you consider (INSERT ITEMS LISTED BELOW) as very important, somewhat important or not important at all?

a) Previous experience	☐ 54–1	☐ –2	☐ –3
b) Recommendations	☐ 55–1	☐ –2	☐ –3
c) Performance on tests of ability	☐ 56–1	☐ –2	☐ –3
d) Age	☐ 57–1	☐ –2	☐ –3

Finally, for <u>unskilled workers,</u> do you consider (<u>INSERT ITEMS LISTED BELOW</u>) as very important, somewhat important or not important at all?

a) Previous experience	☐ 58–1	☐ –2	☐ –3
b) Recommendations	☐ 59–1	☐ –2	☐ –3
c) Performance on tests of ability	☐ 60–1	☐ –2	☐ –3
d) Age	☐ 61–1	☐ –2	☐ –3

7a. Do you get any Negro applicants for jobs here?

       No ☐ 62–1 (SKIP TO Q.8)

       Yes ☐   –2 (ASK Q.7b & 7c)

b. Out of the last 20 people <u>applying</u> for work in each of the following groups, about how many were Negro . . .

                                              63–

. . . Among professional and white collar applying? _____ People 64–

                                              65–

. . . Among skilled workers applying? _____ People 66–

                                              67–

. . . Among unskilled workers applying? _____ People 68–

c. Out of the last 20 people <u>hired</u> in each group, about how many were Negro . . .

. . . Among professional and white collar hired? _____ People 69–

                                              70–

. . . Among skilled workers hired? _____ People 71–

                                              72–

. . . Among unskilled workers hired? _____ People 73–

                                              74–

                                              195

8. What would you estimate the proportion of Negroes to be among your employees on these three levels: 6–

    a) Professional and white collar? _____ Percent 7–
                                           8–
    b) Skilled workers?..................... _____ Percent 9–
    c) Unskilled workers?................ _____ Percent 10–
                                           11–

9. Some companies have been going out of their way lately to hire Negroes whenever possible. Is this mainly true, partially true, or not true at all of your company?

             Mainly true.................. ☐ 12–1

             Partially true............... ☐ –2

             Not true at all.............. ☐ –3

10. Many companies who have tried to hire Negroes have given up because their workers objected so strongly to working with Negroes. How do you think your employees would react to Negroes working? Would they have a negative or positive feeling or would they feel indifferent if Negroes worked . . . (READ GROUPS BELOW AND CHECK APPROPRIATE BOX)

	Negative	Indifferent	Positive	DK
. . . As professional and white collar workers?	☐ 13–1	☐ –2	☐ –3	☐ –6
. . . As skilled workers?....................................	☐ 14–1	☐ –2	☐ –3	☐ –6
. . . As semi-skilled and unskilled workers?.........	☐ 15–1	☐ –2	☐ –3	☐ –6

11. Other companies which have tried to go out of their way to hire Negroes have found that there were very few qualified Negroes to hire. In your experience is this statement justified in the hiring of . . . (READ GROUPS BELOW AND CHECK APPROPRIATE BOX)

	Justified	Unjustified	DK
. . . Professional and white collar workers?........................	☐ 16–1	☐ –2	☐ –6
. . . Skilled workers?..	☐ 17–1	☐ –2	☐ –6
. . . Semi-skilled and unskilled workers?............................	☐ 18–1	☐ –2	☐ –6

12. Do you think that companies in this city have a social responsibility to make strong efforts to provide employment to Negroes and other minority groups?

             No........................... ☐ 19–1

             Yes......................... ☐ –2

             Don't know............... ☐ –6

196

13. Some employers have had trouble with Negro workers. Therefore, they feel it is best to be especially aware of the potential problems with Negroes so that, if necessary, they can take special measures for the good of the company. Please indicate whether you strongly agree, slightly agree, slightly disagree or strongly disagree with the following statements that concern this problem. (READ STATEMENTS AND CHECK APPROPRIATE BOX)

a. Negroes are apt to be less well trained than Whites, so hiring many Negroes will either decrease production or increase training costs.

Strongly agree...................................... □ 20–1

Slightly agree .... □   –2

Slightly disagree.................................. □   –3

Strongly disagree................................. □   –4

Don't know.. □   –6

b. Negroes generally tend not to take orders and instructions as well as Whites and, therefore, to hire too many of them may raise costs of production.

Strongly agree...................................... □ 21–1

Slightly agree...................................... □   –2

Slightly disagree.................................. □   –3

Strongly disagree................................. □   –4

Don't know.. □   –6

c. Since many Negroes have been involved in civil rights demonstrations and acts of civil disobedience, by hiring too many Negroes you risk bringing trouble makers and agitators into your company.

Strongly agree...................................... □ 22–1

Slightly agree...................................... □   –2

Slightly disagree.................................. □   –3

Strongly disagree................................. □   –4

Don't know.. □   –6

d. Since Negro crime rates are generally higher than White crime rates, hiring many Negroes could easily lead to increased theft and vandalism in the comapny.

Strongly agree...................................... □ 23–1

Slightly agree...................................... □   –2

Slightly disagree.................................. □   –3

Strongly disagree................................. □   –4

Don't know.. □   –6

197

e. Negroes are apt to have a higher rate of absenteeism, therefore, hiring too many Negroes may upset production schedules.

Strongly agree..................................... ☐ 24–1

Slightly agree...................................... ☐   –2

Slightly disagree.................................. ☐   –3

Strongly disagree................................. ☐   –4

Don't know.. ☐   –6

(INTERVIEWER CHECK)

Establishment in top 10 sample... ☐ 25–1

Establishment in sample of firms with 100 or more employees............ ☐   –2

198

RETAIL MERCHANTS

Sometimes store owners and operators have a better knowledge of what is going on in the neighborhood than most city officials or even the average resident. We are interviewing retail merchants in this and other areas throughout the country for this reason.

1. As a retail merchant in this city, what are your major problems?_____ 6–
   _____ 7–
   _____ 8–
   _____ 9–
   10–
   Is there anything else? (PROBE)_____ 11–
   _____ 12–

2. Some merchants in neighborhoods like this feel that the main thing is to provide special services to their customers, like staying open late, cashing payroll checks, providing credit, and so on. Do you agree strongly, agree slightly, disagree slightly, or disagree strongly with this feeling?

Agree strongly	☐	13–1
Agree slightly	☐	–2
Disagree slightly	☐	–3
Disagree strongly	☐	–4
Don't know	☐	–6

3. Other merchants say the main thing to do is to buy bargain merchandise so that they can keep their retail prices low enough for people to afford. Do you agree strongly, agree slightly, disagree slightly, or disagree strongly with this feeling?

Agree strongly	☐	14–1
Agree slightly	☐	–2
Disagree slightly	☐	–3
Disagree strongly	☐	–4
Don't know	☐	–6

4. Still others feel that the best way to stay in business in a neighborhood like this is to bargain with each customer and take whatever breaks he can get. Do you agree strongly, agree slightly, disagree slightly, or disagree strongly with this feeling?

Agree strongly	☐	15–1
Agree slightly	☐	–2
Disagree slightly	☐	–3
Disagree strongly	☐	–4
Don't know	☐	–6

199

5. Finally, other merchants feel that in business the main thing in a neighborhood like this is to learn how to price their merchandise to cover the extra costs of poor credit risks, petty thievery, and the likes. Do you agree strongly, agree slightly, disagree slightly, or disagree strongly with this feeling?

Agree strongly...................................... □ 16–1

Agree slightly...................................... □   –2

Disagree slightly.................................. □   –3

Disagree strongly................................. □   –4

Don't know... □   –6

6. Here are some services that some stores often, sometimes or never extend to their customers. How about yourself. Do you . . . (READ STATEMENTS AND CHECK APPROPRIATE BOX)

	Often	Sometimes	Never
a) . . . Cash payroll checks?	□ 17–1	□ –2	□ –3
b) . . . Help fill out applications and other forms?	□ 18–1	□ –2	□ –3
c) . . . Extend credit to people other stores wouldn't help?	□ 19–1	□ –2	□ –3
d) . . . Make contributions to local churches and charities?	□ 20–1	□ –2	□ –3
e) . . . Give advice to customers on personal problems?	□ 21–1	□ –2	□ –3

7a. Do you have customers whom you could call you personal friends?

Yes □ 22–1 (ASK Q.7b)

No □   –2 (SKIP TO Q.8)

b. How many customers whom you consider personal friends do you have?

_____ People 23–
24–

Some store owners complain about problems they have in dealing with Negro customers. How about your dealings with Negro customers? In other words, for each of the following statements that I will read to you, do you agree strongly, agree slightly, disagree slightly, or disagree strongly? (READ EACH STATEMENT AND CHECK APPROPRIATE BOX)

8. Some merchants claim that Negroes are poorer credit risks than Whites, and therefore, they should be given less credit and charged higher interest rates. How do you feel – do you . . . (READ LIST)

. . . Agree strongly?.............................. □ 25–1

. . . Agree slightly?.............................. □   –2

. . . Disagree slightly?.......................... □   –3

. . . Disagree strongly?......................... □   –4

Don't know................................... □   –6

200

9. Some merchants claim that Negroes are less apt to appreciate a good bargain than Whites; therefore, they are more apt to be cheated than Whites. How do you feel about this statement. Do you . . . (READ LIST)

. . . Agree strongly?.............................. ☐ 26-1

. . . Agree slightly?.............................. ☐   -2

. . . Disagree slightly?.......................... ☐   -3

. . . Disagree strongly?......................... ☐   -4

    Don't know................................... ☐   -6

10. Some store owners say Negroes are less likely to complain if they feel they are not treated fairly; and therefore, they are less likely to be treated as fairly as Whites. Do you . . . (READ LIST)

. . . Agree strongly?.............................. ☐ 27-1

. . . Agree slightly?.............................. ☐   -2

. . . Disagree slightly?.......................... ☐   -3

. . . Disagree strongly?......................... ☐   -4

    Don't know................................... ☐   -6

11. Merchants sometimes complain that because Negroes are more likely to be involved in shoplifting and vandalism than Whites, it is necessary to keep a watchful eye on them when they are in the store. How do you feel about this? Do you . . .

. . . Agree strongly?.............................. ☐ 28-1

. . . Agree slightly?.............................. ☐   -2

. . . Disagree slightly?.......................... ☐   -3

. . . Disagree strongly?......................... ☐   -4

    Don't know................................... ☐   -6

12. Store owners who have locations in Negro areas of the city often spend a lot of money making their stores burglar-proof because Negro neighborhoods are high crime areas. These store owners feel they are acting wisely. How do you agree with this? Do you . . .

. . . Agree strongly?.............................. ☐ 29-1

. . . Agree slightly?.............................. ☐   -2

. . . Disagree slightly?.......................... ☐   -3

. . . Disagree strongly?......................... ☐   -4

    Don't know................................... ☐   -6

J10-875 O - 68 - 14

13. Sometimes you hear that Negroes are more likely to pass bad checks. Therefore, it is best not to cash their personal checks. How do you feel about this statement?

    Agree strongly....................................... □ 30–1

    Agree slightly....................................... □   –2

    Disagree slightly................................... □   –3

    Disagree strongly.................................. □   –4

    Don't know.. □   –6

14. Some merchants feel that since Negroes many times seemingly don't care much about good manners, there is no special need to make an effort to treat them as politely as Whites. How do you agree with this?

    Agree strongly....................................... □ 31–1

    Agree slightly....................................... □   –2

    Disagree slightly................................... □   –3

    Disagree strongly.................................. □   –6

    Don't know.. □   –6

15. Finally, some people feel that, because Negroes are seemingly so different from Whites, there is no point in trying to be friends with people of another race or color. How strongly do you agree or disagree with this?

    Agree strongly....................................... □ 32–1

    Agree slightly....................................... □   –2

    Disagree slightly................................... □   –3

    Disagree strongly.................................. □   –4

    Don't know.. □   –6

16a. Last summer, did your store suffer damage from vandalism?

        Yes ☐ 33–1 (ASK Q.16b)

        No   ☐ –2 (SKIP TO Q.17a)

b. (IF "YES" TO Q.16a, ASK:) How much damage occurred?

34–
35–
36–
37–
38–
39–
40–

_____

_____

_____

c. Do you feel that the damage was especially directed at your store, or was it a result of more general disturbances?

        Damage done especially directed.............................. ☐ 41–1

        Damage result of more general disturbances............ ☐ –2

d. Why do you feel that way?_____

42–
43–
44–
45–
46–
47–
48–

_____

_____

_____

                                          (ASK Q.17a)

17a. (ASK EVERYONE) if there were a riot in this section of the city, do you expect that your store would be damaged?

        Yes ☐ 49–1

        No   ☐ –2

b. Why?_____

50–
51–
52–
53–
54–
55–
56–

_____

_____

_____

c. Have you taken any special precautions to protect your store in case there are riots here in the future?

        Yes ☐ 57–1

        No   ☐ –2

203

464

18. Store owners and managers usually have some complaints about their customers. Would you say that it is largely true, only partially true, or not true at all that . . . (READ EACH STATEMENT BELOW AND CHECK THE APPROPRIATE BOX)

	Largely True	Partially True	Not True At All	Don't Know
a) . . . Customers around here are rude to retail merchants?.................................	☐ 58–1	☐ –2	☐ –3	☐ –6
b) . . . Customers in this neighborhood try to take advantage of shopkeepers?...............	☐ 59–1	☐ –2	☐ –3	☐ –6
c) . . . Customers hereabouts are slow in paying bills?.............................	☐ 60–1	☐ –2	☐ –3	☐ –6
d) . . . Customers around here often try to steal from the stores?.............................	☐ 61–1	☐ –2	☐ –3	☐ –6
e) . . . Customers in this neighborhood are hostile to shopkeepers?.............................	☐ 62–1	☐ –2	☐ –3	☐ –6

19a. There has always been a certain amount of disagreement between many merchants and their customers. Now, with regard to prices and quality of merchandise, do you feel that the merchants are trying to take advantage of the customers, that the customers around here are trying to take advantage of the merchants, or is it about equal?

Most merchants take advantage of customers.. ☐ 63–1

About equal.. ☐ –2

Most customers take advantage of merchants.. ☐ –3

Neither taking advantage of either... ☐ –4

Don't know... ☐ –6

b. With regard to manners, do you feel the merchants hereabouts are impolite to the customers, that the customers are impolite to the merchants, or is it about equal?

Most merchants are impolite to the customers... ☐ 64–1

About equal.. ☐ –2

Most customers are impolite to the merchants... ☐ –3

Neither, both are polite... ☐ –4

Don't know... ☐ –6

c. With regard to credit, do you feel that the merchants around here charge too much interest, that the customers generally are bad credit risks and should be charged high interest rates, or that there is a pretty equal balance on this score?

Most merchants charge too much interest.. ☐ 65–1

About equal.. ☐ –2

Customers bad credit risks and should be charged higher interest rates........... ☐ –3

Don't know... ☐ –6

204

I would now like to ask you some specific questions about your store and your job in it.

20. Do you personally deal with customers as they come in?

Yes ☐ 66–1

No ☐   –2

21a. Do you live in this neighborhood?

Yes ☐ 67–1 (SKIP TO Q.22)

No ☐   –2 (ASK Q.21b)

  b. How far away do you live? _____ Miles 68–
69–

22. Which of the following best describes your store? (READ LIST AND CHECK APPROPRIATE BOX)

Small grocery store... ☐ 70–1

Supermarket.. ☐   –2

Hard goods store (furniture, appliances, etc.)....................................... ☐   –3

Soft goods store (clothes, linen, etc.)... ☐   –4

Restaurant, snack shop, bar.. ☐   –5

Liquor store... ☐ 71–1

Car dealer... ☐   –2

Drug store.. ☐   –3

Novelty shop.. ☐   –4

Department store or Discount house (variety of goods)..................... ☐   –5

Other (Specify)_____ ☐ 72–1

23. Are you the owner, manager, or employee of this store?

Owner... ☐ 73–1

Manager... ☐   –2

Employee... ☐   –3

24. How long have you been personally working in this neighborhood?

_____ Months 74–
_____ Years   75–
76–
77–

205

25. What is the approximate annual gross income of this store?

$ _____

6–
7–
8–
9–
10–
11–
12–

26. How difficult is it to keep up with your competition? Is it very difficult, somewhat difficult, or easy?

Very difficult.. ☐ 13–1

Somewhat difficult............................... ☐ –2

Easy.. ☐ –3

27. How many people are employed in this store? _____ People

14–
15–
16–

28. How many of these are Negroes? _____ Negroes

17–
18–
19–

29. About what percent of your customers are Negroes? _____ Negroes

20–
21–

30a. Do you extend credit?

No ☐ 22–1 (SKIP TO PAGE "A", Q.1)

Yes ☐ –2 (ASK Q.30b)

b. (IF "YES" TO Q.30a, ASK:) Do you charge for this service?

No ☐ 23–1 (SKIP TO PAGE "A", Q.1)

Yes ☐ –2 (ASK Q.30c THROUGH 30g IN SEQUENCE)

c. (IF "YES" TO Q.30b, ASK:) About how much do you charge a customer per $100.00 of credit?

$ _____ Week

$ _____ Month

24–
25–
26–
27–

206

467

d. Are there any people or groups to whom you do not extend credit?

        No ☐ 28–1 (SKIP TO Q.30g)

        Yes ☐   –2 (ASK Q.30e)

e. (IF "YES" TO Q.30d, ASK:) What people or groups are these? _____

        29–
        30–
        31–
        32–
        33–
        34–
        35–

30f. Do you collect overdue bills, or do you have some collection agency do it?

        Self.......................... ☐ 36–1

        Agency................... ☐ –2

g. Do you sell your credit installment contracts to banks or other finance businesses?

        No ☐ 37–1

        Yes ☐ –2

207

468

POLITICAL PARTY WORKERS

1. From your experience with the people who live in this district, what are the major things they are concerned with as problems?

Is there anything else? (PROBE)_____

2. Compared to other parts of the city, do you think people in your district feel they are better off, worse off, or about the same?

Better off ☐ 13-1   Worse off ☐ -2   About the same ☐ -3   Don't know ☐ -6

3. Every district is made up of different groups who may have different opinions about the way things are going. I will read you a list of different groups of people. Please tell me how satisfied you feel each group is with the general way in which this city is run. Do you feel (GROUP) are very satisfied, somewhat satisfied, somewhat dissatisfied, or very dissatisfied with the general way this city is run? (CHECK APPROPRIATE BOX FOR EACH GROUP LISTED)

	Very Satisfied	Somewhat Satisfied	Somewhat Dissatisfied	Very Dissatisfied	Don't Know
a) Old people......................	☐ 14-1	☐ -2	☐ -3	☐ -4	☐ -6
b) Adolescents....................	☐ 15-1	☐ -2	☐ -3	☐ -4	☐ -6
c) Young adults.................	☐ 16-1	☐ -2	☐ -3	☐ -4	☐ -6
d) Store owners..................	☐ 17-1	☐ -2	☐ -3	☐ -4	☐ -6
e) Landlords......................	☐ 18-1	☐ -2	☐ -3	☐ -4	☐ -6
f) Negroes........................	☐ 19-1	☐ -2	☐ -3	☐ -4	☐ -6
g) Whites.........................	☐ 20-1	☐ -2	☐ -3	☐ -4	☐ -6

4. In some districts party workers have noticed changes in people's attitudes in the last few years. How about your district? Here are changes that some have noticed. Have changes like this occurred here? (READ EACH CHANGE AND CHECK APPROPRIATE BOX)

	Yes	No	Don't Know
a) People are more determined to get what they believe they have coming to them..	☐ 21-1	☐ -2	☐ -6
b) People are more fed up with the system, and are becoming unwilling to work with politicians..	☐ 22-1	☐ -2	☐ -6
c) Young people have become more militant................................	☐ 23-1	☐ -2	☐ -6
d) Middle-age people have become more militant...........................	☐ 24-1	☐ -2	☐ -6

208

469

I want to ask you a few things about your own background and activities.

5. How long have you been a political party worker in this district? (RECORD EXACT NUMBER OF YEARS)

_____ Years 25–
26–

6. What is your present position within the party in this district?

_____ 27–
28–

7. How did you get this position—that is, were you elected by voters, elected by a local party organization, selected by party officials or by some other means?

Elected by voters... ☐ 29–1

Elected by local party organization............... ☐   –2

Selected by party officials............................. ☐   –3

Other (SPECIFY)_____   –4

8. On the average, about how many voters do you talk with every week?

_____ Voters Per Week 30–
31–
32–

9a. About how many hours a week, on the average, do you spend talking with voters in your district?

_____ Hours Per Week 33–
34–

b. Do you have regular hours at which voters can come to talk about their complaints and their problems?

Yes ☐ 35–1   No ☐ –2

10a. Do you have any say in who gets jobs in this district?

Yes ☐ 36–1 (ASK Q.10b)   No ☐ –2 (SKIP TO Q.10c)

b. (IF "YES" TO Q.10a, ASK:) Are persons cleared with you or do you recommend people for job vacancies?

Cleared ☐ 37–1 (SKIP TO Q.11)   Recommended ☐ –2 (SKIP TO Q.11)

c. (IF "YES" TO Q.10a, ASK:) Does anyone in your political party have a say over who gets jobs?

Yes ☐ 38–1 (ASK Q.11)   No ☐ –2 (ASK Q.11)   Don't know ☐ –6 (ASK Q.11)

209

11a. (ASK EVERYONE) Do you receive requests for help from the voters?

        Yes ☐ 39-1 (ASK Q.11b)   No ☐ -2 (SKIP TO Q.12)

  b. (IF "YES" TO Q.11a, ASK:) Can you help them almost always, usually, or just sometimes?

        Almost always............... ☐ 40-1 (ASK Q.11c)

        Usually......................... ☐   -2 (ASK Q.11c)

        Sometimes.................... ☐   -3 (ASK Q.11c)

        Don't know.................... ☐   -6 (ASK Q.11c)

  c. What kinds of requests for help do you receive most often?

                                                                        41-

                                                                       42-

_____ 43-

_____ 44-

_____ 45-

_____ 46-

                                                                       47-

12. If you wanted to, could you get in touch with (NAME OF PERSON) to discuss problems in your district? (ASK AND CHECK APPROPRIATE BOX FOR EACH PERSON LISTED IN GRID BELOW)

13. Have you ever gotten in touch with (NAME OF PERSON)?

	Q.12 Could Get In Touch With		Q.13 Have Gotten In Touch With	
	Yes	No	Yes	No
a) The Mayor?...	☐ 48-1	☐ -2	☐ 49-1	☐ -2
b) Your City Councilman?..............................	☐ 50-1	☐ -2	☐ 51-1	☐ -2
c) Your U.S. Congressman?...........................	☐ 52-1	☐ -2	☐ 53-1	☐ -2
d) The Police Chief or Commissioner?...........	☐ 54-1	☐ -2	☐ 55-1	☐ -2
e) The Head of Sanitation in your area?.........	☐ 56-1	☐ -2	☐ 57-1	☐ -2
f) The Head of Welfare in your area?...........	☐ 58-1	☐ -2	☐ 59-1	☐ -2
g) The Head of Building Inspection in your area?..	☐ 60-1	☐ -2	☐ 61-1	☐ -2

210

Now, I want to ask you a few things about the people in your district.

14. About how many voters live in your district?

_____ Voters

62–
63–
64–
65–
66–
67–

15. Of those eligible to be registered in your district, about what percentage actually are registered at the present time?

_____ Percent

68–
69–

16. Now, of those who actually have registered, about what percentage vote in a <u>local</u> election?

_____ Percent

70–
71–

17. Some people in this district are more politically active than others. Are old people, for example usually active, or usually inactive in registering and getting out to vote? (CHECK APPROPRIATE BOX FOR EACH GROUP LISTED)

Card 4
5–4

	Usually Active	Usually Inactive	DK
a) Old people?	☐ 6–1	☐ –2	☐ –6
b) How about middle-aged people?	☐ 7–1	☐ –2	☐ –6
c) The young adults?	☐ 8–1	☐ –2	☐ –6
d) The high-income people – those in business and professions?	☐ 9–1	☐ –2	☐ –6
e) The low or moderate-income people – workers and clerks?	☐ 10–1	☐ –2	☐ –6
f) The unemployed?	☐ 11–1	☐ –2	☐ –6
g) The Negroes in general?	☐ 12–1	☐ –2	☐ –6
h) The Whites in general?	☐ 13–1	☐ –2	☐ –6
i) The civil rights militants – particularly Negroes?	☐ 14–1	☐ –2	☐ –6

211

Now I would like to ask you a few questions about the young people of voting age.

18. About how many of them are (<u>READ STATEMENTS BELOW</u>)? Is it almost everyone, many of the young people, some, or just a few of them? (CHECK APPROPRIATE BOX FOR EACH STATEMENT LISTED)

	Almost Everyone	Many	Some	Few	DK
a) Very interested in getting the best man elected?	☐ 15–1	☐ –2	☐ –3	☐ –4	☐ –6
b) Restless and hard to control?	☐ 16–1	☐ –2	☐ –3	☐ –4	☐ –6
c) Industrious and want to learn in order to be successful?	☐ 17–1	☐ –2	☐ –3	☐ –4	☐ –6
d) Too militant to work inside a political party?	☐ 18–1	☐ –2	☐ –3	☐ –4	☐ –6
e) Afraid of authorities that they do not know personally?	☐ 19–1	☐ –2	☐ –3	☐ –4	☐ –6
f) Apathetic?	☐ 20–1	☐ –2	☐ –3	☐ –4	☐ –6

Now, I would like to find out how the people in your district feel about the councilman.

19. Do most people in this district feel that the councilman is a friend who is fighting hard for them, or is he thought of as a part of the city government which must be asked continually and repeatedly in order to get things done?

Friend fighting for the people............... ☐ 21–1

Part of city government....................... ☐   –2

Don't know... ☐   –6

20. How do the voters feel about the councilman for this district? (READ EACH STATEMENT BELOW)

	Yes	No	DK
a) Do they think he is militant enough?................................	☐ 22–1	☐ –2	☐ –6
b) Does he get things done quickly?......................................	☐ 23–1	☐ –2	☐ –6
c) Does he follow the line of his party too much?.................	☐ 24–1	☐ –2	☐ –6
d) Does he help the people in this district a lot?...................	☐ 25–1	☐ –2	☐ –6
e) Do they think he is powerful?..	☐ 26–1	☐ –2	☐ –6

21. How easy is it for a person to get a parking ticket fixed in this city? Is it very easy, somewhat easy, somewhat difficult or very difficult?

Very easy...................... ☐ 27–1   Somewhat difficult............... ☐ –3

Somewhat easy............... ☐   –2   Very difficult....................... ☐ –4

Now, let us consider the services available to people in your district.

22. From the city or other organizations, is (are) the (<u>NAME OF SERVICE</u>) excellent, good, fair, or poor? (CHECK APPROPRIATE BOX FOR EACH SERVICE LISTED)

	Excellent	Good	Fair	Poor	Don't Know
a) Telephone service......................	☐ 28–1	☐ –2	☐ –3	☐ –4	☐ –6
b) Garbage service...........................	☐ 29–1	☐ –2	☐ –3	☐ –4	☐ –6
c) Street lighting............................	☐ 30–1	☐ –2	☐ –3	☐ –4	☐ –6
d) Street cleaning...........................	☐ 31–1	☐ –2	☐ –3	☐ –4	☐ –6
e) Street repair..............................	☐ 32–1	☐ –2	☐ –3	☐ –4	☐ –6
f) Police protection..........................	☐ 33–1	☐ –2	☐ –3	☐ –4	☐ –6
g) Recreational facilities.................	☐ 34–1	☐ –2	☐ –3	☐ –4	☐ –6
h) Schools.......................................	☐ 35–1	☐ –2	☐ –3	☐ –4	☐ –6
i) Building inspection......................	☐ 36–1	☐ –2	☐ –3	☐ –4	☐ –6
j) Fire department..........................	☐ 37–1	☐ –2	☐ –3	☐ –4	☐ –6
k) Ambulance service.....................	☐ 38–1	☐ –2	☐ –3	☐ –4	☐ –6

213

Now let's talk about leadership of organizations in your district.

23. Is (are) the __(NAME OF ORGANIZATION)__ very influential, somewhat influential, or not at all influential in your district? (CHECK APPROPRIATE BOX FOR EACH ORGANIZATION LISTED BELOW)

	Very Influential	Somewhat Influential	Not at all Influential	Doesn't Exist Here
a) Churches..	☐ 39–1	☐ –2	☐ –3	☐ –9
b) NAACP (National Association for the Advancement of Colored People)...........	☐ 40–1	☐ –2	☐ –3	☐ –9
c) CORE (Congress of Racial Equality).....	☐ 41–1	☐ –2	☐ –3	☐ –9
d) City newspapers..................................	☐ 42–1	☐ –2	☐ –3	☐ –9
e) Local newspapers................................	☐ 43–1	☐ –2	☐ –3	☐ –9
f) SNCC (Student Non-Violent Coordinating Committee).....................................	☐ 44–1	☐ –2	☐ –3	☐ –9
g) Urban League......................................	☐ 45–1	☐ –2	☐ –3	☐ –9
h) Labor Unions.......................................	☐ 46–1	☐ –2	☐ –3	☐ –9
i) Merchants Associations........................	☐ 47–1	☐ –2	☐ –3	☐ –9
j) PTA (Parent-Teachers Association).......	☐ 48–1	☐ –2	☐ –3	☐ –9

24. Now let us consider how militant are different groups of Negroes in your district in insisting on their rights. Are the ___(NAME OF GROUP)___ very militant, somewhat militant, or not at all militant?

	Very Militant	Somewhat Militant	Not at all Militant	DK
a) Older people..	☐ 49–1	☐ –2	☐ –3	☐ –6
b) Middle-aged people..	☐ 50–1	☐ –2	☐ –3	☐ 6
c) College students..	☐ 51–1	☐ –2	☐ –3	☐ –6
d) Non-college young adults..	☐ 52–1	☐ –2	☐ –3	☐ –6
e) Adolescents...	☐ 53–1	☐ –2	☐ –3	☐ –6
f) High-income people—those in business and the professions...	☐ 54–1	☐ –2	☐ –3	☐ –6
g) Low or moderate-income people—workers and clerks...	☐ 55–1	☐ –2	☐ –3	☐ –6
h) Unemployed people...	☐ 56–1	☐ –2	☐ –3	☐ –6
i) Civil servants and city employees.........................	☐ 57–1	☐ –2	☐ –3	☐ –6

215

Appendix B

RATING DIMENSIONS FOR CITY ELITE INTERVIEWS

PUBLIC OFFICIALS

Staff Rater: _____

City: _____   Date: _____

A. Mayor

Autonomy (ability to make decisions independently) ....

Potency (ability to carry out decisions and cause action to be taken)

. . . .

Accessability (to black community)   —To moderates ....

—To militants ....

Sympathy-antagonism (to black demands) ....

Responsiveness (to black demands) ....

General Competence and Leadership Ability ....

B. City Council

Autonomy (ability to make decisions independently) ....

Public Officials (*continued*)

Potency (ability to carry out decisions and cause action to be taken)
. . . .

Accessability (to black community)   —To moderates . . . .

                                                              —To militants . . . .

Sympathy-antagonism (to black demands) . . . .

Responsiveness (to black demands) . . . .

Black Representation on Council (proportionate) . . . .

C. Miscellaneous Ratings

Information and sophistication about the black community on the part of the mayor . . . .

Information and sophistication about the black community on the part of the city council . . . .

Note: "10" = High
         "0" = Low

MASS MEDIA

Staff Rater: _____

City: _____   Date: _____

Salience of mass media in interviews . . . .

NOTE: IF LITTLE OR NO MENTION OF MASS MEDIA IN INTERVIEWS DO NOT FILL OUT THE REMAINDER OF THIS RATING SHEET

A. Newspapers

1. General Press

Coverage of civil rights events in the general press . . . .

Coverage of other black community events in general press . . . . .

Mass Media (*continued*)

Accessibility of general press to black moderate leaders ....

militant leaders ....

Sympathy-antagonism to black demands and grievances ....

2. Black Press

Presence (P) or Absence (abs) of Black press ....

Moderateness-militancy of Black press ....

Importance of Black press in black community ....

B. TV and Radio

Coverage of civil rights events in black community in TV and radio news ....

Sympathy-antagonism of coverage to black demands and grievances
....

C. Some General Ratings

The press and other mass media in this city systematically suppresses news items concerning black events in order to keep the level of tension in city from rising ....

The tone of coverage of civil rights events is such as to case some comic or ludicrous aspects into highlights ....

The press and other mass media eagerly cover civil rights events in order to play up their "sensational" aspects ....

COMMUNITY STYLE RATINGS

Staff Rater: _____

City: _____   Date: _____

A. Importance of Groups in City Decision Making and Agenda Setting
    (within city)

	Informant Group	
	Whites	Blacks
Mayor and Mayor's Office	_____	_____
White Ethnic Groups	_____	_____
City Council	_____	_____
Major Industries	_____	_____
Black Organized Groups	_____	_____
Banks and Other Financial Institutions	_____	_____
Labor Unions	_____	_____
Major Merchants	_____	_____
Organized Political Groups in White Community (e.g., Political Clubs)	_____	_____
Catholic Church	_____	_____
Other Churches	_____	_____
Chamber of Commerce or Other Civic Clubs	_____	_____
Public Agencies (e.g., O.E.O., Welfare)	_____	_____
Other Groups (list: _____)	_____	_____

B. Style of Political Decision-Making

Issues are usually controlled by a strong political
machine   _____ _____

Issues are usually controlled by a strong civic elite _____ _____
Issues usually involve disagreement between
sizeable political factions, interest groups, and
ethnic groups, etc.   _____ _____

Community Style Ratings (*continued*)

    Issues usually involve disagreement between a
large number of small and temporary groups   _____   _____

    Issues usually involve great public conflict   _____   _____

    Public conflict over issues is more or less
continuous rather than sporadic and episodic   _____   _____

    Issues tend to be settled by gradually building
consensus, rather than forcing through decisions
over the opposing groups   _____   _____

C.   Global Ratings of City Leadership

    Elected officials are powerful, co-ordinate
(co-ordination in this section is viewed as a
component of power)   _____   _____

    Elected officials are divided into a number of
sizeable blocs which are sometimes in conflict   _____   _____

    Elected officials are weak, dispersed, fragmented   _____   _____

    Civic elites are powerful, co-ordinated, (if elected
officials are also powerful, an alliance is assumed)   _____   _____

    Interests are divided into a number of sizeable
blocs, each with some influence   _____   _____

    Interests are dispersed; diverse groups and
individuals compete for access; a good deal of
"citizen participation"   _____   _____

D.   Styles of Handling Opposition

    City officials and elites pursue a policy of
repression   _____   _____

    Black leaders are quickly coopted into leadership
structure by jobs, positions, etc.   _____   _____

    Public officials and elites prefer to do things for
people rather than involve them in decision
making   _____   _____

E.   Mood of City

    Blacks are tense, uneasy, apprehensive and ready
to blow   _____   _____

Community Style Ratings (*continued*)

	Informant Group	
	Whites	Blacks
Whites are tense, uneasy, apprehensive and ready to strike back	_____	_____
Many whites are losing confidence in city administration's ability or will to control black discontent	_____	_____
Most black leaders have no faith in public officials good will and regard them as white racists	_____	_____
Most white leaders see the black community as led by militants who hate whites	_____	_____

LOCAL ISSUES IN RACE RELATIONS

Staff Rater: _____

City: _____   Date: _____

(These are ratings of saliency: How often an issue appears in the interviews and with what intensity of feeling and the amount of conflict between whites and blacks on those issues.)

	(High = 10)	
	Salience	Conflict
A. Housing and Related Areas		
Quality of housing available to blacks		
— public housing	_____	_____
— private housing	_____	_____
High rentals, high purchase prices, discriminatory mortgage policies, poor maintenance	_____	_____
Urban renewal, redevelopment, highway construction and their impact on black community	_____	_____
Discriminatory practices on rental and purchase markets	_____	_____

Local Issues in Race Relations (*continued*)

B. Welfare

Adequacy of welfare program for needs of blacks ——————   ——————

Dependence of blacks on welfare program   ——————   ——————

C. Police Practices

Police brutality, hostility, lack of politeness in
handling blacks   ——————   ——————

Police protection in ghetto areas   ——————   ——————

Civilian Review Board (or other kinds comm.
control)   ——————   ——————

D. Exploitation of Blacks

Exploitation by retail merchant in ghetto   ——————   ——————

Exploitation by employers in wages and
promotion   ——————   ——————

Exploitation in credit and loan practices   ——————   ——————

E. Employment

Discrimination against blacks in

public employment   ——————   ——————

private employment   ——————   ——————

union membership   ——————   ——————

F. Public Education

General quality of educational system   ——————   ——————

Provision of special black subjects (e.g., Swahili) ——————   ——————

Community control of schools   ——————   ——————

School desegregation (also bussing)   ——————   ——————

WELFARE POVERTY PROGRAMS AND MODEL CITIES

Staff Rater: _____

City: _____   Date: _____

A. Welfare Department (Agency which administers AFOC General Assistance, OAS, etc.)

    1. Welfare Officials

        General competence and adequacy of welfare officials   _____

        Accessibility of welfare officials   _____

        Sympathy-antagonism of welfare officials to black demands   _____

        Representation of blacks among officials   _____

        Responsiveness of welfare officials   _____

        Potency of welfare officials   _____

    2. Welfare Rank-and-File

        Sympathy and Antagonism   _____

        Representation of blacks   _____

        Responsiveness to black demands and grievances   _____

    3. General Ratings

        Adequacy of welfare support   _____

        Competence of agency   _____

        Punitive versus nurturant stance vis-a-vis clientele   _____

B. Poverty Program (essentially CAP, Manpower Retraining Programs, etc.)

    Autonomy of program from other public officials   _____

    Competence of program officials   _____

    Representation of blacks on levels of rank-and-file workers officials   _____

    Adequacy of program   _____

C. Model Cities

    Competence of officials   _____

Welfare Poverty Programs and Model Cities (*continued*)

     Representation of black among rank-and-file workers officials _____

     Adequacy of program   _____

WHITE COMMUNITY

Staff Rater: _____

City: _____   Date: _____

(These ratings refer to the larger body of white residents of the community and surrounding areas—rank-and-file citizens and low level leaders as opposed to public officials, school officials, business, elite, etc., which are rated separately. NOTE THAT THE GEOGRAPHIC REFERENCE IS TO THE METRO AREA AND NOT MERELY TO THE SPECIFIC CITY INVOLVED.)

                                       (Mark "abs" if not present, otherwise rate for importance)

A.   Specific Activities

     Anti-black political or parapolitical organizations (e.g., KKK, White Citizens Councils, Wallace Orgn.)   _____

     Attacks on blacks or confrontations initiated by whites   _____

     White support for nonviolent civil rights activities and organizations   _____

     Movement among whites to arm themselves   _____

     Interracial stable neighborhoods   _____

     Interracial church movements   _____

     Prominent white leaders who are sympathetic to black demands and grievances   _____

White Community (*continued*)

B.   Global Ratings

Reputation of being on the whole a liberal
group sympathetic to black demands as
opposed to very racist:

— for lower income whites   _____

— for upper income whites   _____

— for elected officials and candidates for
office over past decade or so   _____

PUBLIC EDUCATION

Staff Rater: _____

City: _____   Date: _____

A.   School Superintendent

Autonomy of School Superintendent (ability to make
decisions independent of other public officials and
school board)   _____

Potency of school superintendent (ability to make
changes in eductaional policy and see that they in fact
occur)   _____

Accessibility of school superintendent to black community   _____

Sympathy-antagonism to black demands   _____

Responsiveness to black demands and grievances   _____

B.   School Board

Representation of black community on school board   _____

Accessability of school board to black community   _____

Sympathy-antagonism to black demands and grievances   _____

Responsiveness to black demands and grievances   _____

Potency of school board   _____

Public Education (*continued*)

C. Miscellaneous Ratings

Quality of educational experiences offered   Whites*   _____
to students   Blacks*   _____

Representation of blacks in rank-and-file levels   _____

Progressivism, innovativeness, flexibility of system   _____

Degree to which special efforts have been made to
provide educational opportunities specially tailored
to black population   _____

Extent to which local communities are permitted or
encouraged to participate in decisions about education
(e.g., community schools)   _____

BUSINESS AND LABOR

Staff Rater: _____

City: _____   Date: _____

A. Business Elite

Importance of business elite in working of community   _____

Support among eilte for business organizations oriented
toward correcting conditions in black community
(e.g., National Alliance of Business, Urban Coalition) _____

Business organizations in community (Chamber of
Commerce, Civic Clubs, etc.) are behind efforts to
provide employment for blacks, better housing and so on   _____

Sympathy-antagonism toward black demands and
grievances in the area of employment   _____

Responsiveness of business elite to black demands and
grievances   _____

---

*Rate according to the general statements made by informants about the quality of education offered to blacks and whites in the system.

Business and Labor (*continued*)

B. Labor Unions

Importance of labor unions in the workings of the community   _____

Sympathy-antagonism toward black demands and grievances in the area of employment   _____

Responsiveness to black demands and grievances   _____

C. Miscellaneous

Adequacy, quality of job opportunities available to blacks   _____

Adequacy, quality of job opportunities available to whites (especially considering the lower end of the white economic scale)   _____

POLICE OFFICIALS AND DEPARTMENTS

Staff Rater: _____

City: _____   Date: _____

A. Police Superintendent (or Equivalent Top Policy Making Police Official)

Autonomy of police superintendent (ability to make decisions independent of other public officials   _____

Potency of police superintendent (ability to make decisions which appreciably change operations of police department)   _____

A. General competence and leadership ability   _____

Accessability of superintendent   — to moderate blacks   _____

— to militant blacks   _____

Sympathy-antagonism to black demands and grievances   _____

Responsiveness to black demands and grievances   _____

B. Police Rank-and-File

General competence as a police force   _____

Police Officials and Departments (*continued*)

Honest–corrupt _____

Sympathy-antagonism to black demands and grievances _____

Representation of blacks on the police force _____

C. Miscellaneous Ratings

Information and sophistication about black community
(who are leaders, nature of movement organizations, etc.)
on the part of police officials _____

Police style of handling militants, demonstrations,
picketing, etc. of movement is permissive as opposed
to repressive _____

Police style of handling dissidents in general is
permissive as opposed to repressive _____

Extent to which local communities are permitted or
encouraged to participate in decision about the police
(e.g., Civilian Review Board) _____

BLACK COMMUNITY

Staff Rater: _____

City: _____   Date: _____

	Influence with*		
	Present (P) or Absent (Abs)	White Leaders	Mid Cl Blacks	Lower Cl Blacks

A. Presence and Influence
   of Black Organizations

NAACP _____ _____ _____ _____

Urban League _____ _____ _____ _____

---

*Influence with white leaders is to be interpreted as having an effect on their actions as well as being paid attention to by such leaders. Influence on blacks is to be interpreted as playing a leadership role with middle class and lower class blacks respectively.

Black Community (*continued*)

CORE	_____	_____	_____	_____
SNCC	_____	_____	_____	_____
SCLC	_____	_____	_____	_____
Black Muslims	_____	_____	_____	_____
Local "Black United	_____	_____	_____	_____
Front" †	_____	_____	_____	_____

Other Organizations:
(List by name)

_____	_____	_____	_____	_____
_____	_____	_____	_____	_____
_____	_____	_____	_____	_____

B.   Presence or Absence of Specific Activities

	Present (P) or Absent (Abs)
Afro-American Cultural Center	_____
Movement for community control of schools	_____
police	_____
ghetto businesses	_____
Movement for Police Civilian Review Board	_____
Black-white communal riots	_____
Guerrilla style attacks on police, burning of public buildings, interference with public utilities, and so on	_____

---

† E.g. "United Negro Protest Committee" in Pittsburgh, "United Negro Front" in Washington.

Black Community (*continued*)

	Present (P) or Absent (Abs)

Boycotts directed against

— Schools   _____

— Stores and retail business   _____

— Major employers   _____

— Other (specify_____)   _____

Demonstrations and picketing

— Landlords   _____

— Stores and retail business   _____

— Employers   _____

— City Hall and public agencies   _____

— Other (specify_____)   _____

— Schools   _____

Organized opposition to urban renewal or redevelopment or highway construction   _____

Spontaneous confrontations with police (other than major riots)   _____

C. Global Ratings of Civil Rights Movement Styles   Rate 0–10*

A few middle class blacks have been selected by white elites to "represent" the black community   _____

The blacks who are regraded by the leaders of the white community as the key people in the black community are actually looked down upon with contempt by the black community   _____

A number of civil rights organizations compete for leadership with individuals acting primarily as representatives of the organizations   _____

---

* Rate according to the degree to which black community fits the statements with 10 being the closest fit and 0 being the worst possible fit.

Black Community (*continued*)

A number of individuals compete for leadership shifting from organization to organization or devising new organizations to attract followers   _____

The leadership in the black community, whether organizational or individual, presents a unified front to the white leaders   _____

Leadership is divided with cut-throat competition for supremacy

Leadership in the black community is so transistory that it is difficult to judge whether a particular organization or individual's claim to leadership are correct   _____

D.   Militancy of Black Community   Rate 0–10

Grievance Orientation: Movement directed mainly toward correcting specific conditions (e.g., discrimination in specific organizations, increased welfare payments)   _____

Integration Orientation: Directed toward getting policy statements from white leaders which would make integration in public accommodations, housing, schools, and employment a matter of public policy   _____

Participatory Orientations: Directed toward having community and its leaders consulted on issues involving black community   _____

Autonomy Oriented: Directed toward having a separate but black controlled set of community institutions (schools, retail businesses, local police force, etc.)   _____

Black Community (*continued*)

Radical Goal Oriented:	Rejection of given social order as "sick" and substitution of alternative social order of a radically different kind	_____

E. Some Miscellaneous Ratings

Potential or actual solidarity of black community in voting for black candidates on local elections _____

Potential in community for explosive types of upheavals among black youths _____

Negro respondents characterization of white community as tending towards genocide, white racism, etc. _____

Negro leaders acceptance of whites in the movement _____

Negro respondents talk of arming black community _____

Negro trust, confidence in white leaders in public office (e.g., Mayor) _____

Negro talk of violence as response of black community to inaction or poor policy moves on the part of the total community _____

F. Age, Militancy, Leadership   Rate 0–10

Degree of influence-control over older blacks by the following:

a. White official and community projects: (e.g., OEO, Community Relations Councils, Church Action Groups _____

b. Moderate black organizations and leaders (NAACP, Urban League, moderate black ministers, etc.) _____

c. Pragmatic black community action organizations (Mothers for Adequate Welfare, New England Grass Roots Organization _____

d. Militant-ideological black organizations and leaders stressing black identity and culture, emphasizing global rather than specific goals) _____

Black Community (*continued*)

e. Armed black radicals and revolutionaries (e.g. Panthers, "Swapman") _____

Degree of influence-control over *younger* blacks by the following:

a. White official and community projects (e.g., OEO, Community Relations Councils, Church Action Groups) _____

b. Moderate black organizations and leaders (NAACP, Urban League, moderate black ministers, etc.) _____

c. Pragmatic black community action organizations (Mothers for Adequate Welfare, New England Grass Roots Organization) _____

d. Militant-ideological black organizations and leaders (stressing black identity and culture, emphasizing global rather than specific goals) _____

e. Armed black radicals and revolutionaries (e.g., Panthers, Swapman")

G.   More Miscellany

    a. Militant discontent among black youth _____

    b. Spontaneous protest action by black youth _____

    c. Militant discontent among older blacks _____

    d. Spontaneous protest among older blacks _____

                                        P-Abs.

    e. Presence, importance of welfare rights movement _____ _____

INDEX